Lila's Child

Books by Dan Glover

Philosophy

The Art of Caring: Zen Stories
The Mystery: Zen Stories
Apache Nation

Mermaid Series

Winter's Memaid
Mermaid Spring
Summer's Mermaid
Autumn Mermaid

Gathering of Lovers Series

Billy Austin
Lisa
Allison Johns
Tom Three Deer
Justine
Yelena

Short Stories

There Come a Bad Cloud: Tangled up Matter and Ghosts
Mi Vida Dinámica

Lila's Child
An Inquiry into Quality
Dan Glover

Published by Lost Doll Publishing at Amazon

This book is a work of fiction. Places, events, and situations in this story are purely fictional. Any resemblance to actual persons, living or dead, is coincidental.

Table of Contents

Prologue

The Lila Squad began as an Internet email list in August of 1997. The discussion group, devoted to Robert M. Pirsig's second book, Lila: An Inquiry into Morals, originally consisted of seven members. Over time, the list grew to over a hundred members of all ages from many different countries all around the world. This book began as an attempt to chronicle that discussion.

The idea for Lila's Child was not my own nor did I belong to the group during the early discussions chronicled here. When I did have the honor of joining the group in June of 1998, it didn't take long to notice that the discussions taking place had been going on for some time. The archives seemed well organized though not all the contributors used proper subject lines in responding to messages nor did they always address to which discussion their posts pertained. I suppose at the time each contributor just knew. I had problems returning to certain posts I wanted to read again and I suspected others might have the same difficulty.

When Bodvar Skutvik, one of the original members of the group (who knew of my fondness for the archives), approached me about making an attempt to organize the early Lila Squad discussions into a readable format, my first thought was, "He's got to be joking." With over a thousand posts in the archives from just the first six months, it seemed like a task that might take years to complete. Bodvar asked me two more times before it dawned on me that he was actually serious and I agreed to take on the challenge. I had grave reservations as to the value of such work but put those thoughts aside with the conviction that taking on any project meant my full attention was called for despite all the misgivings I harbored. The project began in autumn of 1999 by gaining the permission of the contributors, constructing an outline of the posts, and finally uploading a rough draft to a website early the following year.

Lila's Child has taken a great deal of perseverance to complete. The hours that went into Lila's Child perhaps ought to have gone into more productive endeavors, such as growing the business that keeps bread on my table and the lights turned on, practical matters instead of a flight of fantasy like putting together a book. I really should have known better. After all, I've been told time and again by people I respect a great deal that I have no right involving myself in a project such as this. I'm not a scholar. I should leave this to someone more qualified, a person with a degree in philosophy perhaps, a name with game. I have no disagreement with this point of view but I found myself drawn to the work. I couldn't seem to shake the Lila's Child project despite the many obstacles to its completion that cropped up over the years, including my own complete indifference at times.

What possesses a person like me to take on a project such as putting together a book? To begin answering that question brings back faded memories of the first author I had the opportunity to meet. I don't recall his name but I do remember a bit of the time. I grew up close to a river where as a boy I spent many hours fishing and exploring up and down the wild and overgrown riverbanks with my brothers and friends. The water was so polluted by the small-town Laundromat and open sewers that tall stacks of soap suds and unmentionables would oft times float past our fishing lines, making the fish we caught uneatable but nonetheless fun to catch.

At a secluded site alongside the river crouched an old crumbly concrete house that appeared to us boys for the whole world like a medieval castle might look. I recall that every season the house seemed to mimic the color of the river and surrounding woods; summertime green moss growing in profusion over the foot thick cement slab outer walls would turn brown in the winter just like the filthy river water once the algae had gone dormant with cold.

Being naturally inquisitive as boys tend to be, my brother and me knocked on the door one day. An old white haired man answered and greeted us as if we were old friends. I must have been ten years old or maybe eleven, my brother a little younger. He seemed delighted we had stopped by as he invited us in, almost as if he'd been expecting us. Of course, we'd been warned about strangers but we followed him through the big wooden door anyway. I can't say exactly why now. He said he had something he wanted to show us boys so we simply followed him. He led us down a stone hallway to a room in the back of the house. It was a library, with shelves from the worn wooden floor to what must have been a fourteen-foot high ceiling.

Picking up and balancing a pair of Ben Franklins on the end of his nose, the old man walked to a dilapidated wooden ladder held together via tarnished brass fittings with little brass wheels on the bottom. Placing one foot on the first step and with a push of the other he scooted half way across the room, continuing his climb as the ladder creaked its way along the balustrade on which it was mounted, finally coming to rest at just the spot predetermined by his initial push. Looking down through his bifocals he took one of the dusty books in his hand, tucked it under his arm, and climbed down the ladder.

He showed us the cover of the book, pointed to the name there, and said that it was his. He wrote it many years ago. A twinkle in his eyes as he looked over his glasses at us and a shy smile as he underlined his name on the cover of the book with his finger related together at that moment to give me the odd feeling that he was both embarrassed and proud at the same time.

I know now, after my work on this project, that he had accomplished something special. Perhaps he simply wished to share that feeling of pride and embarrassment with someone, anyone, even two little boys who came knocking on what to them was a castle door, simply out of curiosity. I don't remember what I said, or if I even said anything at all to the old man (my brother has always been more the talker), but now I know that a book is not an easy thing to put together. Perhaps that is what the old man really wanted to show us, not the book itself, but rather the feeling that comes from holding it in your own hands.

The old mossy cement castle is gone now. A no longer remote sanitary ranch-style house stands in its place. I haven't been inside but I'd bet a dollar to a donut that there is no library in that house. The river is much cleaner these days and I hear a person can even eat the fish they catch out of it now, but boys can no longer explore or fish along its banks. The influx of big expensive houses crowding the river's once tangled and brambled banks all seem to have yards that come pre-equipped with "No Trespassing" signs. Something tells me that the occupants of those houses would not be so happy to greet a couple of curious little snot-nosed boys knocking at the door as the old man seemed to be so many years ago. There are no paths to explore any longer other than the manicured walking trail where the old railroad tracks once ran. That old man is most certainly long dead and all those books rotting in a landfill but he too has a part in the Lila's Child project with his love for books.

I've always had a love for books too. In approaching them from a reader's point of view though, I didn't know how difficult assembling a book could be. If I knew when I started this project what I know now I would have politely but firmly refused Bodvar's invitation to write the Lila Squad story. Perhaps it is the same for all authors (not that I am really an author). There were times when seeing this book in print seemed about as remote as my walking on the moon while other times that I could almost hold it in my hands and leaf through the pages. I can say with a sense of certainty that without both the support and criticism of many other people over the years that I would have forgotten about and given up on the project a long time ago. I thank you all.

When I began the Lila's Child project I had no idea that Robert Pirsig himself would stumble across the rough draft on the Internet several months after I had uploaded it, much less be impressed enough with it to write a letter to Bodvar about it, as I was informed of in the autumn of 2000. I was too close to the work to tell if Lila's Child had value or not, but this helped confirm my suspicions that perhaps it did.

After a return letter from Bodvar, Mr. Pirsig agreed to provide an introduction and annotations for the manuscript. Those annotations are represented by bracketed numbers within the text, leading to the footnotes at the end of each chapter. In addition, Mr. Pirsig was good enough to answer some questions regarding those annotations. This exchange constitutes the epilogue at the end of the discussion.

Finally, I would like to thank everyone involved in Lila's Child: Anthony McWatt, Platt Holden, Ken Clark, Margaret Hettinger, Donny Palmgren, Doug Renselle, Bodvar Skutvik, Hugo Alroe, Dave Thomas, Struan Hellier, Magnus Berg, Keith Gillette, James Marshall and other contributors. And of course a big Thank You to Robert Pirsig!

Introduction

By Robert Pirsig

It was fortunate I stayed out of this online discussion of my books, Lila, and Zen and the Art of Motorcycle Maintenance. Not many writers get to read a body of criticism of their work as intense and diverse as this. It could never have achieved its insights and discoveries if I'd been participating in it, dominating others with my "expert" opinion.

One of the most valued members of this group has written that this discussion should not even be published at all because it is not a finished work. Much of what is said here sounds amateurish and mistaken. People will laugh at it, it was said, because it sounds so ill informed. I believe "crap" was the word used. I don't agree with this at all, but think that the objection is an important one that needs a close examination.

What we see in the following pages is what I would call "real philosophy" rather than "philosophology." This term, philosophology, is one I find myself using all the time to make a point that most academic philosophers seem unaware of: that when they speak of the ideas of such famous philosophers as Plato or Hegel they are giving us a history of philosophy, an "ology" of philosophy, not philosophy itself. Philosophy itself is opinions of the speaker himself about the general nature of the world, not just a classification someone else's opinions.

This may seem a minor point but I remember hearing many years ago how a professor of art, Jerry Liebling, was outraged when he heard that an Art Historian told one of his students that he should give up painting because it was obvious the student would never equal the great masters. At the time I didn't see what Liebling was so upset about but as the years have gone by I understand it better. Liebling loathed this attitude of Art Historians because, while they thought they were preserving the standards of art, they were in fact destroying them. Art is not just the static achievements of the masters of the past. Art is the creative Dynamic Quality of the artist of the present. Neither is philosophy just the static achievements of the masters of the past. Philosophy is the creative Dynamic Quality of the philosopher of the present.

There are similarities to chess. Both are highly intellectual pursuits in which one tries to manipulate symbols within a set of rules to improve a given situation. In chess, one can benefit greatly by studying the games of the masters. In philosophy, one can also benefit greatly by studying the writings of the great philosophers. But the important point here is that studying chess masters is not chess itself and studying philosophy masters is not philosophy itself.

The real chess is the game you play with your neighbor. Real chess is "muddling through." Real chess is the triumph of mental organization over complex experience. And so is real philosophy.

Although what we see on these pages could be classed as philosophological, that is, the study of someone else's work, what we see is dominated by the philosophy of the members: nothing is cut and dried, nothing is asserted with mind-numbing scholarly precision, no big reputations are at stake, there is just the happy process of thinking about things. The participants don't always get it right and no one expects them to. They are just trying out different ideas against each other just to see how they work out. The fact that everyone knows that everyone else might be wrong makes it much more interesting, and as you read along you see that the thinking gets better and better.

Personalities emerge: there is Magnus, dour at times but insightful and to the point; Bodvar, loyal, honest, and combative for what he believes in; Hugo, brilliant and discriminating; Maggie, putting things into a social perspective; Platt, hitting bulls-eyes like a Zen archer; Horse, solid as a rock; Doug, ahead of the pack with a suitcase full of Dynamic acronyms; Ant, who is doing his Ph.D. on the Metaphysics of Quality, and has to face academic opposition head-on. There are many others and you can discover them for yourself.

Dissenters also abound: there is Donny, who wants to put the MOQ in a larger philosophological context. There is Keith, who is such a model of courtesy and fairness and care that you immediately pay close attention to what he says. His questions go to the root of the difficulty many people have in understanding the MOQ. And there is Struan, Keith's mirror image, who makes an art form out of the personal insult. It's been said in philosophy that, "Where there is no heat there is no light." Struan has generated plenty of both.

But if dissenters didn't exist we would have to invent them because no set of philosophic ideas is worth much until it is tested by dialectical opposition. In the usual printed academic essays dissent comes weeks or months later in the form of reviews. But here, on the Internet, affirmation and dissent appear together. If a writer tries to belittle someone else in the manner of a polished literary critic, he can find himself belittled right back three minutes later. It makes for more careful criticism.

After reading through these and many other comments, I've concluded that the biggest improvement I could make in the MOQ would be to block the notion that the MOQ claims to be a quick fix for every moral problem in the universe. I have never seen it that way. The image in my mind as I wrote it was of a large football field that gave meaning to the game by telling you who was on the 20-yard line but did not decide which team would win. That was the point of the two opposing arguments over the death penalty described in Lila. That was the point of the equilibrium between static and Dynamic Quality. Both are moral arguments. Both can claim the MOQ for support. Just as two sides can go before the U.S. Supreme Court and both claim constitutionality, so two sides can use the MOQ, but that does not mean that either the Constitution or the MOQ is a meaningless set of ideas. Our whole judicial system rests on the presumption that more than one set of conclusions about individual cases can be drawn within a given set of moral rules. The MOQ makes the same presumption.

Finally, you will see that throughout the discussions I've added notes of my own. With them has comes the question, "Why make them?" Having done so well so far by staying out of this discussion, why don't I just continue the good work and keep staying out of it?

One justification for the notes is that there are questions raised here that only I can answer and this is probably the only time and place that I can answer them. But beyond this are a lot of comments that can only be classified as kibitzing.

A kibitzer is the guy who stands behind your shoulder in a chess match and tells you all the great moves you could have made if only you were as smart as he is. Not a very popular thing to do, but that is surely what is being done here. I have tried to keep it to a minimum and passed over much that I disagree with where it does not seem to destroy the Metaphysics of Quality, but it's still kibitzing.

After worrying about this for weeks, I finally found an alibi. Kibitzers only interrupt current chess games and current conversations. These discussions are now several years old and getting older every year. They're historical. I am not talking about current philosophy but about the philosophy of the past. That makes me not a kibitzer but a philosophologist. As everybody knows, philosophologists are not kibitzers but responsible dedicated wellliked respectable people!

Chapter 1

The outstanding achievement of twentieth century physics is not the theory of relativity with its welding together of space and time, or the theory of quanta with its apparent negation of the laws of causation, or the dissection of the atom with the resultant discovery that things are not what they seem; it is the general recognition that we are not yet in contact with the ultimate reality. We are still imprisoned in our own cave, with our backs to the light, and can only watch the shadows on the wall. —Sir James Jeans, The Mysterious Universe

More Quality, More Levels

Jason:

Several levels seem to be missing, including a quantum level below the inorganic, and at least one higher level (ascendant Quality, perhaps?) above the intellectual. Also, the interrelation between the current levels is sometimes elusive. Some experiences (such as friendship, for example) seem to span many levels, thus leading to confusion when applied to the MOQ.

I believe that two different approaches can be taken in addressing this problem. First, we can rethink our present attitudes toward language, replacing ambiguous terms with more specific ones, which exist on only one MOQ level. This would be a daunting task! However, not all languages seem to exhibit this dualistic nature. (Any comments regarding your own experiences?)

A more practical approach would be to carefully define the relationships between levels (and possibly to evolve new relationships/levels). This would allow us to retain our current language basis, while moving forward toward a more holistic worldview.

First off, I must begin by stating that the concept of additional levels in the MOQ is not solely my own nor can I take exclusive credit for its creation. Doug (a fellow Pirsig follower and correspondent) and I have been discussing this and related issues for about six weeks. Doug is very well read, and has a much stronger background in quantum physics than I. (I have told him about his list and hopefully he will be joining us soon.)

Quantum level phenomena are not directly observable through our senses (although the dark adapted eye can detect a single photon); therefore, unfortunately, I cannot provide real world examples of such phenomena that are easily apparent in our everyday experiences. Numerous documented scientific experiments strongly suggest that quantum level microworld phenomena exhibit characteristics that are inconsistent with our macroworld experiences. Examples include wave/particle duality, quantum communication (which seems to occur instantaneously between quanta, i.e., faster than the speed of light!), Einstein's relativity theory (energy equals matter and matter equals energy), and Heisenberg's uncertainty principle (it is impossible to simultaneously determine the exact position and momentum of a subatomic particle).

These phenomena are universally accepted among physicists, yet they are entirely unlike any macroworld experiences that we might have. For this reason, Doug and I agree that a new quantum Quality level should be appended to the MOQ below the inorganic level. [1] Inorganic patterns of value emerge from quantum phenomena, just as biological patterns emerge from the inorganic. For further background in a highly approachable non-technical format, I suggest the following:

The Dancing Wu Li Masters by Gary Zukav

The Tao of Physics by Frijof Capra

The Quantum Society by Danah Zohar

These three books will provide an excellent introduction to the concepts that I've only briefly alluded to here if read in the order shown above. If anyone has a specific question related to the implications of a quantum level of the MOQ, please reply! The ascendant level is something that Doug and I have both arrived at independently. In short, we intuit the existence of additional levels above the intellectual simply by interpolating from the existing structure. Even though we may not currently possess the (physical or intellectual) ability to recognize such levels that does not mean that they do not exist.

We should refrain from imposing artificial limits on our new metaphysics and limiting our own growth just as the Subject/Object Metaphysics (SOM) has done in the past. The new disciplines of chaos and complexity theory may in some ways be related to higherlevel phenomena, but this is primarily speculation at this point. Doug has also suggested that genetic mutations may be Nature's attempt at a higher level of Quality. I would be quite interested in hearing about any of the other ideas that each of you might have related to this subject.

Bodvar:

Jason referred to Doug for hinting to a new level above intellect. This is a very interesting point and in my view, the MOQ allows for a never-ending escalation of moralities, but the ascending value is Dynamism itself at work and doesn't qualify as a new static level. For completeness let me add my opinion of the vague borders between the different static levels that Jason brought up.

As to the vague borderline [2] between the different static levels, I would say that this doesn't endanger the Quality idea. According to it, the static patterns are like waves—patterns in an underlying Dynamic medium—different from other patterns but of the same stuff. No one can tell where matter ends and life begins [3] or where an organism ends and a society starts [4] (a body can be regarded as a society of cells [5]), nor the difference between communal cooperation and cultural activities. Still, one recognizes it when one encounters the experience itself.

The friendship term (any other emotion for that matter) is a good example of the interplay: as sexual (erotic, etc.) attraction, it is a biological value; as love (loyalty, sympathy, etc.) it is a social value, but as Platonic love (empathy, etc.), it is an intellectual value. I admit that this is ambiguous and may be debated, but the beauty of the MOQ is that it integrates emotions. In contrast, in

Subject/Object Metaphysics (SOM) such phenomena that play such an enormous role are subjective non-entities.

One must keep the basics clear: permanence as such is static value; what isn't is Dynamic value. The quantum level below the static inorganic level displays no patterns [6], is principally uncertain, and as such, is Dynamic. A level above the static intellectual level? This is a very interesting idea and in my view, the MOQ allows for a never-ending escalation of static patterns, but ascending value is the Dynamic force at work and doesn't qualify as a static level.

Jason:

I'd like to take this opportunity to respond to Bodvar's comments and also to clarify some of my own. Concerning the matter of a quantum level (no pun), you wrote: "The quantum level below the static inorganic level displays no patterns, is principally uncertain and as such Dynamic."

I agree that uncertainty and probability play an invaluable role in our present (theoretical) understanding of this phenomenon. However, I think that many modern physicists would take issue with your comment that quantum level phenomena display no patterns. [7] The patterns that do exist are both static and Dynamic, just as is the content in each of the levels in the MOQ. Take the Schrödinger wave equation as one example: it can be used to describe the definite (i.e., static) probability of any number of potential (Dynamic) outcomes. Dynamic Quality, as Pirsig has presented it, seems to refer to the intangible substrate out of which all reality emerges. It is the constant life force of the universe. Incidentally, Danah Zohar's book, The Quantum Society, presents a coherent new scientific hypothesis involving the necessary influence of such a phenomena throughout all of reality.

In order for Dynamic Quality to have an effect on the static levels, it must interact and influence them in some way. Therefore, static quality cannot accurately be described as exclusively permanent. If this were true, all levels would be fixed, with no potential for further evolution. Static and Dynamic Quality are not isolated entities. They are complimentary aspects of a continuous flux of being/becoming. I see quantum physics as an excellent illustration of this interaction. Furthermore, try to imagine a world without a static quantum level—a level involving patterns of creation and destruction, matter and energy—a constant complimentary dance, if you will. Without this fundamental prerequisite, there would be no raw material facilitating the emergence of inorganic quality, and hence no biological, social, or intellectual quality. Because we cannot directly experience quantum level Quality events through our senses, we naturally overlook or disregard them in our conventional notion of reality.

If the MOQ is to survive as a cogent, holistic system of thought, it must subsume all phenomena. As for the ascendant static level, I entirely agree with your interpretation. The term ascendant does have strong Dynamic implications and for this reason should probably not be used to describe a static level. However, the prospect still remains for additional levels, and it will likely be necessary to refer to such levels in our discussions. Does anyone have any suggestions for an alternative name?

Lars:

Hello, everybody! It's great to finally find other people interested in Pirsig and I'm really looking forward to discussing the MOQ with you. I had a brief discussion with Bodvar earlier this year and had planned to invite him to join this list, but that now seems unnecessary.

Pirsig describes static quality as an agent that works behind the Dynamic forces and tries to preserve what they create. Using this idea on the levels of Quality seems to imply that a hundred million years ago during the reign of the dinosaurs, long before the arrival of man or even our ancestors, the great apes, the levels of social and intellectual quality did not yet exist. I'm less certain on whether it means that entirely different levels of Quality might have arisen in their place had the dinosaurs not died out.

I think this also means that the intellectual level is fairly young, about 2500 years, and that no further levels have yet appeared, although they almost certainly will, if all goes well. Also, with regard to the quantum level—how would you argue that it is not part of the inorganic level? Would you say that the levels of Quality are really continuous, and that the levels are just terms applied to static quality by humans, but not really present in that quality by itself?

Kelly:

I rather suspect that these levels are latent, awaiting the proper patterns to emerge within the static realm in order to be manifested. In terms of evolution, could the emergence of intelligence be merely the emergence of the ability to perceive Quality? If so, then there are gradations in Nature as animals certainly make judgments of value, even if they are rudimentary (my cat turning her nose up at the generic brand cat food placed before her, for just one example). Perhaps brains are those organs that have evolved for the sheer perception of Quality itself. Therefore, the more refined a given brain's ability to make Quality statements, the more evolutionarily advanced the brain.

Lars:

Right, these levels aren't only subjective to human nature (human intelligence and human social behavior) but all of Nature in general. Intellectual quality is a high level that resides throughout Nature. It might appear to be human-centric but this is only because we embody the highest known intelligence—the highest level of Quality—in Nature. Pirsig is really saying something positive about mankind!

Kelly:

A fascinating thing would be to learn just what Quality statements are made by, say, the Orca or Humpback whale populations. Perception must be Dynamic in nature, but it must emerge from static patterns. Is the history of the Universe the tale of its march toward the apprehension of Quality?

Andrew:

As far as higher levels of quality, I think such ideas are pure speculation (as if the rest of this isn't, right?). What do we know of that is of higher Quality than thought? What could morally usurp an idea? Dynamic Quality.

I have a question regarding the Zen practice of meditation as a technique to experiencing Quality or Enlightenment (Buddha). First, I think we should draw a parallel between Phædrus' experience with Quality in the bedless bedroom, staring at the wall for three days and three nights, and a Buddhist monk's Enlightenment experience. This parallel is illustrated in The Guidebook to Zen and the Art of Motorcycle Maintenance quite well. Now, my question: would this quiet meditation be a way of removing Dynamic Quality or directly experiencing it? I use Dynamic Quality since the experience seems to be far from static quality. Any thoughts?

Magnus:

I'd pick the latter. Without having read the Guide you mentioned, I'd say that it would be a case of ritual Pirsig talks about. The staring would become so automatic that all conscious thought would halt. So, the only thing left would be Dynamic Quality. The only thing removed would be almost all levels of static quality, at least the intellectual, social, and biological levels.

Jason:

I agree with this response. There is a strong tendency in the West to promote rational, logical thought, often denying or repressing its irrational, intuitive counterpart. I think meditation is a vehicle, developed in the East, for overcoming this crippling habit and realizing our full selves. As Andrew suggested, meditation offers a way to directly experience the Dynamic substrate that permeates and defines/creates our lives. Pirsig himself strongly promotes such practice as a path to enlightenment.

There is definitely a place and time for rational thought; the key here is to complement this with creative, intuitive experiences. It seems that good art and some religious practices offer alternative paths to this same goal. Pirsig's primary thesis in ZMM (Zen and the Art of Motorcycle Maintenance) was that this holistic experience could (and should!) be extended to the hum drum everyday events of our lives through caring and wholehearted engagement.

MOQ Puzzles [August 1997]

Jason:

Placing all inorganic patterns of value in one class involves an enormous amount of generalization. After all, we're talking about phenomena as small as the first static, distinguishable quantum events, and as large as planets, solar systems, and even entire universes, excluding all Dynamic Quality and phenomena falling into any of the three upper levels, of course.

Bodvar:

Yes, it is an enormous generalization, but a metaphysics professing to cover everything must start at this general level, and of course, the inorganic level is the material universe.

Jason:

If we are to avoid defining an infinite number of new static levels, then there must be some definite gradation within each of the currently existing levels.

Bodvar:

No irony, but I can't see the need for that. For an instance of gradation within the organic level, consider an amoeba. It is as much alive as a human being, biologically seen, even if it is exceedingly simple; however, if we think of man as a social being or capable of symbolic exchange then we have entered other moral levels, particularly the intellectual one.

Jason:

To get the most benefit from this new system, especially when viewed as an ethical tool, the next step must be taken in developing guidelines that resolve conflicts involving static patterns of the same level.

Bodvar:

You have a point here. As I see it the MOQ doesn't present readymade specific ethical guidelines like the Mosaic Law or the Koran, thank Goodness. We have had enough of commandments.

But it solves a series of age-old moral dilemmas—for instance, the problem of evil and free will.

Jason:

Perhaps some real world examples will help. Is a mountain or an ocean more valuable than an atom or a photon? Is this relative to the situation?

Bodvar:

A deep one, this; can you can stand another round of MOQ basics? A mountain, an ocean, an atom, and a photon are within the same quality dimension—the inorganic—and as such equal, but to the other levels (the organic one preferably), they are evaluated very differently. But nothing is dispensable or valueless in a MOQ sense.

Jason:

What distinguishes a high quality intellectual idea from a lower quality one? [8] All things being equal (i.e., same static level), is complexity a valid measure of the amount of quality that a given pattern possesses?

Bodvar:

Another puzzle, but the same goes here. An idea is an static intellectual pattern and as such no more high or low quality than any other thought, but when manifestly applied to a society (in the cultural sense), it may be a catastrophe or a blessing. Remember the insanity part of Lila? The complexity of an idea is no valid measure, as I see it. My hope is that MOQ will make it into society, because it is the highest Quality idea ever.

A MOQ Worksheet [September 1997]

Doug:

Hello, Lila Squad. Robert Pirsig told me to check out Bodvar's site. I have downloaded his paper [http://home.online.no/~skutvik/] but I have not read it yet. It sounds like he does not want to extend the four levels.

Pirsig has already agreed that there is a level under his former bottom level. Plus one may not deny the fractal nature of everything in the multiverse. I am glad that you are seeing the value layers as an ethical system.

Bodvar:

This I find very intriguing. Do you refer to Robert Pirsig's 1995 Brüssels paper, Subjects, Objects, Data and Values (SODV) [http://www.moq.org/forum/emmpaper.html] or another source? Please quote the full passage.

Doug:

Thanks for touching base with me. I am curious about your work on MOQ, et al. Note that Pirsig's SODV paper was written in response to the folk in Brüssels who saw the relationship between the Pirsig system (philosophy) and quantum theory.

Thus, my answer has to be that the whole paper is the passage you seek.

I sent Pirsig the worksheet that now appears on the Lila Squad [http://www.quantonics.com/MoQ.html] and he sent me the Einstein Meets Magrïtte (EMM) paper in response. He affirmed by letter agreement with the added quantum pattern level.

Pirsig's philosophy unifies the subject/object dichotomy in the macroworld. He calls this SO. He says this unification can only happen in the context of Quality. We get SOQ. But we are still in the macroworld. Why? Because Pirsig started at the inorganic level and worked his way up. The inorganic level is the atomic level from a physics perspective. The macroworld is everything above atoms: e.g., molecules, crystals, water, DNA, cells, proteins, organs, life forms, and so on. The microworld is everything below the atomic (inorganic) level. The quantum level represents the next level below the inorganic level. At this level and below, I speculate that we will find a different kind of unification. [9] Could we call it "soq"? For me this is another unification. Note that we still have Pirsig's Dynamic Quality unifying both. Something like this: DQ(SOQ,soq).

I hope this is not too technical. If you find it so, I will attempt another pass at simplification.

Platt:

In response to where the quantum level should be placed in MOQ, I think Pirsig includes it within the inorganic level even though he talks about it separately. First, he states flatly at the beginning of Chapter 12 of Lila that the four levels include everything: "If you construct an encyclopedia of four topics, Inorganic, Biological, Social and Intellectual, nothing is left out." Second, the quantum level exhibits the same intrinsic pattern of preferences (to exist or disappear) that marks all four levels. Third, when you start to subdivide the levels, you begin to lose the elegant simplicity of Pirsig's theory, which, perhaps more than any other factor, points to its truth.

Bodvar:

I don't pretend to be an official MOQ spokesman, but I protest Doug's introduction of God knows what in his MOQ worksheet. He admits that it is purely speculative, but goes on to say: "It may be useful for you in addressing the Pirsig system."

Hardly. If anyone surfs on to the site, spots this, and believes it to be a table of the MOQ, the person is sure to leave as soon as possible and never come back. I would at least. It revolts me because I feel it goes against the grain of the Quality idea, which is to simplify the mess that Subject/Object thinking has led to, and I cannot in my wildest fantasies believe that Pirsig has vouched for this. Doug had better come up with some documentation that he has his OK, and until it is presented I suggest the thing be removed from the page. He may write whatever he wants on the internal mailing list, but to have it up on the billboard isn't fair.

Doug says this is a graphical distillation of Chapter 12 in Lila. I have just re-read it and how and where he finds grounds for introducing additional static levels above and below his essential four ones is incomprehensible. The said chapter opens with the statement, "They are exhaustive. That's all there are."

Doug's diagram heading "Dynamic Value Patterns" is a misnomer too; if one thing is for sure, it is that Dynamic value has no patterns to it (let's keep the fractal nature of chaos aside). It shows that Doug has not grasped the very essence of the Quality idea.

Sorry for sounding so zealous, but I find it terribly important to keep the Quality idea from being polluted. Doug may add tables to his heart's delight if they are underpinned by the fundamental simplicity; for instance, the social interactions are truly baffling and may give employment to his fertile mind for years, but don't mess with the fundamentals. The Einstein Meets Magritte paper will soon be available on the site, and everyone can see that Doug has no back up from Pirsig for his assertions.

Jimmy:

This is my first posting to the Lila Squad; this means that I have dropped (belly first) into the middle of a (lot of) discussion(s) so I hope you will have patience with me. I would like to start with praising the Internet. We are very fortunate to be able to meet and share our thoughts with other people who live in different parts of the world. In the first posting I received the question, "Which has more quality, a mountain or an atom? And do some ideas have more quality than others?"

My answer to the first one would be "mu" (Zen and the Art of Motorcycle Maintenance, but I can not remember where). A mountain can be beautiful, full of life, and of potential. An atom can also be beautiful and full of potential. Of course, they both have quality, but when the above question is asked, an Aristotelian split is made between matter and substance. It is that kind of splitting that the MOQ is turning away from. The question is faulty. We can say: an idea is an idea, but an atom is not a mountain.

I have a spontaneous thought that popped into my mind—if Dynamic Quality is filled with too many levels, do we not lose the flexibility and power? If a quantum level is added, then it sounds to me that it is just sucking up to modern science. Is quantum theory the only theory (that is valid today) that explains matter?

Magnus:

Sucking up. :-)

26

Yeah, I'm also a little skeptic about adding new levels—static levels that is, not Dynamic, but I guess that was a typo. That got me thinking about what it takes to define a new level. What makes two static levels different? If this can be defined, you could match the new level against the others and see if it really is a new, different level. Here's an attempt at this. Feel free to argue. Who am I to stop you guys anyway?

I'd say that the answer is in Lila, where else? Pirsig states that any static level above another is more moral than the other. So, take set A containing patterns belonging to the new level, and a reference set B containing patterns belonging to a known level, then, if all patterns in set A are more (less) moral than all patterns in set B, this would mean that the new level is above (below) the known level. Repeat this with reference sets from all known levels and you could place the new level in the correct place.

Apply this to quantum physics and I'd say that inorganic patterns are more moral than quantum fluctuations.

Doug:

I agree but Pirsig says Dynamic Quality is in the background of the static patterns, but pervades them. I wonder if the quantum level is where pervasion originates. Perhaps quantum flux is a form of pervasion. Pirsig suggests that probability value only has one possible home among his four layers, the inorganic level.

I hereby retract the MOQ table I formerly submitted to the Lila Squad site. I have thought about this a lot. For me Pirsig is about unification of ideas and new patterns of value, especially unification of subject and object. Pirsig is about Dynamic Quality (DQ), which allows new memes to spontaneously arise. I want to be part of that process.

It is clear that my perceptions do not align well with those of Bodvar. I sense a rift, caused by me, in the early stages of the development of the Lila Squad. I do not want to be responsible for damaging your efforts. I am for good, positive energy. I believe that negative energy destroys!

Jimmy:

First, let me say that I do find it possible to find other levels. In Lila, Pirsig says that the intellectual level is quite new but I also think that new levels will be new, something that develops from the intellectual level. But let's return to the question about the quantum level. I have snipped something from a discussion of quantum theory that I have been observing. (To make a very short and very simple resume, when the subatomic particles are not observed, they do not exist.)

"Measurements are always, in principle, repeatable. Once a measurement is carried out and a result is obtained, the state of the measured system must be such as to guarantee that if that measurement is repeated, the same result will obtain (given no tampering in the interim). Subatomic particles are, when not observed, in a state of superposition. When measured or observed, the effect of measuring an observable (quantum mechanic lingo for measurable properties of physical systems) must necessarily be to change the state of the measure system, to collapse it, to make it jump from whatever it may have been just prior to the measurement into some particular state. Which such particular state it gets changed into is determined by the outcome of the measurement. And what determines what state? According to another tenet of quantum mechanics, probability, it is at this point in quantum mechanics, and at no other point other than this one, that an element of pure chance enters into the evolution of the state vector of an observable. We cannot repeat the measurement and get identical results. Since we cannot know how the state vector of an observable will collapse, except probabilistically, we must be uncertain of the outcome."

This must mean, if I understand it correctly, that before we measure the particle it is in superposition. We might say that before it is measured it does not exist. It is nothing but pure Dynamic Quality (this might sound mystical), but when we measure it (give it value), it springs into existence as an inorganic value pattern. This means that quantum scientists look at particles that are formed from nothing.

Doug:

Yes. Pirsig says this is essentially the same as the Quality event. From Pirsig's EMM paper: "The Quality event is the cause of the subjects and objects...this Quality event corresponds to what Bohr means by observation."

Anders:

Hello all. I'm new to this list. Since this is my first posting, I'll just give you all a (very) short rundown of who I am, so you'll know what to expect from me, or not. My name is Anders. I live in Denmark. I've studied physics before, but I've become much more interested in philosophy. I've taken some philosophy classes at the University but I find them completely boring, so I'm studying Computer Science and Mathematics now, while reading philosophy in my spare time, and trying to learn ancient Greek.

But let's get back to my letter:

What Jimmy seems to be doing is to try to interpret quantum mechanics in a Dynamic Quality, static quality framework, in a somewhat intuitive way. I can understand how one might be led to think Dynamic Quality is a somewhat chaotic thing, something we cannot grasp or get hold of. How a particle behaves before it's observed is also something one cannot put a finger on. So both are sort of "chaotic" (in a very, very loose sense of the word), but there is a difference.

You cannot think or talk about how the particles are when they are "non-observable," that is, when they are in a state about which there is no potential way of knowing anything about them, not just the state they were in just before we observed them. The difference between a particle being in a state that is such that we have no potential knowledge of it, and merely being in some state that changes when we observe it, is quite big.

I think there is a general misconception about this, and that is probably where the Schrödinger's cat "paradox" comes from; but that's not for discussing here. I'm going to write an article or something about that later. Now, about the short quote, "The

Quality event is the cause of the subjects and objects…this Quality event corresponds to what Bohr means by observation."

Unfortunately, I have not read the whole paper from which this is taken, but it seems to correspond somewhat with what my impression of the Quality event is. It is basically the same thought that all of Phenomenology (Husserl, Ponty) builds on—that basic experience is the foundation of all knowledge and that the world (objects) and the soul (subject) are really just different kinds (or patterns) of experience. This correlates quite well with Quality as it's explained in ZMM, and what you call the Quality event. But how this relates to the four levels, I've yet to understand fully.

Bodvar:

This morning there were new postings, and I was happy to find Doug's offer for withdrawing his table among them. We must be extremely cautious to modify Pirsig's teachings at that fundamental level and at this early stage. There is something between carved in stone and written on water. In Lila, there is a passage where Pirsig describes how life found foothold in matter and he says, "A Dynamic advance is meaningless until it can find some static pattern with which to protect itself from degeneration back to the conditions that existed before the advance was made, a static latching on of the gain that has been made, then another Dynamic advance."

Some latching of his teachings is needed for it to find foothold and make progress. Another parallel (from ZMM) is when Subject/Objectivism was just a fleeting idea held by a little "Socrates Squad" in a predominantly sophisticated culture; they fought like wolves to keep the teachings pure. Now history is in the process of another turn, where SOM is to be replaced by another grander overview. At this early stage, it is a fragile touch and go. The MOQ must be nurtured carefully—no pruning or experimental additions, please.

A last go (for me) at the confounding additional levels issue— our bickering over this reminds me of Albert Einstein and Niels Bohr during their famous fight over the interpretation of quantum theory. Bohr said, "There is no quantum world. There is only an abstract quantum physics description. It is wrong to think that the task of physics is to find how Nature is. Physics concerns what we can say about Nature." I have an impression that what Jimmy earlier (and Bohr) pointed out is not heeded sufficiently. There is no physical/objective realm that metaphysics may or may not agree with. Theory comes first.

The last sentence is madness in a Subject/Object context, and as young Phædrus of ZMM knew of no other reality, it blew his mind. Luckily, he survived the trip outside our Subject/Object Mythos and came back to tell of another perspective.

Einstein never reconciled himself with the uncanny consequences of the Copenhagen interpretation and searched for the hidden parameters that would make quantum theory into ordinary Newtonian physics. The search for new levels is a parallel to Einstein's hunt; a MOQ after such a modification would be another subject/object, physics/mysticism a la Capra and/or Danah Zohar. I have read both and particularly Zohar shows how it is possible to be close to a Quality breakthrough, but not making it completely.

One last thing—I accused Doug of not having grasped the basics of the MOQ. From what he writes, I take that back with apologies. He may be the best ambassador of our common cause.

Quality? [September 1997]

Jason:

After a brief period away from our discussion, I must say that I was pleasantly surprised to find a pile of messages waiting for me upon my return. To my dismay, however, it seems that our usual cooperative and mature exchange has given way to much bickering and egotism. (Particularly Bodvar's harsh criticism of Doug's diagram!) Good, heated debate is one thing, but it seems that many of our recent posts have served the sole purpose of defending strongly held personal positions without offering any hope for the possibility of collaboration and mutual growth.

A very respected man once told me that one has no right to take issue with an opposing position until he is able to restate his understanding of that position sufficiently enough to receive the other's approval. Perhaps this sort of active listening would serve us well.

In regard to the frequent allusions to Pirsig's personal position on the issues being discussed, I see this as a moot point. Pirsig has offered us a very solid foundation for a new worldview. However (regardless of what he has or has not written), this system is not carved in stone; it is Dynamic! Once the fundamental concepts are understood, it is time to move on and to allow the MOQ to evolve on its own.

Is it the intention of this group to study ZMM and Lila as sacred scripture? (I trust that we are all aware of the distinction between philosophy and philosophology.) Granted, we do share a definite need for a strong common foundation (i.e., static quality) for further progress to be possible. An important point to bear in mind at this juncture is that Dynamic Quality, that ever-present potential for further growth, reigns supreme over all that is or ever will be. No metaphysical system will ever entirely capture this for our finite intellects. My point here is simple. We must allow the MOQ room to evolve.

Turning to the highly debated issue of a quantum level, let me attempt to summarize my understanding of the positions being expressed. Doug has suggested that quantum (i.e., microworld) phenomena possess some static characteristics, which distinguish them from inorganic patterns. Therefore, Doug feels a need for an additional level in the MOQ below the inorganic, which would specifically address such phenomena. (I personally see this as a valid opportunity to enhance our awareness of the many embodiments of static quality.)

Bodvar seems to appreciate the simplicity of the existing framework to the extent that he entirely rejects the notion of additional levels (except perhaps for those above the intellectual). He also rejects a need for gradation within each of the existing levels. From my reading of his comments, Bodvar is content with the MOQ as it stands. This is a valid position. Granted, one can subsume all experience within an ambiguous system. My question is related to the usefulness of such a system—are we truly getting all we can out of the Dynamic/static split? My contention, viewing the MOQ as an ethical guide, is that we are not.

I do believe that a definite distinction can be made between atomic and subatomic phenomena. According to my second hand interpretation, atomic phenomena are for the most part static, observable, and measurable. Atoms do not spontaneously appear and disappear. They do not exhibit wave/particle duality. They are not spontaneously created and destroyed, at least not under the conditions that we are most familiar with, that is, standard atmospheric temperatures and pressures. These general statements exclude radioactive elements, which do in fact spontaneously decay. The very essence of subatomic patterns, conversely, involves a constant interplay between existence and non-existence, creation and destruction, being and becoming.

As I've stated before, I do not pretend to be an expert in the area of quantum mechanics, but I would like to pursue this thread further and to offer a first attempt to answer your question. Dynamic Quality (a.k.a. the Quality event, measurement, experience, observation, etc.) plays a vital role here. Prior to this event, a subatomic pattern of value does not exist. The closest we can come to describing what is taking place here is to say that such a pattern is Dynamically created out of an elusive vacuum of potential. (The concept underlying the vacuum here does not lend itself well to verbal interpretation. It is incorrect to say that the vacuum is nothing, since it contains within itself the potential for all things. It is also incorrect to say that it is anything, since it possesses no distinguishing characteristics prior to the moment of the Quality event.)

Drawing this conceptual distinction between the atomic and subatomic levels emphasizes the necessary and sufficient role that Dynamic Quality plays in producing all static patterns.

Immediately following the Quality event, the subatomic particles (over two hundred of them identified to date) do in fact exist and do possess characteristics, which completely distinguish them from the higherlevel atomic patterns that they enable. If these phenomena are neglected (or grouped together with atomic patterns), then how can the MOQ account for such documented phenomena as wave/particle duality and Heisenberg's Uncertainty Principle? Certainly, we cannot describe these as characteristics of Dynamic Quality itself, since by definition it is a creative event, possessing no distinguishing characteristics of its own (except perhaps an inherently evolutionary or synthesizing tendency, hence facilitating the emergence of static patterns of value).

Bodvar:

This site has in a few days developed into one of the hottest spots on the philosophical Internet (can we keep up this pace?) and I appreciate Jason's effort to keep the exchange polite and positive. I also see his point in trying to counterbalance my rhetoric, but when something interests me or goes against my opinion, I can't manage to stay quiet. The subatomic level debate meets both criteria so here I go again. Jason upholds his view of a distinction between sub and regular atomic phenomenon, and says among else, "Atomic phenomena do not exhibit wave/particle duality. They are not spontaneously created and destroyed," etc.

Regarding the first, particle compounds (atoms/molecules) don't, but protons and neutrons do, and they are atomic according to Jason's criteria in the sense of being permanent, observable, and measurable (not elementary of course). If used in the double slit experiment they appear as waves or particles depending upon the setup, and as everything is made up of particles, the double nature (Dynamism) underpins everything upwards.

Regarding the second, I don't think the atom is a useful borderline except in the sense that the simplest atom (in molecular form) is the lightest element of the macroworld. I feel that Jason's subatomic realms are the more elusive host of particles that hardly live long enough to be detected (only relativistic effects in particle accelerators make it possible), and yet when those particles occur they are stable inorganic patterns. A particle is not a substance that obeys laws: "It is the law, or the pattern, or the value, itself! It is a little moral order." (Lila, page 392) We must keep in mind that the stability term (of the MOQ patterns) has nothing to do with durability in time. [10] A pattern can be discontinuous both in time and in space.

It is here, with all respect, that I feel a little misunderstanding may introduce itself and forgive me for stressing this point: The subject/object myth of various objective substances—subject to natural laws—is left completely behind in the MOQ. The static inorganic patterns (along with all patterns of all levels) are morality patterns, continuous or discontinuous, permanent or perishable, it doesn't matter. Even the virtual particles that don't live long enough to be registered are stable patterns the immeasurable instant they exist. The rest is Dynamic. There can't be a pattern to Dynamism. It's self contradictory (I disregard the new fractal and chaos theories in this context. They counter the old void nature of vacuum, but not the MOQ, to the contrary).

Finally, as the organic, the social, and the intellectual patterns are based on the inorganic, I fully agree with what Jason says about "written on water." Metaphysically seen, Dynamism is at the root of everything, but there can be standing waves in a Dynamic medium.

Lastly, I'm not negative towards Danah Zohar, and I would be happy to discuss her ideas. I only said she is very close to a Quality understanding without quite making it, and members of the Lila Squad can't possibly blame me for thinking that only Pirsig has made the full transition.

I don't go for any worship Pirsig style; I don't think he would like any messiah role. I have had my scares regarding his ideas, but when they always seem to come out on top, I can't help sounding a little awed.

Jason:

Bodvar's analysis of my most recent quantum level message was particularly exciting. I finally feel that we have come to a point in this quantum level discussion where we truly understand one another. I fully agree with all that you (Bodvar) offered in this last piece. Further debate concerning the inclusion/exclusion of a quantum level seems unnecessary from my perspective.

Artificial Intelligence [September 1997]

Magnus:

A little diversion from the deep discussions about quantum theories as requested—I've been trying to figure out this so-called "intellect." When I think about it, I always come up with two different kinds. First, we have these static intellectual patterns of value that are supposed to devour society and use it for its own purposes. Then, we have the intellect that enables us to walk, talk, and function as human beings. From time to time, I simply wanted to split them apart and call the first something else. The definitions, or rather the examples of its manifestations today, have been like Bodvar's "individual freedom." Don't get me wrong; I also think that individual freedom is better than social tyranny. It's just that in all the history of static quality, this scenario has never appeared before. What's more important, it does not conform to the MOQ. The scenario is that patterns of level A (humans) are used to form patterns of level A+1 (society), and when level A+2 (intellect) appears, level A patterns suddenly pop up from nowhere and take command. It doesn't make sense!

The usual case would be that level A+2 would take control over level A+1, still leaving level A at the mercy of level A+1. And level A will have no idea what's happening. It's totally unaware of level A+1's manipulations, so is level A+1 about A+2's. I realize that we don't have that many analogies to work with here: 3 levels in a row in a 4 level hierarchy only make 2 constellations. Second, analogies might not be the best approach to the problem. After all, the levels are separate for a reason—they're different! But it's the only approach I can come up with.

OK, let's drop down a level and see what happens. Set the inorganic level as level A. Level A+1 (the organic) uses level A to form organisms and level A has no clue, so far so good. Then, a strange thing happens. To form a society (level A+2) out of organic patterns, you can either take whole organisms, i.e. sheep, to form a herd. Or, you choose simple organic cells to form one sheep! So what level does the sheep belong to? [11]

It gets even stranger if you choose humans instead of sheep, because the humans that form society are fully aware about the society they're supposed to have no clue about! I don't know if anyone else has had similar thoughts. It usually starts with thinking about the intellectual level and why you can't get a grip on what exactly it is. But you can really start with (almost) any level and find the same problem. Until recently, I just fought the thought off thinking that, surely I didn't grasp MOQ enough to understand it. But with you guys on the other end, I thought I might at least formulate some questions, and as usual, I try to answer them myself, so here we go.

Maybe you're already guessing what I'm getting at, or maybe it's been clear to you all along, and it just wasn't sufficiently explained for me in Lila. The answer is that the "objects" we see around us can be viewed and used as any level up to and including its highest level. Sheep can be used as inorganic, organic, or social patterns of value (assuming that sheep do not have intellect), depending on what you're interested in. And a human can be used as patterns of any level. This would mean that any society, even a classic SOM society, should have patterns of all levels up to and including social.

Hmmm. Where are those organic ones? You could argue that we are the organic patterns in a SOM society. And in some early societies I guess we were the only organic patterns, but not in a modern society. Today, societies without schools, fire departments, police, and so on are considered to be very primitive ones, just as early collections of cells are considered to be very primitive forms of life.

So, you argue that all parts of a SOM society need people to function, and I'd say, yes, today, but not conceptually. The only thing society needs is the function that the different organs perform. It needs a fire department to extinguish fires, it needs schools to train new members of society, and so on. It does not need intelligent people!

A question for the think tank—if social patterns use the "functions" of the organic level to build upon, what do other levels use their lower level for? Is that the difference between the levels? I mean, imagine a society exploiting the function of single atoms, or even smaller particles. The smallest society we recognize today is a cell, right? Maybe we should consider an atom to be a society too. Or maybe I'm being confused by Bohr's atom model being constructed like a society. We really like constructing societies all around us, don't we.

The next question is really about this. Why did humans with intellect start building societies in the first place? According to the MOQ, that is immoral! And, according to Pirsig, we are just now on our way to break loose of these chains we constructed for ourselves thousands of years ago. I must confess though, that considering the life the people of the time led, forming a society was quite moral! Why? I guess they had no choice. It was either that or being back on the organic level struggling for survival every day. Note though, that our individual intellectual patterns are supported by our individual social patterns called our bodies. Many intellectual patterns supported by our SOM society have not yet emerged! Or…?

I think that we would be able to recognize it if it had emerged. On the other hand, I wouldn't expect us to recognize patterns of a higher level some of you have mentioned. We're supposed to have no clue about higher levels, static levels that is. So, back to this elusive intellect of ours, I'd say that the only intellectual patterns we see today are our own individual ones. The reason we have societies is to make survival easier. Unfortunately, we have had to run society more or less by ourselves. But that time will soon come to an end and we can let society run things for us and intellectualize as much as we want, as we are here on Lila Squad!

The question has popped up in my mind a couple of times during the discussion here about quantum levels, but also when Bodvar suggested a new thread about "the most elusive top notch." My question is—are static levels really and absolutely dependent on the next lower level?

As some others in the Lila Squad, I studied computer science and am now working with computers every day. So I often get to think about artificial intelligence, wondering if it is possible to get intellectual patterns of value [12] into a computer, which rather would be, get intellectual patterns of value to devour the inorganic patterns of value called the computer. [13] According to Pirsig, this would be utterly impossible because it involves skipping not only one but two static levels [14] and this really bugs me! Is there no way in h-ll anyone, anywhere or anytime, can build such a thing?

A real world observation—a research team (in the States I think) is making small mechanical insect-like robots. The robots can walk on their six legs and communicate with each other. The idea is to send them to Mars or somewhere similar and explore the vicinity. This team of robots (I think they were talking of about six) is worth much more together than any of them alone. Each robot can have a unique ability in some area but basically every one is similar. This is a team, and when I'm saying team, I mean team as in a static social pattern of value. The robots themselves are expendable; any robot can fall into a cave and break into thousands of pieces, but the team is still there.

From now on, I'll assume that this team really is a social pattern of value. [15] So this is a good place to write your thoughts about that. There are, at least, two ways out of this dilemma. You say either that static patterns of value are independent of the next lower level, or you say that the robots are artificial organic patterns of value.

I'd go for the latter, and I'll try to explain why. The static patterns we see around us are built using lower levels of static patterns. Why? Because at the time they appeared there was nothing else around to build it upon. Or rather, the lower patterns that formed were the first pattern that the higher level could use to build upon. Just because our world looks like it does in terms of what specific patterns of each level have formed doesn't mean that it has to be that way.

An analogy from Lila would be the novel that is able to exist on paper, on a disk, or in the computer's memory. It's still the same novel. This is why I say that the robots in the team are organic patterns of value. [16] The problem seems to be the name given to that level. Organic life is not the only possible manifestation of this level. It is one of many possible groups of patterns belonging to the level.

My answer to the original question would be, yes, a pattern of a higher level is dependent on some pattern of the next lower level, but not necessarily as we know it. So maybe one day it will be possible to build that machine I mentioned earlier using artificial social and organic patterns in between. Maybe the Internet will develop intellectual patterns one day.

Bodvar:

This puzzle looks like a blow to the very core of the MOQ idea and I congratulate Magnus for providing this most crucial acid test of its validity. I also congratulate him on his own solution to it, a most impressive piece of work, this. My own answer to his first point is— yes, definitely. A static level is dependent upon the next lower one, but I also agree that artificial intelligence is possible in the MOQ universe. Only in that, I will add, because in the Subject/Object worldview the awareness or consciousness concepts put up an impenetrable defense. And yet, as Magnus points out, this produces an impasse—how can static intellectual patterns arise directly out of static inorganic patterns (matter equals machines) skipping two levels altogether?

He goes on to say: "According to Pirsig, this would be utterly impossible because it involves skipping not only one but two static levels. And this really bugs me! Is there no way in h-ll anyone, anywhere or anytime, can build such a thing?"

I don't think Pirsig has said anything about this particular theme, but I acknowledge Magnus' deduction—so how can this be reconciled? I think Magnus delivered a valuable and valid solution himself—it is only in a superficial sense that levels are bypassed. The robots/machines may constitute an artificial society as well, and that leaves only one static level missing, i.e., life. But may it be discussed if not there is an artificial organic level too? Yes, I would even omit the artificial term in a metaphysical sense.

Then Magnus says something that is a bit ambiguous to me: "The static patterns we see around us are built using lower levels of static patterns. Why? Because at the time they appeared there was nothing else around to build it upon. Or rather, the lower patterns that formed were the first pattern that the higher level could use to build upon. Just because our world looks like it does in terms of what specific patterns of each level have formed, doesn't mean that it has to be that way."

I agree fully to the first part, and also to the last if he by this means what building block (element) the Dynamic forces used for introducing life on to matter (carbon) was a coincidence, but I uphold that the matter-life-society-intellect sequence is inviolable.

Magnus:

Thanks for the clarification Bodvar. When I'm writing, it's hard to see what others will see reading it.

Annotations by Robert M. Pirsig

1. I've never had strong objections to this. My reason for not doing so was that the quantum level is inorganic, and the addition of another level adds complexity to an already difficult book without strengthening the basic thesis.

2. This seems to be a recurrent objection to the MOQ. It occurs, I think, because I didn't get into enough detail on these borders. I'll try to do so now as questions of vagueness come up.

3. Life is matter that has been configured by DNA. The distinction is very sharp.

4. In the MOQ all organisms are objective. They exist in the material world. All societies are subjective. They exist in the mental world. Again, the distinction is very sharp. For example, the "President of the U.S." is a social pattern. No objective scientific instrument can distinguish a President of the U.S. from anyone else.

5. This is a stretch that seems to destroy the meaning of the word "society." One could say "an atom is a society of electrons and protons," but that weakens the meaning of the word without gaining anything.

6. The quantum level displays precise mathematical patterns, and as such has to be primarily static.

7. Right.

8. Its truth, mainly. Also the magnitude of the questions it answers or problems it solves. Other things being equal, its rhetorical "elegance" is also important in the mathematical sense of that term.

9. I don't think so. The "quantum level" is a part of the inorganic level. This addition of Doug's distinctions is not untrue, and I have written this to him, but neither is the omission of these distinctions untrue. You can have it either way. But it seems to me that to include these extra distinctions lowers the clarity of the MOQ, particularly to someone who has never read it before.

10. Yes. Unfortunately "static" and "Dynamic" have a meaning in physics that refers to space and time and motion and this can be confused with the static and Dynamic of the MOQ.

11. Using the MOQ description of biology as objective and society as subjective, it is clear that sheep are biological. A herd of sheep is also biological.

12. Both hardware and software are formed by intellectual patterns of value.

13. "Devour" is normally a biological function that I wouldn't use in this case but if you want to extend it to intellectual level you can say that when the programmer programs the computer to do something the intellectual patterns are "devouring" the hardware of the computer.

14. I don't recall saying you can't skip levels, but in this case none are skipped. The hand that taps the computer keys is biological. The school that taught the computer programmer how to program is social. He had to learn programming from somebody through social interaction unless his name is Von Neumann. But Von Neumann didn't grow up in the jungle. Social institutions had to educate him.

15. This assumption destroys the system of classification set up by the MOQ. Social patterns are subjective. Robots are not.

16. This also destroys the system of classification set up by the MOQ. Organic patterns contain DNA.

Chapter 2

Character is like a tree and reputation like its shadow. The shadow is what we think of it; the tree is the real thing. —Abraham Lincoln

Useful Interpretation of MOQ [September 1997]

Jason:

I do see the need for a more evolved MOQ, which might answer the underlying ethical question that prompted my "Quality?" post— how can the MOQ be interpreted in such a way that it becomes useful and practical as a tool in making our everyday value judgments?

Pirsig led the way in Lila by demonstrating how some patterns take precedence over others (e.g., ideas vs. social norms, doctors vs. germs). What I am seeking is a more refined system that will answer subtler questions. Bodvar has taken Pirsig's ZMM approach to the question, offering something like "you will know it when you see it." This sort of statement, unfortunately, does me no good. Intuition is a powerful aspect of consciousness, but its significance should not be convoluted as an easy "out" in a rational debate.

Ultimately, how can we more carefully apply the MOQ to conflicts in our everyday life, aside from the obvious case of inter level conflicts? Perhaps I'm missing some important aspects of the existing framework. If so, I hope that someone on the list can point me in the right direction.

Platt:

One way I use MOQ is to help me analyze an individual's value system so I can better understand his basic philosophical assumptions. For example, from Jason's original "Quality?" post I compiled the following list of his likes and dislikes:

Positive Values vs. Negative Values

Maturity—Egotism

Cooperation—Bickering

Collaboration—Harsh criticism
Mutual growth—Defending strongly held positions
Active listening—Ideas carved in stone
Evolution—Sacred scripture
Potential for growth—Philosophology
Enhanced awareness—Ambiguity
Usefulness—Convolution
Practicality—Easy outs
Refinements—Hard and fast systems
Subtlety—Highly structured
Rational debate—Begging the question

From this I conclude that Jason comes down on the side of evolutionism, rationalism, relativism, and pragmatism. The only one of these assumptions Pirsig agrees with is evolutionism. He is critical of pure rationalism (subject/object thinking), relativism (all assumptions are equally worthy), and pragmatism (a static social pattern retarding the evolution of truth and Dynamic Quality). Now you can argue with my conclusions about Jason's assumptions (and he probably would) and about my interpretation of how Pirsig might view them. But that's not my point.

My point is I find useful and practical the intellectual framework MOQ provides that helps me uncover the assumptions (often hidden) in philosophical discussions, as well as "everyday" interactions with family, friends, and associates, thus "enhancing" my "awareness" of what's really going on. If I make a mistake the other party is usually quick to correct me, sometimes justifiably, sometimes not.

As for deciding which assumptions are true, I like Pirsig's art gallery analogy in Chapter 3, "…simply to enjoy and keep those that are of value." [17]

Jason:

Thank you for the time that you took to address my question. I found your comments highly valuable, but I do have several questions regarding your interpretation of Pirsig's work that I hope you can clear up for me.

First, I'll accept your point on rationalism. I have (consciously) favored such an approach in my prior posts, but I do appreciate the undeniable importance of intuitive experience as well. I agree that Pirsig heavily promotes the value of intuition, but you can't deny the fact that his writing and thinking is highly structured and analytical at its core. After all, the MOQ is a rational system. That is the point that I was trying to make here. If we're going to promote a coherent metaphysics—one that is to be accepted on a global scale—we must continue that endeavor through to the end. Perhaps there will come a point where rational tools can take us no further. Rational methods must then wisely give way to complimentary intuitive ones, as exquisitely illustrated in many Eastern philosophies. My humble suggestion is that before we render them obsolete we get what mileage we can out of our familiar rational tools.

I must be a bit more harsh with your comments regarding relativism, that "all assumptions are equally worthy." What I am offering is that we carefully and completely consider all ideas, suggestions, assumptions, etc., before denying their relative value. After such consideration, I do believe a distinction must be made between high quality ideas and lower quality ones. (My question regarding characteristics of this valuation process still stands.)

Finally, I entirely disagree with your comments regarding pragmatism. After all, the original impetus for Phædrus' philosophical quest (back in ZMM) was to develop a worldview that would more closely coalescence with real world experiences than that resulting from the restrictive Subject/Object dichotomy. I believe that Pirsig's static/Dynamic split effectively serves this purpose. Do you feel that attempting to apply the MOQ as an ethical system has the effect of "retarding the evolution of truth and Dynamic Quality"? Isn't the central theme of your message essentially an (thoughtful) example of the pragmatic virtue of Pirsig's thought? I think this is an important point that requires further elaboration and discussion.

You personal application of the framework was very interesting and insightful. Thank you again for taking the time to share your thoughts.

Platt:

I enjoyed your most generous and thoughtful letter. It gives me a chance to demonstrate another "pragmatic" way I use MOQ which goes back to your original question: "How can MOQ be interpreted in such a way that it becomes useful and practical in making everyday value judgments?"

You raise several apparent paradoxes in your letter that Pirsig might call "platypi." Following your good advice, permit me to rephrase them so you can tell if I understood them correctly.

The first one was—how could MOQ be critical of rationalism when it is itself a rational system? The MOQ answer is that trying to create a perfect, rational metaphysics can't be done. As Pirsig says in Chapter 9: "The game is supposed to stop when it is agreed that a particular line of reasoning is impossible. This is supposed to be similar to checkmate. But conflicting positions go on for centuries without any such checkmate being agreed upon." I think Pirsig might say that, although his metaphysics is rationally constructed to communicate it to others in our current culturally approved universe of language and thought, its value is provisional and should only be accepted until something better comes along.

Your second paradox was—how can MOQ be critical of relativism when it asserts that what is true is whatever a person believes is good? The MOQ answer is that good is direct everyday experience and thus allows more than one set of truths to exist. But since truth is a universal concept, it transcends relativity.

For example, in logic, if one asserts that all is relative, he asserts an absolute, non-relative truth. Pirsig says in Chapter 29: "Truth's a metaphysical subject that everyone disagrees about. There are many different definitions of truth and some of them could throw a whole lot more light on what was happening to Lila than a subject/object metaphysics does. If objects are the ultimate reality then there's only one true intellectual construction of things, that which corresponds to the objective world. But if truth is defined as a high quality set of intellectual value patterns, then insanity can be defined as just a low quality set of intellectual value patterns, and you get a whole different picture."

An aside: when I first learned of Gödel's proof that in math and logic there will always be certain true statements that cannot be proved true, my opinion of rationality as high quality value pattern dropped down several pegs.

Your third paradox was—how could MOQ be critical of pragmatism when I attempt to show in this letter and the previous one the pragmatic virtue of Pirsig's thought? The MOQ answer is that pragmatism is a social pattern of good. For example, political correctness is a pragmatic method of promoting social harmony, but by punishing heretical thought it blocks Dynamic Quality. Pirsig says in Chapter 29: "The Holocaust produced a satisfaction among Nazis. That was quality for them. They considered it to be practical. But it was a quality dictated by low level static social and biological patterns whose overall purpose was to retard the evolution of truth and Dynamic Quality."

I assume Pirsig has no objection to my using a personal form of pragmatism (such as I'm demonstrating in these letters) so long as I don't try to impose it on others.

Jason, whether my pragmatic application of MOQ to these paradoxes is of high or low quality is for you decide. I'm sure you'll find some of it puzzling and perhaps downright mistaken. I'm also aware that in Lila, like in the Bible, one can usually find an idea or a quotation to support a particular viewpoint. But for me that's the magic. Pirsig has given us a sweeping new intellectual framework, magnificent in its breadth, depth, and explanatory power, but simple enough so even someone like me can begin to grasp it.

Intellect from Society Theorem [September 1997]
Magnus:
I don't think there's any difference between what we usually call a society, and a society of cells. [18] Social patterns of value

combine organic patterns of value into something more valuable than the sum of its parts. [19] A society can be recursively divided into smaller societies until the parts no longer can perform its function without the society. The larger society in each step uses the function (the organic property) of the organs within it. It does not care whether they in turn are societies or not.

In Lila, Pirsig describes the cell as two organs, the Dynamic and fragile core and the protective shield. [20] They are organs [21] to the cell-society. [22] Separately, they are inorganic; inorganic patterns of value that can perform a function for a society are more valuable than other inorganic patterns. This discrete criterion marks the division between inorganic and organic patterns of value. [23]

Lila tends to give that impression. But I also think that the society of robots I mentioned in an earlier post is a society, i.e., social patterns of value. And they can't reproduce themselves, but they are organs anyway, to that society. This is also why I never use the word biology when I talk about organic patterns. [24]

If a society needs a chair, it must have a chair maker in case the chair breaks. In that case, the chair would be organic patterns of value, which should make us a little more careful about what we say about the organic level, i.e., not set it equal to what we call "life" and so on.

Social patterns use the function of its organs.

I think Lila only describes the different level's manifestations we can see here on earth. But they are only examples, not the definition. And since we are talking about static patterns, a definition should be possible.

Bodvar:

That is exactly the way language/intellect developed, namely as a survival tool for society. This is in fact an important part of Pirsig's idea. He says so in Lila (on top of page 306, Bantam Press): "The intellect's evolutionary purpose has never been to discover an ultimate meaning of the universe. That is a relatively recent fad. Its historical purpose has been to help a society find food, detect danger and defeat enemies. It can do this well or poorly, depending on the concepts it invents for this purpose."

All value patterns started their "career" in the service of the parent level, but gradually they took off on their own and became a new value dimension. [25] I don't think that humans, or even humanoids, ever have been below the social level threshold; even apes live in societies with strict rules and hierarchical structures.

Magnus:

The languages our individual intellects are built upon are the language provided by our social patterns of value called our bodies. [26] It hit me when you wrote, "...in the invention of language." How can a language, and now I mean a conventional language used to communicate thoughts, needs or warnings, be invented without intellect?

Bodvar:

Here your "intellect as consciousness" surfaces again. Symbolic abstract language is the intellect! It is an intellectual activity to convey ideas/thoughts. Needs and warnings may be conveyed much more effectively by other signals by all animals. There might be a conference held on the needs of the hungry or on the threatening global pollution, but that takes place in the intellectual realm.

Language is the birth of intellect, but thousands upon thousands of years went by with human beings capable of speech but still "submerged" in social values. Also, you sensed the extremely important effect that language had on creating the subject/object division. In a way, subject/object metaphysics itself can be viewed as the first intellectual manifestation! "Pursuit of rationality!" Just great! Objectivity (truth) was the first "SOM as intellect" breakout.

Yes, "in the brain," just as a novel can reside in magnetic orientations, print, or in your memory, but it is not the inorganic medium. The words are static intellectual patterns.

Deep down we have a reptilian brain from that period of evolution, then a limbic brain common to all mammals, and so on upwards until the special human neocortex and frontal lobes. Of course, the intellectual patterns have a home in the organic body in the sense that every level builds upon the next lower, which builds upon the next, etc. In that capacity, all levels have a home in matter. Society and intellect have a home in biology, but intellect (of the MOQ!) does not emerge from organic body directly; it grows from society. Sorry for hammering so strongly on this point, but I have a feeling that when (Magnus) the term "organic body" is used here, it is really its inorganic (matter) aspect that creeps in.

And if the SOM's "consciousness produced by brain" notion enters, it messes up the MOQ completely. We are not in disagreement, as I see from the previous that you have written. Brain is a prerequisite for intellect even in an MOQ context, but like a Jesuit, I am out to exorcise every vestige of the Subject/Object "consciousness out of matter" idea (which leads into the age old blind alley of: everything is matter or everything is mind). The neural system had to reach a certain complexity for the Dynamic forces to use it as a vehicle for the intellectual development (just as matter had to have a volatile element like carbon for the forces to use as a vehicle of life). But, again, brain is biology and matter while intellect is all levels. The brain (Penrose's "tubulae" or whatever) as "producer of consciousness" is foreign to the MOQ. [27]

Magnus:

Bodvar, as I understand it, my view of the intellectual level differs from yours as follows. My view:

Our individual intellect are intellectual patterns of value built upon our bodies, which are social patterns of value built upon (to simplify things) one human, which are organic patterns of value built upon inorganic patterns of value called matter. Our individual intellectual patterns of value are influenced by other individual's intellectual patterns of value in the same way that inorganic patterns of value are influenced by other inorganic patterns of value and so on.

Your view:

Our individual intellects are carriers of intellectual patterns of value built upon the social patterns of value called "the society," what I called a SOM society in my original post. This society is built upon organic patterns of value called our bodies, which are built upon inorganic patterns of value called matter. The intellectual patterns are dependent on society.

My view needs to deal with this dilemma:

It's hard to separate the social patterns of value called our body, and the organic patterns of value also called our body. My solution goes something like this. The social patterns of value called our body are built upon the different organs of our body. The body uses these organs as organic patterns of value; they are however also social patterns of value in that they in turn use different sub organs to make up the organ. You might think this sounds very SOM oriented, and I say, yes, but social patterns are very SOM oriented in that it's very hierarchical. I wrote that a chair might be used by some society and in that case, the chair would be organic patterns of value.

Let's say that a society needs an organ for another organ to sit on. This organ could be a chair or a horse. The difference, and the only difference, between the chair and the horse, is that the horse is selfreproducing whereas the chair is not. Therefore I say that it's not the organic (as in carbon based, "self reproducing life form") property of organic patterns of value that are of interest to the social level, but the function of the organic pattern. As soon as inorganic patterns of value are able to perform a function for a society, it can be used by the society as organic patterns of value, i.e., it has raised one level on the static scale. The dissection of societies inside societies stops where the function stops.

Your view needs to deal with this dilemma:

If we are only carriers of the intellectual patterns of value supported by the social patterns of value called the society, then how did the Indian in Lila (I don't remember his name) who opposed the priests and was banned and excluded by his society, survive? You can't say that only the organic patterns of value called his body survived, because he came back with his intellect intact, destroyed his native society, and constructed a new one.

Bodvar:

Your summaries about our respective views and the dilemmas they face were well formulated. You even formulated your own view's problems very fairly. Also congratulations on the Züni Indian example, but the dilemma for (my view of) the MOQ I fail to see.

It proves it. Being banned from one's society is a harrowing experience, and may cause the individual to "loose its mind" (going mad if you still live in a human society or turning into a wolf if you live among wolves). That proves the point. The reason that the brujo survived was that he was so firmly anchored to an intellectual vision (ideas are the most powerful means ever brought to bear) that the loss of tribal contact did not affect him. He saw himself belonging to his people in such a deep sense that the priests couldn't shake his social value foundations. Those who aren't visionaries are more vulnerable to rejection; we all are more or less. However, no particular social relationship we live in is the (objective) social value dimension of the MOQ.

Principally the MOQ's static intellectual "dimension" has nothing to do with smartness, intelligence, or ability to think. There are calculating prodigies who can come up with the most amazing results in seconds, so their "thinking" is not the least affected even if they are intellectual and social nitwits. Also, consider the immense neural calculations (organic value/mind) taking place for us to be alive (do you know Tor Nörretranders' Mærk Verden?).

Magnus:

This is starting to look silly. First I give you a dilemma that I thought would disprove your view of the MOQ, and you regard it as proof for it. Now, you gave me another one, and I'll do exactly the same. Either we don't understand each other's points of view, or we're plain stupid.

About the wolf society dilemma—what it shows to me is that "our society" is needed to develop what "our society" considers intellect. In the same way a wolf society is needed to develop what a wolf would call intellect; stay clean, lie down when the big chief growls, and so on. It shows to me that wolves and boys are able to develop static intellectual patterns of value that....

A few comments on your earlier post: you say, "Symbolic abstract language is the intellect!" I'd say that symbolic abstract language (i.e., most human language) is the base on which static intellectual patterns of value are formed on top of a SOM society. Today's manifestations of such patterns are libraries, databases, the Internet, and so on.

Then you say, "Needs and warnings may be conveyed much more effectively by other signals by all animals." But those signals are also a language. It is the language that enables an animal to perform a function for its society. The only language a child knows at birth is the built in one—cry when hungry, loud voices and spankings are bad. If the child had no language, it would be totally impossible to communicate or affect it. I'm beginning to think that this is the core to our disagreement. You think of language as human language communicated, spoken, written, or whatever. I think of a language as any type of output that becomes input and affects the receiver, or to put it in MOQ terms, something that the receiver values or not.

Now on to your answer to my dilemma for you—you say: "Ideas are the most powerful means ever brought to bear." Yes, ideas (i.e., intellectual patterns of value) are more powerful than social patterns of value. But it isn't the society that carries the idea. It's the human. A human can be a part of one society, grow an idea, and then apply that idea to another society. It sounds to me like you think that an individual can hold on to a thought only by saying it to himself over and over.

On your last point: "Principally the MOQ's static intellectual 'dimension' has nothing to do with smartness, intelligence or ability to think." I totally agree. That is partly why I think it's so hard to define what "intelligence" is, and now I mean what we usually call intelligence. Most agree that it is not "Jeopardy" knowledge, which is static. Intelligence is Dynamic.

Bodvar:

Voila! We have arrived at a common understanding. You admit that our society is needed to develop our intellect, and that a wolf society produces a wolf mind (even if a human organism is involved). But trust Magnus to have a new twist ready: the sneers and growls are "what a wolf would call intellect." Of course, it is valuable for a wolf to understand it, but animals cannot express themselves via abstract concepts and ideas (tautology). That is the intellect's privilege! If you insist on calling the baring of fangs "language," even "intellect," who am I to stop you? Admittedly, it is communication (the term "sign" can be mistaken for human sign language that can be used for abstract purposes as much as the written or spoken one), but the wolf's body language is all about signaling biological wants and needs and the position within a social hierarchy.

What your ofullende sentence, "It shows to me that wolves and boys are able to develop static intellectual patterns of value that…" is supposed to mean, I'm not sure, but if it is a "society of brain cells," I cry. Neural activity is a prerequisite for any organism, the more complex, the more complex its experience; it goes for amoebas as well as human beings. Dogs (wolves) have listened to human language for eons, but still don't have a clue what's going on, and never will. Its "odour mind" is beyond humans—we can't fathom the richness of its smell universe—but the human mind of (abstract) language is out of bounds for it.

Other primates show an ability to understand and express themselves by signs in a more complicated form, but there is a border that is impossible to cross for animals; the intellect's abstract land is closed to them. Note that "abstract" in the MOQ vocabulary is not opposite to "real" as in the Subject/Object Metaphysics. It is for instance impossible to torture an animal, but to a human being the "imagined" pain of the intellect is twice as painful as the biological one. (Imagination is another platypus in the SOM.)

Was it all these silly platitudes that confirmed your views? The Metaphysics of Quality contains the Subject/Object Metaphysics. It is possible to understand the latter from the former, but not the other way round. The "transformation" procedure still lacks, and even if mathematics is part of the intellect's realm I am a cripple there. Wouldn't it be a task for you or Doug to work on it instead of the endless gnawing at what should have been understood from the beginning? What about erecting yourself a monument by creating the "famous Magnus/Doug transformations."

Thrones and Chairs [September 1997]

Magnus:

I said that a chair is a part of a social pattern, and since social patterns are built on "the second level," the chair is of that level, not social.

My suggestions about what a specific level needs from its lower are not complete. I think the social level needs the function of the organic. And I think the intellectual needs the language provided by the social. But I can't put my finger on exactly what the organic needs from the inorganic, that's why I asked you guys about it last week.

I do think, however, that it's the only way to define the levels— to determine exactly what one level needs from the lower. What made a certain level appear when it did? What patterns of the lower level existed after but not before that instant? If social patterns need the function of organic patterns, then both are defined, not only the organic. Social patterns are what use the function provided by organic patterns.

Gene:

I'd like to note that a chair (as almost everything else) is a combination of value patterns at its creation without regard to how that chair is used: inorganic (wood or, "oh horror," plastic), biological (ergonomically designed for humans), social (made not to allow us to sit with our legs up), intellectual (if designed by

Wright). In Chapter 20, Pirsig discusses "celebrity devices." He means specifically human society when he speaks about social patterns of value. That's why he mentions anthropology as a science concerned with social values. We can speculate about human intellect only, and I would not expect any of it to be produced by a very developed society of ants. No matter how ingeniously they find their way into my kitchen cabinets, they are just a bunch of pathetic looters that my society does not value at all.

It's my first time barging into a conversation like that—sorry if I broke any social rules. Please, let me know what is the proper etiquette.

Bodvar:

Welcome aboard to Gene. I think that the discussion over what category a chair or any other material application belongs to is futile. A material object is inorganic value. That is all the MOQ says and is interested in.

I read the portion of Lila you referred to, and you are right; he speaks about various things as "celebrity devices." The line opens by his saying that celebrity is Dynamic Quality within a static social level of evolution (like sex is on the static biological level). Okay, I may be painting myself into some corner here, but this is the way I interpret this—it is the celebrity that is the value, and only human beings can be celebrities. It touches on the term "power," the Dynamics that formed and glued together societies of old and still does in many ways but I am not so sure if this Quality can be said to reside in the "devices" themselves except as my Oxford dictionary says: "Invented for a purpose," a symbolic purpose. The two topmost patterns utilize symbols to a great extent. The concepts of language are inventions for intellectual purposes.

Money/wealth is another side of celebrity complex (fame and fortune), but the value symbols coins/bills are but devices for payment. A bill is worthless the moment it is found false, and a Rolls Royce car loses its worth in a fuel crisis. Even pyramids are just heaps of stone now that the symbolic forming society (of people) is gone. (Sitting down to decide what level each and every thing belongs and what subtle shifts take place when it is moved from place to place baffles me.)

Let's call chairs merely sitting devices and thrones celebrity devices. So did Pirsig. Running the risk of Magnus boycotting me, I uphold that this leads nowhere.

Magnus:

Yes, I agree that our society is needed to develop our intellect, because what we call intelligence requires much more than static intellectual patterns of value. It requires the ability to change them— Dynamic Quality. What I try to do, as I explained in my post yesterday, is to isolate the different static levels from Dynamic, otherwise it's impossible to define them. What I don't agree with is that our static intellectual patterns of value are dependent on our human society. I would still be able to think even if the earth vanished and I was left in a space suit.

By the way, you're quite right about the end of my unfinished sentence—so just start crying. Where would you place neural activity in a MOQ framework? Neural activity is used for communication between brain cells. And communication needs a language so that the receiver understands what the transmitter sent.

And isn't it you who is putting us humans on the demigod throne now? You say that it's impossible to torture an animal and I assume you mean even if you don't lift a finger to hurt it. Well, a friend of mine has two cats and when one of them was away for a few days, the other one was clearly missing it. She still had an abstract image of the other cat and missed what it represented. And as closer you get to humans on the evolutionary scale, the more abstract thinking is possible—so where do you draw the line?

Celebrities allow societies to change, just as sex allows species to change. That's just another way of putting what you said but that's never in vain. And I hope no one is keeping anything inside just because of fear of painting oneself into a corner. God knows

I've been painting all over the place. I just hope there will be a door open where I hit the wall.

Hugo:

On the chair discussion I tend to agree with Bodvar on that it is futile to discuss which level an object belongs to as such. This seems reminiscent of an objective ordering of the world. But there is good sense in talking about how objects can be understood in light of the MOQ (and I think this is what has been discussed) because this is not a simple "transformation." Pirsig's concept of value is very much like some semiotic views of the world, where the "meaning" of an object (sign) is "decided" by the interpreter, at least to some degree. The value of an old chair is determined (more or less depending on which kind of relation we look at) by the valuer. It may be trash to you, money to an antique dealer, and a precious sign of my granny to me. And as Pirsig shows so well, value has effects; it is empirical and showing itself everywhere in this world.

Now this is not at all easy to come to terms with; there are lots of issues that need to be resolved. I have been interested in the consequences for our notion of scientific objectivity and the relationship between ethics and rationality, to mention a few. There is much to learn and much to be done, so keep on working and discussing!

Bodvar:

Magnus, you accused me of suddenly claiming demigod status for humans. The intellectual value level is a higher morality than the social one, so in that capacity we have occupied the high ground and dominate the lower, but in no way do we have a (demi) God's eye view of objective reality. I do not deny your cat a rich experience: wisdom, emotions, ability to "think," miss its pal, etc., but not by way of symbols or language. In the old days, there was a famous American author/advisor, Helen Keller (Platt may remember her?), who was born blind, mute, and deaf.

In her autobiography, she describes the event when she crossed into the realm of language and intellect. Her tutor had tried to bring her over by writing in her palms, but Helen had not grasped the connection between words and sensation, until one day when she poured water over one of her hands and wrote "water" in the other. She describes it as a flash, a revelation, she suddenly "saw." From then on, it was plain going and she became an intellectual celebrity (!) giving "chautauquas" in magazines and newspapers. There is no smooth transition from the social to the intellectual. It is another dimension.

Magnus:

Bo, I don't know if I've expressed this clearly enough, but I do think that our human society has the capacity for intellectual patterns on top of it, and that most animal societies don't. And that, in turn, depends on exactly what I think you've been saying, that we have a language advanced enough to support intellectual patterns. I'm not really sure exactly what those patterns are though, or if they're really there. The intellectual patterns I mostly talk about though are the ones on top of what I think as a society of cells, our body. These are two different things, SOM wise, but in the MOQ, they are the same.

The Number of Angels on Needle Points [September 1997]

Bodvar:

Dear Friends and Quality seekers—the Lila Squad was my first encounter with so-called mailing lists and I guess my hope of it being about applying Pirsig's ideas to various fields was in vain. This is about applying the various member's own ideas on the MOQ. OK, it can't be helped; this goes for all system builders.

First, it was Doug with his sub-inorganic and super-intellectual "exercises," then Magnus hit with his organic vs. social antics. I am just waiting for someone starting about where life borders on matter and intellect vs. society. I said so in my opening letter…there is no "objective" point in time or space where you find a sign: "You are now leaving the Biology Sector." Seen from within, each domain stretches from eternity to eternity.

Of late messages have been flying about what levels are "aware" of what, above and below, as if "static value patterns" are objective entities with a subject/object consciousness of their own. The Medieval scholastic councils on how many angels could sit on needle points comes to mind. Perhaps my long admonishing "epistles" has been part of it. Anyway, nobody wants a "chairman" (ZMM!) on this board.

At times, I have the urge to ask this question (I don't...this is just a draft)—if you once found the MOQ valuable and credible, it must have been for it being a solution of the Subject/Object paradoxes. Why then the efforts to plunge it back into the very ugliness? Why pondering over what this and that "really" are? Objectivity is left behind along with subjectivity (awareness, consciousness, and mind).

Keep up the debate, but read a little of Pirsig in between and try to find documentation for or against what you say. It would raise the Quality.

Hugo:

On the content of Lila Squad—in my view we cannot discuss the MOQ without in some way applying it (and how one "applies" an alternative metaphysics is something we all have to learn). We can of course discuss internal incoherence in the MOQ, and this is important too...Pirsig has not entirely finished philosophy off.;-)

But if we consider the MOQ a potential alternative to the SOM dominating the Western culture and science, and not just an interesting intellectual toy, we have to address how the metaphysical structures of understanding might be probed. Pirsig has done enough in his books to make me want to walk his path, but others might be less pre-adapted to the MOQ or more sceptic. If we are to make any difference for those who haven't paused to question SOM then we have quite a job ahead. I see Pirsig's recent paper as yet another probing analysis of metaphysics, and I might have a shot at a comment later (like probably most who have grown up in our Western culture, I find thinking Pirsig's way very hard to do).

Anyway, speaking from my experiences (good and bad) on other email-lists, we should be very wary of excluding any threads (or worse, persons) as long as they are within the limits set for the list. On Peirce-l, which is the most successful list I know of in achieving a community-like feeling, the criteria is simply that the mails should be of relevance to the philosophy of Peirce. Not that Peirce should be mentioned in every mail, but one should be able to show the relevance if asked by the list manager. And this is a second important thing, I think. Nobody but the list manager should confront members of the list on the irrelevance, offensiveness, or the like of their mails. If someone finds a mail offensive or a thread of mails irrelevant they should address the list manager directly and not the sender. This is such a difficult media to keep keen discussions friendly in—we all have to contribute towards making this a place we like to be a part of. Addressing the issues you yourself find interesting, reading those you care for, and deleting the rest could be a working strategy. Whichever way we chose, it seems important to come to some agreement on this.

Magnus:

About Bodvar's latest, you're so right. We must remember why we got together like this; we are more alike than different. One thing Pirsig always wanted was to join the "romantic" and the "scientific" people. I guess we're approaching the MOQ from two different directions and sometimes that's very hard.

I'm sorry for being such a PITA for some (all?) of you. I tend to get quite academic (if that's the right word) from time to time. I guess it's my way of "using" the MOQ. Just shout, "Shut up and have a beer" if I'm annoying.

Gene:

It seems that the value of a chair is in the eye of the beholder, and it's not practical, in my opinion, to try to sort values by patterns in general. The boundaries are fuzzy. Instead, we should learn to use the value diagram to help us to "do the right thing" when value patterns are in conflict, which happens in every step: watch TV or read a book; read a book or play a silly game with your child so she/he will not watch TV, etc.

Bo, I don't think there is any distinction between MOQ intellect and SOM mind. Both terms denote the same product of Dynamic Quality. You said yourself, "That seen from within, any level fills every nook of the universe," but by putting intellect into "another dimension" we would deny Dynamic Quality to other levels. I like Magnus' idea of life as Dynamic Quality of the biological variety. May be we should view the value diagram as seen from above with Dynamic Quality as a shimmering foundation permeating every other pattern. I guess, riots, revolutions, parliamentary debates would be the Quality events of the social level then. What would be Dynamic Quality of inorganic level?

Magnus:

Radioactivity—Schrödinger's cat is the primary example. Also any matter that is warmer than absolute zero K (most!) has some unpredictable attributes. The general rule here is, the smaller things get (the fewer atoms involved), the more uncertain is the behaviour of the set. Large numbers of atoms behave very predictably because each atom behaves equally unpredictable.

I'm sure Jason or Doug could elaborate and correct this, but I think it covers the basics.

James:

Do you mean that inorganic Dynamic Quality boils down to quantum chance? Or could we say that matter is static quality and energy Dynamic? But then what about those biochemical processes that lead to the transition to the next level?

Magnus:

Hi James and welcome to the Lila Squad! Well, the term "inorganic Dynamic Quality" is like "intelligent stone" or something. There's no such thing. What you probably meant was, "Dynamic Quality influence on inorganic patterns." But yes, since we cannot predict (all) quantum events, we could call them Dynamic Quality until, and if, we can predict them.

No, we cannot call matter static quality and energy Dynamic Quality. Have a look at $E=mc^2$. It says that they are both interchangeable and predictable. That would not be the case if energy were Dynamic Quality. I don't think we should talk about "transitions" to the next level, rather that the next level at a certain point became able to use the patterns of the lower level. Even if inorganic patterns suddenly are used to form organic patterns, the inorganic patterns are still there, untransformed.

Bodvar:

A value, however shifty (as in the counterfeit money case) is not subjective. The subjective term, as well as the objective, is foreign to the MOQ. The value of an inorganic artifact or of a biological organism (a pet for instance) seen from the higher levels' point of view is as real as real comes, in that value level's context.

I once said that seen from within, any level fills every nook of the universe. Life regards everything as leading up to its creation, sustaining or threatening it. So does society. Everything dead (inorganic) or alive (organic) is positive or negative social value. Values from below are everything from minor nuisances to outright evil while the value of the intellect is transparent or invisible. Dirt (inorganic value) at wrong places diminishes my social status as a clean person. Burping at the table (or worse sounds) may destroy it completely. Life's more powerful values, sex for instance, must be directed into acceptable channels, the "evil" greed or lust given some acceptable social form.

The same goes for the intellect. Seen from its high ideas/rationality perch every bit of the universe is high or low intellectual value. We do our discussion from intellect's premises, and my error was to try to decide how society looks upon this in an intellectual way. It's impossible; metaphysics cannot be employed at other value levels other than the intellect, only Quality can. Human beings, when focusing on the social (or lower) level are not intellectual. When we start rationalizing why we like this and hate that we're back on the intellectual level. This why it is so horribly important to get the distinction between the MOQ intellect and the SOM Mind sorted out.

Focus can only be in one level at a time. The transit is like the Gestalt psychology "two profiles or one vase perception." One moment you see one reality, the next another. I am sitting at the keyboard totally submerged in the intellectual but a headache or a feeling of hunger, and in a flash, I am a biological organism. I may even go all the way to the inorganic when I die (excuse the socially unacceptable morbidity). Reading Lila Squad mail is intellect, but then I see a sarcastic remark and suddenly my (hurt) social self is in focus. Even the Internet and the Lila Squad are small pocket societies with rules and status.

Magnus:

Patterns of all levels still have all attributes from the lower levels. I have mass, colour, gravity, etc., although I'm not daily considered to be inorganic.

A human with a warm coat and a good pair of shoes is a society (a composition of organic patterns) that can better withstand cold weather than a human can without them. Therefore, the coat and the shoes (and the human) are organic patterns to that society.

Platt:

Magnus has always insisted that the social level can be applied to any group of elements. The statement above is the latest example. Nowhere in Lila do I find any references to society other than a society of people. What Pirsig means by the social level are things like tribes, cities, nations, Victorians, Indians, anthropology, status, celebrity, constitutions, police, etc. He doesn't mean ants, baboons, wolves, lions, whales, or elephants, which are also social creatures. He certainly doesn't mean that a human wearing a coat and shoes is a society.

In my opinion, a synonym for the social level is cultural level. [28] Pirsig didn't use the word "cultural" because it's loaded with political overtones; he deliberately used the more neutral word "social." (He does use "culture" in some references to the social level.)

Intellect is infamous for its ability to rationalize and "spin" any point of view. Besides being a pointing tool, it's also a dividing/combining tool. If you ask intellect, "How many things in a thing?" It will answer, "As many as you want." If you ask it, "What is everything?" It will answer, "The Godhead, the Cosmos, the Ultimate, the Void, the Absolute, the Brahman, the Tao, the Quantum, etc."

Between these two extremes, it will divide and combine in any and every way imaginable, even changing the meaning of words and inventing new ones to suit its purposes. There's nothing mysterious about the four levels. The inorganic refers to earth, sky, fire, and water; the biological to plants, bugs, and animals; the social to people, institutions, and artifacts; the intellectual to language, math, and philosophy. We can divide and mediate the levels to a "fare thee well," but even an eight year old can recognize the levels for what they are and tell the difference between them.

The original version was animal, vegetable, or mineral, like a popular radio show in my youth. Once given the category, the four person panel had twenty questions to identify the subject's "secret," whether an occupation, book, or unusual feat. The panel rarely failed, usually getting the answer in fifteen questions or less. Pirsig merely combined animal and vegetable and added social and intellectual to suit his thesis, which is not about levels so much as about the omnipotence of values, no matter how you divide the world.

Retrospect [September 1997]

Jason:

Much of the (very fruitful and sometimes frustrating) discussion that has taken place on the list has centered on an apparent ambiguity in our understanding of each of the four static levels. Based on the impressive grasp of Pirsig's work that I have seen demonstrated in each of your posts, I would love to hear each person's own attempt at a set of definitions and/or criteria that might distinguish phenomena in each level.

Hugo:

I will follow Jason's invitation to present our views of the levels of MOQ, as this might be a way to better pin down what we agree on and where we disagree, and a view of the levels seems to capture a lot of what MOQ is about. My view has a kind of semiotic bent (surprise!), and I will give a quick and dirty outline of how it looks right now (it seems to change even faster after I joined the Squad):

The levels:

A: Physical level
B: Organic level
C: Social level
D: Intellectual level

The character of the "jumps" from one level to the next: A to B: The emergence of (individual) mind and autonomy

(please bear with me on the terms for a while) the vehicle being mediated relations in that some (organismic) relations are maintained by way of other relations, as opposed to the physical level with only unmediated relations. A simple example is the chemotaxi (swimming in a preferred direction in the presence of a gradient concentration of a chemical) of bacteria, where one relation is used as a sign of another relation. And the self-sustaining, against gradient, chemical pumps, etc., are basic organismic features.

B to C: The emergence of the cultural mind or society, with yet another level of mediated relations—the use of organismic relations in order to maintain cultural relations. To pick some examples, the tail of the peacock, the antlers of the deer and probably some human characteristics too, are organismic features that play a part in social relations, and thus are "unfit" to the naked neo-Darwinian eye. Various forms of programmed cell death is an example in the society of cells forming our body.

C to D: The emergence of the intellectual mind or "the world of ideas" (anyone with a better term?), where ideal (idea-like) relations utilize the cultural relations in sustaining the intellect. Some examples are revolutionary ideas transforming or disintegrating societies. But somehow (?) the "realization of self," the emergence of selfconsciousness, seems like an essential part of this transition. Any ideas?

Jason:

Thank you for sharing your thoughts. I think that your post has made a great stride in moving the discussion forward and promoting a better understanding of the fundamentals of the MOQ. I'm sure others will take issue with some of the details, but you have focused in on the central issues and given us a common starting point for discussion.

My initial reaction regards your suggestion that self-consciousness or self-awareness [29] may fit best at the intellectual level. The problem that I foresee is that of an isolated individual or organism raised in virtual isolation, that is, with only minimal social contact. Wouldn't you agree that such an individual would have some sort of self-awareness? (I'm intentionally avoiding the use of the term "consciousness" here, because I think that the ambiguity of the term may lead to conflict and confusion.)

Based on this hypothesis, I would suggest that the most fundamental aspects of self-awareness (including emotions) reside best at the organic level (I think Pirsig briefly comments on this in the SODV paper, see the top of page 15). As such, the intellectual level would contain only the abstract and creative "world of ideas" to which you referred. I adamantly agree with your observation that the emergence of such ideas is dependent upon the shared wisdom and knowledge of the social level.

The obvious potential problem with the "self awareness as organic" suggestion is that some "social organisms" do not seem to demonstrate full self-awareness. In my opinion, this is simply due to the fact that these organisms have not evolved to the degree that we as humans have. If they possessed the same sophisticated brain structures, I believe that their fundamental "awareness" would be similar to our own. As our nearest neighbors in the animal kingdom, the primates may provide the best example of such evolving "awareness." Each time I visit the zoo I am amazed at the similarity between primate behavior and our own.

Hugo:

We need to be very careful with the terms concerning consciousness…on that I absolutely agree. I think we have to address this crucial notion though, while trying not to include more than necessary in the discussion. Here is a fuller version of my present view on this—I distinguish between a basic sort of consciousness or awareness in the same sense as in "knocked unconscious," and self consciousness or awareness in the sense of reflective consciousness of one self. The basic awareness is connected with being an autonomous entity, because being autonomous means heading for an embodied goal despite hindrances on the road (this is the basic form of learning, changing behaviour upon interaction with the world), and this implies the entity has to be aware of the world around it, described as its umwelt.

The reflective awareness is connected with what we may term "free will" (yes I believe I have to include this), meaning the ability to change one's will, with "will" being basically the autonomous goal mentioned above. The realization of one self means for one the realization of one's autonomous goal, of where one is bent on going. And realizing where one is going entails realizing that one could go somewhere else, hence free will. This is the basics of intellect and imagination (forestillingsevne). These arguments need to be probed more!

I share your fascination of primate behavior, and parts of the above view arose upon watching apes. I remember seeing a scene on television with a chimpanzee and a mirror, and you could literally see at some point how suddenly she realized that it was herself in the mirror, upon which she tried out various hilarious moves and faces. More scientifically, tests have been made on whether an animal realizes (upon first having been acquainted with mirrors) that the spot in the face in the mirror is on its own face (it has been put there under anesthesia). Apes can do this and children from about the age of three as far as I remember.

Anyway, it is evident that although we try to find these sharp distinctions between levels (and I believe they are sharp in some sense), there is a tremendous amount of gradual and continuous change inside levels too. More directly on your question of the isolated individual, I believe we are somewhat misled with the myth of the rational hermit, Robinson Crusoe, and no, I don't believe a human being could grow up in total isolation (so much for science fiction test tube babies). There would of course have to be some basic interaction just for the physical needs although these could be kept to a minimum. But the kid would die anyway. Humans are basically social animals and cannot develop in a non-social environment. I don't even believe adults can survive for very long without any social relations, but this is debatable.

Then we can take some middle example as the kid growing up among wolves, and yes, this child could grow up because we are so like wolves. And it would get some level of self-awareness, though which level I don't know. The reason for believing this is that self awareness presumes social awareness, the awareness of other, and wolves would do fine in that respect.

Platt:

In response to Jason's invitation to define the four static levels, here's my simplistic view, based on high school curricula:

Inorganic: Physics, chemistry

Biological: Biology.

Social: History.

Intellectual: English, math.

From this elementary structure, the "divide to conquer" intellect takes off on a reductionist romp. Just to take one example, the Earth Sciences (inorganic level) get knifed into mineralogy, petrology, geochemistry, geophysics, geomorphology, paleontology, hydrology, oceanography, meteorology, etc. Similar slices can be found in all branches of knowledge.

Reductionism has worked so well to expand knowledge and improve the quality of life that that we worship at its feet. But with the discovery of the quantum world, those feet have turned to feet of clay, requiring an entirely new metaphysics that steers intellect away from its now stymied and flummoxed methodology.

Enter Pirsig. Instead of viewing the world as consisting of wholes and parts (the basic assumption of reductionism), Pirsig suggests we view the world as a moral order.

Boom! Suddenly all the favorite interests of the intellect shift. Definitions take a back seat to examples and metaphors. Things like harmony, beauty, elegance, and artfulness take center stage. Occam' s razor is elevated to prominence. A child's innocence becomes an indicator of truth, and intuition lights the path.

So I think I'll stick to my simplistic definitions lest I get lured backed into the labyrinthine tunnels of the old intellectual edifice where, as Pirsig says, nobody wins (except perhaps those rascally robots).

Annotations by Robert M. Pirsig

17. I highlight this because it helps respond to later criticism that presumes the purpose of the MOQ is solely to provide a single right answer to every moral question.

18. In Lila, there is a difference, although I neglected to state it. Cells are objective. Societies are subjective. No objective scientific instrument can detect a society.

19. In Lila, societies are quite separate patterns that emerge from and are superimposed upon organic bodies of people, but they are not combinations of these organic bodies of people.

20. I believe I described the virus as two molecules.

21. No, they are molecules. The confusion that follows comes from imprecision in the use of terms.

22. In Lila, there is no such thing as a "cell-society." Organic patterns are not social patterns.

23. In Lila, the criterion is strictly the presence of DNA in a self-perpetuating pattern.

24. But biology is organic patterns. We must all use terms as they are described in the dictionary or we lose the ability to communicate with each other. That is what happens (to me) in the next sentence.

25. This is okay. In Lila, I never defined the intellectual level of the MOQ, since everyone who is up to reading Lila already knows what "intellectual" means. For purposes of MOQ precision, let's say that the intellectual level is the same as mind. It is the collection and manipulation of symbols, created in the brain, that stand for patterns of experience.

26. Bodies are not social patterns.

27. Well said!

28. For precision I think I would say that a culture contains social and intellectual values, but not biological or inorganic.

29. The MOQ, as I understand it, denies any existence of a "self" that is independent of inorganic, biological, social or intellectual patterns. There is no "self" that contains these patterns. These patterns contain the self. This denial agrees with both

religious mysticism and scientific knowledge. In Zen, there is reference to "big self" and "small self." Small self is the patterns. Big self is Dynamic Quality.

Chapter 3

Stillness is what creates love. Movement is what creates life. To be still and still moving, this is everything. —Duc Yung Cho

Do Atoms Experience? [September 1997]

Platt:

As I understand it, the MOQ equates Quality with direct experience. In turn, experience creates static patterns of value. The problem is—how could inorganic static patterns be created unless inorganic entities like atoms were able to experience? [30]

If atoms don't experience, at what level did experience arise? And, how could experience arise from a lower level of no experience? [31] This seems to be a subject/object platypus. Is there a MOQ solution?

Magnus:

You said it yourself; experience is Quality, which creates static patterns of value, not the other way around. You also use the word "experience" as both a noun and a verb, which helps to create the platypus. By using it as a verb, you assume that the atom existed before it was created by "its" experience. Pirsig deals with this causation platypus in Lila, Chapter 8.

What's equally important; remember that substance is another major platypus removed by the MOQ. Everything we call substance is nothing without experience. The only way we can describe substance is by describing how we experience it. Then we invent this model we call substance to fit it into the SOM framework (Lila, same chapter).

Bodvar:

Platt's "experience" term indicates a sentient capacity, possibly even consciousness or awareness, at least the ability to think or learn, isn't it so? To come to grips with this requires a step back to square one of the MOQ. Its first postulate is that the great divide between subject and object is shifted over to between Dynamic and static value. The still more basic assertion that everything is value is just as true or untrue as the mind and matter presuppositions. At this level Gödel's Theorem hits all who come down from mountains with stone tablets.

Once this metaphysical rearrangement is done all the countless subject/object dualities of mind/matter, psychic/physic (see Chapter 7 of Danah Zohar's The Quantum Self for additional dualities) lose their absoluteness, merge, become relative. Mind is everything and nothing in a MOQ sense; experience becomes the world. A human's mind is humankind's world, a frog's experience is a frog's world, and, with my tongue in cheek, an atom's (or any other particle's) experience is the world of inorganic patterns.

The frog reality is simple (but complete, no foggy version of man's as the SOM indicates). It is only the inorganic and the organic values, while mankind's reality is the most baffling aggregate ever assembled. It contains the said realities plus the social and the immensely complex intellectual one, which include heaven and earth, language, music, art (ZMM page 244), but in no way are we "aware" in the "objective God's eye" sense that the subject/object notion of "being able to think" suggests (see footnote). Subjectivity as well as objectivity has become subsets under the grand MOQ overview. It is a Copernican revolution where (as Pirsig of ZMM says) the center shifts—subjects and objects become planets that circle the sun of Quality instead of their former role as reality itself. Nothing changes, yet everything changes.

Footnote: the SOM phrase "ability to think" means in MOQ lingo the ability to manipulate static intellectual values: language, mathematics, etc. This is no longer the subject/object ghostlike, "abstractions in the mind," but as real as real comes, intellectually seen, and resolves the nihilistic trap of SOM where it can be easily proven that there is no reality outside ourselves. Only humankind has entered the intellectual level, but perhaps other primates are in the fringe zone.

This was intended to answer your first point, Platt. Inorganic static entities (patterns or particles) are the inorganic static experience, just as we humans are all subsequent levels of the Quality experience. In a SOM context, this sound like mysticism, but it is the reality that naturally unfolds itself seen from the MOQ platform. The second question of how experience could arise from no experience, or how mind could emerge from matter, is, as you suggest, the biggest platypus ever to have roamed the subject/object world. The above gives the MOQ solution, but I am at your disposal for another round if useful. Your own knowledge of Pirsig's work (and the more pragmatic application of his ideas) surpasses mine I admit.

Jason:

Yes, I think I understand what you are saying here. Perhaps you could share your views regarding this resolution of the so-called problem of consciousness as it relates to artificial sentient beings. Do you believe that a machine could be created which would have the same conscious experiences that we enjoy as humans? [32]

Bodvar:

Maybe I am overexerting myself. In my reply to Platt, I said something about humankind's experience being humankind's mind (or consciousness). This sounds trite, but is really the fulcrum on which the MOQ rests. I don't blame you Jason for not noticing it and keep returning to "the same conscious experience as we men," as if the intellect of Quality is identical with consciousness of the SOM.

But first allow me to air an idea that may clarify the MOQ morality levels, and their relationship. If I have said this before please forgive. As you know, the Quality duality is between Dynamic and static values, not between mind and matter. About the Dynamic half, not much can be said except about it being the background of it all, but the static levels are also different realities in a way. It seems complicated and I had a bit of trouble with this, until I got the "dimension" input. We are familiar with physical space and the three dimensions (vectors) that constitute the spatial continuum.

Nobody can tell where width ends and breadth starts or both are replaced by height; these dimensions can be endlessly combined but still keep their unique quality. Isn't this a good analogue of the MOQ levels? We humans are the four planes of reality, all the time. They intersect and interplay in an unending number of configurations while what we call "mind" is the reflection of what dimension at a given time dominates.

Well then, over to the MOQ intellectual dimension and my definition of it, which is: the level where the value of the individual (self) as different from its society is recognized.

In this sense, it is related to the SOM awareness (or consciousness or mind) term (if one manages to keep the "aware of objective reality" connotation of SOM at bay). I also said that frog's experience is the frog's consciousness. I refuse to put it in brackets because it is so in its fullest sense. This does not mean that a frog "thinks" (hey, I am a frog, what am I doing here?) in the sense of using symbolic language, but it senses and experiences its organic reality according to its neural complexity. We humans may easily slip down to the organic level too; in pain or lust, we experience without "thinking" or "language" (the social level experience is also dominated by emotions, but heavily intersected with language).

Language and/or thinking's, "Hey, I am a human being," are static intellectual value patterns. It is a marvelous dimension, to repeat: "It contains heaven and earth," etc. (ZMM page 244). It is every bit as real as the other levels (even more valuable as the top position), but as the great divide no longer is between subjectivity and objectivity, it does not represent "reality as it is."

I anticipate Jason's next argument as: yes, but the manipulation of language's concepts in rules of semantics and grammar are abstractions! The concrete/abstract duality is also a subject/object offshoot, and does not apply in the MOQ. This is simply infuriating. In the SOM, this creates another platypus as it is easily proved that there is no reality outside language, i.e., the world is an illusion. Thinkers who dare these paths have pulled back in horror or plunged into the nihilistic void (Nietzsche, for example).

In Lila, Pirsig shows how the intellectual values of freedom from society's bonds came to dominate the Western political scene (as late as around WW II). He also points to its first steps in that direction to around Homer's time (see also Jaynes' Bicameral idea), so yes, in a sense can Subject/Object metaphysics itself be seen as its endeavour to conquer social values. But this does not mean that the Dynamic forces hadn't tried to latch on for tens of thousands of years. Brain's neural capacity (language, thinking) has been well developed for perhaps fifty thousand years— caveman's art was even better—but the point is that tribal/communal values dominated what was in their minds. It's been an enormous and tortuous path until now when intellectual values dominate.

This was supposed to be about artificial intelligence, but I did not reach that point. Jason's very intelligent questions force me to "resolve a metaphysical dispute at the end of each sentence." (Lila, page 64)

Gene:

Pirsig categorized values according to the order of their historical development. For example, procreation was put into the biological set. Therefore, if those pesky robots decide to "procreate," no matter by what means, we can still say they are attracted to a biological value. Boundaries between sets of static values are not crisp, I think. We are "suspended in language," and in Western culture; that's why Pirsig had to use a classical diagram to convey Zen perception of reality. I believe we should use fuzzy logic to define sets of values. This way our cats will be classified to harbor intellectual values to some degree, but not, of course, to a degree members of the Lila Squad do. This allows us to agree with both Magnus (having a cat of my own) and Bodvar (it's nice to be a demigod).

Hugo:

On the issue of other incarnations of intellect, up until now we have been inventing and using different sorts of intellectual tools, such as books, calculators, and computer systems. I call them tools because they have not interacted autonomously and directly with the rest of the world, but only through us humans; we have used them as intellectual tools.

No doubt able to develop directly interacting versions of these tools, we call them robots. There are several aspects of interest here. For one, this can be a kind of test of our understanding of the levels in our own incarnation of intellect, and secondly, this understanding of ourselves might throw some light on the nature of robots.

To be truly another incarnation of intellect, they have to be separated from our own, at least more than they are at present. Now suppose we decide to do this (or more likely just let it happen) and succeed in doing it—what are we faced with then? Some hints could be taken from the hype surrounding the various versions of artificial pets being marketed as we speak. They are premature versions of beings on the social level (like a cat) and though they are in many ways dependent on their owners (a main aspect of "being a pet") they possess the features that allows us make a social bond with them— one consequence being that people wish to bury them when they pass away. This indicates that basic ethics will apply to robotic creatures once they are created.

We know we can make social (interacting and mutually representing) robotic creatures and we know we can make intellectual tools with rational powers comparable to our own. I see no reason why we should not be able to make robotic intellectual creatures. The question is whether we should, and here some advance understanding of their nature would help in making such a decision (though judging from the way the development runs today, we probably won't take time to decide before we act. Dynamic Quality has its dark sides as well).

We ourselves have been pretty nasty towards our fellow passengers on spaceship Gaia, and indeed, we may only constrain ourselves, by way of reason, in order to keep the spaceship functioning. I am afraid robotic creatures would not even have this concern. There are all sorts of questions popping up in my mind, on "human rights," power structures, and so forth, which really are questions concerning our human world as well.

I am not afraid of robots; there are surely many steps to take in order to make them truly autonomous, but I am afraid of us. We who make up Western culture (which has almost become the human culture) seem to be taken by a religious sort of compassion for rationality, and building robots is just a symptom.

Turing Test [October 1997]

Lars:

What do you feel a computer must do to enter the intellectual level? I don't think passing the Turing test is sufficient. What would you consider sufficient? And what would it mean, calling a piece of silicone "intelligent"? Would it have human rights? In what way would its intelligence be different from our intelligence?

The Turing test is not really acknowledged as a good test, as quite a few things can cause trouble with it. In fact, Joseph Weizenbaum wrote the famous Eliza program to prove how easy it is to pass the test. Eliza is a very simple program that pretends to be a psychoanalyst of a particular school of psychologists that had a very simple therapy that mostly consisted of asking the patient questions.

So Eliza asks you a lot of questions based on the last thing you wrote, which just twists the dialogue a little, changing me to you, etc. Eliza fooled many people, including Weizenbaum's secretary, who demanded to be left alone with the program, claiming that only it understood her. Although Turing was in a sense the father of modern computation, he died before anyone had much experience with computation. In fact, his most important results, like the halting problem proof, predated the first computers. So he's not such an authority on this as it might seem.

For those of you who don't know what a Turing machine is, it's a simple computer that you can construct on a piece of paper and which follows a set of very simple rules. You can "run" it on paper as well.

Doug:

To me, in order for a third party to distinguish these two hypothetical static patterns of value (SPoV) aggregates, the third party would have an insoluble problem knowing when to stop asking questions. If they were equal, you would never find a contradiction. If they were not equal, you still would not know when to stop, assuming you never arrived at a contradiction, even if they aren't equal.

Magnus:

This is a rather elegant criticism of the test, Doug. I liked it. I think what you write is correct, but it still doesn't mean that the test can't work. The probability that both parties would answer the same even once is infinitesimal. The probability that they would do it say fifty times is for all practical purposes zero.

Bodvar:

If one intelligence (a human being) cannot distinguish between a "program" and another human being (both out of sight and communicating through print) the conclusion is that there is no difference!

Magnus:

First of all, this communication channel used would cripple a human intellect and force him to statically intellectualize all that he wants to communicate to the receiver. The communication almost strips all Dynamic Quality away, which makes the two "competitors" much more equal. Secondly, I didn't think you considered one human to have an intellect; I thought you thought humans were just biological.

Lars:

I don't agree with this. If this is to be a criticism of the Turing test you'll have to specify what kind of information is "stripped away" that makes it more difficult to decide whether the entity on the other side of the screen/keyboard is intelligent or not.

Magnus:

The thing is, I can't specify what is stripped away because it is Dynamic Quality, and Dynamic Quality is impossible to specify. The human at the other end of the keyboard has to intellectualize all answers before typing them. OK, this is true for most types of communication but I think the written language is more static than, say, the spoken one. You have to think one step further to write a thought than to speak it.

You still talk as if intelligence is something you can define in the same way as you define the operation plus or minus something. Imagine that a definition is possible—what would it say? List all the right answers to the questions. Then it would be quite easy to fake such an intelligence, just as all computer manufacturers try to optimize their computers to the current Benchmark tests. This is very similar to Doug's rational criticism of the test.

I think the minimum requirement for true artificial intelligence is that it has to be able to surprise its creators. The answers must not be rationally deducible from the input.

We can't rationally tell Dynamic Quality apart from simulated Dynamic Quality because when we intellectualize them, they become the same.

Bodvar:

Magnus says that Turing wasn't aware of Dynamic Quality, but doesn't Dynamic Quality reside as comfortably in a digital circuit as in the brain cell of a human being? [33]

Magnus:

I don't think so. We made our best to rule Dynamic Quality out in digital circuits. Dynamic Quality is there all right, but it has no chance to affect the circuit so much to make a one out of a zero or vice versa. The reason we did rule it out is because we don't want it! We want a computer to be absolutely static and predictable. I think true artificial intelligence would mean letting go of that control and that could, as many science fiction movies (and Hugo) tell us, be dangerous. Dangerous to us that is, not to Dynamic Quality! [34]

Bodvar:

I think life can be faked (as Magnus once called it) and so can intelligence; it is only "artificial" regarding the material involved. What if it becomes possible to grow neural tissue?

Magnus:

To grow neural tissue would mean letting go of absolute control and predictability.

Bodvar:

No, we must keep the intellect of the MOQ apart from intelligence. Aren't animals smart?

Magnus:

Yes! And yes!

Lars:

This is exactly what I disagreed with. Verbalizing is distinct from intellectualizing, and even intellect has Dynamic Quality.

Magnus:

Intellect has Dynamic Quality, yes, but after intellectualizing, a static pattern of intellectual value is formed. This static "thought" is then transformed into words.

Lars:

Think of poetry. There's nothing in the test that says the judges can't ask the participants to write a poem. In fact, it encourages it.

Magnus:

This is true for most types of communication but I think the written language is more static than, say the spoken one. You have to think one step further to write a thought than to speak it. I don't think the actual words of a poem are Dynamic in any way. Once written, they don't change. The Quality event that is triggered when reading a poem doesn't come from the poem itself, but from the "state of mind" it puts the reader in. (Now I'm really off topic.)

Lars:

This sounds like a possible starting point for a rejection of the Turing test. You still have to specify exactly how this invalidates the Turing test. Why does it make it possible for a non-intelligent being to pass the test?

Magnus:

Because I think what we call intelligence involves a great deal of Dynamic Quality. And with this stripped away by the intellectualizing and writing, there's nothing left and the true intelligence becomes more equal to the static artificial intelligence. I think the minimum requirement for true artificial intelligence is that it has to be able to surprise its creators. The answers must not be rationally deducible from the input.

Lars:

This happens even with something as simple as a web server. Optimizing one for full speed can be very difficult. By this criterion alone, innumerable programs are already intelligent. In fact, I once made a Scheme interpreter that sometimes surprised me by rebooting my computer in the middle of a computation, and I never could figure out what did it.

Magnus:

That's what I'm getting at. I don't think a Turing machine will ever be considered intelligent because a Turing machine is predictable. A true intelligence is able to come up with hypotheses never thought of before and not deducible from the currently valid axioms.

Machines Perceiving Quality [October 1997]

Maggie:

I just don't see how the possibility of artificial intelligence discussion affects the MOQ. If people create artificial intelligence, it will be based on all human social patterns, otherwise humans would not call it intelligent. And, if the future society of robots decides to discard all life/biology on Earth, they will just loose one of the levels. Amended, the MOQ will still be useful to them as an explanation of their reality. They will still be thankful to the once necessary biological level as a facilitator of social and intellectual levels.

Anders:

Yes well, let me ask a question then—if we presume there's intelligence at least as advanced as our own somewhere in the universe, will these aliens then be able to use the MOQ as a way of describing their reality, or is the MOQ a human-specific metaphysics?

Maggie:

I would think that the aliens might be able to come to understand the MOQ and use it if it is valuable, just as when one human society meets another human society it can adopt those patterns it finds that are valuable to it, often leapfrogging to new levels of capability without having to go through all the steps (and structures) that the original society had to create.

The aliens might not be able to even see (observe or comprehend) the human intellectual patterns (including the MOQ) at all, not having their own similar intellectual patterns to observe them with. The aliens might not be able to observe the social patterns, not having their own human social patterns to compare them to. The aliens might not be able to observe the biological patterns for the same reason. It seems, though, that any aliens who originated within our galaxy (or our physical system, any thing that we would define as a "place") might be able to recognize the patterns of the inorganic level, and be able to observe from them that here on Earth, something exists that is different from their own habitat (or maybe not, if the changes in the inorganic level are in a different spectrum than they are used to observing).

Whether the intellectual patterns of the MOQ are useful to the aliens, the levels and structures that MOQ describes would still exist. And the aliens could make use of them to the extent that they are perceivable and valuable. I think, however, that it is more likely that we will be able to apply the MOQ to the study of the existence of the aliens rather than the other way around.

Anders:

I think of making artificial intelligence not as much as making an artificial human, but more of making an artificial intelligent alien, because then you don't have to explain why it can't do humanspecific things like dancing or handstands, etc. If the MOQ is not completely human-specific, constructing an artificial intelligence will be making a machine perceive Quality.

Maggie:

I think we already have machines that can perceive Quality. We certainly have social and intellectual patterns that perceive quality and make decisions (allow static quality or even Dynamic Quality to operate at a particular balance point) thereupon. The human individual is not the choice maker here. The human individual is often a cog in the wheel, a cell in the organism.

For an example, the ATM machine (an inorganic pattern set up by the mediation of social, biological, and intellectual patterns) decides whether or not you get money when you stick your card in. Some human has programmed it, but the point of decision (the Quality event) happens at the inorganic level if the reason you are rejected is due to your card being bent or the machine experiencing a power surge, or a strong magnet nearby; or at the social level if the cause of rejection is the fact that someone in an office messed up your account records; or at the intellectual level if some boundaries have been set by the bank and your balance has gone out of bounds.

Anders:

All this is still a matter of faith (I believe artificial intelligence is possible, others don't) as no one has given any constructive recipes of artificial intelligence programs, but on the other hand, I don't think it's fair to say that you've proven that artificial intelligence is impossible.

I don't think you'd be able to call a task specific program intelligent, if the criterion of intelligence is passing the Turing test. A conversation with an automated car pilot, for example, might go:

You: "Good evening James, take me to my Parent's House."

Car: "And their address is still Farum Hovedgade 35, is it?"

You: "Yes it is."

Car: "Shall I take the scenic route, or the highway?"

You: "Oh. Hmmm. Well I've got time to spare, so let's go by the coast."

Car: "Very good sir, we shall be arriving around 8 o'clock sir, make yourself comfortable."

And that's probably stretching it a bit. You'd never be able to converse with it about poems, jokes, or recent political events and such (mostly because that kind of intelligence isn't necessary for an automated car pilot).

As far as I see it, the only thing able to perceive Dynamic Quality is a human or rather a sentient being, but not society, and certainly not atomic matter! Saying that Dynamic Quality for the inorganic static patterns is the quantum flux is pure nonsense to me. I'm sorry to sound so harsh, but really, I don't understand what people mean when they say this. [35] To back this point I will offer a quote from Lila.

Here, Pirsig is talking about the (im) moralness of the death-penalty: "And beyond that is an even more compelling reason: societies and thoughts and principles themselves are no more than sets of static patterns. These patterns can't by themselves perceive or adjust to Dynamic Quality. Only a living being can do that." (Page192, Corgi Books, paperback edition)

Doug:

The key phrase here is "by themselves." Do you agree that Pirsig makes it clear that any SPoV in DQ has potential for change? Do you agree that no biological patterns could exist were it not for the inorganic patterns of value being in DQ? Do you agree that inorganic patterns of value evolve and invent new biological patterns of value and so on up the MOQ static pattern ladder? [36] Other members of TLS have broached the topic of how far down the ladder we go before the constituents of the SPoVs are not living. The classical humancentric SOM view is that only humans are sentient.

Anders:

Yes, but that's pretty much obvious. You take a rock, and break it in two. Then you've changed it. But would you or Pirsig claim that a rock strives towards a situation of higher quality, an "organic lifeness"?

Maggie:

Maybe it seems odd to think of a rock striving toward higher quality, but when I consider the universe as a system of many kinds of matter spinning and reacting to each other and Dynamic Quality, and see that rock as part of that great movement, it doesn't seem so far fetched. I think it's the difference in time scale that makes it hard for us as humans to perceive a rock's perceptions.

At any rate, Pirsig's example of the most Dynamic "rock" (the carbon molecule, which is balanced in such a way that it is not as susceptible to static inorganic patterns, but was instead free to become the basis of something radically different) is a small percentage of the inorganic matter in the universe.

(I hope I haven't misunderstood your conversation and put my foot in my mouth.)

Magnus:

Hi Anders. I like your straightforwardness. I'll try to explain what I mean.

It seems that you think, for example, that quantum flux will be understood one day and we will be able to predict it accurately. I hope so too, and I think it also, but I also think that a full understanding of quantum flux will not enable us to predict everything. I think we will always have some domain left that we don't understand.

This domain that we don't understand, I call Dynamic Quality. It might sound outrageous to move this border as we go along…it's supposed to be the first and absolute split of Quality, of everything. But I see no other way.

You also think that only sentient beings can perceive Dynamic Quality, but that brings up the mind/matter SOM platypus. (Hey Bo! My turn to preach.) What in sentient beings enables them to perceive Dynamic Quality? They consist of nothing but non-sentient parts. I think it has to come from "beneath."

Bodvar:

In the Artificial Intelligence/Turing Test question Anders came to my rescue so I think that one is settled. What Anders call "task specific" fits nicely in with what I call "intelligence," i.e., what keeps an organism alive in its normal environment. This must be kept separate from the intellectual level, which builds on the social level.

Anders asks if the MOQ is valid for extraterrestrial life as well. He believes in its main tenet, Dynamic/static quality, but has doubts about the four static levels, they being too fuzzy and human specific for his liking. [37] Even if the aliens may be biologically different from earthly life and also have different social relations as well as an alien intellect, the inorganic level is at least common throughout the universe.

Agreed! I once said that a theory that doesn't account for artificial intelligence isn't worth much; this goes for aliens too. A theory of everything does by definition profess to cover all eventualities. But it is an important aspect to our situation—never before in history has a person sat himself down to construct a metaphysics (until Pirsig everybody believed that metaphysics was what unfathomable German philosophy concerned itself with). The mind/matter division was the way the world had been assembled from eternity on.

Quality's aim is to wholesalely replace the Subject/Object Metaphysics and does thereby claim universal validity, anything less is impossible. It stands or falls; there is no middle way. This is exactly the trouble I have with extension or improvements to the MOQ. Once the basics are laid down, all efforts to improve it only worsens its trouble if it is infested with weaknesses from the start. I have yet to find weak spots with it, and feel no need for modifications.

Anders went on to say that he did not put much value to the four levels, because they were far too fuzzy and human specific. Fuzzy perhaps, but it has been found that fuzziness works better than clarity (logic), so why is the fuzziness so detrimental regarding the four levels? (Remember my space dimensions simile? Who knows where height ends and breadth begin or depth takes over? Fuzzy all the way, but still discrete, and universally valid.)

No, I believe that the static part of the MOQ is just as valid for Proxima Centauri as it is on Earth. Not only the inorganic level, but also the whole sequence is. Already by calling it extraterrestrial life, we have introduced the biological level, and their intellectual perception of reality will necessarily be based upon their society. It will most likely not match the human one, but will still be static patterns of intellect. Of course, the MOQ is a human intellectual construct, but what escapes that condition?

What haunts us is the Mind of SOM; it keeps surfacing repeatedly because it has not been understood that it is eradicated from the MOQ, not replaced by Dynamic Quality. For instance does Anders say that only sentient beings can perceive Dynamic Quality, not societies and certainly not atomic matter. (Bravo Magnus, you spotted that this brings us right back to the mind/matter platypus jungle.) Could Anders please tell what distinguishes a sentient being from an insentient one?

The "perception of Dynamic Quality" or "sense of value" sounds suspiciously like good old consciousness. Quality's first axiom is that there is nothing but value. Matter isn't material atoms perceiving Dynamic Quality, or sensing inorganic value. It is stable inorganic value itself—a morality! So is the rest of the quality sequence. There is nothing but value, but there are four moralities! The living organisms sense biological value. The social organisms sense social values and the intellectual organism (up to now only terrestrial human beings) sense intellectual value.

According to Pirsig, to perceive Dynamic Quality is a religious experience, easily mistaken for madness, but instrumental for making the transition to a new metaphysical platform (a horrifying experience and nothing worth pursuing). I don't find the talk of Dynamic Quality very useful. Our experience is in the static part of the scale; the Dynamism is nothing we should mess with unnecessarily. Admittedly, each value step is more Dynamic, freer, better than the previous one; the top notch volatile enough to react to Dynamic Quality, but static nonetheless.

Anders:

Let's try not to get religious about it, shall we?

We can't very well discuss anything, if you are willing to accept contradictions in the text.

It's not like we're at a Bible study-session down at the local Jehovah Witness Hall.

But we do have an advantage that Moses didn't have when he had to explain the Ten Commandments. We can go to the source and ask questions—so how about we write up a letter pointing out the contradictions we seem to be stuck upon, and giving Robert Pirsig (or "the great author" as you people insist on calling him) a chance to elaborate on what he meant? [38]

But in any event, if you feel that the multiple context idea explains Pirsig's (seemingly) contradictory statements, please explain this. Set up the relevant contexts, etc. This might be a bit of a task though.

Mediation [September 1997]

Maggie:

In several different threads, I noticed questions that seemed to be wanting a concept, one that I kept wanting to refer to in order to speak to your ideas. I'll try to throw it out, and then we can see if we can use it. Magnus seems to have asked:

"How can static intellectual patterns arise directly out of static inorganic patterns (matter, machines) skipping two levels altogether?"

There's a concept called mediation that seems useful here. I first encountered it in education theory, studying Lev S. Vygotsky. I have not studied this to the extent I would like. I'm only a beginner at formal educational theory. I hope I can do justice to it and its application to MOQ. Please take all of this as starting points for discussion.

I'll start with a quotation from Marx:

"Tools created in the process of work lead to particular production systems and social organizations. Thus, human labor transforms both Nature and human experience."

It looks like he is saying that a lower level object (the tool) transforms society. However, if we look at that tool from Pirsig's perspective of a tool being the concrete embodiment of an idea, then we can see that it is an idea of a pattern of work—embodied in the tool, and passed on to people to use—that mediates the transformation in social patterns and Nature (biological and inorganic patterns).

Lev Vygotsky, who lived in much the same social and intellectual environment as Marx, took this idea and went further. He said that:

"Psychological tools (rather than tools of work) bring about the transformation of human consciousness."

This parallel statement, when viewed from the MOQ, shows that Vygotsky was working on, and defining, how the intellectual level is created and how it functions, again, through mediation— exactly of what and how is another interesting puzzle. But within the MOQ, they are parallel, and that, to me, is exciting. Let's drop back down to the interaction between social and intellectual. It's more concrete.

Vygotsky's socio-historical theory of psychological development includes the idea that speech (and therefore thought) is a social pattern that has been mediated by something particularly human (that the MOQ would call intellectual patterns). The body of mediated social patterns has become culture and knowledge. Speech, a social pattern, is observed in biological humans, but it is not contained in the biological level. It is not an innate biological skill, but is a set of patterns contained in the society. So is knowledge. (I would go further and say that speech and knowledge support both static intellectual patterns and the capability of forming new ones, but are not part of the intellectual level, either. This is not Vygotsky speaking here at all.)

As a practical matter, mediation can be deliberately used, and managed. Vygotsky uses the term "sign," which may turn out to be synonymous for a static intellectual pattern that is chosen to be the agent of mediation. The act of making the choice would seem to be a Quality experience. A person makes a list for himself or others to follow, and that is use of a sign, deliberate mediation. A number used as a label or instruction is also a sign.

Here's how I think mediation is useful in MOQ. When a pattern in any level experiences an interaction with a higher level pattern or a Dynamic Quality event, the lower level pattern is changed in substance or direction. For instance, in Lev Vygotsky's sociohistorical perspective, the social level has been changed by the mediation of intellectual patterns. It is not possible to see the original "pure" social level any more. Intellectual patterns throughout human history have altered the social patterns so that much human behavior seems to be intellectually based. In fact, most of it is purely social, but the patterns themselves have been influenced by intellectual.

Mediation played a part here, and the original link between biology and society has been lost. You can't get to human society from biology. The structure is not only a standing structure (as in standing up from the base), but has some element of "hanging" from the higher level. A paradigm shift happens when the new structure reconnects with the base in a different spot. (Just skip this if it doesn't work for you, but sometimes I can really see all this. It seems physical.)

Let me play through another example—one suggested by the group—the Internet. The physical Internet is an inorganic level pattern that has been formed by the mediation of intellectual, social, and biological level patterns. There is no way that the organic components of the Internet (data packets traveling through phone cables to servers and little dots showing up on my screen) could have developed from the inorganic components directly. It was the mediation of biological patterns (people working in the computer factories meeting their needs for food and shelter) that put the physical components into place so the new inorganic patterns were formed (electricity, keyboards, cables).

At the same time, it was a very complex system of social patterns that made it possible for those biological patterns (people) to meet their survival needs by putting in work time and receiving a paycheck. This system has been formed (over time) by the mediation of intellectual and social patterns on lower levels.

Many different social patterns have had their effect on the inorganic web called the Internet. And if, as we probably believe, it was Dynamic Quality that mediated the creation of the MOQ (an intellectual pattern) it is also worth remembering that Dynamic Quality has its effect at all parts of this process. Sometimes, the new organic pattern is one in which the mediating forces (patterns? vectors?) no longer have much visible interaction any more. The patterns needed the mediation of higher levels in order to have been set, but not to be maintained. They can be maintained (often) from below. (This, I believe, might be applicable to the problem mentioned at the beginning, the apparent skipping of levels where a link actually did exist at some point.)

When, after being altered by mediation, patterns cannot be adequately maintained from below, other cross level changes occur. For example, current practices of human society cannot always be maintained by the natural environment, and things happen because of that. It is in this way that lower level patterns can effect change in higher level patterns, but I don't think this is the same as mediation. Lower levels support (or do not support) higher, but perhaps only higher levels mediate lower.

At any point in this process, both when patterns are balanced or when they overreach and are broken, Dynamic Quality is an active agent of redirection. One aspect of this that I personally think is worth pursuing is that it seems to me that a balance (some sort of gravity-like equilibrium) between patterns or streams of patterns is most likely to allow the influence of Dynamic Quality, whereas in situations where patterns overreach or are broken, the new direction is likely to be set by conforming to the direction of lower level patterns. I think this has something to do with the question of why new different lower levels are not easily formed.

I'm aware that I just brought in some undefined thing about direction, vectors, and influence. This seems integral to this concept, but I can't define it. I would like to see it defined.

I guess it's time to take a breather. This was intended to be short. I hope it doesn't seem rude to be dropping this big thing on you, but once I get started, I can't find the place to stop. Your discussions have started all kinds of things spinning in my head again.

Is mediation a useful concept? Does it help anybody?

Magnus:

Indeed it does! Especially when you say, "When a pattern in any level experiences an interaction with a higher level pattern or a Dynamic Quality event, the lower level pattern is changed (in substance or direction)."

It seems to me that too many are still focused on that notion that Dynamic Quality has to be the agent involved when a step up the static ladder is to be made. Mediation from an already existing higher level works just as good, and I also think that the lower level's experience of the change is equal, regardless of the agent involved.

I also appreciate your examples. They are a little less constructed than mine are and probably more accessible to most. But beware of Dynamic Quality sneaking in here and there. That's mostly why I try to avoid real life examples; they are too crowded with Dynamic Quality influence. And I guess I'm not quite ready for that yet. First, I have to figure out static quality.

As to my thoughts about artificial intelligence—I think I should brief you on my current view on that. I really think that computers are topmost intellectual patterns of value. No Dynamic Quality in sight though—we have ruled that out on the electrical level. The social patterns are the composition of the components in a computer and the different parts are the organs built using inorganic patterns. The intellectual level is supported by the language between the organs, the electrical language.

Another very interesting thing in a computer are the ones and zeros. I think those are inorganic patterns supported by the computer in the same way our inorganic patterns are supported by a lower level. The ones and zeros in turn are used by organic patterns, subroutines, objects, and they are in turn used by the social level, the programs.

Maggie:

The concept of fractals comes to mind here. We have these (four?) major streams of (growth, life) that the MOQ labels Inorganic, Biological, Social, Intellectual. They grow out of each other. At the juncture of departure from the lower level, there is a function of support by the lower level (consistent direction toward static level quality), as well as the function of opposition (originally towards Dynamic Quality, but a new static quality once it is set).

The streams have another kind of effect on each other, like gravitational attraction or like the pull of one current on another. The existence of a new level affects the direction of all the other levels as well. Within each of these major streams (except perhaps inorganic), there are other streams, like multiple strands in a rope, having within them the same types of interactions and shapes, being "pulled" away from the stream's center (static quality) by Quality, or "pulled." The thicker the rope, the stronger the pull. This "pull" is, I believe, the same concept as mediation, but in this image of streams and ropes, "mediation" sounds silly.

Your example of the computer seems to me to be a rope in the intellectual stream, having its own full set of levels within itself. Do you think so?

I have to go teach. I feel a little guilty about popping off things like this. I start to make a simple, straightforward observation, and end up drawing pictures in the air. In any other situation I would hold off and not send this, but believing that Dynamic Quality often appears as "spur of the moment," I'll just say thanks to you for triggering this stuff, and let it stand.

Magnus:

I don't know if I followed you all the way through your rope analogy. Let's just say that I consider a computer to be a static version of the human intellect. That would mean a very thin rope, no?

"I have to go teach."

Quality, I hope.;-)

The Four Levels [September 1997]

Doug:

Magnus, I am enjoying your posts and comments enormously! You and DQ keep us "on the track." We periodically refer to Turing's work. Allow me to add some material here that may be useful in understanding part of what Turing accomplished. I am quoting from Douglas Hofstadter's work entitled Metamagical Themas (paperback version), Hofstadter's review of Hodges book on Turing, Chapter 21, pages 483-491. In turn, Hofstadter quotes from Andrew Hodges preeminent work, Alan Turing: The Enigma.

"In 1931, the Austrian logician Kurt Gödel devastated Hilbert's and Russell's hopes of creating a perfect formalization of all mathematical reasoning. Gödel had demonstrated that there were undecidable propositions in any consistent axiomatic system of the Hilbert-Russell sort, propositions based on famous paradoxes of logic that had plagued logicians ever since the Greeks. What Gödel had left unsettled, however, was the question of whether, given an axiomatic system and an arbitrary proposition in it, one could determine mechanically whether that proposition was undecidable in that system. (Page 485.)

"Alan Turing chose to work on this question. To his surprise, he discovered that for very Gödelian reasons, no machine could be built that could infallibly recognize undecidable propositions. He went further and showed that a very complex type of Turing machine, called a 'universal' Turing machine, was capable of being fed a single number that encoded the structure of any other Turing machine, much in the way DNA codes for the structure of an organism.

"Turing's death blow to the hopes of logicians such as Russell and Hilbert was delivered in two stages. First, he supposed that a machine for recognizing undecidable propositions exists; then he showed how that assumption leads to self-contradiction. In short, through Gödel's and Turing's work, mathematics was revealed to be unmechanizable...no matter how complex the machine involved." (Page 486.)

And I thought this particular quote belies the intuition, beauty and vibrancy of the MOQ: "Thus Turing's seemingly negative result about machines can be seen as a positive result, in that it sheds new light on how physical objects might reflect on themselves, and even consider themselves to be conscious, deliberating beings." (Page 487.)

I have left much out. You get the basic idea here; formal logic is incomplete! And Gödel and Turing showed clearly that nothing could be completely proven by rational means. And Pirsig showed us why this is true in a metaphysical sense. So, when we toggle back to SOM we enter a world that produces incompleteness and paradoxes. MOQ, quantum physics, and the great author show us that the formal (rational) world based on SOM is a bad place to be if you want nonparadoxical perspectives of reality.

Magnus:

I'll continue on the theoretical trail one moment, bear with me. I'm not acquainted with Hilbert-Russell systems but I assume they are not always, I think the word is, complete. A complete axiomatic system is where every proposition is decidable. One might wonder why anybody would want to construct an incomplete axiomatic system. Generally, because the more powerful and expressive a system is, the harder it is to evaluate propositions. And to describe "reality," very powerful systems must be used.

Doug:

The classical scientists wanted decidable systems for the same reason that Einstein said God doesn't roll dice: determinism, guaranteed predictability. This is SOM stuff, reductionist stuff, limited-thinking stuff. I agree that undecidable systems can be richer. I like to call us "quantum mechanics." I do that because from my perspective we are built from endless quantum systems, all defined by their interrelationships with all other quantum systems. (What does that sound like?) The probability patterns of value among all quantum systems create them and concurrently make them intrinsically undecidable. (All of this is my opinion. I doubt many quantum physicists would say it the way I did here. But I said it, I hope, with some fidelity to how the great author would say it.)

Magnus:

Now, what does this have to do with the MOQ? What we should do with the static levels is to construct a consistent and complete axiomatic system in which it is possible to express any static phenomenon. It's probably better to construct four systems, each corresponding to one level. It's of course possible to use various already existing systems for this. What we gain in splitting the systems up is the same as the old "divide and conquer" approach. What the MOQ provides is the glue between the systems, which must be equally waterproof.

Doug:

This approach feels good, but it may feel good because it has the SOM-reductionist flavor which Bo decries. If we can say the above paragraph in MOQese, it might provide an approach of: "What...to do with the MOQ." Is our goal to make the MOQ more accessible to all? If the great author sees us as the vector for a purpose, we should decide what that is. Can we do that and still have the threads? Is that OK with the Lila Squad? Bo?

Magnus:

This "divide and conquer" approach is partly what makes the MOQ superior to SOM in describing static phenomenon, and we must use it wisely. We must not extend the systems beyond completeness because then we're entering the domains of Dynamic Quality.

Doug:

Yes! And we must also remember that much of humanity is more SOM-like and our approach must wean them off of SOM onto MOQ. We have to remember how brilliant the great author is. He tacitly chose to use familiar SOM techniques corrected and retuned with MOQ to help us transition from SOM to MOQ. Matt and I have been discussing the apparent fact that SOM, as practiced, is something more like QSOM. I think Matt used that acronym first. So, in a sense SOM is already being evolved by DQ. QSOM is an intermediate, as practiced, stage of that evolution. If the world practiced pure SOM, nothing would work!

Magnus:

This might sound as if we just think real hard, we will eventually be able to capture Dynamic Quality within these systems also. I don't think we need to worry about that though. For example, today it looks like quantum flux is very much influenced by Dynamic Quality, which would actually contradict the fact that each higher level is more Dynamic than the lower, which in turn is an argument to include it in the inorganic level. Maybe we'll one day be able to describe quantum flux as complete as our description of matter is today, but there will always be undecidable Dynamic phenomenon somewhere.

Here's another big difference between the SOM and the MOQ. The SOM either tries to explain "reality" with one gigantic incomplete axiomatic system or "gives up" and says, it's impossible, don't bother. The MOQ on the other hand has the freedom to explain as much of "reality" currently possible and leave the rest to Dynamic Quality, and still be amazed by and have faith in DQ.

Doug:

Yes, one big axiomatic system is like one, absolute, deterministic truth called the GUT (Grand Unifying Theory) which Einstein, et al., have sought, fruitlessly. I agree with most of the above, Magnus. Many truths to you.

Magnus:

Are there more than one?

Doug:

Yes, there is a new one immediately after each Quality event. And, each new us (resulting from the "flux of us": Flus) in the DQ can be in any one, or more of an infinity of contexts (each affected by other "local" and "non-local" contexts), each with its own "quasilocal" truth(s). (Pretty, rich, vibrant, Dynamic, and MOQetic, eh? Ahh…the music…the poetry…the joy.)

Many truths to you, Magnus.

James:

As a new member, I hope it's OK if I make some general remarks on MOQ, say where I stand on some issues, and in particular give my interpretation of the levels of Quality. I am sorry if I am crossing over some threads here, but what I have to say seems unified to me.

I am very fond of the levels of Quality because they encourage analogical thought, and they are especially useful in that they provide a rich source of examples in which we can trace the action of Dynamic Quality. There is a Dynamic relationship between any two adjacent levels characterized by two functions: (1) a function of support and (2) a function of opposition. It's a love/hate relationship—as if the lower level helps the higher against its will, or is tricked into giving the higher level its opportunity.

Each level depends absolutely on the level below it (as a whole) and feeds off it like a parasite, or a rebellious slave turned master, always seeking to achieve a sort of independence by broadening its application. It liberates itself by finding alternatives and making choices between them. (Of course, I'm anthropomorphizing here, but I do the best I can with the language I have. Language has its traps. For instance, I am sure we have all unconsciously used the subject/object division a hundred times each in this forum. What we really need is a new vocabulary.)

The higher quality arises from the "need" of the lower form, but then starts to exhibit aberrations. For instance, if we say that existence over time is the need of the inorganic level, organisms fulfill this need by the trick of reproduction, but it looks strange in

101

comparison to the values of cohesion, size, etc. otherwise dominant. Moving up a level according to Richard Dawkins, the survival of the gene is the ultimate value of biological evolution. But soon you get the deer antlers that Hugo spoke of, and you need to explain things on a social level because they seem "unfit" on the lower level. Finally, it is clear that a lot of intellectual behavior appears aberrant at the social level, even if it is finally justified.

Once the higher level is established it then turns on the lower levels and starts to influence them. The intellect, for instance, "mediates" the other levels by means of tools both inorganic and cultural. Impulse turns into manifestation. For example, social conflicts throw up economic theories which begin to influence society, and whose effects are felt right down to the inorganic spinning machine. History shows that individual experiments (mere chance from a social perspective) throw up inventions (e.g., the steam engine, the Web) that had not been thought of much before they were invented. In other words, technology drives society as much as society drives technology, owing to the powerful if uneven development of intellect in recent history.

The higher level cannot altogether forget the lower level it stands on, any more than a diplomat can permanently forget the people he is supposed to represent. For instance, our tools have given us great control over Nature, but we could not continue this discussion without the indulgence of the sun. Another example: our intellectual edifice of science, mathematics, and literature has had great successes, but it was developed in societies on just one side of the world; Western thought is not fully representative of the social level worldwide. In relation to the development of Quality I would have to disagree with Bo when he says, "I don't think one morality can make much impact on the next higher morality." The higher values arise from the lower values and are, alas, conditioned by them.

In considering the progress from one level to the next, it is tempting to think of a final Ideal State, in which material, biological, and social values would be present in their totality, but would only be signs in a cosmic show. Theists will think of God; another try is Hegel's Absolute, the "unity of the Subjective and Objective Idea," caught thinking about itself from Bertrand Russell's description. One must also consider the possibility that levels beyond the intellectual will evolve.

In my opinion, computers present a challenge to the levels of Quality theory, for here, we seem to have static intellectual patterns directly superimposed on inorganic patterns, [39] the whole being characterized by a notable lack of Dynamic Quality. I can't buy Magnus' ideas about social patterns in computers, in either hardware or software, but perhaps there will be more of a case for this idea if agents become genuinely popular. (Agents are autonomous, goal fulfilling programs which persist over time, mostly in a state of waiting.) Also, there is a lot of science fiction potential in the growth of the Internet as an intellectual super being.

Perhaps it is premature here to discuss such a tricky concept as Dynamic Quality before settling matters about the levels but it would be highly interesting to see how it could be related to the latest theories of evolution, systems theory and emergent properties, and Hegel's dialectic (especially for me since I have no special knowledge of any of these myself).

Bodvar:

James, welcome to the Squad. I am most impressed by your opening message; it is a deep and important analysis and I am looking forward to seeing your biography and future contributions. The little disagreement with me is insignificant. My point was merely that the morality of a higher level is not changed by a lower one. For instance, life's purpose is to transgress matter, which is adamant, but of course, there are plenty of reverberations in the organic realm of what happens on the inorganic level.

You also see the challenge for the MOQ posed by artificial intelligence. This issue has not been probed fully because each time we have been stuck in the confounded subject/object "mind" in contrast to the Quality "intellect," and did I spot the same "difficulty" with you, James? That those computers must enter the (MOQ) intellectual level to be declared intelligent? Magnus, in his usual fashion, waved off Alan Turing's test for intelligence, but Turing is after all the father of computation as we know it, so if he couldn't come up with another criterion of intelligence (than not being able to distinguish it from a human being), I doubt if we can do any better. Alan Turing himself could not come up with another definition of intelligence.

Magnus:

That's because he was trying to define it, and I don't think that can be done since Dynamic Quality is very much involved in what we call intelligence. Static intellectual patterns should be possible to define though.

Bo, please, sometimes I'm not sure if I'm totally incapable of transferring my view or if it's you who refuses to see what I'm saying.

A rational definition of intelligence is not possible because what we call "intelligence" has so much to do with Dynamic Quality: intuition, fantasy, inspiration, association, etc.

I actually didn't think of that particular definition of intelligence when last I waved it off—I probably mixed it up with someone else's. However, I don't consider that a very good definition though. Since Turing didn't know anything about Dynamic Quality, he thought everything could be defined using rational means; that was the only way. He probably thought that one day the intelligence of humans could be defined using rational means. [40]

James:

I have always felt that Turing's test is good as a test, but that it is often mistaken for a definition. For instance, if I wish to see if my stove is hot, I might touch it and test it. Does this mean that we should define heat as "that which seems hot to experts" or "that which is similar to good examples of heat such as fire"? Clearly not. Similarly, we have not come far in our understanding of intelligence when we say that it is intelligent which seems intelligent. We sense a Quality from examples, but if static forms such as definitions are to have use then the Quality must be related to other qualities.

Perhaps Magnus is right when he says that Dynamic Quality pervades the concept of intelligence too much to allow for definition, especially since Dynamic Quality appears to grow and quicken with each higher level and we are still struggling with Dynamic Quality at the inorganic level. If that is so, it is bad news for artificial intelligence. Each level depends absolutely on the level below it (as a whole) and feeds off it like a parasite, or a rebellious slave turned master, always seeking to achieve a sort of independence by broadening its application; it liberates itself by finding alternatives and making choices between them.

Reading over Pirsig convinced me that the struggle for the independence of intellect from society began around the time of the Greek cosmologists. It was the emergence of what I call "declarative thought" from "procedural thought." Procedural thought knows of ways and means; declarative thought knows of existence and models. The first man who made that remarkable leap of abstraction was the man who went from, "This is the way to do it," to "This is the way it is." Just who that was is a matter for philosophologists.

Maggie:

This is interesting. My gut feeling (and this is not a criticism) would have been that "declarative thought," as you define it, would have been first, followed by "procedural thought." If you are right, then perhaps it is my habit of looking at life from the perspective of a person who has been raised in a culture in which the intellectual level is accepted, one in which the naming seems primary. In past times, before the intellectual level was firmly established and its effects disseminated throughout the social level, the way social man "learned" was by doing the accepted thing, without thought or intellectual evaluation. So that makes "the way to do it" come before the abstraction.

That's what you said. I just had to work my way around to it. Wow!

Earlier, James wrote: "The rational thought system of Western civilization is very stable, with a proven record of supporting human/social needs, but it is not so successful at representing individual emotions, hence the need for art. In general we are still very much in the middle of the struggle between the social and the intellectual, for instance, it is still more common to condemn intellectual theories because they encourage bad social practices than it is to condemn social practices because they reflect poor judgment."

I'm going to agree with you here. I also think it is possible for a lower morality to affect the higher. For example, the AIDS virus is a development in the biological level that has profoundly affected the higher levels.

In bringing up the virus, I was trying to think of something that developed naturally within the biological level, not as a result of mediation by something in another level. Now I am wondering whether that was an appropriate example. Is the AIDS virus something that developed within the natural processes of the biological level? It's a genetic mutation, right? Maybe that's not biological process at all, but an example of how Dynamic Quality can affect inorganic patterns directly, able to work within pockets of balance within the biological patterns.

James wrote: "In considering the progress from one level to the next, it is tempting to think of a final Ideal State, in which material, biological, and social values would be present in their totality, but would only be signs in a cosmic show. Theists will think of God; another try is Hegel's Absolute, the unity of the Subjective and Objective Idea, thought thinking about itself from Bertrand Russell's description. One must also consider the possibility that levels beyond the intellectual will evolve."

It may be happening now, and any new levels would be expected to be faster moving, closer together, and less distinct. Perhaps it is our own human grounding in the social/intellectual realm that makes it seem so. (Sorry. Any moment now, I'll be drawing more pictures in the air. I have this strange urge to do that. I keep thinking that someday I'll see a diagram of four-dimensional mathematics describing some natural process and I'll be able to say, That's it! That's how it works on all the levels! Wouldn't that be something?)

Back to reality. :-)

James:

Has anyone suggested yet that what is needed is an entirely new language? That is, a language will all of the flexibility of a natural language, but none of its philosophical assumptions, replacing them with MOQ style constructs.

Platt:

Welcome Maggie! Your contribution is wonderfully thought provoking. A question—is mediation another word for causation? When I substitute the words cause and causation where you used mediate and mediation, they seem to fit. Example:

Original: "For instance, in Lev Vygotsky's socio-historical perspective, the social level has been changed by the mediation of intellectual patterns."

Using cause: "For instance, in Lev Vygotsky's socio-historical perspective, changes in the social level were caused by intellectual patterns."

I must be missing something in the concept of mediation, but if it does mean the same as causation, then it can be related to Pirsig's "patterns of preferences" and Dynamic Quality, which he defines as a force for transformation and change, always seeking something better.

Maggie:

Even though your substitution seems to work, my gut reaction is that mediation is not the same as causation. This is a challenge I will try to address as soon as possible. It's boiling in my head. Let me give you an example.

Magnus wrote, "If you really mean this, we're really starting to understand each other. A human with a warm coat and a good pair of shoes is a society (a composition of organic patterns) that can better withstand cold weather than a human can without them. Therefore, the coat and the shoes (and the human) are organic patterns to that society."

Now, about that coat—the substance of the coat is inorganic value. If it is a fur coat, the form of the material (the shape of that inorganic substance) is set by biological value. The inorganic patterns were mediated by biological patterns. The process of reproducing these new patterns is stored in the DNA of the raccoon who first wore the fur.

The habit (pattern) of putting on a coat over the human body when chilly is social value. Whatever habits people had before they discovered putting on coats have been supplanted by a new pattern that resulted from Dynamic Quality mediation. (This happened long enough ago that it seems OK to assume that the intellectual level had not formed.) That Dynamic Quality insight has been stored in the shared custom of humans. The reproduction of this mediated social value (covering the body) is managed by a process that is different from learning algebra. It is a social process that is accomplished by imitation, not thought. The biological level has been mediated as well (just ask the raccoon). The process of the reproduction of fur pieces for coat material has been stored in human biological patterns as well, as the maintenance of this process has become linked to the biological welfare (paycheck equals food) of the trapper, merchant, salesman, and banker (thus, of course, creating and affecting other social patterns).

The knowledge of varieties of ways to sew a coat and the many different intellectual patterns that mediate the social patterns of the coat industry are all intellectual patterns. These patterns were mediated by Dynamic Quality and that Dynamic Quality is stored as static intellectual patterns that are available to be shared among people only if they can be stored in some lower level pattern for transmission and reproduction. The chain of mediation continues downward from there, to the point where the inorganic patterns that make up the coat may be something totally different (i.e., petroleum based).

The status recognition is a social pattern of value, but only to the extent that it is unconscious imitation. If the wearer has heard from someone else that wearing a certain coat is "cool," and makes a deliberate decision to wear that particular coat to enhance his social status, then he is using an intellectual pattern of value, one that gives him more control over social patterns. The wearer might also have a Dynamic inspiration of the rightness of this coat, which allows him to evaluate and choose between different social patterns.

Once that decision has been made, the person may have changed his own internal set of valued social patterns, and the putting on of that coat may be following a social pattern of value again, i.e., a habit, an unconscious action, unchallenged until a new situation forces or allows reevaluation.

The word "evaluation" is tricky here. It comes closer than any other non-MOQ term to describing human participation in the Quality event, but I think that evaluation is most commonly used to describe an intellectual Quality event. There may be a social Quality event that is also included under the term evaluation, three different processes, hard to distinguish. According to the MOQ, they should have predictably different results.

These differences could be important. If I live long enough, I'd like to catalog them.

Bodvar:

Applied to the garment issue, when a person dresses to comply with fashion, the suit, coat, or whatever, is regarded as artifacts to enhance the wearer's social status, but if the person is dying from cold the clothing enhances his/her biological survival. What they are in themselves besides inorganic patterns (the shoe's animal hide is inorganic in this context) is intellectual deliberations.

Maggie has a point about intellect's interference. One's reasoning may make one decide to give a damn about fashion and wear rags instead (perhaps starting a new fashion trend). There is however a point I must stress—the focus shifts extremely quickly. On your way from the wardrobe locker to the mirror, you may change from social awareness to intellectual reasoning many times. Even the freezing person may change to social value and give away the lifesaving coat to a friend.

These quick shifts may make it look like the value levels are merging, but they are discrete. On your way from the proverbial locker, you may step on a tack and in a flash are the intellectual deliberations and social urges gone while simple organic pain overwhelms you for a moment.

The evaluation bit was good.

Annotations by Robert M. Pirsig

30. I think the answer is that inorganic objects experience events but do not react to them biologically, socially, or intellectually. They react to these experiences inorganically, according to the laws of physics.

31. Since experience is the starting point, it doesn't arise from a lower level of no experience. Logically speaking, a starting point that arises from something else is no longer a starting point.

32. Since the MOQ states that consciousness (i.e. intellectual patterns) is the collection and manipulation of symbols, created in the brain, that stand for patterns of experience, then artificial intelligence would be the collection and manipulation of symbols, created in a machine, that stand for patterns of experience. If one agrees that experience exists at the inorganic level, then it is clear that computers already have artificial intelligence. A question arises if the term "consciousness" is expanded to mean "intuition" or "mystic awareness." Then computers are shut out by the fact that static patterns do not create Dynamic Quality.

33. I think the brain cell has to be classified as a static pattern and does not "contain" Dynamic quality.

34. I think there may be a confusion here between Dynamic Quality and chaos, which is certainly undesirable in a computer. However, many engineering and scientific discoveries are made by an apparatus not doing what it is are supposed to in a way that is discovered to actually be better than what it is supposed to do. This betterness is then incorporated into future designs. That, then, is a Dynamic process.

35. I don't think it is nonsense but I think he is right. "Dynamic" in physics and "Dynamic" in the MOQ do not have the same meaning.

36. The MOQ as I understand it does not conflict with Darwinian explanations and does not say that molecules invent cells any more than giraffes invent long necks. It just says that when something that works better occurs and is sustained, that is evolution. Without the term "better" there is no way to distinguish

evolution from degradation. The undefined "better" is Dynamic Quality.

37. I don't think they are fuzzy.

38. That is what is supposed to occur with these notes. The "Great Author" is a sarcasm used by Richard Rigel, not a term of respect.

39. No, there are always some biological fingers in there somewhere. Computers don't do anything without the fingers, and these fingers are directed by cultural forces.

40. For precision in the MOQ it's better to limit intelligence to symbol manipulation, as defined earlier. I think that a lot of perceived fuzziness of these levels can come from expanding terms beyond their ordinary dictionary meanings when there is no need to do so.

Chapter 4

MOQ grant us the serenity to accept the things we cannot define, courage to define the things we can, and the wisdom to know the difference. — Magnus

To Define, Or Not To Define [October 1997]

Platt:

Perhaps there is something to be said in asserting that Pirsig's four levels of value patterns cannot be explained intellectually. So, what are we to do? [41]

How can we possible get someone to understand us by directly experiencing the four value patterns? I used the high school curricula to define the four levels because: 1) most people have had the high school experience, and 2) while in high school have sprinkled iron filings over a magnet, viewed pond water through a microscope, touched a cultural artifact, written a book report, and solved a problem in plane geometry. The distinctions between those kinds of experience are clear even though we can never know what it's really like to be an iron filing, a little critter swimming in pond scum or a Buddhist monk living in Hong Kong.

So when sitting around discussing the MOQ with friends and someone asks me to define an inorganic value pattern I say, "In high school physics class did you ever sprinkle iron filings on a magnet and see the filings cluster around the poles? Well, that's an inorganic value pattern." [42]

The challenge for me has always been to find ways to explain the MOQ to people who have no interest in philosophy and/or are so set in the static pattern of subject/object that to say the world is values engenders either an incredulous stare, a patronizing smile, or an gently phrased retort like, "Are you nuts?" As Pirsig says in Chapter 9, "If you're going to talk about Quality at all you have to be ready to answer someone like Rigel. You have to have a ready-made Metaphysics of Quality that you can snap at him like some catechism. Phædrus didn't have a Catechism of Quality and that's why he got hit."

Magnus:

I really want to have definitions of the static levels. They are static, they have always been, and will always be static. OK, you can give examples till you have exhausted the vocabulary but if anyone can do that, he/she must have some internal rules where to put each word from the vocabulary. I want these rules. [43]

Without definitions, we are confined to inductive use of the MOQ. Deduction will be totally closed to us and I'm not very thrilled about that perspective. And yes, the concept of definitions is intellectual, so what? That's what we use intellectual patterns for, so that we can look into the future and predict predictable events, and to affect the future.

Doug:

On definition and whether to define or not define, can we return to the words of the great author? I decided to look at some of the many places where he considered the issue, "to define, or not to define." The truth is, he sounds just like us. We are experiencing the same throes and anguish, all of what Bo calls the ugliness. I think he needed (and so do we) to do it. In ZMM, he (apparently) goes insane doing it.

If you recall in ZMM, he decided that Quality was not definable. [44] But in Lila he decided that, regardless how large and difficult the task, he must define Quality. Here you can see him arguing with himself about proceeding (this reminds me of the discussions we have seen the past few weeks on TLS): "Since metaphysics is essentially a kind of dialectical definition and since Quality is essentially outside definition, this means that 'Metaphysics of Quality' is essentially a contradiction in terms, a logical absurdity." Page 73, Lila.

Phædrus says to himself, "Don't do it (i.e., define Quality). You'll get into nothing but trouble. You're just going to start up a thousand dumb arguments about something that was perfectly clear until you came along...." Page 74, Lila.

"The trouble was, this was only one part of himself talking. There was another part that kept saying, 'Ah, do it anyway. It's interesting.' This was the intellectual part that didn't like undefined things, and telling it not to define Quality was like telling a fat man to stay out of the refrigerator, or an alcoholic to say out of bars....." Page 74, Lila.

As you can see, right here in Lila he decides to go ahead and do it, fusing the SO mind/body dichotomy with the two intermediate static levels: social and biological. And further fusing the four static levels and DQ with DQ's evolutionary tension constantly applied to the four levels, and finally establishing the five moral codes. I think he set an example for us, here. He would, in my opinion, suggest that we define the "Architecture" of the four static levels, not the infrastructure, but the Architecture. [45]

In SODV, he explains the above further:

"I will point out to you that for centuries rhetoric instructors in our culture have been paid to pass and fail students on the quality of their writing without ever having any viable definition of what that quality is or even if there is such a thing at all. That is a bizarre practice that I tried to end." Page 11, SODV.

"Quality is real even though it cannot be defined." Page 12, SODV.

It sounds as though he is waffling here, but if you read the surrounding text, you will see he is not. He says Quality may be derived from Subject and Object and their interrelationships: the quantized Quality events that occur when Subject becomes aware of Object.

"The bottom box shows inorganic patterns. The Metaphysics of Quality says objects are composed of 'substance' but it says that this substance can be defined more precisely as 'stable inorganic patterns of value.' This added definition makes substance sound more ephemeral than previously but it is not. The objects look and smell and feel the same either way." Page 14, SODV.

"The fifth evidence of similarity is that probability itself may be expressed as value, so that 'a static pattern of inorganic values,'

115

which is a definition the Metaphysics of Quality gives to 'substance,' is the same as a 'pattern of probabilities,' which is a definition quantum theory gives to substance. If the atomic world is composed of probability waves and if probability is equal to value then it follows logically that the atomic world is composed of value." Page 16, SODV.

An ominous situation, that. But for us, TLS, in Lila he decides to define Quality.

Bodvar:

A splendid example of intellect's impotence is in describing the taste of chocolate. [46] My guru of old, Colin Wilson, had a favourite example of "language inadequacy" (as he calls it) to distinguish between the taste of an orange and a tangerine. This goes for any taste, not only differences. It goes for all values of the organic level and, well, and partly the social ones although here language starts to interfere. I think poetry is the linguistic attempt that probes deepest downwards from the intellect, but then, it is art.

Colin Wilson has a hope that in the far future language will achieve this capacity, but that is in vain. Language can like no other medium convey intellectual ideas, which is its mission, but the "language" of the body does this so marvelously well so why bother.

Now, what is society and what is culture is another difficult border definition. [47] Right now, we have the Algerian fundamentalist atrocities. It is completely insanity from our usual rational political standpoint, but I think the MOQ puts it in perspective. The communal value-focused Islamic culture (Semitic religions are social values made into eternal ones) fights back against Western intellectual influence. In Lila, Pirsig puts the fascism and Nazism of the Second World War in this same context, which makes a lot of sense.

Doug:

One of the reasons I say "Many truths to you" at the end of my emails is that one of the most powerful aspects of MOQ is it (like QM and vastly different from SOM) eliminates paradoxes via the reality of many truths. MOQ and QM are compatible with many truths, while SOM is compatible with one absolute truth (yes/no, true/false, etc.).

But MOQ's code of ethics is not locally relativistic as "many truths" may have you believe. MOQ works as an ethical system because it is the best metaphysics of reality man has today. But its "many truths" nature carries extra responsibility and work for its practitioners. We are used to living in a SOM world. Some of us, in my opinion, have become lazy in our thinking habits. Let's see if I can explain why I think this is true.

I ran the above paradox past Pirsig a couple of years ago, but he did not bite. I also distracted him with a textbook by Christopher Alexander entitled Notes on the Synthesis of Form, that appeared to him very SOM like. Actually, the book was about context. I think context is a very important part of MOQ. If I am wrong I need to know, and perhaps more important TLS needs to know.

I stated the paradox to Pirsig a little differently:

A: Statement B is true.

B: Statement A is false.

If you place both of these sentences in one context (which is what SOM does with everything) you get, guess what, paradox (es). You feel this kind of brain locked looping stupor. It makes you dizzy. My point to Pirsig and to my fellow TLS mates (this paradox is not new, I did not originate it, countless others have used this example; except I have not seen anyone else solve it the way I am about to show you. If you know of another person who has already done this, please share) is that MOQ and QM and the concept of many truths eliminates the paradox.

They do so by implying that if there are many truths there must be many contexts. All we have to do to eliminate the paradox is create a separate context for the two statements, say a local "true" context and a local "false" context. Then place the two sentences in each context. When you get a contradiction, switch to the other context to make the sentence, which is contradictory true. Caveat: we now have the added responsibility of keeping track of multiple contexts for ourselves and those with whom we are communicating. This is not easy. It is easier to be SOM-like, assume a single context, and allow the paradoxes to spew forth abundantly.

The reason I am spending so much time on this is that I see this as part of the problem we have deciding which example and its static patterns of value fits in which level(s). Then we seem to have trouble knowing which context we are in and communicating that consistently to our fellow TLS mates. I see this concept as imperative! It, at least for me, points the way to gaining consistency of understanding and communication of the four levels in MOQ. Each level is a different context within the MOQ. Yet, we need to use MOQ itself in an unlimited variety of cultural and other contexts. Each example we discuss may be in its own local context and yet prefer multiple precondition MOQ levels. (As an example think of Eskimo culture vs. Victorian culture on sexual mores.)

It says to me we need to do several things (this is a lot of extra work, so you may want to say, "Doug, we are having fun. Just take your many truths/contexts and go away."):

We need to be sure we state our assumptions:

Including which local context we are in,

Including which MOQ level(s) we are in, and

State when we change to another local context,

State when we change MOQ level(s), and

There may be more.

Note that in the SOM paradox, which we solved using MOQ's many truths, there are two different moralities, just like there are two different moralities in the Victorian vs. Eskimo mores. When you view the other context from your local context, you can judge the other context's code as immoral, but within your local context, your own code is moral. If there is something wrong in your local context MOQ will help you assess that negative value and find ways to correct in the direction of "better."

We may be assessing our own personal moral code compared to other cultures' codes, our own culture's codes, or a friend's code within our mutual culture. In my opinion, in each case, if we are responsible practitioners of MOQ, we must know and state the context(s). If we do not, we will confuse us and we will confuse those SOM folk we wish to adopt MOQ.

I see this as the major source of confusion in TLS when we discuss the four levels and their applications to various examples. So now you see I am very serious and intent when I say—many truths to you!

Anders:

Isn't it just a basic requirement of rational thought (and comprehensible speech/writing) not to contradict yourself during an argument? And so if I were to do it anyway, for example, in the form of a sentence like, "All people named Anders lie all the time," I'd break this "law" and hence make no sense (make a meaningless uttering). I don't think this has anything to do with SOM?

Your multiple context idea appeals to me on a subconscious level but I can't grasp it fully; so could you show some examples where you use this idea?

Doug:

That's the thing about paradoxes and belief systems that generate them. They keep people confused and dizzy for millennia. Imagine the coming revolution when MOQ moves to the fore. There are many examples, but if I give you a few simple, real life ones you will be able to invent your own "better" ones.

Visualize: a residence in a small neighborhood. Man and wife at home. Home has lots of windows. One front window is open. Car is in driveway. Passenger window is down. Weatherman says rain is coming. Man and wife decide to go to movie. They go to the car and jump in. Man says to wife, "Honey, will you please close the window."

Visualize: a man in Toronto wants to know how to get to Denver. Has a friend in LA and a friend in Chicago. He calls each for directions. Friend in Chicago gives directions from Chicago to Denver. Friend in LA gives directions from LA to Denver.

Visualize: you are in church. You are instructed to, "Turn to page 34." You have a hymnal and a Bible on your lap.

Anders, see if these help. The big thing here is the SOM dumb assumption of a single, absolute context (e.g., Einstein and his Grand Unifying Theory) versus the MOQwise awareness of many truths and their concomitant, many contexts (e.g., Niels Bohr, et al., and complementarity).

Many truths to you, Anders.

Gene:

There is something similar in fuzzy logic where each truth is true to some degree. Most useless ones are 100% true (when it's raining water comes down from the skies), but really interesting truths always depend on the context (to borrow Doug's terminology). Fuzzy logic theory is very well developed (Lofti Zadeh, Bart Kosko) and it is conducive to silicon implementation. Expert systems we program now are based on fuzzy logic as opposed to the "if...then...else" rule trees.

Doug:

I made an inference from what you said above that formal logic is a SPoV invention of the SOM types. Do you agree?

Gene:

Yes, Boolean (yes/no) logic separates everything into sets with crisp boundaries the same way SOM does. This simplification of everyday reality is useful in many cases, but very artificial. It does not allow to simulate an expert, who very often makes decisions without being able to formalize them into a crisp yes/no tree.

Doug:

I also infer that fuzzy logic is more MOQ-like. Is that what you are hinting?

Gene:

I do feel similarities. Of course, fuzzy logic is just one of the patterns in the MOQ structure. I'd like to be able to define the similarities, but not sure how important that is. I look at the fuzzy logic mostly from engineering point of view (I use it in my programs), but I originally was attracted to it on a higher level by its "many truths" possibilities.

Doug:

If so, then could we use a kind of fuzzy representation of the four levels and their contexts, relationships, etc.?

Gene:

I think we already did, when the Lila Squad writes about interdependency and mutual mediation of levels. It seems to me that level boundaries are not crisp, they overlap. For example, it's very difficult to pinpoint where inorganic stops and biology begins. [48]

Doug:

As I understand it, fuzzy logic is still not continuous; it has multiple, settable, discrete levels instead of the formal dichotomies and trichotomies, right?

Gene:

Sets in fuzzy logic overlap; they are continuous. Degree of overlap is "context" specific. Let's say, we wanted to separate all people into two sets of "tall" and "short." According to the Boolean logic we would establish a threshold, let's say 6 feet. In that case, a 5'9" person and 6' person would belong to the two completely different sets, despite the fact that we all understand that they are pretty close in height. Expert system based on Boolean logic would trigger two different rules to handle these two people. According to the fuzzy logic, we would create two overlapping sets, "short" from 0' to 6' and "tall" from 3' to 9'. Each person would belong to both of these sets with a different degree of membership: 4'6" person would be "short" to a degree of .5 and "tall" to a degree of .5, 5'9" person would be "short" to a degree of .03 and "tall" to a degree of .1997, 6' person would be "short" to a degree of 0 and "tall" to a degree of 1. These numbers (.1997 and 1) reflect closeness in height of 5'9" and 6' persons. Fuzzy logic based expert system would trigger several rules to a different degree, based on the each person's membership functions. In this case, 5'9" and 6' persons would be treated very similarly.

Doug:

Thanks for the input, Gene.

Platt:

Of course, our discussion occurs in the rational SOM mode, which, as Doug points out, leaves something to be desired. (I think Doug's email about "many truths" is extremely significant.)

Magnus:

Indeed, but I also think that the MOQ says something about these contexts. It orders them according to their morality, and I think there's a very good reason to do this. Any level (context) is not aware of the levels above, so it cannot judge it. So, I don't think even the MOQ should be used to resolve self contradictory assertions such as the one discussed earlier. Both assertions recognize the other and can therefore not be placed in different levels. If you place them in different contexts, however, those contexts will have nothing to do with the levels of the MOQ.

By the way, I found the quote in Lila I talked about earlier (at the end of Chapter 11): "...The shift in cell reproduction from mitosis to meiosis to permit sexual choice and allow huge DNA diversification is a Dynamic advance. So is the collective organization of cells into Metazoan societies called plants and animals."

I guess it's open for different interpretations, but I interpret it as Pirsig says that plants and animals are social patterns of value. [49]

Platt:

There are several SOM paradoxes in the MOQ itself. For example, the quality of the rational Metaphysics of Quality cannot be proved by rational thought. Still, so long as we admit to being in a rational SOM mode, self-contradictory assertions need to be challenged. When we want to go beyond the SOM mode, we can drop in a poem.

Magnus:

Then who decides it is a poem in the first place? And who decides that the sense made of it is OK?

Platt:

I was hoping you would pick up on that. It goes to the heart of a huge platypus in intellect's logical pattern, the platypus of "who decides?" For instance, the scientific method depends on verification. But who verifies the verifier? Before you know it, you're into infinite regress. Enter a social pattern. To prevent infinite regress, verification relies on communal confirmation. That is, to verify a proposition, others following the same assumptions, context, and methodology used by the originator should arrive at the same conclusion. Science bases its truths on others being able to repeat experiments, thereby requiring a social element.

The great advantage science has over other means of establishing truth is that scientific social verification is tied to data provided by biological patterns. The validity of evolutionary theory relies on measurements of tangible bones. The validity of quantum theory relies (please correct me here) on measurements of particle traces seen on a computer screen. But, to verify the meaning or "truth" of Shakespeare's Hamlet or Pirsig's Metaphysics of Quality is another matter. In that case, verification depends not on physical measurement but on the social and intellectual patterns of those who have seen the play or read Lila and who are qualified to render a judgment based on life experience, philosophical understanding, and educated opinion. Biological patterns, while not entirely irrelevant, are not as critical to the verification process as they are in science.

Given that a social element is required in any verification, and given that a poem and the making sense thereof is not subject to scientific verification, the artificial intelligence test I propose will necessarily require a panel of qualified "experts" to decide if it's a poem and if the sense made of it is okay. Similarly, the Lila Squad is a panel of self-appointed qualified experts judging the validity and value of the MOQ.

Of course, we could always hook up another artificially intelligent computer to determine if the first computer created a poem, and another computer to check up on that, and another to check on that, ad infinitum. Which is why I believe true artificial intelligence, one able to mimic the entire spectrum of human capabilities, will always be just an intellectual pattern's dream.

So in one sense we end up with Doug's "many truths." Trouble is that assertion is self-contradictory because it is framed as a single truth. And around and around we go again. Ultimately, the only thing that stops infinite regress and answers the question, "Who decides?" is one's own innate sense of quality. It stops when an individual human decides, "That's a good truth."

I just don't think it's fair to take written words too literally. First of all, the intellectual pattern becomes static as soon as it's printed as words. And second, language is limited and ambiguous. OK. So why are we hung up on defining the levels? Even the best definition will be limited and ambiguous.

Maggie:

I think rhyme must be a social pattern, because it seems to be a very powerful and basic component of primitive language, which was social. I don't think it's coincidental that rhyme also involves aural pattern matching, a biological ability that may be more direct (nonintellectual? non-social?) than other types of human pattern matching, such as visual. Rhythm is important in poetry, and rhythm is a very strong biological pattern, one that has a close (can it be connecting?) counterpart in primitive social patterns.

I wonder whether music and poetry don't owe their unique power to some close link or balance that affects or involves all the levels in the same reaction, i.e., Dynamic Quality operating at more than one level (whereas in most interactions, the matching, or breaking, or decision event involves one level).

Next Level [October 1997]

Platt:

Recent posts have gotten me SOM thinking (always a problematic pursuit) about the next level above the intellectual.

Pirsig hints at such a level, calling it "a code of Art." What does he mean by "code" and "Art"?

Pirsig's reference to the possibility of a "code of Art" is in Chapter 13, page 163 of my hard cover edition of Lila. It goes like this:

"First, there were moral codes that established the supremacy of biological Nature over inanimate Nature. Second, there were moral codes that established the supremacy of the social order over biological life—conventional morals—proscriptions against drugs, murder, adultery, theft and the like. Third, there were moral codes that established the supremacy of the intellectual order over the social order—democracy, trial by jury, freedom of speech, freedom of the press. Finally, there's a fourth Dynamic morality which isn't a code. He supposed you could call it a 'code of Art' or something like that, but art is usually thought of as such a frill that the title undercuts its importance. The morality of the brujo in Züni—that was Dynamic morality."

Could the MOQ be the next level, trying to establish supremacy over the subject/object metaphysics of the intellectual level, necessarily including the SOM level but transcending it? Putting the two together, the next level above the intellect, a code of Art, would be a comprehensive collection of laws about Quality or simply Laws of Quality. And what would that be? The Metaphysics of Quality itself.

Doug:

I found this in Lila: "Lila then becomes a complex ecology of patterns moving toward Dynamic Quality." (Page 412 of the Bantam paperback.) Taken out of context we might infer this Lila to be MOQ, or at least part of MOQ. Could this implied goal be what Platt is asking about?

From Zukav's Dancing Wu Li Masters: "'When I studied physics in Taiwan,' said Huang, 'we called it [physics] Wu Li (pronounced Woo Lee). It means Patterns of Organic Energy.'" (Page 31 of the 5x8 Quill paperback.) Zukav avers over 80 different meanings of Wu Li together. (Very highly implied context sensitivity. Hebrew is similar.)

Zukav says Li is organic patterns, universal order, universal law. He says Wu means energy. Wu Li also means: nonsense, my way, I clutch my ideas, and enlightenment. Interesting, eh? Can't you just hear Sinatra? "I did it...."

Speaking of art, from Capra's The Tao of Physics, Needham translates li as "principle of organization" and gives the following comments:

"In its most ancient meaning, it signified the pattern in things, the markings of jade or fibers in muscle. It acquired the common dictionary meaning 'principle,' but always conserved the undertone of 'pattern.' There is 'law' implicit in it, but this law is the law to which parts of wholes have to conform by virtue of their very existence as parts of wholes. The most important thing about parts is that they have to fit precisely into place with the other parts in the whole organism which they compose." Quoted by Zukav from J. Needham, Science and Civilization in China, vol. II, pp. 558, 567, page 290.

Then, on page 291, Capra says, "The Eastern sages, therefore, are generally not interested in explaining things, but rather in obtaining a direct non-intellectual experience of the unity of all things."

Back on page 87, Capra talks about "lila": "The basic recurring theme in Hindu mythology is the creation of the world by the self sacrifice of God, 'sacrifice' in the original sense of 'making sacred,' whereby God becomes the world which, in the end, becomes again God. This creative activity of the Divine is called 'lila,' the play of God, and the world is seen as the stage of the divine play."

Capra's further comments on "lila" in the context of Brahman and Maya are significant analogues of our recent discussions on TLS. Capra says if we view "lila" from the wrong vantage, we will become confused. If you have time, I suggest all TLS read Capra's and Zukav's words around Li, li, and lila. It all fits/complements MOQ in an artistic and wonderful way.

So, Lila could be a code. I anxiously await other TLS members' responses to Platt's proposal that MOQ itself be the next higher level. (I am fearful of broaching this topic directly—myself.) Platt, hopefully the above quotes leverage a codified and artistic bent in our considerations of the MOQ.

Platt:

How is the MOQ presented? Not as a SOM paper, essay, or philosophic treatise but as a work of art in a novel called Lila. As a work of art, the MOQ is primarily a static intellectual pattern, while as Art it invokes Dynamic Quality through the aesthetic sense. I would be so bold as to assert that all of us on the Lila Squad, to one degree or another, for one fleeting instant or more, have experienced while reading Lila, a Quality event of high order. That is, a QE with a preponderance of DQ.

Bodvar:

I tend to follow my own lines of thought and not pay much attention to other inputs, but Platt's "Next Level" entry broke through. First I must admit that Pirsig's hint of a new level as a code of art has passed me by, but Platt's reflections about it is a major Quality insight in its own right. The MOQ itself as the next level? At first, I saw no need for an extension of the present four-tiered system, but it did not go away and after a while, it struck me as quite plausible, perhaps inevitable, but like Doug, "I anxiously await other TLS members' responses to Platt's proposal that MOQ itself be the next higher level."

Still, let me offer some tentative thoughts. A while back, we spoke about the emergence of intellect and I said that in a way Subject/Object Metaphysics could be seen as identical to the intellectual level of the MOQ! [50] This fits nicely in with Platt's proposal. If the top level of the static sequence is SOM, then the MOQ (as a totality) necessarily must transcend intellect. Platt went on to say:

"For further evidence that the MOQ is the next level up, consider that the lower levels fight against it. (James and Doug have brilliantly explained why.) Not only have social patterns bastardized the meaning of "quality," associating it with the white, heterosexual European male world view and all the supposed social evils thereof, but the intellectual level ridicules the idea that the world is a moral order, employing such vitriolic language as found in the two critical reviews on the Forum, brazen attempts to intimidate the curious into apathy and silence. (The fights for dominance among levels can indeed be vicious.)"

Yes, the academic/intellectual resistance against the MOQ is an indication that it may be the first effort from a new level to free itself from its parent. Remember that Pirsig's says that all value levels start as part of, and in the service of, the lower one. The time aspect is of course enormous and we will never know if our speculations are valid, but it is an idea well worth pursuing.

Finally, we agreed that a lower level does not recognize the next higher, as such, except as danger along its own perimeter. The intellectual level can't or won't recognize the MOQ, while we the Lila Squad, from a still higher perspective, do! I have always had this problem when people ask me what the MOQ is. It doesn't fit any category and escapes every box you try to put it into. Is this why it is so elusive?

Thanks Platt, you brought in a new dimension to our discussion.

Magnus:

Hi Platt, your recent post was really interesting, thanks for your thoughts. You requested our thoughts so here's mine:

I see at least two arguments as to why the MOQ would not be of a higher level. The first one is plainly because we can comprehend it, intellectually. The second argument is a comment to your words: "For further evidence that the MOQ is the next level up, consider that the lower levels fight against it." This doesn't mean that the MOQ is of a higher level. Different patterns within the same level can have as vicious fights as patterns of

128

different levels; just look at communism vs. capitalism. I'd say that the resistance against the MOQ is one intellectual set of patterns resisting another. [51]

Because we, in the "metaphysics" context of the MOQ, want to use it to model physics. And yes, the model will probably always be incomplete and ambiguous but as I've said before, I don't want to be surprised every time something falls to the ground. I want to be able to predict predictable phenomena. We do this every day, call it common sense, so you can't just close your eyes, and pretend you don't do it. I don't think it's a big difference trying to express this common sense in writing.

I'd place the core of our disagreement here. We've approached the MOQ from different directions. But that's OK, that's what it's supposed to do, join seemingly different people around the same core. Your approach is homing in on the "inquiry into morals" part, whereas mine aims for the "metaphysics" part. And this metaphysics part has very much to do with the composition of man-made objects, as well as non-man-made objects.

Platt:

Excellent point. For me the metaphysical thrust is secondary to the morals thrust. Thanks for making the distinction clear. It illustrates the value of Doug's advice to bring our assumptions out into the open. Since our assumptions are so near and dear to us we often don't recognize them for what they are, and it takes someone else to point them out.

Magnus:

Great! One thing worries me though. I really hope that in stating which context a post belongs to, everyone will still read that post and not deem it irrelevant because it belongs to the "wrong" context. We have so much to give each other and this inter context exchange is maybe the most important part of what the Lila Squad is about.

Awareness of Upper Levels [October 1997]

Doug:

Where I get confused on the levels and their contexts is when I hear some of TLS say that the lower level is not "aware" of its next higher level. I find many examples in Lila where Phædrus asserts just the opposite.

Magnus:

News flash for me—could you point at some so we can start thrashing?

Doug:

To me there are three glaring examples in Lila of the social level being aware of the intellectual level:

1. Pirsig's extended discussion on the battle between the Zũni priests and the brujo. The social immune system was "aware" of the new intellectual pattern threat to their control by the brujo's new ideas.

2. Pirsig's brief mention of the same thing happening to Joan of Arc.

3. Pirsig's brief mention of the same thing happening to Galileo. This example certainly juxtaposes the Catholic Church condemning Galileo for his intellectual threat to their "non-intellectual flat earth-centric" traditional social patterns. Many within the Church then and now condemn intellectual freedom of belief and/or thought. I see these as examples of a lower level keenly aware of a higher level. I also think there are other examples of other levels, too. [52]

Magnus:

So it would seem, but it takes a human to intellectually realize the danger to the society and then act on it, either alone or make the society act. It all comes down to our (my) different views of the social and intellectual levels. I see both human societies and human bodies as social static patterns of value. To translate the brujo example above to a human body society, it would sound something like this:

A man has a bad liver and it needs to be replaced. The body society would fight such a violation to its integrity but the intellectual patterns of value realize the need and accept the

130

operation. I should "confess" though that one reason I started my reorganization of what things belongs to what level comes from the assumption that lower levels are not aware of higher levels but considers this mediation as Dynamic Quality.

Anders:

Wasn't this more a case of resistance to influence by Dynamic Quality (the whole latching idea)?

Doug:

Yes, but the consuming, provocative meme of the MOQ is the architecture of morality and correct application of hierarchical moral codes. In SOM-land, the social level resists any DQ that is rationally against the current patterns of tradition. As a result, the SOM-landers are incapable of correct moral judgment when DQ uses a higher level to impose "better" changes on that tradition.

In MOQland, the problem is fixed. The four SQ levels and the five moral codes tell MOQlanders which DQ QEs at which levels to adhere/inhere and which to reject. Am I wrong, or are we really making progress now? Another time when I get confused is when I hear some of you (Magnus most recently) ask the question, "Are the levels absolute or otherwise?"

Magnus:

I asked it because I sensed the confusion where I have no doubt. And this might be because I haven't thought about it enough. I was trying to get to your unanswered questions.

Doug:

In the Lila review I did last April for www.amazon.com, I mentioned scaling. Let me try an example to see what you mean by absolute. Seems that other TLS members have already averred something like this, but I can't recall who/when. If I said that there is social "behavior" in either of the two lowest levels, you would disagree, right?

Magnus:

Right. As soon as I see a society, i.e., parts, organized to make it more valuable than the sum of its parts—for example, a motorcycle— I call it social patterns of value and the parts organic patterns of value.

Platt:

So, in one sense we end up with Doug's "many truths." Trouble is, that assertion is self-contradictory because it is framed as a single truth. And around and around we go again. Ultimately, the only thing that stops infinite regress and answers the question, "Who decides?" is one's own innate sense of Quality. It stops when an individual human decides, "That's a good truth."

Doug:

If you stand in SOM, I see how you can make the observation about "many truths" which you made. However, I do not see you standing in SOM. Much the opposite; you understand, as Bo has said, MOQ better than most of us (TLS). I do not frame my "many truths to you," in SOM. My context for that phrase is MOQ. To me both MOQ and QM (quantum mechanics) prefer a precondition "many truths." Perhaps I should add the word "potential," but if we intuit MOQ and not SOM, Mtty seems okay, by itself, without the extra word "potential."

Also, "Mtty," in my opinion, subsumes SOM's one, absolute, deterministic truth as just one of the infinity of truths. This places SOM in its proper perspective—just one SPoV relegated to some obscure tiny corner of the unifying and inclusive MOQ. That is how I think about it. If it lacks MOQesque, please help me see how. One more item—I see QEs as "decisions."

Platt:

I feel we're both trying to push the envelope of the MOQ into uncharted spaces (as are others on the Lila Squad), struggling to overcome the limits of SOM intellectual patterns in order to pierce the resistant core of the ineffable.

Your "contexts" solution is elegant. I think it's similar to "modes," a word I've used once or twice without realizing its significance until you excellent email of October 15. I still have trouble keeping track of multiple contexts, but take some relief from your caveat that, "This is not easy." I'm also attracted to

Gene's fuzzy logic although its mathematical context raises a curtain of opacity that I who have trouble adding up a restaurant check find difficult to penetrate. As you pointed out in a previous post, "many truths" contains the inherent danger of promoting the idea of "truth is relative" as a postulate for the virtue of tolerance. We must guard against the implication that because there are many truths, one can never be right, thereby killing the quest for the good, the true and the beautiful that we MOQites value so highly.

All this is a very round about way of saying I see your "many truths" as being entirely compatible, indeed essential, to the MOQ. But permit me to add some thoughts to your statement, "I see QEs as decisions." "Decisions" implies some sort of deliberation, a pause for reflection, a considered opinion, a mulling over of options. Better I think to see QEs as esthetic judgments: immediate, intuitive, undeliberate, and involuntary, leaving no room for conscious application of standards, criteria, rules, or precepts.

In other words, I see QEs as instantaneous whole judgments totally free of static patterns whereas "decisions" suggest to me a secondary step, a derivative of a QE.

Doug:

Yes, you are right. I have no disagreement with your view. I include your view in my broader definition of "decision." It is much like the Master's words in Herrigel's Zen in the Art of Archery. The student (Herrigel) tries diligently and SOM dumbly to intellectualize the bow, arrow, his body, and the target. Where the Master unifies all in a Zen framework, the student analyzes. The Master makes it easy. The student makes it hard.

I understand this. But I do not yet know how to do it. I am, as yet, unenlightened. I sense "Its" imminence, but I am not there yet in spite of great progress. This quote from Herrigel seems apropos (page 38):

"Out of the fullness of this presence of mind, disturbed by no ulterior motive, the artist who is released from all attachment must practice his art. But if he is to fit himself self-effacingly into the creative process, the practice of the art must have the way smoothed for it. For if, in his self-immersion, he saw himself faced with a situation into which he could not leap instinctively, he would first have to bring it to consciousness. He would then enter again into all the relationships from which he had detached himself, he would be like one wakened, who considers his program for the day, but not like an Awakened One who lives and works in the primordial state. It would never appear to him as if the individual parts of the creative process were being played into his hands by a higher power; he would never experience how intoxicatingly the vibrancy of an event is communicated to him who is himself only a vibration, and how everything that he does is done before he knows it."

...To play and to be played...that is the decision...to awaken and to be Awakened...that is the decision...to latch and to be Dynamic...that is the decision...to value and to be Value....

Many truths to you, Platt.

Hugo:

The way I see it, Pirsig uses "moral" in an unusual way (not that I mind but just to be clear on what we are talking about) where the common sense of moral is closely connected to the concept of free will. We don't hold people morally responsible for actions they did not do out of free willing, whether it is due to war, insanity, selfdefense, etc., just like we don't hold the cat morally responsible for killing the mouse.

The way Pirsig uses moral (and value) is obviously different, perhaps more like the discussions of "The Good" in ancient Greece and later in theology. In Greece, they used the concept aretê, which does not really translate well to English. It is often translated as "virtue" but it means something more like fullness and functionality; "to fill ones place" (da: fylde); the aretê of a hammer is its ability to fulfill its function as a hammer; the aretê of a warrior is to be a "proper warrior," filling the role and life of a warrior. While obviously having to do with value, aretê is not very similar to the present day moral of good and bad.

The Wikings had a similar conception of moral, the good people filling their place in life and society and the not-good (value-less) people not living a full life but rather living a shallow existence. Hence, the Wikings would value the well-done killing in the heat of the moment, because it was well done, even if there were no cause to kill. (This does not mean such a needless kill did not cause them trouble. Fees had to be paid or a feud might arise.) Kierkegaard similarly distinguished between the proper (or true) and non-proper existence (da: egentlig og u-egentlig eksistens), where proper existence is living by the will of one self while non-proper existence is living by the conventions of society.

Is there a connection between areté and fullness and the higher value of higher levels in the MOQ? If one takes a very broad view on what evolution is about, then the ever growing filling of places, the ongoing simultaneous creation and filling of "roles" or "niches" could be an appropriate picture, the becoming of levels being a step into a new possibility space of existence. Incidentally, I believe this nothingness—this empty possibility space—is the very potency or dynamis, which causes evolution.

Given this evolutionary picture, the moral good (in Pirsig's sense) of higher levels is that they increase the "space to fill" of existence, and hence the world would in a sense be less rich without them. This then, given that the very existence of higher levels is conditioned on the constraining or limiting of the possibilities of the already existing, is this what Pirsig calls a moral code?

Bodvar:

Yes, exactly, the gist of the MOQ is the constraint on a(ny) higher moral level from the lower one (one level cannot exist without its foundation). The most sensitive aspect of this doctrine is of course the intellect/society moral code (which has been grandly misunderstood by many critics and readers who thinks Pirsig is out to bash the poor blacks of America to revenge the murder of his son Chris). Being the top notch, intellect is not limited from above and interferes with society's own struggle to constrain the biological forces.

This, and what you wrote before, was good, Hugo. Even if the "creating and fulfilling of roles" idea was a new approach to me (is it from Charles Peirce?) I think this interpretation of morals is more in line with Pirsig's than the (post Christian) "responsible for one's own actions" one. That the world would be less rich without the higher levels is correct (still, impossible without the lower ones). Particularly the intellect has unfolded a new universe. Still, the dependencies upon the lower ones are mandatory.

Hugo:

No, it is not straight from Peirce, I believe, although Peirce plays a part. It came to me as part of an answer to the question of what drives evolution towards ever more complexity, when I wrote my masters thesis (on evolutionary theory) in 1989, and I did not know Peirce at the time. I don't believe I have snatched this particular idea from anyone else, but one never knows. It is closely connected with the idea of actualizations preventing other actualizations, which you refer to below. The ideas behind it can be found way back in Aristotle's potentiality/actuality distinction (which, come to think of it, may have arisen out of the potentiality involved in aretê?), which Peirce later used. Popper's work has many similarities with Peirce though he apparently did not know Peirce when doing it, and I was inspired by Popper's work on probability theory back then. Pirsig discusses something like this as well in the last part of Chapter 12 and the first part of Chapter 13.

Bodvar:

That the "Quality term is identical with the Greek aretê" is after all Pirsig's main thesis. See the section in Lila where he follows the rt trail (page 386). I seem to think that you, Hugo, once said that the filling of a role/niche closes the window upon others trying to reach it. A while back, we spoke of other species, primates preferably, on the verge of entering the intellectual level (realization of freedom as more valuable than social constraint). I think this is true. Humankind has closed the door behind itself. No other life form on earth can now develop societies advanced enough to support intellect.

Hugo:

Actually, I am not quite sure this is right. I would say that no other kind of intellect could develop where one is already present. This does not preclude that other lifeforms or artificial creatures can enter "our" actualization of intellect; in fact, this is exactly what I see happening today. We are teaching various animals different sorts of languages, for instance, such as the sign languages taught to Bonobos, our human kind of language. And we are creating artificial creatures in our own image. I am not enthusiastic about the latter, rather I say "are you sure you know what you do?" in a sort of anxious way.

Bodvar:

Also do I think that you are right when comparing the Viking's seeming callousness to aretê. In my view the Viking culture was a "hibernation" of the arch quality metaphysics, long after it had been replaced by the Subject/Object one (later to become the morals of Christianity) in the Middle East/Mediterranean region. The question then is if the MOQ is a regression. In my opinion, yes, but in a spiral sense; on a higher level.

Hugo:

These ideas on ancient Nordic ethics I took from a book with the funny name Odin and the Hard Disc (only in Danish I believe) on the Nordic worldview and morals, written by John Carlsen. He did not link it to aretê, but the similarity is obvious.

Bodvar:

I had started to write in response to Doug's examples (in Lila) of the social level being "aware" of the intellectual one, but in the meantime Anders suggested that Doug's Züni priest example is an example of resistance to Dynamic Quality. Anders is right; what that particular passage really tells about is Pirsig's conception of the Dynamic/static dualism (after he had rejected the Romantic/Classic split).

But Doug's observation is highly interesting. What you say about the social level's "immune system" is valid. I covered the "awareness" question a while back and I still maintain that from within, each level only sees itself. To society everything in the universe is social value (of course society knows about Life and Matter, but they are what leads up to society, while intellect is not recognized, as such, except as dangerous social experimenting.

The Züni priests saw themselves as preservers of the tribe's values and looked upon the brujo's insolence as a threat to their static society. They did not recognize his effort as a necessary adjustment to a new factor that, if not heeded, would destroy the tribe (the white man's culture). Or, the MOQ can regard him as an intellectual whose ideas forced a society to change.

This goes for the Galileo/Catholic Church conflict too. As a social institution, the Church regarded Galileo as socially destructive. It's impossible for a society to recognize anything except "good for (that) society" or "bad for (that) society." There possibly was an individual Cardinal or a Pope who silently recognized his intellectual achievement, even foresaw the development, but when doing so, they did it from the intellectual mode (of value). The moment they were assembled to vote for excommunication of Galileo they had put on the social hat again.

The fact that Galileo later, from the victorious intellectual level, is declared a hero just proves the point: this historical event is now regarded as infringement of intellectual value (freedom). The intellect peers down its own nose and sees everything as good or bad for the intellectual values. However, the MOQ is a tool that makes us able to see this connection and give unto Caesar each level what belongs to that level.

Doug

This really helped me. Believe it or not, after all this time, I had not distinguished that we assume those in SOM-land have blinders on in a level while they are in that level and cannot see the other higher levels. But those who reside in MOQland can see all the levels all the time. I am ashamed to admit I seem to have missed the most important point of all.

Profoundly, thank you!

Defining SOM [October 1997]

Lars:

Do any of you know of any good definitions of the terms subjective and objective? Can you think of any thing/idea/concept/whatever that would be purely subjective or objective? (I'm now trying to think entirely within a SOM framework, disregarding MOQ for the time being.)

The idea I have is that there might exist ideas that are purely objective. (I've no idea yet what it would mean for something to be purely subjective.) The way I'm trying to go to find them is towards completely objective representations of something. Something like the symbol "1" or the equation "1+1=2;" however, currently I'm a little lost as to on what kind of level this objective entity should exist.

What I'm thinking is that if something is purely objective all subjects should have the same interpretation of it (provided they understand it correctly). Formal mathematical systems might be a way to go to achieve such a thing. Anyway, when I find the time I'll it down with a stack of paper and try to work this out and see where it's taking me. For now, these are just high quality questions for me. What I'd really like is to hear what kinds of responses this sparks off in the rest of the Squad, just to feed the bubbling in my head.

My hope is that by trying to find things that are really subjective or objective I'll get a better understanding of the difference between the SOM and MOQ paradigms. Maybe the S/O dichotomy is really a continuous scale, maybe it doesn't make sense at all—I don't know yet—but I'd like to find out.

Bodvar:

Nice try Lars, but you are reinventing gunpowder. The very reason for Pirsig to come up with the quality idea was that anyone who tries to find what is "really subjective and objective" is doomed to frustration. You tentatively put forward numbers as an example but where are the mathematical truths? Point to them! You state that you are trying to think entirely within a SOM framework, disregarding MOQ for the time being. Exactly. Within SOM's framework, you have to admit that everything (except matter) is in our minds— subjective! The case is water and airtight. Really, upon second thought, even matter is perceived by our subjective senses and ends up in Kant's mysterious Ding an Sich realm. It's no good protesting: but everybody knows this is silly, etc. This paradoxical outcome is the inevitable result of SOM thinking, what broke Phædrus of ZMM and led to his declaring SOM's division invalid.

Lars:

What I was uncertain of was whether one could create an intellectual structure that all people would interpret the same way. Peano arithmetic would be a good example. It uses two symbols: 0 and S. 0 is zero as we know it (i.e., what you get if you compute 5-5), S is the successorship function (i.e., add one to the argument.) So S0 is 1, SS0 is 2, etc. Add the concept of addition, and you have it.

It's kind of hard to imagine anyone disagreeing on what these concepts actually mean and it doesn't matter if they do because as long as they follow the rules they'll get the same results. This is a formal system, so theoretically one can throw away the interpretations and just view it as a game, idly doing string manipulations on a piece of paper.

However, we'll all have different associations connected to these symbols and the way the rules work. For instance, I'm instantly reminded of programming languages like Miranda and no doubt you connect this with other things. So, are the theorems of Peano arithmetic objective? Do they exist independently of the subjects, like Plato thinks, and do they have to do so to be objective or is it enough that all subjects agree on them and their interpretation?

Bodvar:

Ideas, including numbers, mathematics, etc., are intellectual patterns of value. On that level, they are as "objective" as an atom on the inorganic level, a living organism on the biological level or a country on the social level. What's purely subjective or objective does not apply within the MOQ, and afterwards I cannot see how you can disregard it. It is like declaring modern cosmology suspended for the time being and looking for what "pure" crystal sphere upholds the moon in its orbit.

Don't misunderstand me. The subject/object classification is necessary for the intellect. Rationality requires a temporarily subjective/objective division. It was your "purely" that got me. Remember, we arrived at consensus that the intellectual level of MOQ can be viewed as SOM itself, but this has become reality itself within Western culture. (Have you been sleeping in class? :-)) The MOQ is an enormous effort to, like Munchausen, lift ourselves by the hair (bootstraps) out of this quagmire.

Lars:

I know, but for the purposes of this "investigation," I'd like to disregard that for a while. I want to really know why SOM must be rejected and then see how MOQ solves the problem. What I really want to get at is why the concept of Quality is necessary and exactly what it means. I have a superficial understanding of all this already, but I want to get it under my skin.

Doug:

I think your statement above, "What I really want..." is what we are all after. One of the best reasons we must reject SOM is because it improperly classifies value! There are many other reasons too. Carefully study Lila starting on page 66 of the hardbound edition and page 76 of the paperbound (both Bantam). Starting with the quote: "The value is between the stove and the oaths. Between the subject and the object lies the value," Pirsig begins a complex sequence of answers to your question. The essence of the answer is in this quote, but Pirsig's extended prose around the four platypi, the three puzzles, and the five moral codes finish the task.

Hugo:

Lars, let me take a shot at your pursuit of the objective, and then you can say whether it did you any good. I think I understand your concerns. I have been working with the question of objectivity in science, and ventured into the Metaphysics of Quality partly in order to provide a satisfying answer to this very question. And perhaps discussing this in some detail will add one more perspective to our present view of the MOQ.

First, I think we have to distinguish between the objectivity of methodology and "objective knowledge," [53] as the term is used by Popper, where objective knowledge is supposed to be provided by objective methods of inquiry. Popper was on the right path (say I) on the methodology, providing the foundation for what has later (Donald Campbell) been termed "evolutionary epistemology." Put shortly, characterizing science as a Popperian sort of objective method, I would emphasize the public nature of science, involving both the openness to and concern for public critique, and the common goal for the inquiry (the quest for truth).

This is a very general description of objectivity, which goes along with your description. And I think it is one that is generally acceptable to modern science. But, even if this view avoids some of the problems of more crude views of objectivity, there seems to be a residue of "objectivism" hidden in our view of objective or scientific knowledge. Saying this, I would to some extent agree (with others on the list, I forget who) that a change of metaphysics would not alter the results of science. But it would alter the way we look upon scientific knowledge, and the way we use it, and as a consequence of this it would probably alter the practice of science.

The main problem with "objectivity" in science is a neglect or lack of concern for the contextuality of inquiry, and subsequently for the contextuality of knowledge. A discussion of the issues of contextuality involves the various positions of "objectivism" and "subjectivism" or relativism. These positions can be (and this "can be" entails a lot of effort, beyond Pirsig's initial effort, but I believe they can be) shown inadequate, but there are few people who have avoided falling into one of those pitfalls in the process of proving the other wrong, or at least a few that are more or less well known now. Among those are Pirsig and followers (us in all modesty) and some of the American pragmatists (Peirce, Dewey), with roots in Aristotle (yes, I know) and, I have recently learned, Schelling (and perhaps Bohr, Bateson, others?).

I believe the idea of objective knowledge has roots back to Plato's world of ideas, where the things in our world were more or less poor copies (shadows; in the cave scenario) of the eternal, perfect ideas. I believe this metaphysical view to be wrong. And I am afraid that Popper, whom I value highly, had a kind of Platonistic view, with his three worlds: the real or physical world, the subjective world of our thoughts, and the world of objective knowledge (I have yet to investigate in more detail the influence of this idea in his philosophy of science). As an aside, this Platonistic metaphysics is not uncommon among mathematicians, and I know Roger Penrose holds a view much like Popper.

Objective knowledge, true theories, mathematics, etc., are often taken to be true no matter where and when. We know the idea of eternally true natural laws, for instance (well, perhaps that was more the view in the previous century?), and Lars has given some mathematical examples. I believe all knowledge is contextual, even in the form of scientific theories, or mathematical systems. Scientific theories are not mere "ideas," they refer to the lower levels of reality (in Pirsig's sense), they evolve, and they are used by being applied. Theories entail a (more or less explicit) context of application, and expectations (often in a mathematical form) on the outcome of such applications.

Some of the major events in physics in this century can only (or so I say) be understood in the light of some such contextual view of knowledge—quantum mechanics, where Bohr made some headway with his complementarity principle, and relativity theory, the interpretation of which is still (I claim) paradoxical due to the lack of a contextual frame.

As for mathematics, I have read too little to refer to others. But as for my own view, answering Lars' question of whether arithmetic is "purely objective," I would say that even the theory of numbers, the rules of addition and so forth, are contextual. The context assumed here is that of a world of "individual things," of entities, and the rules of addition would do you no good in adding piles of dirt; you would never get more than one pile of dirt. Addition works fine if we keep the relevant context of application in the back of our minds. Other parts of mathematics and logic have other (often tacitly) assumed contexts, but they are not without context of application, and this is important when they are applied (and when not, they may be looked upon as some form of art!?).

Interestingly, logic, and mathematics is characterized by their "detachment" from the world, by the lack of reference, and they have become more and more detached through history. Most notably, perhaps, is Hilbert's attempt at founding geometry without any reference to visualisation (anskuelse) of the objects of geometry— building an entirely formal system where the points, lines, and planes might as well be thought of as chairs, tables, and glasses, as he puts it. Magnus gave a quote by Einstein on this, I think, saying something like—math is only true to the extent that it does not refer to the world; and I am very uneasy about this view of mathematics.

As for more complex actions than the piling of dirt, neglecting the contextuality of our knowledge and the implications of this contextuality is, I believe, behind many of our present and future problems.

Annotations by Robert M. Pirsig

41. I would argue that the four levels can be explained intellectually.

42. Right. And the magnet is an inorganic value pattern of atoms choosing to cling to each other and so are the iron filings. Everything that has not been created by life (defined as DNA) is an inorganic value pattern.

43. They're here now, in these notes.

44. It is only Dynamic Quality I think is impossible to define. I think definition is both possible and desirable for the static levels. I just didn't do it because these levels seemed so obvious. But in view of all the trouble people are having, I'm doing it now in these notes.

45. Very good. But the infrastructure can also be defined if you are willing to work at it. It's like defining justice. One can say justice is so hard to define we might as well just not make the effort. But over time it has been discovered that even though definitions of justice are imperfect they are better than nothing. And we call these imperfect definitions "the Law." The same can be done with the MOQ.

46. Not so you can tell someone about it in common language. However the taste of chocolate is a distinct chemical entity that can be defined with precision by flavor chemists. (I once wrote articles on this for General Mills Research Laboratories)

47. I think a culture should be defined as social patterns plus intellectual patterns.

48. Here we go again. The virus is the boundary because it is the simplest organism that contains DNA. I have read there is some dispute about the virus being living or dead, and I take this dispute as evidence that it is the boundary.

49. "Societies" is used figuratively here as a more colorful word meaning "groups." If I had known it would be taken literally as evidence that cells belong in the social level I would not have used it. Maybe in a future edition it can be struck out.

One can also call ants and bees "social" insects, but for purposes of precision in the MOQ, social patterns should be defined as human and subjective. Unlike cells and bees and ants, they cannot be detected with an objective scientific instrument. For example, there is no objective scientific instrument that can distinguish between a king and commoner, because the difference is social.

50. This seems too restrictive. It seems to exclude non-subjectobject constructions such as symbolic logic, higher mathematics, and computer languages from the intellectual level and gives them no home. Also the term "quality" as used in the MOQ would be excluded from the intellectual level. In fact, the MOQ, which gives intellectual meaning to the term quality, would also have to be excluded from the intellectual level.

If we just say the intellect is the manipulation of language derived symbols for experience, these problems of excessive exclusion do not seem to occur.

51. I agree with this.

52. After the beginning of history inorganic, biological, social and intellectual patterns are found existing together in the same person. I think the conflicts mentioned here are intellectual conflicts in which one side clings to an intellectual justification of existing social patterns and the other side intellectually opposes the existing social patterns. A social pattern which would be unaware of the next higher level would be found among prehistoric people and the higher primates when they exhibit social learning that is not genetically hard-wired but yet is not symbolic.

53. Even in a subject-object metaphysics this is an oxymoron. It leads to endless confusion.

Chapter 5

As far as the laws of mathematics refer to reality, they are not certain, and as long they are certain, they do not refer to reality. — Albert Einstein

DQ as Flux; the Pre-Socratics [September 1997]

Jarod and Miss Parker:

Is Dynamic Quality to be construed as flux itself, or perhaps the essence of flux? Then if Dynamic Quality is "higher" than static quality, perhaps we have a return to the philosophical urstoff of the pre-Socratic philosopher Heraclitus, who maintained that the essence of the Universe is flux. His classic formulation is "you cannot step twice in the same river, for new waters move on as you take the second step."

Hugo:

We could go even further back to Anaximandros (600-550 BC), by some considered the first metaphysicist (that we know of). Despite the obvious sources of error and misunderstanding, I will give an (my) English translation from a Danish translation of the reproduction of Anaximandros words made by Simplicius. There are other interpretations of course.

"Simplicius: Anaximandros said, that it is 'apeiron' which is the 'arche' and essential element of the existing things; he was the first to use this word 'Arche.' He thinks that it is neither water nor any of the other so called elements, but something else, apeiron, of which all worlds and their order [or structure] arises. Anaximandros: 'That, which the existing things arise from, is the same [that] they are annihilated to by the law of necessity, for they serve sentence and pay penalty to each other for the wrong they are doing, according to the order of time.' Thus, he expressed it in a somewhat odd way. It is obvious, that having observed how the four elements transformed into each other, he did not find it proper to make one of them the principal instance, but to find something else, which was different from them. So he does not let creation arise from the transformation of an element, but from the separation of opposites as a result of the eternal motion."

Beware of language; the terms above are judicial, and we are only slowly establishing an independent language for metaphysics. It is analogous to Bo's (and Pirsig's) use of "morality" in areas where it cannot be used in the same sense as human morals.

According to Anaximandros, becoming makes up a debt, which is to be paid "according to the order of time." Things have to pay back the debt, undo the wrong of becoming, in order for other things to become, and so on. We can see this debt as the "stable unbalance" which is the very static patterns of value in Pirsig's MOQ. An example can be that this (natural) life on earth has to vanish before any other form of life can arise; life on earth is "guilty" by precluding a host of other possible beings.

Apeiron is the limitless, that without distinctions, which cannot be described. And apeiron has (or is) an inner force, an eternal "motion," an urge for being, a potency for becoming. Aristotle arrived at the distinction between potency and act in his unfolding of logic, and Charles Sanders Peirce (1839-1914), in connection with his development of relational logic, distinguished between Potential, Actual, and Necessary (habitual) Being.

This is a second source for a new metaphysics, which may provide something beyond Pirsig, just as Pirsig provides something beyond Peirce, and they seem compatible to me, once the logical side of Peirce is held within its fence. In balance to my remarks on the logical Peirce I can give his triad of evolutionary processes: tychastic (by chance), anancastic (by mechanical necessity) and agapastic (by creative love) from his article, Evolutionary Love. Peirce was a remarkable man.

Platt:

The essence of Dynamic Quality is paradoxical. It's both Dynamic and static simultaneously as expressed in, "The present never changes but everything that changes in the present."

Jarod and Miss Parker:

If the Dynamic and static properties are both present in Dynamic Quality, then why the split of Quality into Dynamic Quality and static quality? I am starting to wonder if we are making an error by speaking of Dynamic Quality all the time. What is prior is Quality, of which Dynamic Quality is a sub-entity. As soon as you tack on the designator Dynamic, you have a categorization.

Platt:

Yes, you're quite right. I should have said, "Quality is paradoxical." Quality is prior to Dynamic Quality. After Heraclitus, there were many philosophers and sages who maintain that the universe is more than meets the rational eye. They also maintain that Dynamic Quality is not pre-rational but trans-rational, that is, above the intellectual level. What has confused many is that since the prerational and the trans-rational (Dynamic Quality) are both nonrational, they must be the same. This is known is philosophical jargon as the Category Error.

When flipped into the air, the coin shimmers and dances in the light. I'm sure I haven't made myself clear, but Dynamic Quality is such an elusive phenomenon that using words to describe it is like trying to thread a needle with boxing gloves. But whenever I want to get in touch with it, I just sit back, close my eyes, and listen to Rachmaninov's Piano Concerto No. 2. A walk in the woods is good, too.

Jarod and Miss Parker:

Music may not be entirely an intellectual pattern, but there is certainly a good degree of that, in the mathematical relationships that govern tonalities. Any introductory course in Music Theory will reveal a vast realm of intellectual pattern behind music, in the relations of keys to one another and in the chord progressions used. Many of the 20th century efforts to abandon tonal systems only replaced them with other systems, or other intellectual patterns, as it were.

Now an interesting question arises. The essence of, say, Mozart's 40th symphony is different from the intellectual patterns that govern it. But in what way is that essence (Quality) dependent on the intellectual pattern? I think there is something more than mere foundationalism, as in the case of the novel's relationship to the voltages in the computer's memory that represent it. Surely there is some dependence, but what? In what way does the essence of the symphony emerge from the intellectual pattern?

Platt:

It (Dynamic Quality) is prior to intellectual division and thus cannot be defined in words or formulas except to say it cannot be defined. It eludes rational analysis just as the experience of listening to Mozart's 40th symphony eludes intellectual talk about keys, tonalities, chord progressions, etc. (Music does not emerge from intellectual patterns. It emerges from the composer's intuition of Dynamic Quality. Intellect tries to horn in and dominate music and the arts just as it tries to dominate society.)

Jarod and Miss Parker:

I would think it better to say that a composer's intellectual patterns make it possible for him or her to formulate an expression of Dynamic Quality in the way that they choose. If music does not emerge from intellectual patterns, then in exactly what way does it relate to those patterns? A symphony's chord progressions are not the symphony itself, but that is not to say that the symphony's essence is not in some way dependent upon them. [54]

Platt:

Good point. Perhaps this is similar to the question—how does math relate to natural phenomenon? Do we impose mathematical patterns on the world or are the patterns built in like Plato's ideals, awaiting discovery? Is the essence of light dependent in some way on quantum mathematics? I vote no. But there are many far wiser than me who say yes. [55]

Jarod and Miss Parker:

I suspect that the answer lies in between, as it always seems to do. The mathematical patterns that underlie music, light, gravity, etc., are there. We cannot deny the existence of those mathematical patterns, and it seems to me that in some way these things are dependent upon them. But the essences thereof are surely not strictly part and parcel of those mathematical patterns. I cannot perceive "red" in the absence of light of a certain wavelength striking my photoreceptors, but you are certainly right in saying that the fact of that causal relationship does not mean that the relationship itself is the essence. Perhaps Dynamic Quality cannot emerge without a foundation based on static quality. Your thoughts?

Platt:

To quote Pirsig (Page 11, Subjects, Objects, Data and Values paper), intellectual patterns are left behind "in the wake of this cutting edge (Dynamic Quality)." So, Dynamic Quality must be independent of and prior to any foundation.

We may be getting into the first cause argument that says each event must be caused by a prior event, ad infinitum. But, quantum theory suggests time and space can be fragmented with no arrow of time present. In that context, to say something happens "prior to" becomes meaningless. At this point I'm in over my head, so I defer to a quantum expert like Doug.

It seems to me that by enumerating acts through which one can apprehend Dynamic Quality is, at least in one key way, a descriptive act. Well, I can describe how to get an experience, but not the experience itself. For example, I can't describe the smell of a rose, the taste of chocolate, or how to ride a bicycle. Can you describe Quality?

Jarod and Miss Parker:

Not in so many words, but I take the act of "pointing to it" to be at least partially descriptive. The point is that one cannot "describe" Quality except through the act of pointing to it as we are doing.

Platt:

Yes, we agree. The essence of intellect is a pointing event, so to speak.

Doug:

Platt, and other eminent members of TLS: Gosh, I wish I could live up to that appellation, "quantum expert"! I can't! Richard P. Feynman said, "...Nobody understands quantum mechanics...." Posthumously, he is as right now about that as he was thirty-plus years ago.

Just so you know, Platt, et al., I am a student of quantum theory and quantum mechanics. I am also a student of the great author, and in doubt whether I will achieve even a fraction of what he intuits. In addition, I study genetics from an information theory viewpoint. I see biological life as the finest earth-bound system we perceive. I am interested in object-oriented (OO) system architectures and wonder with delight and amazement the potential for them if my mind were able to habitually practice MOQ and apply it to the development of new systems. I want to paint systems the way Bo paints pictures. I want to write systems the way Mozart, et al., have written music. I believe MOQ will make this possible. Imagine all system engineers and software engineers practicing their art as the masters practice their Zen arts.

Back to the subject—quantum time and its meaning for students of MOQ. Everything I have read says that quantum time is still an open subject. No one really knows what it means. Much of what I read about it sounds so MOQ-like I am simply astounded. Allow me to serve you just one tiny portion. This is from Paul Davies' excellent book entitled About Time, the paperback, page 178:

"Clearly, the topic of time in quantum physics is a decidedly murky one, and for good reason. First, as we have seen, there is no such thing as a perfect clock in quantum physics—all physical clocks are themselves subject to quantum uncertainty. This smears their smooth running in an unpredictable manner, and might even cause them to run backwards. Second, Einstein's time is not Newton's time; it is flexitime, its malleability inseparably interwoven with the affairs of matter and gravitation.

"Because the strange rules of quantum physics are supposed to govern all things, gravitational fields included, then not just clocks but time itself will be subject to quantum fuzziness."

See, Platt, nobody really knows about time. Some, like John Wheeler, think we will eventually do away with it. I keep pushing the importance of quantum mechanics (QM) to my fellow TLS mates because Pirsig's MOQ is so incredibly like what I have read and know about the quantum world. The topic you just broached above Platt is a perfect example of what I am talking about.

Before I give the quintessence, may I lay just a bit of foundation? In the same book I referenced above Paul Davies describes eloquently two experiments related to the famous double slit experiment first performed by Thomas Young (1773-1829). See pages 168; subtitle Erasing the Past, and 173, subtitle Spooky Signals and Psychic Particles. You can read about these experiments in many other places with many other interpretations, but I think these may be the easiest for you to quickly grasp and get the gist of the rest of my words below.

In the SOM world at the time of Young's experiment his results were paradoxical—it appeared that he could get particles out of the slits during one test and turn around and do it again and get waves. This was the beginning of the great wave-particle duality paradox. Prior to that, Newton argued for particles (he called them corpuscles) and Huygens argued for waves. As you well know, the SOM types insist that it must be one or the other (all their thoughts seem disgustingly and dialectically dichotomous). This argument is interesting in itself, i.e., why were two SOM-types using similar SOM tools and concluding different things?

Later, Bohr tried to explain the whole thing with his complementarity. I think Pirsig did an excellent job of relating complementarity to MOQ (in SODV). I doubt anyone can do better. Anyway, and now we are getting close to crux, Bohr tried to say that particle and wave are just different aspects of the same probabilistic value pattern. Now we have all seen the reception of the MOQ by today's scientists, philosophers, and metaphysicists.

They say, "No way!" Well, those same dipstick SOM-types did the same thing to Bohr! But guess what? These experiments show that Bohr was correct! In spades, he was correct! (And just for your information, Einstein was full of peanut butter.) For me that says (but of course all of us already knew this, right?) MOQ is correct, too.

After you read the two experiments, re-read SODV. Now consider: Quality is where value and the four levels are. Ss and Os are in value, something like this: sVo. SODV says that Os prefer the precondition Quality and come first, and then Ss prefer precondition Os and Quality and come next. Here's the crux: Quality events (QEs) occur when Ss become aware of Os and value that awareness. Until QEs occur, Ss and Os are just there in some, let us say, superposed state. If QEs occur based on probabilistic patterns of value...then (we know, we can assert) they do happen. As QEs occur, we get latched SPoVs as Platt described above—some long entropic stream of QEs and their trailing SPoVs.

The double slit experiments described in the two subtitles I referenced above sound to me awesomely similar to the previous paragraph. The experiments can be set up in such a way to allow the system to in essence be superposed, wavelike. As soon as the experiment tries to observe the (paths of the) wave superpositions, a QE occurs and the system latches to particle-like. I do not understand ("...nobody understands...") this completely, but it appears that when we observe the superposed "quantum quality" surrounding us the observed quantum wave functions experience a QE and latch into reality. That is how I see it. Perhaps now you can see why I am so predisposed on this subject.

I believe the duality twixt MOQ and QM is clear. Now given that QM is the best we have and SOM types are having to convert to this new reality, doesn't QM give us a big fulcrum to leverage MOQ into acceptance? I think it does.

I did all of this basically off the top of my head, quickly, without being critical of my own words. I may have blown some details. I know we have to define some terms like awareness relative to QEs. There are probably more, like experience.

I hope this helps.

Bottom line, Platt—I do not believe that "prior to" is meaningless.

I believe a very few people on this planet understand what I just wrote above, assuming I got it 75% right. Pirsig does. Some of the folk in Brüssels may too.

Many truths to you, Platt, and all the other members of TLS.

Mother of all Relativity [September 1997]

Bodvar:

After reading Pirsig's Subjects, Objects, Data and Values paper, it seems to me that, in an assembly of SOM based people, Pirsig obviously tried to cater to their views as far as he could, so, superficially seen, his came to resemble a SOM approach. It struck me that the search for the reality of the quantum world gives the impression that there (in an MOQ view too) is an objective reality, although on a still more basic level. I had in my essay used the map metaphor, i.e., that reality is the terrain a theory has to match or "represent" to be credible. Pirsig had in a way also, by using the map projection metaphor, and I now realize that he has the better one.

But then, what is it about this experience/terrain that the MOQ map is supposed to match better than the SOM one? I went cold as I saw that I had introduced good old objectivity through the back door, and pondered this heavily. The relief came from the said Dr. Harris (who I still hope will turn up here) who mentioned the Lorenz transformation equations that are applied when going from Newton physics (NP) to General Relativity (GR). I am no expert, but I know that GR in a sense "contains" the NP; it is principally possible to calculate a moon trip based on GR but it is far too accurate. NP suffices with wide margins. Still, when speeds are high enough, as in particle accelerators, GR must be applied. But NP does not give room for relativistic effects and the Lorenz equations are used when switching between the two physics mode.

However, relativity seen from the classic view has the same trouble as the MOQ when addressed from a SOM standpoint. We all know the space distortion quandary—if space curves, what straight measuring rod do we compare to? Or if time dilates what absolute time does it fluctuate compared to? It is used as a layman's "disproof" of relativity but the physicists couldn't care less; GR works perfectly; they use the said transformation procedures and do not speculate about "real" space or time. I guess this goes for quantum physics too. It predicts the outcome with great accuracy, but cannot be understood from a classical point of view.

It struck me that the MOQ is a General Relativity of Metaphysics. History as we know it has been a relentless passage from absoluteness towards relativity. Euclid's absolute flat geometry has given way to a host of special geometry's (see ZMM on Bolyai and Lobachevski), and Ptolemaian cosmology has been replaced by the Copernican universe that ended absolute direction (up/down) and center. Now the mother of all relativity is in the wings. There is no absolute reality; it "curves" due to the Dynamism underlying it all. And the resistance and attempts to overlook it from the establishment recur with tenfold force. Was it Anders who said that the MOQ was an invention of Pirsig just as gravity was an invention of Newton? That shows a deep understanding of what's at stake, and that he has read ZMM!

I wonder if anyone has anything to say about Quality's reconciliation of the evolution versus creation quandary.

Magnus:

Count me in Bo! I think the greatest use we could get from the MOQ is to get a wider view of what kinds of evolution are possible. We have seen, or at least we think we have seen, evidence of one kind of evolution: atoms to molecules to cells to plants to animals and so on.

With the MOQ fully developed we could simulate, imagine, and backtrack all kinds of evolution. And I don't mean only Darwin's biological evolution. I mean evolution of both lower and higher levels. This would however require a MOQ free of dependencies from the one evolution we have witnessed. We can't have level definitions like inorganic patterns are atoms and such; organic patterns are biological life and such, etc. They are too connected to just one kind—our kind—of evolution. How can we expect to see other kinds if we don't allow ourselves to look beyond that border?

In our quest to understand our "reality," we smash particles together in big accelerators to see of what they are composed. But to really succeed and get that Great Unifying Theory everyone is seeking, we have to build particle accelerators the size of the solar system. Well, maybe there's a better way of doing this?

We know four levels—let's have a really close look at them and their relationships, especially the lowest we know. What does that level provide to the one above that is so crucial? Then, how is that done? And with what? Maybe we can come up with some theories about how an even lower level could be detected, or otherwise, what other manifestations of our inorganic level could be manifested and detected? I mean, just look at the formula $E=mc^2$. Isn't it obviously just two different manifestations are on top of the underlying level?

Hugo:

On relativity and metaphysics, Bodvar wrote that MOQ as opposed to SOM may be likened to relativity as opposed to classical physics. There may be some likeness in there being a paradigmatic revolution/change involved, but if you suggest that the metaphysics of relativity is a kind of precursor of MOQ, I am somewhat sceptic towards that. Einstein's theories of relativity rest on a strictly phenomenological metaphysics; it is a world where "observers observing the world" is the fundamental prerequisite. Look at one of his gedanken experiments and you will see that it is always based on electromagnetic (light usually) signals by which an independent observer tries to make sense of what he sees.

Actually, I tend to see relativity theory as a SOM platypus, not in its capacity as a tool for making predictions, of course, but as a provider of an understanding of kinematics, of the way things and "no things" move. There are a number of paradoxes in the metaphysics of relativity, and I believe taking a Pirsigian step back and acknowledging the SOM underlying the theory (and that the paradoxes may arise from here) is a first step towards resolving them. This does not mean that MOQ as Pirsig has explicated it has something to offer here, only that it resembles how he has resolved other metaphysical paradoxes. Or did Pirsig discuss relativity theory critically?

But if we leave out Einstein's solution, I can see how you find the general move from absolutism towards relationism supportive or symptomatic of SOM and MOQ. And I am not advocating a more absolutist metaphysics of kinematics. On the contrary, the paradoxes of relativity seem to arise because Einstein did/could not go far enough towards a relationary foundation. These are very loose arguments, but I think the paradoxes and how they arise can be shown in a rigorous way and I have done some work on it, still preliminary though. I should say I have been an amateur relativity theorist for some years and have some grasp of the Special Relativity issues, but I still know too little of General Relativity to say much on that.

I think they only use Special Relativity in particle accelerator physics, or am I wrong?

Doug:

Before I begin, I want to make a few observations.

First, in my opinion, humankind is an evolved species. Our recent ancestors are Neandertal and Cro-Magnon. We (Homo-sapiens) survived. Why? Because as Richard Dawkins says, "We practice a better evolutionarily stable strategy (ESS)." However, our entire being is moving forward on many levels. It is evolving on micro, intermediate, and macro (all) scales. At the quantum level, we are evolving in the smallest of time increments. Our minds are evolving in millisecond to multi-year intervals. Mentally none of us is near as primitive as we were when we joined TLS.

Using the scales of geologic time—eon, era, period, and epoch— we are evolving as a species at ever accelerating rates. The time period between Neandertal and Cro-Magnon was approximately 210k millennia. Neandertal evolved and lived between 250k and 35k millennia ago and Cro-Magnon evolved and lived between 40k-25k millennia ago. The time period between Cro-Magnon and modern Homo sapiens is much shorter, say less than 50k millennia. I believe that the next iteration is imminent. I call it Neo-sapiens. I believe it will happen within the next 5k-10k millennia. Neo-sapiens will find it difficult to believe why Homo sapiens found MOQ so difficult to understand and use habitually.

Second, in my opinion, any productive, non-dissipative entity in the macroworld, which does not evolve, becomes extinct. Stagnation is not an ESS. Even things which evolve at a rapid pace will be replaced by superior species with superior ESSs.

Third, humans and some other animals in the biological kingdom share architecture which has a biformal bias: two arms (wings, fins), two legs, two eyes, two ears, two nostrils (gills), a bilongitudinal digestive tract, and perhaps most important two brain lobes. This biformal architecture has much to do with current human thinking and MOQ. Our language is extremely constrained by primitive forms. This is true for Western and Eastern languages. The difference is Western languages are more formal and left-brained. The Eastern languages are more artistic and right-brained. But both are constrained by primitive forms (fonts, brush strokes, local contexts, etc.).

This was one of Niels Bohr's greatest concerns. It is why he said we have a language problem. It is why he said we are immersed in language. It is why few of the classical minds understood what he meant by complementarity. (By the way, this is one excellent test of MOQ. In my opinion, MOQ makes it possible to understand complementarity!) The biformal bias is what Phædrus' chatauqua was about when he discussed how the Aristotelians (left-brained analytical types) won (in my opinion, temporarily) the battle against the Sophists (right-brained romantic types) for eminent domain over Quality. All of this is important because, in my opinion, Quality—via the MOQ—is about to regain eminency. I believe TLS is part of that process. I believe we are part of that process!

Finally, why did the Aristotelians win out, short term (epochs-toperiods) over the Sophists? In my opinion, ESS! Homo-sapiens need to survive, just like their ancestors. Their biformal bias gives them the edge, short term. That reason is the king of all metrics in our global society today: speed. The forms of human thought which are the quickest from a survival perspective are binary. Classical science evolved a plethora of binary tools: deterministic classical substance properties (whose presence or absence may be answered yes or no), Hegelian dialectic, tautology, dichotomy, difference, centricity, schism, objectivity, Aristotelian syllogism, deduction/induction, analysis/synthesis, and on and on and on.... Virtually all of these are exclusive and oppositional. Almost none is inclusive. They all bifurcate subject and object. But they are fast! Because of our innate biformal architecture, they are intuitive. They produce ESS results. That is why the Aristotelians won. The sophists (and our children, as Pirsig says in Lila) intuit Quality. Classical science needs speed and efficiency. MOQ values Quality.

Bodvar resides more in his right brain. He is an artist. It is grand that Bodvar makes his living doing what he loves. I have taken tests to discover that I am, compared to most other humans, somewhat balanced: I use both halves of my brain about equally. But you have all seen that I am more left-brained and rational than Bodvar. My guess is that most of the LS are more balanced or more right-brained.

To Bodvar, and all of the Lila Squad, I want you to know my true position, and my allegiances. I think MOQ is the new reality for us. As I said, Pirsig has birthed a wonderful gift. Given my predilections and proclivities, I want to share this gift with as many of our kind as possible. In my opinion, it is the future. There are some caveats, however. I will share those as apropos. Each caveat finds its basis in what I have said above, and each is related to some of the visceral and zealous interactions infant Lila Squad experiences.

The material Pirsig covered in SODV took an incredible amount of research. Pirsig, by his own admission, is no mathematician or physicist. My perception is that he did very well. I read SODV over and over. He captured much. Each sentence is a metastatement like a huge iceberg whose mass is mostly hidden. Pirsig is, undoubtedly, one of the finest minds of the 20th century. In my opinion, Pirsig would not spend the time he did if he did not see the duality (mapping) between quantum physics and MOQ. For me, he bottomlined that when he said, "If the atomic world is composed of probability waves and if probability is equal to value then it follows logically that the atomic world is composed of value."

Pirsig rejects classical science because of its inability to classify quality correctly and its resulting disjunction of subject and object with the latter as the center of worship. If we are adherents of MOQ, we can only agree. This is Pirsig's great discovery! We reject classical science with some concern, though, because in the macroworld it works very well albeit approximately. And look at where we have arrived. But if not for classical science, had the sophists won, Pirsig would not have discovered MOQ in our lifetime. Hmmm, would that have been better?

Now, Bodvar, I must counter a few of your views above. I may be misinterpreting your gist. If so, push back. I mean no offense. Pirsig was not among a group of classical scientists in Brüssels. He was invited by quantum physicists. In my opinion, you cannot be exclusively a classical scientist and a quantum physicist at the same time. Classical science simply does not work or apply in the quantum realm. (One of the biggest problems physicists have is that classical science is intuitive and quantum physics is not. Even quantum physicists revert to classical mental models because they are intuitive. They have to get really good at switching mentally back and forth. I think this is another problem MOQ will help to solve.) The reason he went to Brüssels was because some quantum physicists saw duality twixt his work and theirs. In my opinion, they saw this duality for very, very good reasons.

Einstein, one of the two acknowledged greatest minds in mankind's history (the other is Newton), is an enigma to me. He was a classical scientist. He disavowed non-determinism. "God does not [roll] dice." He claimed quantum theory is incomplete. His argument was the famous (but fatally flawed) EPR experiment. (See David Bohm's effective confutation of the EPR.) Yet, amazingly, Einstein unified space and time, matter and energy, etc. What an enigma! Classical science had a brain-lock on his mind. He believed and had absolute faith that the universe had to be deterministic. That was his failing!

Classical science often produces paradoxes! MOQ and quantum physics often eliminate paradoxes! Paradoxes value the precondition of classical science. Why? Because classical science values the precondition of unclassified Quality subordinated to subject and object. (See Pirsig on the causation platypus, page 119 of Lila paperback.)

Note that both Newtonian physics (NP) and general relativity (GR) are classical science, or at best, steeped in the baggage of classical science. Einstein developed the special and general theories using his own innovative extensions of classical science's fundamentals. I agree with Bodvar that GR contains NP. Both are about the macroworld. Actually GR is about the super-macroworld of cosmology. Quantum physics is about the microworld. NP works approximately in the macroworld, but not in the cosmological world or the microworld. GR works in the macroworld and cosmological world but not in the microworld. Quantum physics works in all three. (But note, even as we speak, its successors are in the wings. Physics is evolving rapidly.)

Thus, in particle accelerators quantum mechanics unified with GR must be applied. I think this particular flavor of quantum physics is called QED, or quantum electrodynamics. P.A.M. Dirac invented QED, and Richard Feynman invented graphical tools to make QED viable.

On the Hendrik Antoon Lorentz transformations, prior to P.A.M. Dirac, quantum mechanics did not appear to obey the Lorentz invariance requirement. Dirac was able, however, to unify quantum mechanics and relativity theory and produce a Lorentz-invariant system. Systems are Lorentz invariant if their axioms remain unchanged across changes in system coordinates. This is but one test of the goodness of a theory or system. Note that Dirac was a prodigy, much like William James Sidis (page 63-5 of Lila paperback), except Dirac did not hide from society.

All of the above is, just as Bodvar intimates, part of the classical ugliness—except for the quantum mechanics portion. Quantum mechanics awakens physicists in the same way that MOQ awakens philosophers. Isn't it interesting that philosophers and physicists now gain enlightenment through provocatively similar metaphors.

In my opinion, it is that provocative similarity which peripherally holds Pirsig's interest and I hope that of the Lila Squad. What I see, and what the physicists in Brüssels see, is that MOQ is a "Quantum Theory of Metaphysics," to paraphrase your words. That phrase is certainly more apt from what I know about NP, GR, and QT. MOQ clearly is more complete than SOM, just as quantum theory subsumes and is more complete than both or either NP and GR.

In my opinion, evolution is the methodology of creation.

I apologize for the length of this response. Bodvar put a lot of challenges on the Lila Squad playing field. Be aware, as I, that I am human and of finite intellect. I have rendered a portion of my static pattern repertoire.

Some of the "real" patterns may have been perturbed by me. Note that this is precisely what Pirsig described as "…one enormous metaphysical problem unanswered…" with ZMM, and "became the central driving reason for the expansion of the MOQ into a second book called Lila." (See bottom of page 12 and top of page 13 in the original SODV.) "Both the Dynamic Quality and the static patterns influence [Doug's] final judgment." Further, note that without this, life would be extraordinarily dull, indeed.

Before Static Quality [October 1997]

Martin:

I'm new so I don't know if you've discussed this before, but I'll just throw it out. The fight and balance between Dynamic Quality and static quality has resulted in an evolution of values, so if we extrapolate this process backwards in time, what can it tell us about the beginning of existence? Just looking for some thoughts. What do you think?

Magnus:

Hi Martin and welcome to the Lila Squad! First, I think the question is very valid and I have pondered it myself from time to time. My thoughts goes something like this—to be able to extrapolate something we first have to make a model of what we already know; that would be the four levels. Furthermore, to use this model to extrapolate outside of it, it would help if it was continuous, which it isn't. So, we must extrapolate outside of a discrete model. This, in turn, requires a very good understanding of the relations involved in the discrete model, and to underestimate things, we're not quite there yet. But I'd be very interested in your understanding as the question implies a quite good one!

Martin:

Well, the answer (as theoretic as it is) has eluded me as well. I've tried using Quality evolution and our knowledge of history simultaneously to shed some light on it. Let's start a journey going backwards in time. A few thousands years ago the first philosophers appear in Greece. Folks like Anaxagoras and Erastosthenes and Democritus, later Socrates, Plato, and Aristotle, but especially the first one we have on record, Thales of Miletus, living around 700 BC. These folks were the first to use their heads to solve problems and this was a whole new set of values, so we can say with some certainty that the development of intellectual static quality was around this time.

As we continue backwards in time along our trans-temporal road, we'll reach a time when people just started to band together, a time when they were shifting from nomadic lifestyles to settlements, plantations, and eventually cities, when governments became necessary for the first time to establish order, and religions became prominent to answer their questions about the world. This was perhaps ten to fifteen thousand years ago (although people may have existed in clans for a hundred thousand years, they certainly didn't have any social values, per se) and we can say with some certainty that social static quality evolved around this time.

Now we travel a long time against a landscape that changes and becomes more simple as we go along (actually backwards), but nothing new appears or disappears for perhaps a few billion years. Eventually we reach a point where life is just starting out. There isn't much of it, it's very simple compared to today's standards, and it's quite inefficient. The world really looks quite different. The oceans are like a thick "organic soup." Methane, oxygen, carbon dioxide, hydrogen, water, and trace elements fill the atmosphere of a violent early earth, full of volcanic eruptions and lightning.

This is a very Dynamic time! This lightning breaks carbon chains in the "organic soup" up and allows them to reunite in longer chains. Eventually a certain kind of carbohydrate—we would see it as proto RNA—comes along. It has the unique ability of gathering other carbon chains and fixing them to look exactly as it looks. After billions of these "proto reproductions," more complex ones come along, and millions of years down the road we have unicellular life. This whole period has introduced another set of values, from our perspective it has introduced biological static quality.

Traveling farther down the road, now for a longer period of time than the all the time it has taken for the last three kinds of static quality to evolve, we see nothing but one kind of static quality. It all follows the laws of inorganic values, and is exactly what Materialists see the world as—it's all physical.

This is the hard part. What happens here? Along our journey, we've been eliminating each kind of static quality in order of decreasing complexity, so logic would tell us that all we have left to do is eliminate the inorganic values. All this time we've been looking at non-MOQ accounts at what has been occurring, so perhaps we can look at some more theories. I've thought about this and have come to two conclusions: 1) in MOQ terms, all the theories look the same so MOQ terms don't shed any light on the beginnings, and 2) It seems Dynamic Quality can't exist before static values!

1) In MOQ terms, at some point in time Dynamic Quality produced the first values. [56] As soon as they became present and continuous in time, they became static. In scientific terms, everything was a singularity (a dimensionless point, having no physical existence, only a position, and containing within itself both all of matter and all of space) until a moment (Dynamic Quality) in time when it exploded (the values were produced). In religious terms, at some point in time a Creator God (Dynamic Quality) created the universe (produced the first values). We intuitively think Dynamic Quality existed before static values did, so we are led to say it caused the first ones. But this statement is so vague it sheds no light on what actually happened. A scientific or religious theory looks the same depending on if we treat Dynamic Quality as a god or that mysterious force that triggered the Big Bang. I'm at a loss here.

2) Upon further reflection, I noticed that time is dependent on matter. [57] A singularity can exist for an infinite amount of time, but time is meaningless without something to notice time by. If two objects move past each other, you can notice that it happens over an interval of time, but if you're staring at black space (and there wasn't any space before the Bang, either!) you might as well be staring at a photograph taken instantaneously. And since Dynamic Quality is the "now," this moment in time, it seems that Dynamic Quality is dependent on time. Whatever is in the past and whatever we hope in the future is part of static quality, but only a

continually progressing "nowness" gives any meaning to Dynamic Quality. Where was Dynamic Quality and what was it doing before the Bang? In creationary terms, the question is practically the same. What was God, our Dynamic Quality, doing for all the "time" before existence? For all practical purposes, there was no time, and consequently there was no "now," and the concept of a singularity, or God, or Dynamic Quality, is meaningless.

This can also be compared to the "train" of existence. The leading edge is Dynamic Quality, but start taking away the sections of the train, one by one, until you take away the last section. Now there is no train left, so there is no leading edge and no place for Dynamic Quality.

It's quite a conundrum. Your thoughts?

Hugo:

Martin, I have wanted to reply to your first mail on the beginning of existence, as it concerns something I have thought a lot about, and now I have to write. First, a point of disagreement on the levels (I am not sure where exactly Pirsig stands on this issue)—I consider the social level and social values much, much older. Sociality is part of most everything of the life we see and enjoy around us. Your view of the levels might be much more common, though.

In Denmark a guy named Simo Koeppe (Danish: Køppe) wrote an interesting book called The Levels of Reality, in 1990. It is a very thorough analysis of the new "holistic" or systemic sciences where he

uses the same major levels as Pirsig. He actually puts the social and intellectual (I think he calls it the psychological level) in parallel, next to each other on top of the biological level, on top of the physical level. I believe this is wrong, and that it comes from trying to preserve the mind (or soul) as something specifically human when moving towards an evolutionary and hierarchic view.

I myself follow Gregory Bateson (see his Mind and Nature for instance). On this issue, Bateson argues that mind is something that we share with the rest of the living. "The big step" is not from

167

animal to man, but from non-life to life. I have argued this before on the Lila Squad, saying that if we bend Bateson into a Pirsigian shape, we get a mindless level and three levels of mind: the first step being a mind (a subject) reflecting its environment (or better, umwelt, the environment as it sees it), the second step being minds mutually reflecting other minds, and the third step being a mind reflecting itself. (And I do see this as a definition of the levels, even though some say that can't be done.)

If we are to place the revolutions of stepping onto a new level in our evolutionary history, I would point to the becoming of life— the Cambrian revolution, that is—as the becoming of multi-cellular (social) life (at least this is the earliest significant trace we have of the social step in the history of life. See Stephen Jay Gould's Wonderful Life). And we are of course in the midst of the third revolution.

The last part of your mail was most intriguing and goes right to the heart of what I have to say in reply to your mail on the beginning of existence. I will go ahead and mail that reply, but first some specific comments. Martin, you wrote, "In MOQ terms, all the theories look the same so MOQ terms don't shed any light on the beginnings, and it seems Dynamic Quality can't exist before static values. In MOQ terms, at some point in time Dynamic Quality produced the first values. As soon as they became present and continuous in time, they became static."

Yes, this is in accordance with Charles Sanders Peirce's metaphysics, where he distinguishes three modes of being: the Potential, the Actual, and the Habitual (or Necessary) being. The first two, the most important distinctions between potentiality and actuality, were original ideas of Aristotle as far as we know. The question being, how a dimensionless point can contain anything, and how there can be a point, a position, before the becoming of space? I am very reluctant towards calling this mysterious force God, at least without qualifying it, because our (the Christian that is) idea of God seems to imply a present force, a God that has a say in our present life, and this is not implied by this mysterious force of the beginning.

Martin wrote: "Upon further reflection, I noticed that time is dependent on matter. A singularity can exist for an infinite amount of time, but time is meaningless without something to notice time by. If two objects move past each other, you can notice that it happens over an interval of time, but if you're staring at black space (and there wasn't any space before the Bang, either!), you might as well be staring at a photograph taken instantaneously."

Exactly! And this means that we have to find a new concept of time, or at least that we have to dismiss the Einsteinian concept of time as a (fourth) dimension. Time is a derivative of motion; hence, we cannot speak of something moving in a pre-existing dimension of time. This has a great many important implications, which I would love to discuss—maybe later?

My major problem is that I find it difficult to convey my MOQlike thoughts without using well-known terms from philosophy and ordinary language, and then I use them in a somewhat different sense than is common; and we as a group have not yet learned to understand each other's MOQ language.

Bodvar:

Our disagreement is about the "age" of society. Pirsig's position, in my opinion, is that all levels start as part of, and indistinguishable from, the parent level. The social values were for aeons in the service of life (according to Magnus a biological body is a society), but as a moral order in its own right, it is younger and more like the picture that Martin paints. The first (human) social manifestation beyond family (which is a transient stage) was the clan/tribe cooperation. In this context, the individual still was a mere member; in Julian Jaynes' book, it is argued that early humans were mindless (did not value freedom from society), but a little bit freer than in the family clutches. Yes, look, the intellect was already budding, but still in the service of society!

Hugo:

My problem with this is that there are so very many social values at play in Nature—wolf packs for instance—that I fail to see this social structuring as something specifically human. It seems to me that what you call the emergence of the social level, I would call the first traces of the intellectual level. I don't find the breakthrough to humanity in the social but in the intellectual. Having said that, I am not at all certain when exactly the social level did emerge. As I have said before, there are huge differences inside the levels too, from the very first crude form of sociality to the complex social lives of mammals, for instance. My only guide in stating when the levels arose in our evolutionary history is the definition I have given of the levels. Hence, if you disagree with these definitions I have no further arguments for my statement.

Bodvar:

Hugo, I find your exposition good, particularly the section about mind as seen by Bateson versus Köppe interested me greatly. I have Bateson's Mind and Nature, could you give the page where he elaborates on this?

Hugo:

I think much of this book is actually arguing this point, though some of my recollection might be from his Steps to an Ecology of Mind. In Chapter 3, three pages in (page 89 in my Danish version), he talks of why he does not think elementary particles harbour "mind" in his sense, because the processes of mind are always processes of mutual interaction, or something to that effect. Here he distinguishes himself from Samuel Butler and Teilhard de Chardin, he says, as they attribute some kind of mental (spiritual?) endeavour even to the smallest particles.

Bodvar:

On the bending of him into Pirsigian shape, I have a few comments to. "Mind" in this (umwelt) sense is the very same that I tend to call "intelligence" (any organism's universe depending upon its neural complexity) to distinguish it from the intellectual level of the MOQ. Your ladder of minds above matter is a "tempting" solution (life equals reflecting environment; society

170

equals reflecting other minds; intellect equals reflecting itself), but is it Quality metaphysics?

Hugo:

I follow your distinction between intelligence and intellect and have no objections to that. And I definitely feel that my solution is a solution within Quality metaphysics (with due respect towards Pirsig's judgment on this).

Bodvar:

I ask because I am not sure. I notice that you use the expression "levels of mind." Can it be understood that you regard life as well as society and intellect as levels of mind? If so why not include matter? Unless you do, it is the old story of "matter at a moment in time becoming imbued with mind"—a larger version admittedly, but still good old SOM.

Hugo:

I can follow your hesitation towards my use of the term "mind" here, and I should have been more careful. When I read Bateson I loved his placing "human mind" inside the larger mind of Nature, but I actually revolted towards his sharp distinction between mind and matter, and I do believe that you are right that he is wrong on this. My solution then was the idea that "things with properties" were not what actually existed—"relations" were primary. And in this, I actually followed Bateson, because I think he was on to this in his talk of information as "differences that make a difference," and not least in his discussions of what properties are (second last part of first chapter in Mind and Nature) and more.

This is where I part with Køppe as well. In his book, he is discussing the iterative analysis of systems into subsystems and their relations, and he rejects the idea that systems were "all relations" because there would be "nothing at the bottom then" (I don't recall his exact words). Køppe sticks to some sort of materialism with undividable objects or particles at the bottom, and if you read my first reference to Mind and Nature above, you will see that Bateson did the same, at least at that time. If one dares to explore the "it's all relations" ontology, one will necessarily end up in a MOQ-like structure, and at some point of reading Lila, it dawned upon me that that was what Pirsig was on about.

To get back to our discussion, I would have no problem with a terminology of four levels of mind (Peirce talks of matter as the "stiffening of mind," so I don't think he would disagree either) with non-reflective mind and three kinds of reflective mind. I don't see mind as something which is "imbued on matter," I just used the term to describe the more complex (i.e., reflective) forms of existence. On the other hand, I do think such a terminology (four levels of mind) might lend itself to be misunderstood as saying that everything in the universe was part of some larger mind (e.g., God), in a way that I do not intend.

There really is no easy way out of our problem with using SOMlike language to discuss and describe MOQ-like ideas, but I don't think we disagree on the above, Bodvar. Thanks for addressing these issues.

Bodvar:

Martin, allow me a few general thoughts about your "Before Static Quality" entry. It seems that you take the Big Bang creation myth dead seriously. I am not saying that it is wrong or that the Steady State is more MOQ-like, but bear in mind the short (limited at least) lifetime of such theories (best used before year 2000).

The insight that made young Phædrus of ZMM leave his scientific studies was that there are a limitless number of theories that fit any observation. "Truth is an intellectual static pattern," says Phædrus of Lila. We must not be seduced into believing that there is an absolute (objective) endlösung to anything, only the ever better one. To press the point home, take for instance the theory of what makes the sun shine. Every schoolboy knows (Bateson) the nuclear fusion model, but is it the truth? Couldn't a still greater context change all that?

The way you (and Hugo speak) about the event that allegedly took place when the singularity expanded into the present universe is very SOM causation-like. In Lila (page 107), Pirsig mentions a Quality version of various scientific disciplines, for instance,

Quality physics where "A causes B," is replaced by "B values precondition A," without it changing any facts of science at all. What this will have to say for the speculations about the emergence of the material world I only have some faint outlines of, but as usual does the Quality notion turn everything inside out and upside down.

Martin:

Well, my intention was to compare what the MOQ would reveal versus current theories. So the first two layers of static values (going backwards in time of course) could be compared to historical accounts. Before that, we leave history and delve into science theories and religious myths (what else is there?). So, I gave a typical abiogenetical evolutionary account (although I like Dawkins' crystal theory better than the organic soup, personally) for the evolution of biological values. Of course, there are others (as I just showed with the crystal theory). And going to the last step, I reviewed the two dominant theories: the Big Bang and Divine Creation. My point was that on that final step, I didn't gain anything by applying the MOQ to either account. I don't know what was so wrong with using those accounts, though.

Hugo:

Well, Bodvar, I see my ideas on this as very un-SOM causationlike! What makes you consider them causation-like? To me the causal is everything that lasts; causality only considers the static patterns of Nature. Hence, there has been much debate on how new things can become in a world of causality, emergence, and so on. And on the interpretation of the quantum collapse, apart from quantum mechanics it seems like any event can be given a causal explanation, yet we have this definite feeling that something is missing from this mechanistic picture; when and where does the new arise?

I find the simple answer in MOQ and Aristotle's "potency act" distinction. The actualization of potentiality, the Quality event, is the answer, etc.

Bodvar:

The reason it sounded causation-like to me was mainly because you and Martin discussed what caused the singularity to expand into a universe, but that was perhaps on Martin's side.

MOQ and Aristotle! Two very odd partners I must say. Phædrus of ZMM saw Socrates and Plato as the villains who had created the foundation for the coming Subject/Object Metaphysics, and Aristotle as the eternal mechanic who had worked it out in detail. As I see it, the sentence "B values precondition A" means exactly what it says; what brought Newton's apple to let go of the tree is the same "process" that brought the material universe to emerge.

Well then, did our "potential world," along with countless others, scan the various conditions (from a pre-Big Bang abode) and decide what it liked? This sounds like the "many worlds" interpretation of quantum physics if you look upon it with the SOM loaded language, but with the Quality precondition accepted, that way of asking does not apply.

There are moments when I become a little scared of what Pirsig has released. He says the quality version of physics won't change the settings of any scientific measuring apparatus, but will it be a motivation for doing research in a MOQ steeped culture. Isn't science built upon the notion of a detached subject viewing objective reality? Phædrus of ZMM found that there are an unlimited number of theories that fit any observation (the implication of this is sobering), and Phædrus of Lila says that science is just as value dependent as anything else (science abhors "value" as you know. It's even worse than "purpose"). Well, who is there to answer? ("Som man roper i skogen får man svar!"— heter det på norsk.)

You mentioned the "quantum collapse" as one of example of how new things can come into existence. The SOM forces one to look for the miraculous and for people who don't want their scientific (rational) reputation damaged, quantum mechanics is a safe haven. Here the miraculous is juxtaposed with the rational. I am not saying that this is your position, but look, the other day there was a new essay in The Metaphysical Review, "On the Relativity of Quantum Superpositions." After a lot of inscrutable mathematics it concludes:

"And yet nothing in orthodox quantum mechanics refers to size, complexity, or consciousness. This means, if we take the formalism of quantum mechanics at face value, there is no 'ontological' difference between an experimenter and an electron as far as superpositions are concerned. There is nothing in principle to prevent one from applying quantum mechanics to the experimenter from the point of view of the electron in the same way we have just applied quantum mechanics to the electron from the point of view of the experimenter. What I mean is instead of regarding the experimenter/laboratory as collapsed (in a definite state) and the (non-interaction) electron as being in a superposition state, there is nothing in the formalism of quantum mechanics itself to prevent us from regarding the electron as being in a definite state and the experimenter/laboratory as being in a superposition state." (My italics.)

See, even quantum mechanics "collapse of the superpositioned possibilities" needn't be the exotic event where the material (causation) world is created by interaction with mind. We, in the macroworld, are just as mysterious seen from the quantum world's side! The "randomness" examples of yours show that Substance metaphysics not only has problems in its interpretation of quantum events, even "ordinary causation" is beyond its range.

Hugo:

Well, I find the source of SOM in Aristotle's work, but I find more. And we are off course in our discussions of the MOQ (including Pirsig, especially Pirsig because he is so good at it) using the logic that Aristotle worked out. Logic is a valuable tool, but our rationalistic culture has taken logic to be the very structure of the world. Anyway, I just thought it fair and humbling to mention that the ideas behind the MOQ are just as ancient as the ideas behind SOM, and that Aristotle worked out some key concepts of both. [58]

I see the many world interpretation as our causation type way of handling the mysterious (to SOM) facts of quantum mechanics, and I find the idea both false and monstrous. And I don't think our world is "chosen" in any specific way, only in the sense of some form of structural complexity that has had to sprout.

I do think that science is not necessarily objectivistic. Karl R. Popper suggested a broader characterisation of science, stressing the public nature of science, both in the sense of being open and wanting of probing, and in the sense of having a common goal of working towards truth. As Popper famously asserted, working towards truth can be accomplished by hunting the untrue, and hence the two sides of the public nature of science can be coined as a quest for "probeable" knowledge. I don't see why the MOQ should bring science (in this respect) to a halt. But on the other hand, the necessary contextuality of science and knowledge, in a MOQ view, will severely limit the scope of objective science, of the science, which stands outside. The one-eyed truths won't be as widespread and influential as they are today, but I still see a very important role for science and a vital use for "probable truths in their proper context."

I don't agree on much of what Merriam has to say. For one, his way of handling the Schrödinger Cat paradox [59] I find fallacious, a fallacy he shares with most who discuss that paradox (as always in my fallible opinion). And the fault lies exactly in the kind of subjectivist interpretation of quantum mechanics that Merriam follows, in the idea that our observation or our mind has some crucial importance in the quantum collapse.

The somewhat cruel experiment goes like this—we put a cat in a box and let a poison be triggered by a single quantum event. The measurement of the spin of an electron will do, up and down spin, for instance, being equally probable and said to be in a "superpositioned" state until measured, and let's say down triggers the poison like the thumbs of ancient Rome. In measuring the spin, this superpositioned state is "collapsed," that is, one kind of spin is measured and the other probable kind of spin disappears. Now the argument goes, if we don't know whether the spin was up or down, we don't know whether the cat is dead or alive. So then, the cat must be in a superpositioned state between dead and alive, just like the electron, and neither dead nor alive. The (subjectivist or whatever) point being that the collapse won't happen until we look. I say, wait a few days and you might smell the so-called superpositioned cat!

SPPMOTNIIABS (Someone please punch me on the nose if I am being stupid), but in my eyes this (subjectivist or whatever) view is quite confused, even though I often meet upon such ideas. I find it evident that the place of the quantum collapse is in the very actualization involved in the "measurement." A quantum measurement device is constructed as to actualize one of a very specific set of possibilities, and the "collapse of the superpositioned state" is the same as "the actualization of one of the possible outcomes."

Given this view of mine (and a few others I guess, at least the Danish physicist and Peirce translator Peder Voetman Christiansen has expressed a similar view, though I haven't seen him touch upon the Schrödinger paradox), one cannot make a "measurement device that triggers" without involving the collapse of the superpositioned state, or so I say—if the measurement turns out a "down" the cat dies, if it turns out "up" it lives until the next experiment.

Hence there can be no "dead or alive" cat paradox, and I am wary of Merriam's arguments as far as he takes off from the assumption that, "As a result, I conclude there is no difference as a matter of principle between the behavior of a quantum mechanical 'cat' and a quantum mechanical 'electron.'"

And further I suspect that his use of the condition "quantum mechanically sealed off" together with the implicit assumption of being able to observe what is going on inside this sealed off place, involves a fallacy, though this would take a closer scrutiny to decide.

Magnus:

Something for the acronym list?;-)

The MOQ also says that every Quality event results in one object and one subject. [60] But at this point, the SOM way of thinking is to say that the subject is the more "advanced" of the two, i.e., the human is the subject and the cat is the object, or, the instrument is the subject and the photon is the object. The MOQ viewpoint is as Doug says the "many truths" one. Either "X-bject" can be called the subject in any Quality event. Each Quality event contains two truths, one resulting from one being selected as the subject, and one resulting from the other being selected as the subject.

The "mind," whatever is left of it, is placed in the subject and has nothing to do with what particular level it belongs to.

Maggie:

Just a comment—I don't think the motivation for doing science will change by adopting Pirsig's MOQ. The values that science frees itself from are the values inherent in the social/biological spectrum. The values that science is dependent on (and doesn't admit to because it doesn't have the MOQ to define the difference) are the values inherent in the social/intellectual spectrum. Nevertheless, the process of a person removing him or herself from the traps of the biological/social world to use the tools of the intellectual is powerful enough it ought to continue, and that step stool to Dynamic Quality will continue to reap its own reward.

Annotations by Robert M. Pirsig

54. Historically music comes before the intellectual analysis of music and therefore is not dependent on it. Musicology, art and literary criticism, and philosophology are described in Lila as parasitic fields that sometimes try to control their host.

55. Light can be described by quantum mechanics, but the essence of light, in MOQ terms, is a baby's first perception of it. Only later does he invent or learn a language and a math that describes it.

56. The word "produced" implies that Dynamic Quality is a part of a cause and effect system of the kind generated by scientific thinking. But Dynamic Quality cannot be part of any cause and effect system since all cause and effect systems are static patterns. All we can say is that these static patterns emerged and that they are better than physical nothingness.

A philosophic tradition of scientific value-neutrality would argue that you cannot say these value patterns are better than physical nothingness because scientifically speaking in the real world nothing is better than anything else. But if these patterns had not emerged there would be no life. And if life is not better than death and the science that life produces is not better than non-science, then this scientific tradition of value neutrality is no better than no words at all. That is, it has no merit.

57. In the MOQ time is dependent on experience independently of matter. Matter is a deduction from experience.

58. Yes, the MOQ only contradicts the SOM denial that value exists in the real world. The MOQ says it does. Thus the MOQ is an expansion of existing knowledge, not a denial of existing knowledge.

59. I think this paradox exists as a result of the materialist history of scientific thinking. Scientists often forget that all scientific knowledge is subjective knowledge based on experience, although science does not deny that this is true. All objects are in fact mental constructs based on experience. If we do not forget this and start with experience as the beginning point of the experiment,

rather than objective quantum particles as the beginning point of the experiment, the paradox seems to vanish.

The existence of collective masses of electrons can be inferred from experience and there is every reason to think they exist independently of the mind. But in the case of the spin of an individual electron, there is no experience. In addition, the nature of the Heisenberg Theory of Indeterminacy prevents any inference from general collective experience of electrons to certify the spin of any individual electron. If you can't experience something and you can't infer it either, then you have no scientific basis for saying that it exists. Thus the single quantum event that is supposed to trigger the cat's fate is a figment of the imagination. It can never exist independently of the mind and cannot have any effect whatsoever on any real cat that does exist independently of the mind. The Schrödinger experiment is interesting to think about, but like an angels-on-pinheads experiment, is impossible in to perform in an objective world.

60. It says subjects and objects are deduced from quality events, but many quality events occur without a resultant subject and object.

Chapter 6

There are moments in our lives, there are moments in a day, when we seem to see beyond the usual. Such are the moments of our greatest happiness. Such are the moments of our greatest wisdom. If one could but recall this vision by some sort of sign. It was in this hope that the arts were invented. Signposts on the way to what may be. Signposts toward greater knowledge. —Robert Henri

The Quality Event [November 1997]

Maggie:

I need some help with the Quality event, which we've talked about, and though I've looked back through past Lila Squad letters, I'm still not clear on it. I'm writing a paper and I need brief background information. I'm okay until the last sentence, I think (although if you catch anything else, please tell me). Here's what I plan to use:

Brief background of the Metaphysics of Quality (MOQ).

The MOQ involves a non-dualistic way of perceiving reality, quite different from the subjective/objective viewpoint that underlies Western thinking and language. In the MOQ, the primary division of all existence is Dynamic/static. The undifferentiated reality, the undefined, pre-existing source of all things is referred to as Dynamic Quality—not a thing, but the event at which the subject becomes aware of the object and before s/he distinguishes it. Dynamic Quality is a non-intellectual awareness, a "preintellectual reality." "Substance" is replaced in the MOQ by "static patterns of value," sometimes referred to as "patterns." All life is described as a migration of static patterns of value toward Dynamic Quality. The MOQ recognizes four discrete evolutionary levels of those static patterns of value:

Intellectual (I)

Social (S)

Biological (B)

Inorganic (I)

Each of these levels offers freedom from the constraints of the level below it, but each is also dependent on the levels below it for its existence. There are five types of struggle between different levels of Quality: chaotic/inorganic, inorganic/biological, biological/social, social/intellectual, and Dynamic/static. The Quality event (QE) is the point at which static and Dynamic Quality interact?

or

static patterns of value interact with other levels or Dynamic Quality (DQ)?

Which is it? [61]

Here's the same question in a the context of a different passage:

In general, the application of MOQ insight to social theory seems to offer the possibility of sorting out conflicting forces into component parts that are not otherwise seen. The leader/follower relationship is a social pattern of value. Leadership is a social pattern that utilizes the non-social behavior or insight of one person to mediate the social patterns of a group, thereby giving freedom from the constraints of static social patterns, creating new ones. The initial connection between leader and follower may be formed by a Quality event at any level, but must be maintained by the social level. [62]

The Leader experiences Dynamic Quality, creates a "DQ mediated" intellectual pattern (the insight), transfers that to an "intellectually mediated" social pattern (message), and shares it with someone. If the person internalizes it, and sets up and maintains a social relationship with the leader, a static social pattern is maintained. If a group of people—a sub culture—adopts the message, it is referred to as a "routinized charismatic message." Here is the question again, context from the paragraphs above:

What is the second person's (the follower's) experience? I'm asking about the important, meaningful experience that sets the relationship. [63] Is it a Dynamic Quality event, or an intellectual Quality event? Or a social Quality event? I expect that most of us think (or have thought) it is Dynamic Quality. Do you still think so?

I welcome anything on this, whether it's the Lila Squad's usual cogent comments, or stray thoughts. Even red pencils would be appreciated.

Bodvar:

Maggie, here is my contribution (the passages in your letter that I have omitted are just fine). For some reason I have become connected with the Quality Event expression (the title of my essay probably), but this is very much a ZMM thing—the mystic Pirsig. In Lila he doesn't speak so much about Quality events and I believe it is because the passage "...the event at which the subject becomes aware of the object, " etc., has some heavy subject/object connotations. In the MOQ proper, it is replaced by the Dynamic/static value division. Well, I bring out my "red pencil" and make the following corrections to your "Brief Background" foreword. It finally became so cluttered that I rewrote it.

Maggie wrote:

Brief background of the Metaphysics of Quality (MOQ). (Please note that the terms value, quality, morals, and good are interchangeable.) The MOQ involves a way of perceiving reality quite different from the subject/object viewpoint that underlies Western thinking and language. The first proposition of the MOQ is that everything is value, and that the primary division is between Dynamic and static value, not between subjects and objects. The undifferentiated, undefined, pre-existing source of all things is referred to as Dynamic Quality, but in this undifferentiated "ocean," there has formed sets of stable "wave patterns" of which the first is the material universe itself. The MOQ recognizes four such discrete value patterns (other terms are: levels, dimensions, and areas). They are in rising order of good:

Static Inorganic Value (Matter)
Static Biological Value (Life)
Static Social Value (Societies)
Static Intellectual Value (Ideas)

The Quality event (QE) is the point at which static and Dynamic Quality interact?

or

static patterns of value interact with other levels or Dynamic Quality?

Which is it?

Bodvar's comments:

If I am to try to define the Quality event, it's definitely the first alternative, Dynamic/static. The interaction between the two is hard to define; a trite example is the relationship between a medium and the message. For instance, (spoken) words are pressure waves in undifferentiated air. Such waves may become changed by the medium itself; new patterns may form. It is said that if a microphone is placed inside a soundproof room, after a while it starts to pick up sounds from its own internal Dynamics.

The greatest Quality event must have been when the material universe formed, but another major one happened when life manifested itself. The next one was the social cooperation among life forms, and finally the step out of the social bonds into intellectual freedom. Now, as intellect is the youngest, it is also most Dynamic, and every time static intellectual patterns (ideas, thoughts) are created and/or a major shift takes place, a little Quality event has happened.

More from Maggie:

"Here's the same question in a context of a different passage: in general, the application of MOQ insight to social theory seems to offer the possibility of sorting out conflicting forces into component parts that are not otherwise seen."

This is correct! Maggie:

"The leader/follower relationship is a social pattern of value. Leadership is a social pattern that utilizes the non-social behavior or insight of one person to mediate the social patterns of a group, thereby giving freedom from the constraints of static social patterns, creating new ones."

This was new to me, but it looks good, definitely.

More Maggie:

"The initial connection between leader and follower may be formed by a Quality event at any level, but must be maintained by the social level."

I am not so sure if I understand the "any level, but, etc." sentence. I think the leader/follower configuration is typical for the social level.

Maggie:

"The Leader experiences Dynamic Quality, creates a DQ mediated intellectual pattern (the insight), transfers that to an intellectually mediated social pattern (message), shares it with someone. If the person internalizes it, and sets up and maintains a social relationship with the leader, a static social pattern is maintained. If a group of people, a subculture, adopts the message, it is referred to as a 'routinized charismatic message.'"

Yes, with a little qualification. Let's take an example from the ancient times before the intellectual level became a motivating moral force, and still part of (in the service of) its parent level. A leader, say Moses of the Israelites tribe, went up on Mount Sinai and experienced a Quality event and came down to his people and delivered his message. He did so by way of language (even written on stone slates!), but I wouldn't call it "intellectual." Even if language was to become the great mediator of intellectual values, it was solely society's servant at that time. (Compare it to before life. The carbon atom was to become the mediator of biological value, but at that time, it was just "dead" inorganic matter. And still is from matter's point of view.) The Israelites did adopt his message and it became what you call "a routinized charismatic message" (ritual).

Maggie again:

"Here is the question again, context from the paragraphs above: what is the second person's (the follower's) experience? I'm asking about the important, meaningful experience that sets the relationship. Is it a Dynamic Quality event, or an intellectual Quality event? Or a social Quality event? I expect that most of us think (or have thought) it is Dynamic Quality. Do you still think so?"

If I stick to my example, the followers' experience was definitely a social event; at that moment, their society was transformed from a multi-God nomadic tribe into God's own people, which they felt was very good. If they had experienced it as bad social value, Moses would have been chased away, and nobody would have heard of it later. But it is just as valid today. In our capacity as biological bodies, we experience only good or bad biological value; as social beings, we experience good or bad social value, and as intellects, we experience good or bad intellectual value. If it is very good, we may even call it truth.

To respond to your intriguing questions was good intellectual value.

Maggie:

Bo, many thanks for the "red pencil." I have used most of it. The ocean and wave simile is awesome. I think it's perfect for beginners, too. I really like the one-word definitions. In speaking to a beginner, that's the way to go.

I'm going to push back on "societies." The more I look at the social level, the more I think it's not societies that comprise this level, but the particular types of behavior (mores and habits, unconscious imitation) that are this level's "substance." In describing this I am stuck with:

Static Social Value (socially proscribed interactions and reactions) The closest one word description I can find is "habits." There's got to be something better, something that includes the connotation of "imitation," but my thesaurus is no help.

Note that this is one of the concepts that really excite me within MOQ. We have this entire evolutionary level that is practically invisible within our language and our ideas. When its effects are mixed in with the effects of the biological and the intellectual, as they usually are, we have so much contradiction and lack of pattern. When separated out, directions and results are infinitely clearer.

Of course, maybe the reason I can't put a one-word label on the social level is that it's the level I am most involved with. I really needed to see these listed with intellectual level on top, so I flipped them:

Static Intellectual Value (Ideas)

Static Social Value (Socially proscribed interactions and reactions)

Static Biological Value (Life)

Static Inorganic Value (Matter)

I decided to leave the "Quality Event" completely out of the introduction. If I actually use QE in my paper, it will have to be pointed to, but what it is might have to be inferred from use, because any explanation will turn off the reader. Perhaps I can talk about it later in the paper. If, after reading, the person sees the value of the concept, I can send them to Pirsig.

This wording is from James earlier post:

"Each of these levels offers freedom from the constraints of the lower parent level, but each is also dependent on that parent level for its existence. There are five types of struggle between different levels of Quality: chaotic/inorganic, inorganic/biological, biological/social, social/intellectual, and static/Dynamic."

This piece is from Pirsig (thanks!):

"This last, the Dynamic/static code, says what's good in life isn't defined by society or intellect or biology. What's good is freedom from domination by any static pattern, but that freedom doesn't have to be obtained by the destruction of the patterns themselves." (Lila)

I'm following up with the "introduction" I settled on:

Brief background of the Metaphysics of Quality (MOQ).

The MOQ involves a way of perceiving reality quite different from the subject/object viewpoint that underlies Western thinking and language. The first proposition of the MOQ is that everything is value, and that the primary division is between Dynamic value and static value, not between subjects and objects. The undifferentiated, undefined, pre-existing source of all things is referred to as Dynamic Quality, but in this undifferentiated "ocean," there have formed sets of stable "wave patterns" of which the first is the material universe itself. The MOQ recognizes four such discrete value patterns (other terms are levels, dimensions, and areas). They are, in rising order of good: [64]

Static Intellectual Value (Ideas)

Static Social Value (Socially proscribed interactions and reactions)

Static Biological Value (Life)

Static Inorganic Value (Matter)

Each of these levels offers freedom from the constraints of the lower parent level, but each is also dependent on that parent level for its existence. There are five types of struggle between different levels of Quality: chaotic/inorganic, inorganic/biological, biological/social, social/intellectual, and static/Dynamic.

"This last, the Dynamic/static code, says what's good in life isn't defined by society or intellect or biology. What's good is freedom from domination by any static pattern, but that freedom doesn't have to be obtained by the destruction of the patterns themselves." (Lila)

(This is a very brief summary. The original concept is found in Lila; An Inquiry into Morals)

Anything here that jumps out as just plain wrong?

When I follow through with this project, I want to attribute to the Lila Squad. How is this done? Directly or generally? Do you want me to?

Platt:

The Quality event is neither where static and Dynamic Quality interacts nor where static values of patterns interact with other levels. The Quality event is not an interactive event but a transformative event. It is the event at which the ultimate reality of the world (Quality) is transformed:

From the one to the many

From the sensation of self to the perception of other

From chaos to pattern

From potential to actual
From unity to relativity
From simultaneity to duality
From present to past
From primacy to derivative
From the Big Now to the Great Divide
From the ineffable to the expressible.

The Quality event is the Organizing Principle of the world, creating patterns and relationships upon which the world became structured and upon which it depends for survival. The QE is the initial, primal static latch required for the world to see itself, to engage in the play of lila, to understand itself.

What the world understands now is the Metaphysics of Oops: the philosophy of science that asserts the world came into being because it just happened, the result of the Principle of Chance. It is known in everyday life simply as: whatever.

What the world will eventually come to understand is the Metaphysics of Quality: the philosophy of Robert Pirsig that asserts the world came into being because it was right that it do so, the result of the Principle of Goodness. It is known in everyday life simply as beautiful.

Doug:

I found the following on the Quality event in SODV (Subjects, Objects, Data and Values paper):

"In the Metaphysics of Quality the world is composed of three things: mind, matter, and Quality. Because something is not located in the object does not mean that it has to be located in your mind. Quality cannot be independently derived from either mind or matter. But it can be derived from the relationship of mind and matter with each other. Quality occurs at the point at which subject and object meet. Quality is not a thing. It is an event. It is the event at which the subject becomes aware of the object. And because without objects there can be no subject, quality is the event at which awareness of both subjects and objects is made possible. Quality is not just the result of a collision between subject and

189

object. The very existence of subject and object themselves is deduced from the Quality event. The Quality event is the cause of the subjects and objects, which are then mistakenly presumed to be the cause of the Quality!"

And:

"The most striking similarity between the Metaphysics of Quality and Complementarity is that this Quality event corresponds to what Bohr means by 'observation' When the Copenhagen Interpretation 'holds that the unmeasured atom is not real, that it's attributes are created or realized in the act of measurement,' (Herbert xiii) it is saying something very close to the Metaphysics of Quality. The observation creates the reality." [65]

And:

"...The possibility or tendency for an event to take place has a kind of reality—a certain intermediate layer of reality— [66] halfway between the massive reality of matter and the intellectual reality of the idea or the image...it is formulated quantitatively as probability and subject to mathematically expressible laws of Nature (quoted in Jammer)."

You should also read Bo's treatise on the "Quality Event." For me, the above paragraphs say it in a way upon which I cannot improve other than to express my own models, examples, and other interpretations.

Without the QE, we get no latching. Without the QE, we get no SPoVs. Without the QE Ss and Os (wouldn't exist in the first place, but if they did) are forever unaware of each other. There is no MOQ reality without the QE. Without the QE, there is no Quality! DQ is profuse, unending, massively parallel, ubiquitous QEs spawning the SQ we call SPoVs.

Bodvar:

I notice that you refer to Pirsig's SODV in your response to Maggie's "Quality Event" request. Okay, nothing wrong with that and quite natural as the QE is treated there, but ever since I saw this paper, I had a feeling that it was attempt from Pirsig's side to

190

make himself understood by an unprepared audience. Nothing wrong by that either—he retreats to the ZMM argumentation stage to make the same impact as this book had on so many readers. You will notice that the cited passage similar to the "getting hotter" on page 233 (of my Corgi paperback).

If one analyses what he says it ends with the assertion that Quality is the cause of subjects and objects, but the opening (the world is composed of three things) easily gives one the impression that subjects and objects are the major components of reality while Quality is a third entity outside of the two. In Lila, however, this trinity is discarded! Doug enters his favourite field of quantum mechanics and compares the MOQ with complementarity and says that QE corresponds to what Bohr calls "observation." All right, Doug surely put this inside the Quality context, but to an "uninitiated" this sound as if the human mind (consciousness) brings the unmeasured particle to materialize, and this is mind/matter, not Dynamic/static, interaction.

The absurdity of the SOM is lifted because Quality "mechanics" says the big divide of existence is not between subject and object but between Dynamism and permanence! But this lands the MOQ into its own dualistic problem. How does the Dynamic/static interaction take place? What "mechanism" is involved? This is what Maggie asks about.

My answer is that the static patterns of the lower levels are more or less unyielding (there is no interaction). The laws of Nature (inorganic value) are the most static values in the world; no wonder, they are the world! Life is less so, but still rather permanent. The value of social cooperation, as such, is also ineradicable, but communal configurations change in big or small scale (politics), and in my answer to Maggie, I call the social leaders' visions "Quality events." Finally the intellect—I have the impression that this level still is regarded identical to the Mind (of SOM) and that it is here that the exotic Quality event is supposed to take place in the deep recesses of quantum size lineaments. (Supposedly to keep the world from disappearing!)

As I understand the Quality idea, the intellectual level is the most Dynamic one (the most free), but nevertheless static. The resemblance to Mind of SOM is because thoughts/language are the "carriers" of intellectual ideas, opinions, etc. Because these patterns change rapidly, one gets the impression that they are Dynamic—and volatile they are—but while they last they are static. And isn't much of our thinking pretty static? The SOM track is so deep worn that our train of thoughts coasts along in circles, but thanks to Pirsig there is now a switching point.

Doug:

I checked ZMM. The phrase "Quality event" occurs three times in ZMM. The phrase is not present in Lila. The word "event" is in Lila, but not in relation to Quality event. I know the phrase appears in Bo's treatise, and it also appears in SODV. On the trinity, I think Pirsig retained it and described it in Lila as, "The value is between the stove and the oaths. Between the subject and the object lies the value." (Page 76 of the Bantam paperback.) This is sVo and SOQ, do you agree?

Bodvar:

Pirsig used the word "trinity" in ZMM, but not in Lila. The objection from my side is the term's implication of three equally real/important entities (as in the Christian religion). Yes, you are correct about the "hot stove" example, but this is also an interim stage. He soon goes on to say that only value is.

Doug:

I did not do this, as you said above: "Then Doug enters his favourite field of quantum mech. and compare the MOQ with complementarity and say that QE corresponds to what Bohr calls observation." Look carefully. I quoted Pirsig's words directly from the SODV paper. Pirsig said that, I did not! [67] As it happens, I agree with that view. Based on modern QM it is correct. I see this and I think Pirsig does too. That view distinguishes classical and quantum science; classical science has no values except the ones Pirsig delineates in SODV, and quantum science is values (the probabilistic interactions of wave patterns).

192

Yes, Bo, you are right. Pirsig and I put that in the MOQ context. For the following segment, assume I am in the MOQ context. Further, assume that I intuit MOQ's DQ/sq first dichotomy of reality. Bo, you have told us often, and rightly, that you fear the SO dichotomy. And above you say you fear misinterpretation of SODV by the uninitiated. That fear appears to have the effect of you wanting to avoid the use of the words Subject and Object. I think if you could trust us to be in the MOQ context without reverting to SOM, your fear might subside, right?

That brings me to the SOQ/sVo topic. From my MOQ perspective, MOQ unifies S and O under SQ division of Quality. Pirsig spends much energy in Lila on this very idea. He used the four SPoVs as a mapping to (and unification of) S and O. That allows MOQites (I like this term, Platt!) to instantly correlate Inorganic to Object (a.k.a. Matter) and Intellectual to Subject (a.k.a. Mind) when talking with a SOM-lander, while retaining the glue of the two intermediate levels. I think this is imperative for us to intuit, because it is a critical success factor (CSF) enabling us to evolve a SOMlander into MOQland. It also allows us to more easily transcribe SOM to MOQ and vice versa (mandatory for context retention).

We need to be able to move back and forth at will. One of you has already said this: "I wish SOM would just go away, but it won't!" So, we must not fear SOM. We must subsume it in that tiny corner of the MOQ where it belongs. MOQ is better than SOM! Pirsig's SOQ unifies S and O very simply in Quality. We need this metaphor to assist us in our shuffling twixt MOQ and SOM. SVo unifies S and O in Value. This metaphor makes it easy for us to derive SQ patterns and infer DQ and its Platt-ineffability from Quality and then subdivide sq into the four SPoV levels while retaining the mapping to S and O.

Bo, I agree that a SOM-lander might interpret SOQ and think in a SOM manner with S and O separate and Q outside them. We have to use SOQ as a means of introducing Q into their thoughts. Just this simple meme is incredibly powerful! It is impossible to look at SOQ without merging them in countless simple ways. This is a first step. A brilliant teacher once used this technique upon a large group of quantum physicists.

Consider the genius of Pirsig to use the one word (Quality) while every human on earth intuits its meaning and ponders its ineffability! Then subsuming S and O by connecting Q. The SOM-landers don't even know what has hit them! That is an incredible advantage for MOQ!

Bo, you are concerned about some of us falling back into SOM. More important than that, I think we need to worry about helping the SOM-landers ascend into MOQ. Pirsig and we need the SOQ metaphor to do that! Once you achieve that, sVo takes you to the next step. Wow!

I have much more to say about this, but it takes too much space and too much of your precious time reading. Bottom line: we need S and O and the mapping of S and O to MOQ's static values to subsume SOM and proselytize MOQ. (All of the above with utmost respect to each member of TLS.)

What do you think, Bo? Does this make sense?

Bodvar:

Yes, lots of sense. After this, I have no worry that you, Doug, have missed any points. Thanks for launching this clarification "mission," and for bearing with my self-appointed role as the "Great Inquisitor."

Doug:

I am looking for the possible ways which TLS can buttress MOQ. Parables are powerful! The new science, to me, has many parables to MOQ. I want (us) to find them. A really fun read which eliminates a lot of "rust" is The Quantum Universe, by Tony Hey and Patrick Walters, Cambridge Press. Lots of pictures and lay level descriptions of what QM is all about. Some other neat historical stuff here too. Isn't it amazing what Maggie has wrought? What a thread!

Maggie:

Many, many, many thanks for your thoughtful and insightful comments. Instead of replying individually at this point, I am going to try and post the work in progress I'm doing that makes use of them. I'm looking at the leader/follower relationship. Here's my starting concept:

The leader/follower relationship is a social pattern that utilizes the non-social behavior or insight of one person to mediate the social patterns of a group, giving freedom from the constraints of static social patterns by creating new ones. This piece started out as a "reaction paper," a homework assignment in a Group Dynamics class. Although I suspect it might be quite different before I'm done, I'm leaving it in that form for now.

You guys are so clear on explanations that I have taken your exact words in many cases. At this point, I'm not even trying to deal with attributing who said what, as that seems like an issue for later, just so you know. In most cases, I took your advice, in some I have gone counter to it. I hope that if, after reading, you still think or feel differently than I do, you will push back. I'm trying to hammer out something, and there's still a lot of hammering to be done.

Another Question [November 1997]

Martin:

I have another question that I just thought of while I was reading Lila again. Each level is evolutionarily advanced from the ones above because it is more free. Dynamic Quality is of course absolute freedom and spontaneity, and all values are trying to reach it (because it is the ultimate Good). Biological values are more free than physical values because they are the first values to be given the ability to not exist. Physical values are strict and rigid and cannot disappear, only change form. Biological values introduce the freedom to exist or not exist, just as a thing can be alive or not alive.

Intellectual values are above social values because they give the freedom of will and the freedom of individuality (among other things). But, what allows social values to be above biological

195

values? It seems that social values do not introduce more freedom, but rather, they take it away. [68] Social values are all about life values adhering to rules, regulations, laws, mores, principles, belief systems, relationships, etc.

Social values are above biological values because social values introduced language, giving awareness freedom to express and manipulate sensory data not physically present. Pirsig is quite clear about language being a social pattern when he tackles the mind/matter platypus in Lila, Chapter 12: "Mental patterns do not originate out of inorganic Nature. They originate out of society, which originates out of biology, which originates out of inorganic Nature. And, as anthropologists know so well, what a mind thinks is as dominated by social patterns as social patterns are dominated by inorganic patterns. There is no direct scientific connection between mind and matter. As atomic physicist, Niels Bohr, said, 'We are suspended in language.' Our intellectual description of Nature is always culturally derived."

Hugo:

My thoughts on this are a little different (if they are contrary to Pirsig please enlighten me). If Dynamic Quality is the source of everything, like Anaximander's Apeiron (the limitless), then how can it also be the goal? [69] As a source, a potency, of origin, "absolute freedom" can be used to describe the idea that "anything is possible" in the sense of "the freedom of no constraints." When some actuality springs from this source, this "freedom of no constraints" is gone, transformed into a "constrained and founded freedom."

The actual serves both as a constraint on the freedom of potency, and as the founding of not previously accessible possibilities, hence I don't find the "absolute freedom" metaphor to be quite adequate. Let me give an analogy in form of the famous Danish toy, Lego. Initially we have a homogeneous plastic substance, and we are absolutely free to give it any form we like. We choose to make a Lego brick form and produce little Lego bricks.

These actual bricks now found and constrain our freedom; we cannot any longer reach the possibility of playing ping pong with little plastic balls made from our original plastic substance. This is a constraint, but we are free to construct a host of new possible forms based on the new substance of our actual bricks; this is the new freedom founded by the actualization of Lego bricks. And, of course, had we chosen to make little plastic ping pong balls, this would have constrained us from building toy houses and so forth.

Get rid of the conscious choice above and insert a "spontaneous breaking of symmetry," or some other term for a divide with no conscious choice involved, and this is a fair analogy of my view on Quality as a source of origin. Do note the use of the Aristotelian terms substance and form here, used in the analytical sense he intended, and not in the absolute sense of material and idea later adopted. And the "potency act" analytical tool is Aristotelian too, alas.

Following my outline, we have to look both for the constraints imposed by social relations, and the new possibilities they found. Social relations are what make our societies possible in the first place—this we cannot close our eyes to. I will give an example, which presupposes the view that sociality is to be found in most of life, not only in higher animals or humans. Life on earth, the Dynamic system of interrelating organisms, which we may, with some sense of awe and wonder, call Gaia, is a Dynamic structure resting on social patterns. [70]

The speedy flight of the hare and the conning ability of the fox are aspects of one and the same social relation, which has evolved through co-evolution. This wonderful Dynamic relation (if you are not the prey) between prey and predator is not the result of some kind of neo-Darwinian optimization towards a fixed goal; it is the result of the evolution of mutual representations, the evolution of social values. [71]

Martin:

Now about your example of social values—I don't understand what advantage that situation gave to the prey and predator. What possibilities and freedoms do they enjoy? What's so much better about it? [72]

Hugo:

I am not talking in the language of neo-Darwinian adaptation. I am saying that in order for there to be prey and predators at all, there has to be social relations. What might confuse you is that I use my own definition of the social level, which I have put forward in previous mails. In short, what characterizes the biological level is representative relations, as opposed to the simple relations of the physical level; what characterizes the social level is mutually representative relations, and what characterizes the intellectual level is self-representative relations (self consciousness).

I am aware that this is not at all agreed upon by others on the Lila Squad, and perhaps Pirsig would disagree too. But this structure is not coming solely from the philosophy of Pirsig. And I think that we have to be careful not to be too reductionistic and think that the four levels of Pirsig will be sufficient to understand the complexity of Nature.

For instance, there has been some done work on hierarchy theory, which I am trying to utilize at the moment, and it looks like this work has been focusing mainly on levels of social relations (in my sense). You probably know the usual sort of systems theory levels, where a new level arises and is maintained via the interrelations of objects on the first level, and so on. These theories have had severe difficulties with describing Nature—I know because I have been trying to use them.

Anyway, the point I wish to make is that we have to work with a hierarchy of levels within the social level, if we are to approach a useful theory of the levels of Nature. And my taking a different stand than others on where we can find the social level stems from our not being sufficiently aware of the fact that we are concerned with different levels of the social hierarchy in our arguments.

Martin:

Organisms living on their own have to spend every waking moment of their lives just trying to stay alive. The introduction of social values, by way of societies, gives living organisms greater freedom because they don't have to spend all their time just trying to stay alive. When people formed civilizations they had enough spare time to start asking religious/philosophical questions.

Hugo:

I agree that there are these "founding" aspects of society as well as the constraining aspects. But we have to be wary of judging certain aspects of life, good or bad, because the judging depends on where you take your stand. There is no biological value in being a prey, but there is social value. Our world is not a cute Disney World—there is killing and eating in Nature too—and what I am saying is that we could not have our wonderful world (we would not be here) if not for the social relations of prey and predator, or plant and herbivore, or host and parasite, or mutualism (mutually beneficial, to the organisms relations). Gaia is a structure built on social value—it is the mutual relations between organisms that make for the complexity of ecosystems.

Gaia is a society in the sense that all the organisms are mainly dependent on each other, and not only on physical Nature, for sustained existence. This, I believe, there can be no doubt about.

Platt:

I like "absolute potential freedom." My description of Dynamic Quality is "undivided present awareness." Putting the two together, we get "APFUPA" (pronounced appfoopah). Absolute Potential Freedom of Undivided Present Awareness. I can't think of a shorter, simpler, better description of Dynamic Quality.

Ken:

Hugo, with regard to your statement that there is no social value in being a prey, I think it can be interpreted as being that there is a social value "to the group" in being a prey. I think that the whole predatorprey relationship is the foundation on which the biological level is founded. Without the regulating function of the predator-prey relationship the system would be unworkable. In a sense, I think Lovelock's Daisy World bears this out. If we consider the ambient temperature to be the predator then predation would be beneficial to Daisy society as a whole.

I would be interested in your interpretation of how human sentience fits into this picture. I have a little trouble with it myself. I think that the picture of the interdependence of groups of organisms in the biological level is a beautiful picture of mutually interdependent benefit although admittedly hard on some of the individuals. If we wanted to stretch a point, we could consider disease organisms from the biological levels as being beneficial to humans as a group.

Hugo:

Yes, I do recognize this point, and I am not at all clear on this myself. I don't know if we can consider disease organisms straight out beneficial to humankind, but they are part of a stable relationship that we cannot get rid of. I am in fact worried that our efforts toward civilisation has made us vulnerable by changing this relationship in ways we have not been sufficiently aware of. Despite the commercialization of the idea, disease organisms seem to have benefited immensely in terms of world wide spreading from our present way of life, and our limited powers of medical defense is becoming evident. But perhaps we should not discuss such depressing topics.

Ken:

I find James Lovelock's idea of Gaia, the Earth as the living organism, powerfully attractive and can't help thinking in those terms most of the time. From that point of view, I don't find these sorts of ideas depressing at all. Instead, I find them stimulating. Although we have the ability to stave them off, in my view we are not exempt from the same forces and pressures that operate to control the other levels of life. If Gaia survives our assaults upon it, and I think it will although perhaps in a much-altered form, then we are probably not the last word in evolution. If we accept the current idea of the expected life of the solar system, then we represent the infancy of the evolutionary process and there is a lot of time to go. I think it is human hubris that compels us to separate ourselves from the biological level.

An unjustified assumption perhaps? It seems to me that the Lila Squad is too dismissive of the implications of the inorganic and biological levels of the Quality idea. In my mind, these are the origins and sources of all else and the social and intellectual levels should entertain no ideas that conflict with these more fundamental levels. Somewhere in the philosophical construct of the MOQ, we should make provisions for the continued existence, if not the health, of the biosphere. I don't know where I am going with this. I am just writhing around trying to fit the good ideas of the MOQ with the necessary ideas of the biosphere. The MOQ is good but I don't see much conflict resolution going on right now.

Any term that you wish to use that encompasses the biosphere will not alter the meaning. It will save a lot of time if we speak plainly to each other instead of speaking elliptically to spare each other's feelings. This is what I have done and I invite you to do the same.

Mark:

Hi, I'm new so please be patient with me!

I agree with your concerns. When I read your post the concept of banishment from the Garden of Eden came to mind. I'm sure it's not original, but it never crystallized in those terms for me. Indeed, we are woefully out of tune with our biosphere; it's almost unnatural, as if we're not of this planet in many respects. Lost sheep.

The power of Pirsig's philosophy is its secularism. Religion has divided our world. Championing one over another leads to war and hatred yet we need a belief system that can only be called a religion to survive. We need to lead the flock back to faith in Good, in God. Lila offers a path back that appeals to the disenfranchised of the world, the people who see truth as the ultimate reality, the intellectually minded, the victims of hypocrisy, and so on. Lila is a compelling argument for the atheist and agnostic.

Long way to go, yes. Ultimately, I hope to see common themes from all religions on which we can unite. Obviously any belief system should contain both static and Dynamic qualities to allow for evolution. Religion today is frightened of this Dynamic. ("Nothing scares the Bishop more than the presence of a Saint in the congregation.") Pirsig pointed to the blueprint of such a belief system but it's up to the world to construct it.

So, I see Pirsig's philosophy as a secular compass that points towards spiritual healing. All of this benefits Gaia. Every last bit of it. Seeing ourselves as connected to one another and all being composed of the same stuff enables us to transform from planet exploiters to planet stewards.

Ken:

Ken here. Welcome Mark. I, too, am interested in applying Pirsig to the human condition. I am still struggling with Lila, in particular how the static patterns of value with their attendant morals and values and "the good," will apply to Gaia, biological ethics, etc., and present day society at the same time. Value and morals are so difficult to define in this context that it is very daunting to me. At present, I have not much to assert but I will do my best to "discuss" if you will throw out the bait. As of now, I am not even sure what constitutes a new thread unless it is just the subject line. Welcome to us.

If we can agree on what truths we are speaking of—that is, I am not speaking of who swiped the cash from the cash box, but truth as it relates to the story of the Universe—then I think that we can equate truth and good without contradiction.

Your thought about banishment from the Garden of Eden jarred with a previously unrealized recognition. It immediately suggests that because of our egocentric concept of humanity we have banished ourselves from the Garden of Eden. It settles nicely into my vision of our situation. I am in agreement that, given the overriding requirement that the needs of the biosphere be met, the reestablishment of the Garden of Eden is a desirable aim. In that case Pirsig's Metaphysics of Quality is a concept that I have no

202

argument with. I am still of the opinion that the concept of Dynamic Quality will only alter the ethical drift of humanity for the good when the Good gains the numerical upper hand since Dynamic Quality operates for everyone and is only a force for good when the previous platform of static quality of the individual encourages that selection of consciousness which tends toward the Good. If that makes sense.

Mark:

You make excellent sense. And how does that individual select something that is essentially outside of our current mythos? By becoming aware of the distinction between the Good and the True. We pledge faith to the Church of Reason today; things of value do not exist—they're "whatever you like." In order for us to see Good, we need to step outside this mythos into the realm of insanity (like Pirsig). That's why a community of folks stepping outside the mythos is far easier to handle than individuals without support.

Environmental activism is working and working well in many cases because of people who intuitively know it's right. But many more are literally taught to ignore those feelings over truths. Others rationalize these feelings as idealistic and impractical. But that numerical upper hand is happening, Ken. I feel it.

Ken:

I am not sure whether you believe in an immortal soul or not. You didn't make that clear. I prefer not to believe that because not only is it a crushing burden for us to bear but it opens the door for too much contention and strife. It is my belief that we didn't have a choice in the matter of being here but now that we are it is our responsibility to care for this fragile blue planet and the other life forms that depend on our good judgment. Our children and grandchildren and theirs, and theirs, will be profoundly affected by the decisions that we make during our tenure. I don't mean this to sound grim because I think that it is exhilarating for us to contemplate this process in which we are embedded. The contemplation of the operation of the Universe as we understand it today is a source of wonder and awe to me and I believe that if everyone understood that story we would be living in a Garden of Eden. I have no objection to a God as long as He does not interfere with that process, but I also have no fear or regret at the thought that I will be returning to contribute my bit to sustaining Gaia.

Mark:

I'd like to hear your ideas on why this notion is a crushing burden. I do believe in a soul, which transcends our physical self. I see this reality as liberating and empowering rather than a burden. Granted, extremist like some Hindus who take their lives knowing they'll return is wrong. Fear of death evokes our egocentricity more than acceptance of the soul. Anyway, help me see what you mean.

God interfere? He's the source and substance of you and I and Gaia. By the way, here you say you will be returning. Perhaps your point above is that you do believe in a soul.

Ken:

If you have time read the last couple of pages of the article [http://www.moq.org/forum/personalview.html] that I posted on the forum, I think that will explain my position better than I can here at the moment. At 72, my mind is not as agile as it once was. Let me say for those of you who are still young enough to be immortal that for me it has gotten even better as I get older. Don't be discouraged; it gets better all the time.

Platt:

I would tentatively suggest to you, however, that even though Pirsig doesn't specifically refer to Gaia, nor could anyone accuse him of being an environmental activist, he does warn against a higher level destroying a lower one. At the end of Chapter 13 in Lila, he talks about how intellect is threatening society and says, "An evolutionary morality says it is moral for intellect to do so, but also contains a warning. Just as a society that weakens its people's physical health endangers its own stability, so does an intellectual pattern that weakens and destroy its social base also endanger its own stability."

204

It seems to me that where you emphasize the risk to society of ignoring biological deterioration, I could with equal vigor emphasize the risk to society of intellectual arrogance, that is, others knowing what's good for you more than you do and enforcing their moral superiority through the strong arm of a trooper with a gun. In fact, for me that is indeed a more clear and present danger to society than the health of Gaia. Be that as it may, I see our respective views as complimentary rather than opposing with both fitting comfortably into Pirsig's metaphysical structure.

One sentence in your letter really jumped out and bit me: "He (Lovelock) did this to counter the charge of teleology that was directed at his concept by other scientists." Now if there's one thing that destroys the MOQ it is the charge of teleology. Science has such paranoia about any hint of God that they will summarily dismiss, usually with condescending giggles and smirks, any suggestion that the universe has a purpose.

What bothers me so much about this is that old bugaboo, intellectual arrogance. Many scientists seem to think that they are the new Gods, standing somewhere outside of the universe, dispensing knowledge to the great-unwashed multitudes. It never seems to occur to these masters of the universe that they were created by the universe, are part and parcel of it, and exhibit purpose galore. Even they, when pressed to the wall by their vaunted logic, will have to admit they have a purpose in saying the universe has no purpose.

I get up on the soapbox about this because I believe strongly in the MOQ. And make no mistake about it, the MOQ is teleological. It says that evolution occurred not by accident, but by the drive for Quality. Pirsig asserts as much in no uncertain terms. "Natural Selection is Dynamic Quality." (Lila, Chapter 11)

Well, I hope you'll be patient to me for sounding off. In my previous letter, I said I felt a kinship with you on account of age. Now I feel a further kinship on account of intellect.

Ken:

Thank you for your kind words. I am just glad that we were able to make our respective positions clear enough to each other to see that we are not very far apart. I was just struggling to make my concept of both the Metaphysics of Quality and my concept of Gaia fit together philosophically. I looked up your Lila reference and I agree with you that it covers my uneasiness. Pirsig could not possibly cover every detail in depth but he seems to have pointed the way in every case so far. I think that I have pushed this thread far enough. It is time to get back to the business of understanding Quality.

I agree that science has become so compartmented that most fields are working with blinders on. Not many people are looking at the broad sweep and trying to tie things together. That's one of the things I admire about Lovelock. He has rejected the regimentation and the scurrying for grants and has financed his researches out of his own pocket. I think he is teaching us more than most even if you don't agree with all of his ideas—a fascinating rebel oddball.

One thing I am not sure of in your mention of teleology. I am not sure whether you are thinking of a guiding intelligence in the operation of Quality or whether you would be content with goal seeking. I absolutely agree that the Metaphysics of Quality is goal seeking but I do not believe that it is purposeful. By goal seeking, I mean that processes respond in an adaptive or conforming way to stimuli. For instance, in summer my skin tans in the sun to reduce the reaction to the radiation. In winter, I turn whiter to allow greater interaction between my skin and the sun's radiation.

I consider this to be goal seeking. If my skin follows the same procedure in response to directions from some higher intelligence or being, I consider this to be purposeful. The latter case is what I call teleology. This I do not agree with, although I do not object if other people feel more comfortable with purpose. As with you and the arrogant scientists, I only object if those other people insist that I must believe the way they do. I think you are correct in saying that evolution is goal seeking. I think this applies to the entire history of the universe, as we now understand it.

I am in complete agreement with you that evolution was propelled by the drive for Quality. In MOQ terms we are living in a sea of Dynamic Quality whose thrust is toward the Good or greater understanding. Still with as many starting levels as there are people but now we have an understandable function in which to operate. I am on my second drink and running off at the fingers. Let me know what you think.

Platt:

I'm content with goal seeking rather than purpose if, as you say, purpose implies an intelligence in the image of a personified God in Heaven directing the activities of everything down here on Earth. But, my dictionary says nothing about intelligence in its definition of teleology. Instead, it says, "Purposeful development, as in Nature or history, toward a final end." In your example of skin responding to stimuli, I would say the goal or final end is survival, which, according to Darwinian evolution, is the guiding principle of history, as, summed up in the phrase, "History is that which survives."

Pirsig takes on Darwinian theory in Lila, Chapter 11, by asking the question that Darwin and his fellow scientists dare not ask: "Why survive?" The Metaphysics of Quality was built as an answer to that question. Pirsig's conclusion is neatly captured in Chapter 30 in a sentence: "Dharma is Quality itself, the principle of 'rightness' which gives structure and purpose to the evolution of all life and to the evolving understanding of the universe which life has created."

That little question "Why?" is what separates metaphysics from physics. We agree that Pirsig's answer is better than anything we've found so far. As you said, "Evolution was propelled by the drive for Quality," to which I would add, "guided by the principle of rightness." Perhaps that's redundant, but it helps clarify the fundamental assumption of the MOQ in my mind.

By contrast, the fundamental assumption of science is that "evolution is propelled by chance," what I call the "Philosophy of Oops." So now we have three basic explanations of existence: God, Good, and Chance. It's very easy for me to equate God with Good for I recall the grace that was said at our table when I was a child—"God is great and God is good, and we thank You for this food." Christians say, "God is Love," which by my lights is the same as God is Good. So, I have no problem with people saying God is the creator as long as God is not a captive of any one social pattern, i.e., religion. Likewise, I would not want to see Gaia elevated to the level of God as I fear some environmental activists would have us to do—Gaia being a biological pattern.

If God and Good are considered the same, that leaves Chance as the only other viable explanation for creation. Whenever science was challenged to explain how Chance could be the basis of order, they had a knockdown reply: "How else can you explain it?" Now Pirsig has given us a knockdown answer, the Metaphysics of Quality. Not only does it explain creation, but it dissolves the inherent puzzles and paradoxes (Pirsig's famous "platypi") that have haunted the scientific worldview since its inception.

However, I give great credit to science for coming to the realization, with their discovery of the quantum world, that their philosophical edifice of Chance was built on sand and that their precious "mechanisms" for explaining the world (such as neural synapses explaining consciousness) are fundamentally wrong. What they discovered instead at the very base of existence was observation, i.e., awareness, i.e., Dynamic Quality, i.e., pure experience uncontaminated by thought. Thanks to excellent posts here on the Lila Squad by Doug and others (which you may not have had a chance to see) I've learned that quantum physics fully supports the MOQ.

Well, you can see how your thoughts spark my own. The sparking I take to be a form of Dynamic Quality, not necessarily the thoughts. I look forward to your comments.

Logic and Gravity [December 1997]

Anders:

There's no objects or subjects any place in logic. There are just symbols, and rules for manipulating them. And logic is rational thinking par excellence.

Hugo:

So, logic needs no logician? You're suggesting it exists in some objective state free from subjective awareness. Did logic "exist" before Boole? I think Pirsig explored a similar avenue with respect to the law of gravity. If I'm not mistaken, he concluded that the law of gravity did not "exist" before Newton.

Anders:

Well, the phenomenon of gravity most certainly did exist before Newton. I hope we can agree on this. Stuff fell to the ground before Newton. In the same way logic existed before Aristotle (not Boole) put the first theory of logic into writing. People selling goats in the streets of Athens knew that they couldn't contradict themselves in a sentence and at the same time say something true. I mean logic was floating around "unspoken" before Aristotle.

It is certainly a viable point of view to think of contradictions not as false, but rather as senseless but that's not relevant to this discussion. But in any event, this doesn't even relate to our discussion, because the theory of gravity most certainly deals with objects as opposed to subjects, and therefore supports the subject/object schism.

Mark:

Sorry to appear tangential to your original thread, but you are using the terms "subject" and "object" in an unusual way for me. Could you please help me understand? Do you agree that "subject" implies the self and "objects" are all that is not self? [73]

Anders:

Well, yes.

Mark:

From ZMM, we know that you and logic are "One" thing-Quality. It is only our dualistic conventions that separate the two for convenience. [74]

Anders:

Yes, everything is Quality, but we can't really get very far with just this idea. We have to make cuts into Quality and divide it to get anything useful.

Mark:

If you are saying that logic deals with things that are not subjects or objects, then, according to Pirsig, you have defined Quality.

Anders:

I don't understand this objection.

Mark:

Logic is not the source and substance of all things (thankfully). If you are trying to say that, look, logic exists independent of any thinker, you are espousing dualistic thinking. So, if you are saying none of these, then you have a different definition for "subject" and "object." This is where I would like help.

Anders:

Logic exists in the same way as gravity does. When we go throughout the world, we perceive quality, and this immediate experience we split into different things. The primary split is that in most quality perceptions there's an "I," and a "something that is not I" (subject and object-I leave the door ajar for the possibility that there is Quality from which no subject and object can be abstracted). And the "some things that are not I" can again be divided into a great many things.

The use of this kind of language is wrong, but necessary. I can't really say that "we" walk around in "the world" perceiving Quality, because "we" and "the world" are abstracted from the Quality itself so really there's only the pure perception (Quality), but it will do.

But we have many perceptions, and we (both as the human race, and as a personal development from infant to adult) have found out that certain patterns exist in these perceptions. There are objects that exhibit stable behaviour. I have perceptions that I can only communicate to you by referring to as objects. I see my computer standing on top of my table, and a heap of books and clothes lying around on the floor, etc. Some of these stable patterns are what we call objects (tables, computers, other peoples bodies, books, etc.) and others are like gravity.

How the two kinds differ is not entirely clear to me. Perhaps gravity is harder to find because its always there, while the books and stuff, I only perceive when Im in my room. I don't know. But logic is to utterances and sentences like gravity is to objects. Whenever you are in a situation with a physical object, gravity acts on it, and whenever you want to make yourself understood, you have to obey logic. It's so universal that it's hard to see.

While logic per definition doesn't deal with objects or subjects, it does deal with the truthfulness of sentences.

Hugo:

This last is a very complex statement. I think I disagree with you and I will try to explain why and how. Logic was first made explicit by Aristotle, and, given my present knowledge of this, logic arose in connection with his work on the categories: his structuring the world in a non-contradictory way. And by non-contradictory I don't intend to say that logic arises from language (which would be a circular argument) but that logic arises as an integrated part of the very nature of representing, whether in language or pre-linguistic. So, is logic something that exists independently of this categorical structuring, or does it arise as an integrated part of such structuring? I would say the latter, and saying this I distinguish myself from the Platonist view of logic and mathematics, which asserts the first.

To paint with the big brush, I take geometry to arise from the ideas of the position and movement of objects, numbers to arise from the idea of "same kind" of objects, and logic to arise from the idea of "different kinds" of objects. If we make a certain structure of representation of the world, like Aristotle did, that structure embodies a certain logic, this logic distinguishing the unambiguous from the ambiguous structure. And the logic embodied in an objective structuring is what we call subject predicate logic, or so is my conjecture. In other words, structuring the world as things with properties embodies the logic we know from Aristotle, which is the logic we use every day.

Moving beyond this "thingish" structure, we cannot avoid rupturing the logic it is connected with as well. (I am not saying Aristotle did not see this; he may well have, I don't know yet, but we have taken a "thingish" categorical structure as our heritage from Aristotle.)

There is nothing un-MOQ as such in this foundation, the point being that it deals with the static patterns (objects) of Nature. The MOQ merely points out that it neglects the Dynamic part of the world, and—with us being Dynamic creatures—this brings forth a host of problems as long as we insist that it is a complete description of Nature (or, in some other SOM way take it for granted). In other words, these, our tools for handling the objective world, are fine as long as we (or, when we eventually) acknowledge the limits of their application.

I am still not quite clear on how modern logic relates to the logic of Aristotle, but one characteristic seems to be that modern logic insists on that it says nothing on the real world, in contrast to the so called material logic of Aristotle and the scholastics (and I would say, common logic). Modern logic claims to have dismissed of the material intent, or the semantics, to be detached from any ontological implications. If this were true, one might wonder how logic can claim to posses anything like truth. And (I am afraid this discussion takes on more and more issues) if we agree on logic saying something on the truth of sentences, what kind of truth is this? Knowing the origin of logic, I propose that the "truth" of modern logic is unambiguity, per se, nothing more, nothing less. And, if we wish to tangle with the other kind of truth, the empirical truth, the truth which has meaning, which has ontological (or less subject object metaphysical) implications, modern logic has no say on this.

It seems to me our everyday logic is bound up within a "thingish" categorical structure, and, since this logic is the foundation of the rational language we use, it is no surprise that it is extremely difficult to move beyond this particular static intellectual pattern.

The thing I am not quite clear on, is whether rebuilding our structuring of the world, as Pirsig does with his Metaphysics of Quality, has implications for not only the logic we have inherited from Aristotle, but for modern logic as well. But I think the implications are something like this: modern logic is fine as long as we are dealing with "things with properties." But since this "thingish" view of the world is not complete, we shall not take logic to be valid in saying something of the not clearly "thingish." Or, put another way, I think the "thingish" worldview is tacitly presumed in modern logic.

Annotations by Robert M. Pirsig

61. It is the point at which static patterns emerge where there were no static patterns before. It is not a two-way street, and therefore the term "interaction" seems inappropriate.

62. In the case of the military, where deserters are executed by firing squad, you can say that leadership is maintained by the biological and inorganic levels; that is, handcuffs and bullets.

63. In the case of business leaders this would be the paycheck. In the case of elected political leaders, it would be intellectual agreement. Beyond all these there is also "charisma" that seems to be related to Dynamic Quality. Interestingly, this term has theological origins.

64. Descending order?

65. It seems close but I think it is really very far apart. In the Copenhagen Interpretation, and in all subject-object metaphysics, both the observed (the object) and the observer (the subject) are assumed to exist prior to the observation. In the MOQ, nothing exists prior to the observation. The observation creates the intellectual patterns called "observed" and "observer." Think about it. How could a subject and object exist in a world where there are no observations?

66. This is the sort of conclusion that subject-object metaphysics forces one into. In the MOQ, there is only one "layer" of reality: experience.

67. This is difficult to untangle. Bohr's "observation" and the MOQ's "quality event" are the same, but the contexts are different. The difference is rooted in the historic chickenand-egg controversy over whether matter came first and produces ideas, or ideas come first and produce what we know as matter. The MOQ says that Quality comes first, which produces ideas, which produce what we know as matter. The scientific community that has produced Complementarity, almost invariably presumes that matter comes first and produces ideas. However, as if to further the confusion, the MOQ says that the idea that matter comes first is a high quality idea! I think Bohr would say that philosophic idealism (i.e. ideas

before matter) is a viable philosophy since complementarity allows multiple contradictory views to coexist.

68. They introduce freedom from hunger and physical danger, which is far more important than the loss of freedom by rules.

69. Good question. The "Gateless Gate" analogy of the Buddhists may be the answer. In this analogy, as one approaches the gate, it seems to be a goal, but after one has passed through and looks back he sees there never was any gate Translating back into the MOQ, one can say that Dynamic Quality is a goal from a static point of view, but is the origin of all things from a Dynamic understanding.

70. This goes outside the intended MOQ understanding of social.

71. If you expand the meaning of "social" to this kind of generality the whole structure of the MOQ collapses.

72. It is not better. It is worse, because these are biological values not social values.

73. In the MOQ, the static self is composed of both body and mind and thus is both subject and object. It is better to define subject as social and intellectual patterns and object as biological and inorganic patterns. This seems to help prevent confusion later on.

74. Here comes the confusion. To prevent it, it is better to say that logic is a set of rules (i.e. an intellectual pattern) that helps produce high quality in other intellectual patterns.

Chapter 7

"In our highly complex organic state, we advanced organisms respond to our environment with an invention of many marvelous analogues. We invent earth and heavens, trees, stones and oceans, gods, music, arts, language, philosophy, engineering, civilization and science. We call these analogues reality. And they are reality. We mesmerize our children in the name of truth into knowing that they are reality. We throw anyone who does not accept these analogues into an insane asylum. But that which causes us to invent the analogues is Quality. Quality is the continuous stimulus which our environment puts upon us to create the world in which we live. All of it. Every last bit of it." —Robert M. Pirsig, Zen and the Art of Motorcycle Maintenance

Free Will [November 1997]

Dave:

In Lila, is Pirsig saying that Quality is capable of make the distinction between right and wrong? If so, where does that leave free will?

Hugo:

In my view, "free will" is a term that can only be used of selfconscious (self-reflective) creatures. [75] "Will" is a term we may use of any organism—of any autonomous entity—describing the goal involved in autonomy. And "free will" is the ability to change that goal; the ability of an autonomous entity to chose between more than one predetermined (as for that entity) goal. This is the ability following from self-reflection.

In discussing these issues, we have to be very aware of which levels and which systems or entities we are addressing. Hence, while the individual non-self conscious organism has no free will, and thus is predetermined (or static) in terms of the organismic goal, being autonomous implies that it is not predetermined (static) in terms of dynamics or behaviour. Being autonomous involves indeterminacy; we cannot talk of autonomy in a deterministic framework. In order to reach a specific goal you have to be free to avoid the hindrances on your way towards that goal.

We only have the philosophical choice between a completely deterministic world, with no autonomy, no free will, no choice, no love, etc., something utterly incomprehensible to humans I would say, and an indeterministic world in some balance between Dynamic and stasis. Many have sought this balance in a dualistic philosophy of mind and matter, while the Metaphysics of Quality takes this very balance as its foundation.

Returning to your question, it seems to me that the way Pirsig uses the term "moral" goes beyond the use in traditional subjectivist or idealist use of the term. Pirsig uses moral (my interpretation for now) in describing the law of evolution. In order for a new level to establish itself, it has to constrain the level it arises from, be that inorganic, biological, or intellectual. Social dynamics constrains biological dynamics, and this is "justified" because this is the only way social dynamics can exist. Intellectual dynamics constrains social dynamics, as it has to do if there is to be any intellectual dynamics at all.

This, I think, is very different from the ordinary use of the term "moral." And in fact I just discovered Pirsig's use of "moral" (if it is his use) is surprisingly similar to Charles Sanders Peirce's use of "ethics" in a novel way (paraphrasing from his short intellectual autobiography, 1904): "Ethics is concerned with the act and process of control…with investigating the controllable and the uncontrollable as they appear in power and resistance."

Be that as it may, my short answer to your question is that Pirsig's morals say that it is "right" for free will to arise in the course of evolution. I am not sure it says anything on the rights or wrongs involved in different exercises of free will.

Mark:

Morals, according to Pirsig, have everything to say about the rights or wrongs in the different exercises of free will. The hierarchy of values is an ordering of morals. Biological exercises of free will are immoral when they negatively affect social values.

Thus, it is moral to imprison a rapist, but imprisoning a political dissident is immoral. Murder is immoral in any context and so on.

Hugo:

Mark, I am not sure I understand you here. Are you saying that the moral codes of Pirsig's value levels fulfill the role as a working moral for us humans?

Mark:

How can they not? If they do not apply to humans, then why not? Lila was not about natural science, it originally was slated as an anthropologically based novel, remember? Yes, they do fulfill the role of working morals for us, I believe.

Hugo:

And I am not sure I understand your example: "Murder is immoral in any context." Does that mean that killing in defense of yourself or your kin is immoral?

Mark:

Killing is immoral, but someone threatening you or your kin is also immoral. Here we judge what feels like the right thing to do. We defend family and ourselves naturally, but that doesn't change the fact that killing is immoral. We live with having killed someone to save our family. Society does not punish this act as it values life but values family more. So, I was trying to say that the act of murder is immoral in any context, but acceptable to society in some instances.

War is another example. Defending against aggression is moral. Aggression is immoral. This is why our modern industrial society has adopted Orwellian double-speak. Note how our aggressive actions are in "defense" of a population, like the United States invasion of Vietnam, or the Soviet invasion of Afghanistan. They turn an immoral act into a moral one with one word.

That said, killing is immoral, whether defending or not. The act of taking one's freedom to life is depriving him/her of the most fundamental human right of all. But what about life as a slave? We make judgments, moral judgments. The Civil War was horrific. But I believe Lincoln's decision to fight was more moral than not to. Slavery denies freedom. Here the immorality to kill was acceptable over the immorality to enslave. You may disagree and that's fine. As Sophists, we do not engage in dialectic, but we do defend the Good.

Hugo:

And we do in fact imprison political dissidents of the more insisting kind. Take for instance Rote Arme Fraktion in Germany a while ago, or the Nazi's of today. How do we decide, using the morals of Pirsig, when dissidents are to be controlled?

Mark:

Ah, excellent question. Here we can look to Lila. Dynamic Quality values freedom. Freedom is Good. But in Lila, we know that certain controls are necessary; an order is required to judge between freedoms. Society has a right to defend against all intellectual values. Morality is on the side of freedom as long as society survives. Thus if an anarchist speaks out on the total abolition of all laws, society has a right to censor, or rather, to not promote. If someone espouses genocide, society has a right to censor, bar from assembly, even imprison. Now, if someone comes up with a new way to share power, for example, which expands freedoms without destroying society, then morally, it should be adopted. What's this, sharing power? You can see why amorality has been promoted in this century. Here is an example between current morality based on the intellectual movement of the early part of this century and the morality that Lila outlines.

A Frenchman wrote a book that claimed the holocaust did not occur. Public outrage was strident. Some intellectuals rushed to defend him, not the content of his ideas, but his right to say them. This is all in line with amoral, "freedom at any cost," intellectual thinking. But, it is not right, not moral. He should never have been allowed to publish that book. In a MOQ world, a judgment on the Goodness of what he was writing would be made. Is this Good for society that we hear this? The answer is an emphatic No. Note the public knew this intuitively and they were enraged.

Lila says that freedom for freedom's sake is wrong. We must judge freedom in some moral context. Our freedom of speech is Good when it promotes freedoms that do not sacrifice social values. Thus, Sakarov's imprisonment was immoral and neo-Nazi's imprisonment moral.

Good luck convincing the intellectual elite of this. The ace that we hold here is that we approach this from a secular standpoint! That's the brilliance of Lila. If we approached society with these ideas from a Christian context, for example, we'd hear the usual separation of church and state and there's no arguing religion. But, we come to the table with a secular, intellectual argument for morality (which is also intuitive for anyone who has a shred of humanity, in my opinion).

Hugo:

I am not altogether against what you are saying—we have discussed ethics on the Lila Squad before—and I agree that there is a new foundation for ethics in the MOQ. I am just not sure it is quite as simple as your answer above suggests. Could you elaborate a little?

Mark:

Isn't the important idea concerning intellectual patterns of value not when they emerged in society but when they sought freedom from the then dominant social values? Intellectual patterns of values have been around since we have. It has been their position relative to social values, which has only recently changed.

The hierarchy of values is a model more for relative value comparisons and less for evolution itself. That is, it does roughly describe our evolution from inorganic to organic to social to intellectual, but the structure is better suited to describe morality of one level of values over another.

I hesitate to posit that, at some point, no intellectual patterns of value existed. It doesn't make sense; it's not intuitive. If I were to teach a five year old what intellectual patterns of value are, I would say they are simply "ideas." He would likely reply, "Why don't you just call them ideas?" Then I'd stand there dumbfounded. The intellectual movement of the early part of this century cut society adrift with no moral compass. Many organized religions have suffered under the hands of hypocrites. Good people now struggle with what is right! The intellectuals (in service of power) are saying one thing, and the church and Bible are saying one thing and my body is saying one thing and so on.

In Lila, Pirsig has constructed an intellectual theory, which supports a moral order. We have a compass back, delivered by someone we can trust, an intellectual. No Rolex wearing televangelist is calling us sinners here, but make no mistake about it, Lila is a tool for judging. This is anathema to intellectuals and why most of us cringe to hear it. What right do we have to judge? Well, the right to judge for society to survive, the right for people to not to die of hunger or be tortured, the right for our planet to live, and so on. With Lila, we have a solid intellectual support for these decisions. They are not capricious or self-serving; they follow a natural order of Quality.

It shouldn't require arcane definitions to succeed. It begs simplicity. We should be easily able to describe it to that five year old.

Who Is Focusing? [November 1997]

Bodvar:

If the world is composed of values, then who is doing the valuing? [76] No one in the Subject/Object sense, but to a human being who straddles all Quality levels, only one is highlighted at a time. Bodily sensations, needs, or urges (instincts) bring focus to the biological level. Impulses from the social "body" we identify with bring focus to that value plane. In our culture, the focus dwells mostly on the intellect. The attic window glass tints reality, but attention shifts easily.

Ken:

I hesitate to step into this because I am still not sure that I have a good handle on the whole Pirsig framework, but...we, each individual, is doing the valuing. Remember undefined Quality from ZMM? Pirsig demonstrated that everybody knows what

Quality is even though it can't be defined. The Quality for each individual [77] results from that individual's current intellectual state as modified by the Quality event. This is supposed to be a force for good because Quality tends to select the good. There is no independent value or valuer out there. The drift toward value is a result of each individual's conception of value as modified by the Quality event. That is why it is important for each individual to prepare his mind to be most receptive to Quality. It will still take a long time but the trend is toward the good. Otherwise, we will have to bring in a God.

Maggie:

Maybe we're getting to the true meaning of those words that are so hard to remember to say—"will be possessed by." A human who has been raised in a society "will also be possessed by" social values. These values may be recognized in the form of beliefs, behavior, speech patterns, customs, and so on. Humans raised in most modern societies are also possessed by intellectual value.

What I've been coming around to, for the past few weeks, makes it seem that the patterns possess me. And if it is the strength of competing sets of patterns that causes my attention, my ability to choose, or ability to evaluate, then "I" am nothing. I don't like this very much.

It came up in my group dynamics class that even in high functioning, "effective," creative groups (which I took to mean those groups that regularly visit the intellectual/Dynamic range) there is a necessary step in beginning an effort that requires the group to identify goals that it can attempt. Not create them, but identify. So, again, who or what is running the show?

This is not the same feeling I originally got from the MOQ. The original feeling is more like this: it feels powerful to be able to discern currents and patterns. It seems as if I have more control. Also, I have more ability to put myself in the path of surprise and wonder because I am not so attached to a particular outlook (e.g., level focus). I can shift as desired, surf on currents of my choice to keep my balance.

Libet [December 1997]

Bodvar:

If I just say "Quality," it sounds a little glib, so let me tell about a scientific finding which is very disturbing for SOM and promising for the MOQ. Yes, the proof I'd say. Back in the early 1960's the American neurologist Benjamin Libet performed a series of experiments, among them one to find exactly when we make up our minds when we act. He chose such a simple feat as bending a finger, but the setup was very complicated and foolproof. The gist of it all is that there is always an electrical "evoked potential" in the brain approximately half a second before a person does a voluntary act, but the strange thing is that however spontaneous the "guinea pigs" tried to be, the potential peaked before they consciously decided to bend the finger! Some "authority" initiates the act before a person makes up his/her mind!

Libet and all other who commented on this (there was a great stir about the "free will" implications) spoke about the subconscious, the subliminal, and "deeper levels," etc. But it is plain that if an entity decides before the subject itself, then it is not subjective, and as it takes place within the person, it is not objective either. It will be argued that even if we aren't aware, we perform billions of acts—yes, exactly. As I see it, this is the Quality at work—pre-intellectual, preeverything! The subconscious of psychology has been classified as "subjective" up to now, but Libet's experiment called the bluff of this platypus.

At what value level does the impulse originate? I would say biology, and that it takes a little time before it "surfaces" intellectually. Libet also found that the act could be aborted which I interpret that the social level has a vote here (if the act had been indecent it would not have been carried out). But neither intellect nor society need interfere; the body performs its best when intellect (thinking) is absent. Who is doing the focusing? The same who initiates the act and who chooses what level to deal with the task or challenge at hand.

Quality all the way!

Ken:

Bodvar, you son of a gun, I thought I just about had Quality figured out; now you have put me back to square one. Taken at face value the results of this experiment indicate that there is an overarching cosmic mind (God, or what have you) that is directing our actions and we have no semblance of free will.

My gut reaction is to reject this out of hand yet if we accept the results of this experiment I don't know where else to go. After thinking the question over thoroughly, about two minutes, the thought occurred to me to wonder whether Libet was asking the right question. In this case the answer to the question the experiment was asking was always the same so that the neural pathway used was also always the same and conceivably could have been set by my previous concept of Quality.

It seems to me that a better way to ask the question would be to wire up all of the fingers on both hands, and maybe even the toes on both feet. Then trigger a random response with an external signal: a light setup or some such. Then see if the response for the ten different functions could be differentiated in the electrical signals in the brain. As an old CW radio operator, I know that if there were a half second delay between characters that I would be an extremely slow radio operator. With this setup we could then maybe manually bend the various digits and see if the neural pathways corresponded, and most importantly see what the time delays were. Then we could go back to the random decisions by the experimental subject and see what information we could extract from the more complete set of data. With a little more thought maybe we could set up a thought experiment and get different results and see if we got anything that supported the idea of each person's Quality being different depending on their level of connection with their personal universe including the information stored in the brain.

This is a fascinating problem. I am thoroughly POed at you for not including the full story of the experiment in this communication. It may be that the remainder of the experiment will throw my ideas into a cocked hat. Please, please, send us the rest of the story.

Mark:

There is still hope! We all agree that we can approach that cutting edge of reality in our pre-intellectual awareness. That awareness is still "us." Remember Pirsig's model from ZMM? Quality is the apogee, then Romantic Quality, then Classic Quality, which is further subdivided into subjects and objects.

When I "think" to move my finger, I'm in that classic domain, I believe. That pulse is perhaps my pre-intellectual awareness. There is an entire universe in which we exist before we think. We can intellectualize about that prospect (as I am now) only in the past. Imagine that the classic quality "I" always shows up to reality five minutes late. The romantic quality "I" is only an instant or two late. Zen masters, for example, narrow that gap until there is no gap at all.

The two "I's" are your greater awareness spread out in time. Free will is saved!

Bodvar:

The Libet Experiment continued—I was about to write a heavy piece with lots of learned talk, references, and quotations, but it is not necessary, it will not shed more light on the SOM versus MOQ controversy. As I told in the first entry did Libet find that our consciousness lags behind (an evoked electric potential in the brain), but it was followed by another series of experiment that revealed even more disturbing facts.

The time lag from the electric "evoked potential" of the brain until the person "decided" was .3 seconds, which is considerable compared to reaction time (for instance, between sitting down on a tack, or a hot stove and jumping). Anyway, just the fact that something went on before the conscious decision is simply outrageous, and it released much ado in scientific and philosophical circles.

However, Libet went on with his experimenting. He was allowed to do things on people who for other reasons had their brain exposed and found that stimuli directly on the brain needed half a second duration for the patient to become conscious of it. And yet, a stimulus on the skin (on top of one hand for example) was registered as simultaneous (a fact we all know). How is this? It takes half a second (a very long time) to become aware of things if the brain is touched (at the spot that corresponds to the top of the hand). But if/when it reaches consciousness it is felt as if taking place before—exactly as much time as to be felt simultaneous with a signal traveling from the spot to the brain (.02 second).

Libet found that sense of touch is forwarded subjectively in time to be sensed as taking place exactly when it took place! There is of course an autonomous neural system that makes us jump from tacks and hot stoves and such, but Libet's findings have a bring on that too.

What I will add for my own account is that this is a biological equivalent to quantum physics. When the mental workings are looked at closely, it also dissolves into so called subjectiveness, but as it is mind itself that is scrutinized the subjective term is not valid. Admittedly, Libet used it, and a lot of other sub words in addition, but if such a maneuver is activated to fool consciousness into believing that it initiates actions and feels touches when it takes place, then it must be a level deeper than ordinary subjectivity (the subject/object/super subject trinity again!).

No, the SOM is incapable of explaining it, but the MOQ, which is built upon the very idea of a ladder of levels, can—at least do I feel its potential here. The intellectual level (in the consciousness sense) is the last instance to be notified, but a lot of "subjective" tricking is needed for it to look as the initiator and arbiter of things. Okay, it can interrupt and override lower level's workings (as can the social level), but then one becomes awkward and "self conscious." (I know it only too well!)

Outside (objective) agents are not at work (unless the occult is invoked), and what is subjective is supposed to be in the mind, and mind is supposed to be consciousness. Perhaps the psychologists, including Freud and Jung, have been at odds with SOM all the time (the ego/super-ego/id trinity), but have not been taken seriously until a "hard" scientist went to work on it.

Doug:

Good old SOM, it will let you down every time. Allow me to put a slightly different "spin" on this.

Libet's interpretation of a backwards in time effect is purely a manifestation of a SOM-ite viewing reality with SOM blinders on. What do we know SOM always does? It limits our thinking to the objective aspects of reality (as you eloquently stated above). It also practices biformal and human centric thought dogma/doctrine (which keeps the SOM-ites forever caught in their underwear of paradice [i.e., paradoxes]).

According to SOM, humans are unique, separate, reducible, local, and isolable. Humans each have (a, one, [1]) mind. The mind is located in the skull ("How could it possibly be anywhere else?"). SOM-ites have a hard time even accepting the fact that animals have minds, let alone lesser SPoVs (Static/stable Patterns of Value). But if they do allow for other SPoVs to have minds, the minds, as always by SOM edict, are located in the skull. Minds are localized according to SOM. Even if we say sentience is a precursor to mind, the SOM-ites still say sentience is unique to humans and it still resides only in the skull.

MOQ, QM (quantum mechanics), and Zen say sentience is not local. Hugo averred this very well recently. Herrigel's experience with the Zen Master and Capra's chapter on "interpenetration" makes it (to some still quite speculatively) clear that sentience scales and is ubiquitous. Sentience appears to be a Dynamic interrelationship among all SPoVs and DQ (Dynamic Quality).

If this is true (and I believe it is, and the quantum physicists resist admitting it, but quite bluntly they have proven it [acknowledging the limits of proof]), it explains why the inorganic level can sense and react far quicker (for the good of Good SPoV's survival) than the intellectual level.

From the objective, "in the skull-centric" context, a subjective backwards in time rationale is the only thing that can possibly be true, as Libet concluded (or else we just have another one of the many classical SOM paradice) but from the non-centric, ubiquitous and scaled sentient context, there is no need for the backwards in time rationale. As you stated, Bo, the sentience at the inorganic and biological levels acted before and without control from the intellectual level.

For me this is further evidence of Pirsig's vast prescience. It is further evidence of the potent analogue twixt MOQ and QM. It is further evidence that MOQ's subsumption of SOM must happen sooner than later (Platt, et al., that is precisely why I am an activist). I don't know about you, but it dismays me that the future of our world is partially/mostly in the hands of SOM-landers. You may assuage my negative energy on this, but still I do not like it! Thanks Bo!

Ken:

I was just sitting here wrestling with autonomous nervous systems and taxis and synapse times in an attempt to explain Bo's experimental presentation when your message came in. It reminded me that I still haven't shaken the SOM mindset. It is more fun for me to ride the coattails of the Lila Squad to a rather slow understanding of the Quality concept. Thanks for the help.

Doug:

Does Lila have Quality?

SOM view: No. None of her objective properties are quality properties.

MOQ view: That is the wrong way to ask the question. The MOQ way to ask that question is, "Does Quality have Lila?" If you ask me that question, my answer is "Yes!" From the MOQ view, Static Patterns of Value inhere no properties. SPoVs are in Quality. Their relationships manifest properties we assess as Quality or not.

Is Lila an angel of Quality?

SOM view: No.

MOQ view: Lila is of Quality. All SPoVs are of Quality.

Can Quality be defined?

SOM view: None given.

MOQ view: Part of it can be defined. The static quality part may be defined. The existence of the Dynamic Quality part may be defined. The interrelationship of static patterns of value to Dynamic Quality may be defined. The essence of Dynamic Quality may not be defined by finite intellect.

Pirsig defined the Metaphysics of Quality by giving it an architecture called MOQ, which is much different from the architecture of SOM reality. He showed us how SPoVs are born, interrelate, and evolve in Dynamic Quality. He showed us the "interrelationships" of SPoVs to Dynamic Quality. He did not show us the total definition of Dynamic Quality. To do so would make Dynamic Quality finite. To do so would make Dynamic Quality an intellectual possession of finite intellect sentience. Dynamic Quality may not be possessed (by sentience) in the MOQ. That is the big mistake that SOM types make. They believe that Quality is inside things rather than vice versa. Dynamic Quality may be "experienced," but not completely defined in the MOQ.

Is Quality really just two things, as some espouse: a preintellectual moment and static quality?

SOM view: None given.

MOQ view: It is two abstractions, but not those two abstractions. Pirsig defines Quality in two divisions: Dynamic Quality and static quality. Static quality composes static patterns of value. We do not know the composition of Dynamic Quality. We experience Dynamic Quality via a pre intellectual moment at the edge of Now.

Does Quality inhere in objects?

SOM view: Yes! All objects are defined by their inherent physical properties.

MOQ view: No! All patterns of value are in Quality. Patterns of value are defined in Quality by their interrelationship properties with other patterns of value.

Dave:

Not sure about this last one; I think this is a large stumbling block for many people, I know it has been for me. On one hand, there's the quote Bo posted from ZMM, which talks about the analogues humans create and then call reality. MOQ is also an analogue and as such is a description of reality, not reality itself. So, in that sense no "object" has Quality because quality is a human mental analogue of what is. But on the other hand, Pirsig, in his SODV article discussing Bohr's experiments, maintains that there had to be data input into the experiment, and the source of the data was Dynamic Quality. So in this case it appears that qualities are resident in the external "object." [78]

So at this point in time, here's my take. Everything has inherent Qualities. All of these qualities make up the el giangundo field that is everything. There, qualities are of and discrete to any individual human, and qualities are of and discrete to all things external to that individual. From that point of view when we ask the question, "how do we know this?" we then move into the MOQ analogues, which are called static, and Dynamic Quality. In static quality, we don't know reality, as it is a priori; we each construct our pattern of static values, which we call reality. Everything outside that pattern is unknown to us and is in the overall field of Quality.

My latest thinking is that this "unknown to us" Quality field is not just Dynamic Quality but a combine of "static quality unknown to us" and Dynamic Quality which is truly unknown to all. So I feel the potential exists for both static and Dynamic Quality events through which the individual's static patterns of values can change, hopefully to a closer correlation to what actually is.

What makes MOQ superior to SOM is that:

It states up front that individual and collective reality is tentative in Nature and as such is subject to change based on newer and better information. Or it can and does evolve.

It defines how change is possible and occurs.

It has, not two, but five interrelated categories with which to constructed and, more importantly, evaluate reality.

It establishes rules and defines a moral order for the overall system.

By carefully and diligently using MOQ one can create an analogue which can more closely approximate that which truly is better than by using SOM.

Some may think that this method will make everything simpler and clearer but I feel that just the opposite is the case. Given this many components and interrelationships to deal with at the most basic metaphysical level vastly increases the complexity.

For example, "this tree." In SOM, we define it by its scientific characteristics (i.e., size, shape, color, species, board feet of lumber, structural properties, cell structure, etc.) and there we generally stop. But in the MOQ—at least when we talk about man's static pattern, "this tree"—we at minimum have to move on up into the social level [79] and talk about what social value does man assign to "this tree." This then leads to the relationship of the static pattern that is "this tree," to the patterns of the forest, and on and on and on—a more complete understanding of "this tree," but also much more complex.

So I would modify your rhetorical question this way—does Quality inhere in objects?

SOM view: Yes! All objects are defined by their inherent physical properties.

MOQ view: Yes and No! All things have inherent values. All patterns of value are in Quality. [Those] patterns of value [which humans assign] are defined in Quality by their static pattern of values and the interrelationship those properties have with other patterns of value.

Doug:

I agree with this.

In my opinion, all humans have finite intellect. We also have finite sensory capability; consider our disproportionate (classical) tactile, auditory, and visual utilization of the full frequency spectrum. Thus (classically) we are limited to "modeling" reality when we discuss it. But our (sensory limited) experience of reality can be (is) more "real" than our ability to use language and symbols to describe it. MOQ as an analogue of reality, in my opinion, is one of (if not) the best models developed to date. It certainly is "better" than the SOM analogue (the evidence abounds for this).

Bo, Gene, Hugo, I, et al., have discussed this at length in prior posts. In SODV, Pirsig shows us just a few of the trials and tribulations of great scientists and philosophers on this subject. This subject is what TLS is about. It is a "better" way we can understand for ourselves, and then help others understand the MOQ. What you said above exemplifies our entrenched western classical interpretation of reality imposed on us (mostly by the Aristotelians) for many millennia.

Classical science, Western culture, and in particular SOM (Subject/Object Metaphysics) tell us (and most of us still intuit) that what you said above is true: the properties are in the objects. That is how we conclude wrongly that Value inheres in objects. By the way, most of classical science still practices this doctrine. The macroworld deceives us that the Aristotelian view is right. The Aristotelians accomplished this deception by accusing their enemy of sophistry. Remember Phædrus' ZMM encounter with this fork in humankind's philosophical journey that occurred so long ago? Isn't that ironic?

MOQ, quantum science, and several Eastern cultures agree: MOQ says what we perceive as reality is static patterns of value (SPoVs) created by Quality at the edge of Now via a Quality event (QE) which values and latches SPoVs. Note here that the values are not in the SPoVs, but in the relationships (data are interrelationships as Pirsig shows in Figure 3 of SODV) among the SPoVs (especially first exposures to: hot stove, music, art, first love, roller coaster, everything we call reality).

The exciting virtue of MOQ is how closely it parallels quantum science. Niels Bohr's complementarity, which Pirsig's SODV (Subjects, Objects, Data and Values) paper reviews, is an analogue of the Dynamic Quality to static quality (DQ/sq) interrelationships.

232

(We can write a quantum dual of the MOQ process described in the previous paragraph.) Complementarity says that the wave particle duality may be described in an analogous manner to Pirsig's Quality creation of SPoVs via DQ/sq interrelationships.

And if you read about the intermix of Eastern culture and modern quantum science (e.g., Zukav, Capra, Herrigel, Zohar, and even Peck!) you get the same analogies, over, and over, and over again. It may be easier to see this if we distill the Eastern culture analogies into one word: interpenetration (of perceived reality and its complement).

Bodvar and God [December 1997]

Bodvar:

If anyone of religious leaning reads this and thinks that the MOQ puts God into the subjective bag and thereby scraps religion (as such) wholesale, it doesn't, and I will explain why. I haven't brought it up in the discussion earlier because I sense, like Platt, that to bring in theology (not to speak about teleology) is the end of all seriousness. But deep down it is my conviction that the MOQ is a revival of something arch religious—namely that everything is God—and that existence, ourselves included, is an expression of God. See how it matches the everything is good and existence is levels of good.

Mark:

This is where I am also. I've been exploring the idea that there exists a level above the intellectual, which seeks freedom from it. This stratum concerns itself with faith, and I've been calling it spiritual values. Mystical experiences would be considered spiritual values. They certainly are not social value nor are they intellectual. What are your first impressions of this idea?

Magnus:

First, I think that all levels have no idea about any higher levels. Inorganic patterns are not aware of organic manipulation and so on. So, we wouldn't intellectually be able to see any higher levels. Second, since this higher level is not definable, mystical experiences would hardly be mystic if they were defined; it is not a static level. Hence, Dynamic Quality is mediating intellectual patterns.

Mark:

True—even though we cannot visualize hyper-dimensions it still doesn't preclude us from doing the math. I think you are suggesting the hypothesis has no intellectual value because it is incapable of being understood intellectually. Does this mean that any superstructure that might exist above the intellectual level is de facto meaningless to us?

We cannot intellectualize a level above the intellect, I agree. But it may be static from its point of view. If we were only intellectual creatures, I would say that your explanation that they are just Dynamic Quality mediated intellectual patterns is sufficient. But we are more than our intellect. That which is before our intellect is not intellectual, social, biological, inorganic, and it is also not Dynamic Quality, which is something much greater, the source of all things.

Magnus:

My impressions are that people suggesting a higher level don't want it to be static in the first place. It seems to be the same kind of misguided reaction to intellectual patterns like the hippies reaction to social patterns.

Mark:

The hippies equated their moral intellectual struggle from social constraints with the biological struggle against moral social controls. I don't seek to attack intellectual values from both sides with this supposition. I contend there are static values "up there" but we just cannot intellectually understand them from "down here." They will never make sense. I do, however, believe we can "know" this level in other ways. Perhaps I am trying to find a place in Pirsig's model for our spiritual selves. Lumping it into the Great Unknown seems to be denying the possibility of knowing this part of us.

Magnus:

Supposing we are more than our intellect (which I think we're not, but never mind), you have to remember that this level must use intellectual patterns for its own purposes. It must also be dependent on intellectual patterns to sustain itself. Maybe a spiritual level would, maybe not. Maybe I'm too submerged in intellectual patterns in the same way Victorians were submerged in social patterns.

I'll be frank here (I usually am), the name "spiritual value" rings a bell for me, connecting it with religious "holier than thou" mentality. Jehovah Witness groups and people from other churches came to my home and tried to convince me to join them. When they noticed that I was into science, they tried to convince me using scientific arguments. But they always got the bottom line of those arguments from the Bible. To me, that says two things: they close their eyes to observations whenever they conflict with the Bible, and they fail to use their intellect when they don't have to. They think it's already in the Bible so why bother. Giving up like that is something that really appalled me.

That is one reason why I back off when I hear "spiritual value." If it means giving up on the intellectual level before we completely gain everything we can out of it, then I don't think it is more moral than intellectual patterns. It sounds more like a sidetrack and such tracks do not exist in the MOQ.

Mark:

Fine—call it pre-intellectual values then. I agree that dogma in religion is as dangerous as dogma in any discipline. Just remember, if you believe Quality is the source and substance of all things, then there exists no intellectual argument for your belief either. It's faith, same as theirs. In fact, you share the same faith, that ultimate reality is Good, God, and unknowable intellectually. We feel God; we don't deduce Him. Quality is experienced pre-intellectually. Intellectual analysis of quality is always in the past, like chasing ghosts.

Now you're just arguing what the Bible means. They cling to it for answers on morality and you prefer to use an intellectual construction for morality, Lila. When it comes to the struggle between the social and the biological, Lila says nothing that's not in the Bible. Morality-wise, you are in agreement for the most part.

So it all boils down to their static social values versus yours. If they failed to make a convincing rhetoric, then fine, you choose your good over their good. I would only urge care in not dismissing that which evokes such passion in others. There's good behind it. This doesn't mean join every religion that knocks on your door either.

If, however, you believe that Truth is our ultimate reality, that God is Truth, then yes, you can use your intellect to sort all experience into that which is true, not true or not yet determinable. For you, faith is simply belief in something not yet scientifically verified. What better way to know truth than by scientific method?

Ken:

Mark and Magnus, I have just been re-reading some of your mail. Mark, acceptance of the Quality idea is not a matter of faith. Quality is simply the growth of the consciousness of humanity through time as prodded by increased awareness. In my lifetime the depression of the thirties taught us humility and brotherhood, the non-combat slaughter of some fifteen million people during the forties taught us forbearance and compassion, the complacency of the fifties and sixties exposed our self indulgence, and the time since then has exposed our cupidity and indifference to the "others."

The level of consciousness and ethics has risen rapidly in the last seventy years because of what we now understand as the Quality principle and because of the increase in the level of education and understanding in the world. It is not faith to be predisposed and prepared for a new level of ethics in advance of being able to articulate it, which is roughly my understanding of what Pirsig means by Quality and awareness. In my opinion, the discussions of the discontinuities at the subatomic and electron shell level are not germane because the action at the gross atomic level is entirely predictable.

236

Bodvar:

Magnus, you point to the fact that those who suggest such a super level seemingly don't want it to be static, and you are right. The level that Mark refers to is probably Dynamic Quality itself; Dynamism is at the root of every level. Quantum physics has revealed the dynamics "behind" matter (inorganic) and the void beneath the rational (intellectual) is known to all who have experimented with magic, yoga, and/or encountered extra-sensory experiences (I may add that also biology and society will reveal similar Dynamism if scrutinized closely). You are right in saying that a new level must be as static as the rest.

Then you go on to say that a static level doesn't know (the value of) the level above. Right, but when you deduce from this that we wouldn't know of any new level above intellect I can't follow you. Human beings aren't solely intellect. Mind isn't unequivocally the intellectual level of the MOQ (this I believe we also agreed on back in the stone age of TLS). Sensation is biological mind, emotion is social mind, and rationality is intellectual mind. We perceive all levels and will incorporate the "mind" of a new level as well!

Ken:

I like the subject line of this thread. It pleases me to see that Bodvar has top billing over God. When I look at the sweep of history I just hope that he will do a better job. Right on, Bodvar!

Bodvar:

I'll try. The first act of Bo is to change the heading! If it stays the same, I am not omnipotent.

Ken:

Bodvar and Squad, please don't change the heading of this thread. I like it. I have been following the discussion with much pleasure. I would like to see if I could sort out my ideas and present them for criticism. I get the feeling that the discussion is still bogged down in an egocentric concept of humanity. It reads to me as if most of you are still looking at humanity as somehow special and separate from Nature. This is not my feeling at all.

When I watch the wildlife and my yard dogs and cat interact, I see similar motivations and anxieties that move humans. I see rudimentary thinking and planning ahead going on that are not a great leap from the position that us humans occupy. If one looks at the sweep of evolution, as we currently understand it, I believe that we can see a fairly linear development of awareness and understanding that leads straight to us.

When I first read ZMM and Lila, my initial concept of the term Quality was that it represented a level of advancement in human understanding and awareness that was desirable but not yet agreed upon by the mass of humanity. That it represented all of those ideas and feelings and vague yearnings that were desirable but not yet accepted into the mainstream of static quality—the horizon of intellectual and ethical human growth. I still have the same view.

My view of the universe is that it is an objective universe that has many mystical qualities because of our lack of understanding. I believe that when we are able to know everything then everything (object wise) will fit into a coherent scheme. The sweep of the development of the universe looks logical to me. It seems to me to progress in a very objective fashion up to the present moment if we allow a little windage for our state of ignorance.

We see that the Earth came here from other parts of the universe and we still see the precursors of life coming in from space in the form of amino acids. We see the necessary energetics operating that is thought to be the motivating force for the origin of life. We see the progression of evolution that has (so far) produced us and is probably still operating. We see plenty of time for all of this to happen. This seems to me to be a pretty coherent picture of our current position.

What I cannot see is the beginning of it all. If the Big Bang occurred, was it planned? If so, it was planned well. Has the universe been in existence forever? That is a staggering concept to me. My mind just won't accept it. Hawking has given us radiation from black holes, which, to my mind, could make the universe everlasting. If this is so then we don't need reasons.

238

Everything just is. If there is a beginning and an end then we are justified in looking for first causes. Could the universe contain many other planets capable of sustaining life? If so, will they all be constrained to follow the same pattern that we have because they will be starting with the same raw materials and energy? Is there a bunch of Lila Squads out there with the same concerns and debating the same topics? Is God a planet farmer?

I don't know the answer. You pays your money and you takes your choice. I am ready for criticism.

Bodvar:

I really appreciate your letters, and read with great interest the charming stories of dogs' behavior, observations of geographical and linguistic particularities, etc. But I also sense a note of despair over the intricacies of the Lila Squad disputes and over Quality in general. You study the universe and find it objective. You study the past and find no great leap from animals to humanoids and "Homo-sapiens." You study your dogs and see rudimentary thinking and ability to anticipate the future.

Absolutely, but this is not contradictory to the Quality idea, more to "ordinary" thinking that requires an inventor of—first— the natural laws and then creator of matter to obey these laws. Then an unbelievable chance that assembled matter into life, and a thinking spirit to enable life—including your dogs—to behave intelligently, and finally a ghostly soul to preserve our human identity.

May I roam a little? I once read an article in Scientific American about a theory called "The Anthropic Principle." It started with telling how every physical constant (the charge of the electron and so on) seems to balance on a knife's edge, not only one such value, but all of them! We know what the chances are for one such feat and then for a whole series to be exact on the point, and stay there—it is exactly zero! So, ordinary thinking (read: SOM) has to concoct such theories as the said Anthropic Principle to account for this miracle, and other wild theories of the same kind, "The many universes theory," for instance. In my younger days, reading of such weird ideas gave me great thrills; now it bores me because all I see is vain efforts to get around their own obstacles.

Instead of Anthropic Principles, why not consider the Quality principles, which say that the physical constants came to attain their values because it was the ones that "offered themselves" to (the formation of) matter. There is no more need for an electron "to have" a particular charge than for your dogs "to have" thinking ability to know when you are going to take them for a walk (they sense the value of what keeps a dog alive and happy) or for a human "to have" consciousness to think. We sense the same biological values as dogs when it comes to the bodily needs and pleasures, but the social value's "feelings" of right and wrong override these to a great extent, which in turn are modified by intellectual values of what is "rational."

PS. The social values of dogs (which we derogatory call pack instincts) may also override their biology. The top dog is the one to eat first and mate the bitch, isn't that so?

Ken:

Bodvar, you are the rock around which we hip-shooters circle. You provide a stable center that gives us the freedom to wander and speculate, and be wrong, I might add. I remember reading the "Anthropic Principle" sometime in the past but I didn't remember any of the details until you reminded me. I agree with you that such constructions are not necessary.

Once we get through the energetics of the presumed "Big Bang" and settle out with the 92 elements that were here the rest of it seems to be pretty much a foregone conclusion. To my mind, it is hard to see how it could have happened any other way. To my mind, the mystery and wonder reside in the beginning—plenty of room there for God or First Causes or anything else. I don't have a problem with the Metaphysics of Quality or any of Pirsig's insights. I think they fit the case better than anything I have seen previously. Their explanatory powers fit well except for the Big Bang.

The thing that causes me to thresh around and try to make everything fit my view, I think, is that I also accept Lovelock's idea of Gaia. That also seems to me to be the best explanation for the physical process that has produced this planet and us life forms that inhabit it than anything else I have seen. Even if the Gaia Hypothesis is not correct, it seems to me to be a good way to view our situation. I sometimes wonder if too much emphasis is not being placed on humanity in isolation when we should be more concerned about our stewardship of the whole thing. That is why I have a problem shunting the inorganic and biological levels off too much. I have a feeling they are central to the concept. An acceptance of the Gaia view by all of humanity would start a trend toward a more friendly attitude toward the biosphere and ultimately result in a more pleasant and sustainable Earth.

Bodvar, as I say, I think we have about the same view of Pirsig's concept. Where we seem to part is in our placement of humanity in the scheme.

I see a primordial soup with the raw materials and the energetics to combine into living aggregations. I see that amino acids are detected coming in from space, a big step toward life. I see a system that almost demands us once we get the basic list of elements established. I see an evolutionary system that looks extremely convincing. I can't think of another way it could have happened. I see myself as being kin as well as being dependent on the other life forms—looks pretty to me. Bodvar, if it weren't for you I would have to think my ideas through before I put them out there. That wouldn't be nearly as much fun. As it stands, I know I can depend on you to pull me back toward the center when I get too far out. Hang in there and don't change the thread name. I like it. I think it is fitting.

Dave:

Looking at the Subjects, Objects, Data and Values paper on the Lila Squad site, I would say Pirsig would put God in the Conceptually Unknown category, which would agree with what Magnus is saying. This could be seen to correspond with Kant's transcendent idea, "We all live in the question of God," which so shocked the world and finally lead to Nietzsche's experience as the death of God. But I think Pirsig dodges the bullet nicely in three ways:

1. In the Conceptually Unknown section he goes on to say that just because an idea is in this state does not mean it is valueless. So the question of God is with us, will remain with us, is beyond our power of reason, but is not without value.

2. To all the worlds' religions he says, in so much as you establish static social patterns that conform to Quality and are evolving toward a greater good; you are morally right. In so much as you are so inflexible and rigid that you allow no moral progress, you are in a pattern of low quality and most likely will die.

3. He moves morality and ethics from a subset way down the philosophical pike to a primary ingredient of the base.

Then finally he restores the fragmented dissections of SOM to a whole which reunites man, Nature, and universe in such a way that the Gaia Hypothesis appears more believable as do most religions that claim God created and is everything. But for man the question is still out and will be out until God decides to resolve the issue.

Bodvar:

Your interpretation of where Pirsig places God and that it corresponds to Kant's "We all live in the question of God," may well be true. Perhaps did Kant have a premonition of something quality-like? Anyway, the eighteenth century wasn't ripe for that quantum leap. The SOM had to run its course into the cul de sac.

Dave:

I'm still hung up on the only (my emphasis) in this referenced quote: "But quantum theory has destroyed the idea that only properties located in external physical objects have reality." (Robert M. Pirsig, page 14 in his paper Subjects, Objects, Data and Values, presented at the Einstein Meets Magrïtte conference, Fall 1995.)

I infer from this that man's reality always has a "subjective" component, which I believe is born out by the quantum theory, but not necessarily that there is no external "objective" component. And that while SOM maintains that we can isolate that "objective" component MOQ maintains we cannot.

Under quantum mechanics if all men die then the does phenomena we observe and call "quanta" cease to be? Would the then remaining universe, other than man being gone, markedly change? Would the sun, earth, stars disappear or change in any way? [80]

Doug:

These, in my opinion, are superb questions! They touch crux. Caveat on my subsequent comments—I am a self-teaching student of quantum science.

Let's give a layperson definition of "quanta": a quanta, one quantum, is the simplest and indivisible quantum system known to quantum science. Allow me to use the mnemonic, QS, for quantum system.

Now my-, one-, an-, answer to your question—QSs exist forever and are either in their latched state, which we see as reality, or in their unlatched state, which we cannot see or fathom as reality. Latched QSs are surrounded by and interpenetrated by unlatched QSs. The MOQ metaphor here is DQ vs. SQ, or Dynamic Quality vs. Static Quality. (Note: "forever" is from our anthropomorphic, finite intellect perspective.)

Peter:

This is my first time on the list and I'm hoping for interesting discussions up ahead. (Unfortunately, however, I am leaving campus in three days and won't be back until late January.)

Did he actually say this? Quantum theory destroyed the idea of a perfectly objective observer, but I'm not entirely convinced that it "destroyed the idea that only properties located in external physical objects have reality." I don't understand what exactly this "idea" is. The "external" here is in reference to what? External to the observer's body? External to some undefined conscience? Kind of a mind body split here?

Dave:

243

This just shows that even the most MOQed of people (Pirsig) has a hard time slipping the bonds of SOM. In my opinion, the "idea" Pirsig is referring to is that Western philosophy (SOM) primarily though the influence of its daughter branch modern science has as Barrett (Death of the Soul) put it:

"Yet, with all its inherent paradoxes, scientific materialism was to become de facto the dominant mentality of the West in the three and a half centuries that followed. It ruled not so much as an explicit and articulate philosophy, but more potently as an unspoken attitude, habit, and prejudice of mind. And in this unspoken form, it is still prevalent today."

And one of the most basic tenants of science that evolved under SOM is the primacy of "objectivity." A brief review of philosophy during the same period shows a decided trend in defining reality similarly. Now science though the quantum theory has called "objectivity" into question, as you said, by "destroy[ing] the idea of a perfectly objective observer." So what Pirsig says is that it's not a scientific problem, or even a philosophical problem, but a metaphysical problem created by a de facto metaphysical split of reality into subjects and objects. If it were not for that split, we would not be having this discussion.

Peter:

This is the crux of the issue, in my opinion. The statement that "man's reality always has a 'subjective' component which...is born out by the quantum theory," is easily understood and correct. The second, "but not necessarily that there is no external objective component," is somewhat harder. It has been an age-old debate between physicists. On the one hand, Einstein and some of his students believed that there is an underlying, objective, unprobabilistic reality. However, many researchers are working today to show that he is wrong and most more or less believe that Einstein was wrong in saying God does not play dice. The "current" body of mainstream quantum theory is really some mathematics, but the most popular interpretation of the math (the

Copenhagen interpretation) does not "believe" in objective physical properties beyond what is observed and observable.

The last sentence is dependent on the outcome of the ongoing battle of quantum physicists to show that there is not a more fundamental reality beyond the quantum. Since modern day science is presumably a product of subject/object metaphysics, and since there is still ongoing research concerning objective reality, we cannot really say quite yet what SOM maintains concerning objectivity.

What do you mean—a "quanta" of what? Everything we observe is quantized, in some way or another. Indeed our reality would markedly change if everything "forever and always" disappeared from our universe. The term "quanta" is usually used to describe some property, i.e., "a quanta of light" or "a quanta of angular momentum" or "a quanta of bread." Generally, it is not very useful or meaningful by itself.

There is sort of a muddled point here. Quantum physics says things about interactions. Period. Namely, any interaction with a particle causes certain things about it to be changed. The reason this has any bearing on metaphysics is because every experimental method we know and use involves interaction(s) with the subject in question. Since there is interaction, there is a corresponding change in the behavior of the observed things.

This question: "Would the sun, earth, stars disappear or change in any way?" is an interesting one. It is essentially identical to the question—does the universe exist after I am dead? The answer, from a strictly quantum theoretical-esque point of view, is mu. You do not exist to perform any experiments on the Universe. Hence, it is meaningless to ask such a question. The trouble is that by asking such a question you have already essentially assumed the objective existence of the Universe.

Dave:

This shows the crux of the problem. Let's take a little time over the holidays to ponder this from a quantum theoretical-esque point of view. Let's assume that the words "subject and object" do not exist— have never been invented—but Quality with the subdivisions Static and Dynamic and the four Static subdivisions were in their place. How would you then answer the question? Don't assume I have an answer because I don't.

Ken:

Dave, being retired I have time to sit here and mull over the back postings and I can see that you have been struggling with the quanta questions lately. According to my understanding the world of the electron shell and the world of the atomic nucleus (all of them) are based on quantum effects. The world is discontinuous within the Planck (very, very small) distance and time and also on the level of the electron shell (much larger) and maybe other places of which I am unaware. The photon is also quantized as well as some, or maybe all, of the other elementary particles or waves. If all of these disappeared, we would certainly disappear, along with the remainder of the universe.

If we all died it should have no effect on the Earth or the universe at the physical level. The Earth was here and functioning beautifully before we came along and would again. In fact, the Earth (or Lovelock's Gaia) would be a healthier organism without us. If all life died on Earth, the Earth as a living organism would also die since it is life that maintains the distribution of the gases of the atmosphere as well as the film of biotic material that covers the Earth. Without life, the Earth would regress to a dead planet as our other planets are now.

More likely, it would not go all the way, since a reservoir of life that can live without oxygen would remain and evolution could start again. The plant life of the earth supplies and maintains the 21% oxygen that is present in the atmosphere of the Earth. Without life this level would be a fraction of 1% and not capable of supporting us. The Earth just happened to be in the correct size range to allow us to happen. Too little and it couldn't hold an atmosphere. Too big and gravity would start the thermonuclear reaction. Aren't we lucky? The quantum discussion on the Lila Squad is purely a human concern, which the Earth and the

246

Universe blithely ignores. I don't know the answer to your "only" question. I wish I did. The more you look at it the more mysterious it gets. We will still be the dunder-headed human race even if we do get it figured out. Keep in mind that we are talking about an eye-blink when we talk about the history of the human race, plenty of time for anything to happen. If we last that long we are probably not the final word in evolution. There may well be millions of other Daves and Kens out there worrying about the same problems. Let's relax and enjoy the ride.

Dave:

I heard a new blurb that somewhere in Europe, Switzerland I think, that scientists have succeeded in "teleporting" quanta but that "Beam me up Scotty" is still a fur piece in the future. As an architect the dream of eliminating the auto from our built world makes me want to live to be a million years old in the hopes that it someday happens.

Nice to hear from y'all, nothing like a dangle of ignorance to bring lurkers out of the woods. Thanks for filling me in on the essentials of quantum theory. I think I've gone far enough off on the tangent of quantum theory in so much as it appears that even the people doing the work are not able to agree on its implications.

Peter:

Actually, it was in Austria. I had an opportunity to meet the researcher doing this work (Dr. Anton Zeilinger) over the summer. (He was my summer advisor's ex advisor.) In any case, he had successfully "teleported" a photon by transporting all its properties (that we could observe) onto another photon several meters away.

Doug:

IBM, et al., is working on this too, as we speak. It depends upon superluminal communication (to be more correct, zero latency communication independent of distance—Einstein, Podolsky, and Rosen attempted to show that quantum mechanics was "incomplete" using the classical assumption that no phenomenon could exceed the speed of light, nor violate the classical principle of locality).

I am still amazed that Pirsig birthed the MOQ without training in quantum physics. What a gift!

Annotations by Robert M. Pirsig

75. Traditionally, this is the meaning of free will. But the MOQ can argue that free will exists at all levels with increasing freedom to make choices as one ascends the levels. At the lowest inorganic level, the freedom is so small that it can be said that nature follows laws but the quantum theory shows that within the laws the freedom is still there. I remember a physicist telling me that according to quantum theory all the molecules of air in a room could of their own free will move to one side, suffocating someone standing on the other side, but the probability of this happening is so small no one need ever worry about it.

76. This is a subtle slip back into subject-object thinking. Values have been converted to a kind of object in this sentence, and then the question is asked, "If values are an object, then where is the subject?" The answer is found in the MOQ sentence, "It is not Lila who has values, it is values that have Lila." Both the subject and the object are patterns of value.

77. It's important to remember that both science and Eastern religions regard "the individual" as an empty concept. It is literally a figure of speech. If you start assigning a concrete reality to it, you will find yourself in a philosophic quandary.

78. No. In the MOQ Dynamic Quality is not an object that contains things inside it. The term Dynamic Quality is equivalent to the Buddhist "Nothingness." I suspect the Buddhists use this term to prevent intellectual encroachment on what they are talking about.

79. A tree is purely biological. The MOQ doesn't require a social description any more than the SOM does. Remember the SOM includes the field of social science.

80. This is the usual argument against the philosophic idealism that is part of the MOQ so it had better be answered here. It is similar to the question, "If a tree falls in the forest and nobody hears it, does it make a sound?" The historic answer of the idealists is, "What tree?"

In order to ask this question you have to presuppose the existence of the falling tree and then ask whether this presupposed tree would vanish if nobody were there. Of course, it wouldn't vanish! It has already been presupposed.

This presupposition is a standard logical fallacy known as a hypothesis contrary to fact. It is the "hypothetical question" that is always thrown out of court as inadmissible. If pigs could fly, how high would they go? The answer is the same as the answer to Dave's question.

Chapter 8

We can call the quintessence of everything merely objective in our knowledge—Nature; the quintessence of everything subjective, on the other hand, is called the "I," or intelligence. The two concepts are set in opposition to one another. Intelligence is originally thought as the merely representing, Nature as the merely representable, the one as the conscious, the latter as without consciousness. There is, however, in all knowing a necessary interpenetrating meeting of both (of the conscious and of the in-itself non-conscious); the task is: to account for this coincidence. [Friedrich Schelling, System of Transcendental Idealism, 1800]

A Note from the Editor

During the initial phase of Lila's Child development, I informed no one I knew in person what it was that I'd been devoting so much time to on the computer. It just seemed better to keep it to myself until there was something substantial; being a bit of a recluse, it really wasn't that difficult a secret to keep. When I finally told some of my closest friends and family that I had been putting together a book, invariably the first question that came up was—so what is it about? I found it impossible to sum that up in just a few sentences or to explain the project to anyone who hasn't read Lila. I finally settled on telling people that Lila's Child is a philosophy book, for it seemed when I said it was a book about Quality, people would just give me an odd look. Working out the principles of the Metaphysics of Quality seems as difficult a feat as explaining Lila's Child.

The discussion group "think-tanked" out the principles of Quality over many weeks and more than a hundred posts. For brevity, it seems best to represent them here in a more or less complete form, though these principles are by no means the only ones offered during the discussions. As with the rest of Lila's Child, size constraints dictate that only specific posts can be highlighted. These selected posts do not necessarily accurately reflect the general consensus of the group or the spirit in which the Lila Squad was conceived.

The Principles of Quality [December 1997]

Bodvar:

Here are my entries for the principles of Quality:

1. What is metaphysics? [81]

The best definition is the one that Pirsig himself gives in Lila:

"Metaphysics is what Aristotle called the First Philosophy. It's a collection of the most general statements of a hierarchical structure of thought—that part of philosophy which deals with the nature and structure of reality."

2. What does Metaphysics of Quality mean? [82]

It means a different structure of reality from the present Subject/Object Metaphysics (SOM), which says that the most basic division of reality is between the objective world and the subjective minds that perceive it. The Metaphysics of Quality's first axiom is that everything is Value and that the division is a Dynamic/static one. The static part is subdivided into four value levels (also used are the terms "patterns," "dimensions," and "areas").

3. Why did Pirsig write Lila? [83]

He wrote it to promote the enlarged version of the Quality idea that had been presented in his first book, Zen and the Art of Motorcycle Maintenance. At first, Lila had been planned as an anthropological study, which would demonstrate the Dynamic/static division by contrasting the nomadic North American Indians to the white European settlers, but he soon realized that it would not do. He would neither be accepted by the scientific establishment nor understood by the public, partly for his lack of anthropological credentials, but mostly because of the metaphysical presuppositions of SOM would mess up his message, so he finally understood that he had to go to the root, to metaphysics itself.

For good measure, I enter my answers to these questions too: What is Pirsig doing now?

He admits to being a recluse, but says that it is not due to any bitterness: "...Even if everyone understood Lila I would be that way. The Buddhist monk has a precept against indulging in idle conversation, and I think the basis for that precept is what motivates me." (Letter of Aug. 19, 1997) What he is doing of writing is not known, but that he is working on something is for sure. I hope that we will soon know.

What are the sales of the two books?

It is well known that Zen and the Art of Motorcycle Maintenance (ZMM) was a formidable success. How many copies that were sold are not known (it still sells), but it is millions. In an interview, he told that only the rights for the paperback version earned him two hundred and ten thousand (1975) dollars! Lila had an initial boom shortly after it was published in 1991, but the sales fell off after a while. Then they picked up again and in 1995 sales tripled in Japan for instance, and the same year the book was published in Chinese (Taiwan), and later also mainland China.

How much of Lila is autobiographical?

This is always hard to tell. Phædrus is obviously only a lightly camouflaged Robert Pirsig, as he was in the ZMM, but Lila herself has no living model that I know of. She bears no resemblance to his levelheaded wife Wendy, that is for sure. The trip down the Hudson River is authentic in the sense that Pirsig brought his boat "Aretê" from the Big Lakes to New York City before the trip across the Atlantic Ocean to Europe in 1980 (?). The "Cleveland Harbour" episode also reflects his sailing experience on the Big Lakes. The hotel episode with Robert Redford may well have occurred as the rights for filming the ZMM was negotiated for a period (his letter to Redford in the Steele and DiSanto Guidebook to ZMM).

What is the public reaction to these books?

The reaction to the first book in 1974 was overwhelmingly positive, as the sales indicate. ZMM is usually regarded as the better novel and Lila as a not so successful sequel, but philosophically it is another story. The first book is the stirring story of how he came to conceive the basic Quality idea and what that cost him; Lila—even if written along similar outlines—is a presentation of the full-fledged philosophical system and necessarily a more difficult book, and for that reason not so popular. The reader who wants to be entertained doesn't always see the importance of what he is reading.

What do other philosophers think of his work?

The reaction that he foresaw for his anthropological venture has more or less been fulfilled by Lila too. Academic philosophers seemingly don't want to look into his Quality idea. Usually new ideas or paradigms are supposed to start within the academic circles and spread into society, not the other way round. The few reviews published have been overwhelmingly negative—outright vicious— and far too violent for a "mere" philosophical idea. Perhaps the unheard of magnitude of what Pirsig is saying and the frustration over not finding the weak point of his MOQ is the reason.

Platt:

Here is my offering of the basic principles of the MOQ. I wholeheartedly agree that without agreement on the basic Principles, a lot of the Squad's exchanges amount to little more than intelligent but insignificant cocktail party talk. What we're dealing with here is nothing less than a huge paradigm shift on a par with Einstein's relativity. If it is to survive and have any influence, it must "latch" with deep taproots of comprehension and believability. I apologize for the length, but to condense a 400-page book that will "cover everything" and still have some semblance of meaning I found a truly daunting task. To what degree I've been successful is for your evaluation.

Principles of the Metaphysics of Quality

1. The Quality Principle: Quality is simultaneously an immanent and transcendent moral force. It created and gave purpose to our world, motivated by the ethical principle of the Good, which is its essence. Quality is synonymous with morality and value. Thus, the world is primarily a moral order, consisting

254

not of subjects (mental things) and objects (material things) but patterns of value.

2. The Awareness Principle: The essence of quality is known to us as awareness without content: pure, unpatterned experience. As such, it's impossible to describe. Whenever we try, we end up describing what we are aware of, not awareness itself.

3. The Dynamic/static Principle: To explain the inexplicable, the Metaphysics of Quality divides quality into two parts, Dynamic and static. Dynamic Quality is the moral imperative to create; static quality is the moral imperative to survive.

4. The Levels Principle: Quality became manifest in our world by an evolutionary sequence of Dynamic Quality events. Left in the wake of these events were four static levels of evolution: Inorganic, Biological, Social and Intellectual. Each level is a static pattern of Quality, organized and governed by its own unique moral laws: the laws of physics, biology, culture, and reason, respectively.

5. The Awareness Hierarchy Principle: Each higher level evolved from and included the lower but expanded awareness. For example, the intellectual level can apprehend mathematical patterns that the lower levels cannot. Also, all levels possess, in addition to environmental awareness, an awareness of values. Even a lowly virus knows what's good for it.

6. The Moral Hierarchy Principle: Because higher levels are more aware, they are more moral than levels below. Intellectual patterns take moral precedence over social patterns, social patterns over biological, and biological patterns over inorganic.

7. The First Dominance Principle: Because a lower level is largely unaware of levels above it, it considers itself to be the most moral and strives to dominate other levels. What is moral and lawful at one level is often immoral and unlawful at another. For example, biological laws defy the laws of physics.

8. The Second Dominance Principle: Static patterns within levels that humans identify as entities are possessed by varying degrees of Quality depending on their affinity to the next higher or

lower level. They often try to devour other patterns to enhance their own survival. This causes suffering, the negative face of Quality that drives the creative process.

9. The Dependency Principle: When a higher level attempts to assert its moral dominance over a lower level, it must be careful that it does not endanger the stability of the lower level on which it ultimately depends for survival. For example, if the intellect in its quest for freedom from social inhibitions causes social instability, intellect will suffer.

10. The Individual Principle: At the present stage of moral evolution, only living beings can respond to Dynamic Quality. Humans, composites of all four levels, are the most capable of responding. However, responses to and evaluations of Quality vary by individual because each has a different static pattern of life history.

11. The Truth Principle: Truth, an intellectual value pattern, is a species of Good. There's no single, exclusive truth, but those of high quality are empirical, logical, elegant, and brief. In any case, it's immoral for truth to be subordinated to social values.

12. The Freedom Principle: To create ever higher levels of awareness, Dynamic Quality strives for freedom from all static patterns. Freedom is the core value and highest Good in the Metaphysics of Quality. Thus, the best social and intellectual patterns are those that promote freedom consistent with maintaining the static patterns necessary for survival.

13. The Proof Principle: That reality is morality strikes most people as loony. But in denying that the world is a moral order, they have to employ moral judgment. They cannot refute that Quality is reality without asserting a value. And they will have to concede that it's impossible to live without assumptions of what is Good. For life requires action, action presupposes choice, choice presupposes purpose, and purpose presupposes values. [84]

Ant:

Here goes my first contribution to the Lila Squad!

The following is an abstract of an essay [http://www.moq.org/forum/anthony.html] I wrote earlier this year. Hopefully, in the process of refinement I've kept in the most basic tenets of the MOQ and ignored the more secondary elements without losing too much coherence. Maybe the examples could be taken out though this might reduce the clarity of the principles. Please speak up if you think I've overlooked anything fundamental.

Robert Pirsig's Metaphysics of Quality

1. What is metaphysics?

Metaphysics is the branch of philosophy that examines the nature of reality, including the relationship between mind and matter, substance and attribute, fact and value.

2. What is the Metaphysics of Quality (MOQ)?

The Metaphysics of Quality is a theory developed by Robert Pirsig to describe and explain the nature of Quality (and its synonym, Value).

3. What does Pirsig mean by the term "Quality"?

Well, in Lila, he states that it is "the first slice of undivided experience." (Lila, Bantam Press, 1991, page 111). That is to say immediate experience before any division the mind may make before internal or external states.

4. So what is meant by "immediate experience"?

Immediate refers to the present or to be more technical where time t = zero. Experience, in this context, is an awareness of the changing flux of reality. Therefore, immediate experience means "awareness of the changing flux of reality at time t = zero."

5. Pirsig divides Quality (or immediate experience) into Dynamic Quality and static quality. So how is Dynamic Quality differentiated from static quality?

Dynamic Quality is the term given by Pirsig to the continually changing flux of immediate reality while static quality refers to anything abstracted from this flux. Dynamic Quality refers to the divine in experience and can only be understood properly through direct apprehension. Hence the use of the term "Dynamic," which indicates something not fixed or determinate. Ultimately, it is apparent that Dynamic Quality can't be defined and that true understanding of it can only be given through a mystic experience such as enlightenment.

6. So what is static quality then?

By static, Pirsig doesn't refer to something that lacks movement in the Newtonian sense of the word, but is referring to any repeated arrangement, whether inorganic (e.g., chemicals), biological (e.g., plants), social (e.g., ant nests), or intellectual (e.g., ideas); any pattern that appears long enough to be noticed within the flux of immediate experience.

7. How do these four static patterns of quality relate? The MOQ recognizes that the four static patterns of quality are related through evolution. If the Big Bang is taken as the starting point of the universe, it is seen that at this point of time there were only inorganic quality patterns. That is to say, chemicals and quantum forces. Since then, at successive stages of history, plants and animals have evolved from inorganic patterns, societies have evolved from biological patterns, and intellect has evolved from societies.

8. Why is evolution an important consideration in the MOQ?

Though each level of static patterns have emerged from the one below, each level follows its own different laws, i.e., there are physical laws such as gravity (inorganic), the laws of the jungle (biology), cooperation between animals (society), and the ideas of freedom and rights (intellect). It is important to note that the different laws of the four static levels often clash, e.g., adultery (biological Good) versus family stability (social Good).

9. How is a code of ethics generated from these four levels?

The MOQ combines the four levels of patterns to produce one overall moral framework based on evolutionary development. The entity that has more freedom on the evolutionary scale (i.e., the one that is more Dynamic) is the one that takes moral precedence. So, for instance, a human being is seen as having moral precedence over a dog because a human being is at a higher level of evolution.

10. So what's the value of such a moral framework?

By removing morals from social convention and placing them on a scientifically based theory of evolution, the MOQ removes much of the cultural subjectivity that is inherent in many ethical beliefs. Moreover, by the use of evolution, the MOQ brings together things previously difficult to relate, such as mind and matter.

Finally, though it may be argued that a metaphysics that incorporates a central term that isn't defined (i.e., Dynamic Quality) isn't a real metaphysics, it can also be argued that the strength of the MOQ is its ability to incorporate the indeterminate divine within a coherent and logical paradigm. [85]

Pirsig on Goal of Existence [January 1998]

James:

My own offering would be that Quality is the "goal" of existence. In other words, the missing link between "Quality" and "reality" is teleological. Ends arise from causes, subjects arise from objects, and the mind is born of matter.

I know that no definition can express Quality very well, but if the concept is to be useful, I thought that a description should add something to the concept of existence (rather than having a one to one mapping with an already known idea). The idea of teleology is just one suggestion. In particular, the idea of progressing from one level to the next, and calling the next a "higher" level, suggests goal-oriented behavior. I do not mean that "Quality" and "existence" are exclusive concepts by any means, but that existence has different aspects, and that it is infused with Quality. Admittedly, if one divides Quality according to the classic/romantic division, then the classic dimension can be identified with causation.

I wonder what other people think about this.

Bodvar:

Hello Ant, are you listening in? I have a vague recollection that the question of a "goal" for existence was answered by Robert Pirsig in a letter to you. That he said that he had been confronted with the seeming paradox that Dynamic Quality was both the source and the goal, but I am not able to remember what his conclusion was, nor am I able to find the actual letter. Could you please look into your files and see if there is something resembling this? Thanks.

Ant:

That Quote for you! Robert Pirsig wrote:

"Hunting for weaknesses, [in your paper] I find that on page one, paragraph four, there is a sentence, 'Fundamentally Pirsig's term is a mystic one, and refers to the undifferentiated, indeterminate, reality from which the universe has evolved (or grown) from.' Although this is true at a Buddha's level of understanding, it would be confusing and illogical in the world of everyday affairs to say that the world is evolving both from and toward the same thing. I have had some reader mail that has pointed out at one place I seem to imply that Quality and chaos are the same and at another that they are different, so I haven't been clear on this myself and have left an opening to attack. To close it up, let us say that the universe is evolving from a condition of low quality (quantum forces only, no atoms, pre-Big Bang) toward a higher one (birds, trees, societies and thoughts) and that in a static sense (world of everyday affairs) these two are not the same."

(Letter from Robert Pirsig, March 29, 1997. The word "mystic" originally in bold not italics.)

Well, I hope that is some help.

Another phrase of Pirsig's, maybe someone familiar with physics (such as Doug or Ken) could help me out with, is the following:

"Atoms are created by the preference of quantum forces for certain stable relationships. These quantum forces are not objects of any kind. They are believed to have existed before the Big Bang and can be shown to exist today in absolute atomic vacuums. They are just patterns of preference that appear out of what is called mass/energy. But if one asks what is this mass/energy independently of its preferences one finds oneself thinking of nothing whatsoever."

(Letter from Robert Pirsig, March 23, 1997)

Doug:

Anthony, a really good book on the material Pirsig shared with you above is a text I previously suggested on TLS, Order Out of Chaos, by Ilya Prigogine & Isabelle Stengers.

You might hold some reservations as you read this, because Prigogine, as did Einstein, leans to the deterministic side. What I really like is the way he puts the second law of thermodynamics in a "better" perspective. He says that entropy has two terms: one dissipative (Ken, pay attention here), and one productive. The latter is compatible with the increasing complexity of life, which we relate to DQ.

It is a good book, but other weaknesses from my perspective are that Prigogine talks about closed or isolated systems. In the quantum and MOQ worlds, neither of these is possible (my perception). The concept of isolation is a classical one. It suffers the illusion that one may observe an object in total isolation. We know that is not true, and that in reality as we observe the object we affect it and vice versa too. That is why I recently introduced the term co-aware in TLS discussions of MOQ.

Platt:

Here's my suggestion:

Morality: Morality is a synonym for Quality. A phenomenon is considered more moral, or of higher Quality, to the extent that it supports and advances freedom.

Pirsig makes it clear in the hot stove example (Chapter 5) that it's perfectly legitimate to think of Quality (awareness) as being divided along a spectrum of low quality at one end and high quality at the other. In the example he uses such phrases as "undeniably low quality situation," "the value of his predicament is negative," "may generate oaths to describe this low value," "without the primary low valuation," etc.

Later (Chapter 9) he ties this high/low spectrum of value to Dynamic Quality: "The negative esthetic quality of the hot stove in the earlier example was now given added meaning by the static/Dynamic division of Quality. When the person on the hot stove first discovers his low Quality situation, the front edge of his experience is Dynamic. He does not think, 'This stove is hot,' and then make a rational decision to get off. A 'dim perception of he knows not what' gets him off Dynamically. Later he generates static patterns of thought to explain the situation."

The way I interpret this is that the front edge of experience, i.e., Dynamic Quality, includes a sense of value (a dim perception) that operates simultaneously with the front edge and makes an instantaneous judgment along the high/low Quality spectrum, causing a Dynamic response prior to static thought. [86]

Following this line of reasoning, Dynamic Quality's sense of high value is freedom from static values; static value's sense of high value is resistance to Dynamic Quality. It may seem strange to think of Dynamic Quality and static quality as having a "sense," but remember that our first principle states that Quality is known to us as awareness. Awareness equals "sense of."

So I see Quality divided two ways in the MOQ: along a fuzzy logic sort of positive/negative spectrum, and a hard logic Dynamic/static split with both occurring simultaneously, not in a separate either/or relationship but a complimentary relationship. [87] We state in the principles: "There are many ways to divide Quality but the best way is into patterns of Dynamic and static value or experience." I agree it's the "best" way (high/low spectrum), even though Pirsig apparently permits another way, because the Dynamic/Static split is the key that sets the MOQ apart from other rationally based philosophies.

Marty:

Is the MOQ a path to enlightenment?

Ant:

I'm not so sure whether the MOQ (being a set of static intellectual patterns) is actually a path to enlightenment and I certainly wouldn't put that on the Internet. However, I think you can say that the MOQ can assist on a mystic journey to enlightenment. [88]

Well, that's my thinking at the moment, subject to change of course. Goodness knows I've been wrong before. I'm just glad to see freedom back in the principles, no matter how it gets there.

Annotations by Robert M. Pirsig

81. Whatever the dictionary says it is.

82. A metaphysics in which the most fundamental reality is value.

83. To explain why people differed about what has quality.

84. This summary of principles is excellent.

85. This is also excellent.

86. Since in the MOQ all divisions of Quality are static it follows that high and low are subdivisions of static quality. "Static" and "Dynamic" are also subdivisions of static quality, since the MOQ is itself a static intellectual pattern of Quality.

87. This seems very good as long as it is understood that the structure of the MOQ puts static and Dynamic above high and low in its hierarchy.

88. It depends on which kind of Hindu you are. Dhyana yoga, which is the same as Zen, bypasses intellectuality. Jnana yoga however uses knowledge as a path to enlightenment. Hindus generally seem to think both work.

Chapter 9

Now, we daily see what science is doing for us. This could not be unless it taught us something about reality; the aim of science is not things themselves, as the dogmatists in their simplicity imagine, but the relations between things; outside those relations there is no reality knowable. —Henri Poincaré, Science and Hypothesis, page xxiv, translated from French in 1905 by J. Larmor, Dover Publications, 1952

Artificial Intelligence [January 1998]

Lars:

I've been reading a lot about artificial intelligence lately and some ideas are starting to bubble somewhere deep down in my brain. They haven't come together just yet, but Magnus' excellent article [http://www.moq.org/forum/magnus.html] got the bubbling started. Basically, I'm a little unhappy with his dismissal of artificial intelligence (and his use of Dynamic Quality in that dismissal).

Magnus:

It wasn't intended as a dismissal really, but I guess it could be interpreted that way depending on your view of artificial intelligence.

Lars:

I did interpret it that way, I must admit. It was especially this part that struck me so: "We inhibited them from being intelligent by building them so static that it is impossible for them to exercise any Dynamic choices of their own. We have crippled them by specifying the voltage levels for ones and zeros so wide apart that there's no chance for Dynamic Quality to have any influence whatsoever."

Magnus:

See what you mean. I guess you could use the Hitch Hiker's approach—a hot cup of tea as Dynamic input. Anyway, this does raise a very interesting question, something that we haven't talked about for a while and I don't remember if we reached a conclusion. The question is—where does the Dynamic unpredictability of Quality events come from? [89] Did it originate in the Quality event of the specific level or from the inorganic representation of the Quality event?

I realize that both my dismissal above and the hot cup of tea approach assume the latter but I'm not at all sure about it. I guess it's the reductionist in me that speaks. The term "mediation" on the other hand assumes the former. Mediation was introduced by Maggie some time ago and means that patterns of a higher level affects patterns of a lower.

Also, the diagram in Pirsig's SODV (Subjects, Objects, Data and Value) paper suggests the former. Pirsig writes: "This seems the best way to represent it." Maybe we're not able to decide it at all. It would mean a definition of an aspect of Dynamic Quality and that's off limits. One way to relate subjectivity/objectivity to MOQ is to scale it down the static ladder. The higher the level, the more subjective a pattern is and vice versa. The problem comes when you literally fall off the edge of reality below the inorganic level. Pure objectivity suddenly becomes very dependent on the observer, which it isn't supposed to be.

Maggie:

I see that you are talking about the static ladder as one dimensional, and of course, it is, I'm not stating otherwise.

Magnus:

It puzzles me that you said that. I think I see the static ladder as more of a tree, perhaps a banyan tree that has the capability of dropping new roots from its branches.

Maggie:

The banyan tree is new to me but I think I get the picture. We might be talking about different abstraction layers here. Let me draw a parallel to computer science. In object-oriented lingo, there's two basic ways to view a system. The object hierarchy shows relationships between objects, and the class hierarchy shows relationships between classes (of objects).

266

The object hierarchy would map to the banyan tree, consisting of patterns (objects) of the levels (classes), and the class hierarchy would map to the levels. This makes the object hierarchy a tree structure, but the class hierarchy would be one-dimensional. It would be like overlaying the four boxes in the SODV paper with the banyan tree. The patterns of the banyan tree would be mapped to their correct level. The more I think about it, the better the object-oriented analogy seems. Maybe I'll make a formal object oriented analysis of static quality. The straight inheritance hierarchy between the levels would capture the inter-level dependency quite beautifully. Anybody have any comments?

Doug:

Magnus and Maggie, again, brilliant! Pure DQ! May I make one suggestion, however? Substitute the term static pattern of value (SPoV) for object. When you do this, remember that MOQ says value (both DQ and sq) is co-within/interpenetrating via the Interrelationships among SPoVs, a la Dusenberry. By comparison, SOM says the Value (it calls values "properties") or properties are in the Objects, a la Franz Boas. It says interrelationships are subjective and thus insubstantial.

A good example I use here is the old DOS command line interrelationship to humans as compared to the Macintosh or modern browser Graphical User Interface (GUI). There is incredibly more Value in the latter than in the former.

Magnus:

Yeah, that's one of the beauties of the analogue. Too bad only computer nerds can appreciate, or criticize it.

But still, nobody during the French revolution wanted to alter the interrelationship between their head and neck.

Maggie:

In MOQ the inter-level dependency, interrelationships are mediated by Dynamic Quality and the five sets of Pirsig's Moral Codes.

Magnus:

267

Yes, the moral codes would be built in, no Dynamic Quality though.

Doug:

I found this presumption really interesting. Especially from your view of and interest in artificial intelligence. You appear to imply that the moral codes are formal. But in the MOQ, the moral codes are indeed static patterns of value subject to the Dynamic force of evolution (to use Ken's, et al., terms).

Magnus:

Yes, the moral codes are of course subject to Dynamic Quality, hence the "no Dynamic Quality though," in the other post. An ObjectOriented (OO) model of static patterns would only be a static model. As soon as interaction gets involved, we leave the MOQ, because interaction is predictable in the OO model but not in the MOQ. The cause of the predictability in the OO model might be that we are able to observe it passively from the outside without getting our noses wet. The entities inside the OO model would not, so it might seem unpredictable to them, would they ever reflect about it.

Eugenics [January 1998]

Bodvar:

I just received this question from a young student who has read Pirsig's books (and found my essay). A baffling query admittedly, does anyone have an idea or draft for an answer? He writes: "The question I have, simply put, is, 'Is eugenics moral?' Now it is easily arguable that eugenics for racial reasons is not, because useful ideas are lost. But what of the mentally handicapped and retarded, those who most likely will not contribute to the intellectual quality in the least? It is impossible for me to believe that these people must be lost, that these people don't have a quality of their own. I hope you can help me, because as of now I can't find an answer in Pirsig's works." [90]

Doug:

Bo, my quick answer is from the context of the bottom three levels, probably not moral but from the intellectual level, probably is moral.

I didn't think much about this—just seems right on first blush.

Magnus:

I'd say that eugenics is moral as long as it stimulates diversity, but it must never inhibit diversity. I've noticed that often when a problem seems difficult, even when applying the MOQ to it, the source of the problem is (always) the Dynamic/static conflict.

It's the old yin and yang, good and evil controversies in a new disguise. I guess there's an upper limit to the amount of diversity being stimulated, but I don't think we'd ever get near it.

And about the mentally handicapped and retarded, maybe they don't contribute intellectually directly, but they sure as h-ll have an indirect Dynamic impact on people around them. Phrases like "he brings out the best in me," and "she made me look at the world through her eyes," are common in this context. The worst form of eugenics is when people inhibit diversity on the arrogant premises that they know what's best in the long run. They don't have a clue! Nobody has.

Hugo:

There has been some resemblance of the arguments of the four levels of reality to the old "natural ladder" idea, conveyed by the idea that the highest level was "the most moral." I myself has not been entirely satisfied with what I see as a maybe faulty confusion between value in an absolute and in an contextual sense, and with the further merging of value with moral. Pirsig speaks of Quality in an absolute sense, as in being the source of reality, or just being reality, and he identifies value and quality in some places. [91] The question is entirely appropriate, and has to do with an important part of Pirsig's metaphysics.

It seems to me that the question in this respect (the nature of Pirsig's "moral") is related to the distinction between absolute moral (as for instance the moral given in religion) and relative or contextual moral. An often posed kind of question goes like this—

some terrorists make you pick one of ten of your companions for execution, or they will execute them all (less drastic questions can do). In Pirsig's world, the question could be, given that intellectual freedom is the most moral—should new ideas always be brought to life? Or, analogous to the question the student posed, is the existence of humans (rational humans) morally superior to the existence of animals (irrational humans)?

I have no ready answer, but it is evident that we are faced with such moral dilemmas in society. Often the outcome of such dilemmas is based on some balancing between opposing interests. The life of the mother opposed to the life of the fetus. The life of humans opposed to wildlife. The question of eugenics varies across some established line of balance. The life of the irreversibly dying person is not sustained in vain. Premature babied below some lower limit of weight are not provided with life support if they show no sign of a will to live. I think the "will to live" has an important say in this question; we should not without cause limit the livelihood of other living beings, but this is of course hopelessly vague.

Dave:

Dictionary definition:

Eugenics: 1) the movement devoted to improving the human species though the control of hereditary factors in mating. Eugenic: 1) causing improvement of hereditary qualities of a stock. 2) Of, relating to, or improved by eugenics.

I don't think Pirsig addresses this directly but I seem to recall a possibly related topic, "the death penalty" for criminal acts, which he says is not moral because of the loss of the potential "good" of that individual. So on the surface one might think it safe to conclude he would say something similar in applied eugenics when "the death penalty" is used as a method of implementing it, i.e., abortions.

But let's set up a real world scenario moving on to eugenics as it is regularly applied in many parts of the world—marriage blood tests for detection of potentially serious birth defects in planned offspring. A couple has done this, no potential was found, have conceived, and now tests indicate a certainty of serious birth defects. What should they do? How can MOQ help them?

I agree with Hugo that when faced with these types of dilemmas we must look at context and balance. But I would go on to say that with the MOQ, we now have five different frames of reference and at minimum three basic moral points of view with which to balance the decision. Does the choice affect freedom on any or all of the four static levels? If so, which way, pro or con? To what degree? Does the choice on one level so dominate the other levels that it will at some point harm or destroy the system? Does the choice increase or decrease access to Dynamic Duality? [92]

So, eugenics, in the context of the social level dominating the biological level by saying immediate families must not interbreed, is moral. Because that choice will limit the Dynamic potential of having a larger and diverse gene pool, the lack of which threatens overall system stability. On the contrary, eugenics, in a similar social dominating biological context, like the Nazi attempt to purify the gene pool to fair haired, blue eyed Aryans, is amoral for exactly the same reasons. So the Zen answer applies.

But my guess is—given the recent flurry of press surrounding cloning and genetics—that the student's question is more rooted in the world of, "should we even be doing things like the Human Genome Project?" In that this starts us down another path of tinkering with highly complex systems with little real understanding of the long term consequences, the risk there I guess would be of too much Dynamism. In which case you don't know until you get there and it then may be too late.

So, the next daunting task for TLS is to conjure up a framework for making decisions on the application level, which is as broad and Dynamic as the basic premise of the system.

Bodvar:

271

Thanks for responding to the Eugenics issue. You have given me valuable inputs that go into my answer. It came to look like this (but is on "hold" for a while if anyone has further comments):

Is Eugenics Moral?

Your question: "Is eugenics moral" requires a little preparation. I don't know how familiar you are with the Metaphysics of Quality (MOQ), but from your well-written essay, it sounded good enough. As you will know, according to the MOQ, everything is moral or value, but not all phenomena belong to the same static value level. This is the reason so many issues take on a confusing taint when addressed from the Subject/Object point of view. Yes, it is the source of all "good versus bad" struggles of this world.

Well, then where in the MOQ hierarchy does eugenics belong? At first glance, the obvious place would be the interface between the inorganic (matter) and the biological (life). Only the organisms able to adapt to changes in environment survive, but this is hardly eugenics in your book—only when the social level comes into play does it take on the ominous quality we usually connect it with.

Society in the MOQ sense is a very wide term. [93] It can be defined as the whole at the cost of the part. And in that capacity groups have always put pressure upon its members to adapt to the group's interest, i.e., an insect colony's highly specialized individuals, and flock animals' total devotion to the common cause (such things are called instincts in SOM). This is the extreme, but even human societies "breed" individuals that can best fill the society's needs. However, this comes naturally, so to say, though eugenics as an idea (political program) is a relative modern phenomenon.

According to Pirsig (Chapter 23, Lila) the time from the turn of the century and up to the Second World War was the last throe of the social level's dominance of Western culture, and the war itself the final shoot-out between the rising intellectual level and the declining social one. Fascism and Nazism were social value presented as political programs: the individual was to sacrifice itself for the common cause (Das Vaterland, the race, etc.), and the unwanted were to be removed (Holocaust).

The MOQ postulates this law—the value of a lower level is low value to the one above. Naturally, for the rising intellect, social value is invariably bad, and the Western culture that is now dominated by intellect looks upon every social effort to control the individuals as infringements upon its chief value, freedom. The death penalty isn't eugenics, but another social value abhorred by intellect.

In conclusion, to the inorganic level eugenics isn't "known." To the biological level, it is amoral, neutral. Life is eugenics itself. To the social level, it is moral, and to intellect, it is immoral. As intellect is the highest value level, eugenics as an idea should not be contemplated; no programs should be worked out to refine the human stock by killing "unwanted" individuals. And yet, it cannot be eradicated and is still practiced under new names: pre-natal tests, abortion, gene manipulation, the Genome project, etc.

If you still insist, "Yes, but is eugenics really good or bad?" There is no such (objective) reality in the Quality universe; there is only this hierarchy of morals. Nothing can be dismissed as really evil without ending up with paradoxes and/or with an incomplete world.

Platt:

First, let me say that your MOQ based analysis of the eugenics issue was a classic! If anyone has wondered how to apply the MOQ to practical moral questions in "the world of everyday affairs," your letter shows the way. It's a model that I'll follow whenever challenged by social/moral conundrums. Regarding the rationality question, my concern was that in using rationalism alone as a synonym for the intellectual level empiricism was left out. In your mind, rationalism includes empiricism, in my mind, not so. Perhaps the following quote from Whitehead reveals the underpinning of my view:

"It is a great mistake to conceive this historical revolt (of science) as an appeal to reason. On the contrary, it was through and through an anti intellectual movement. It was a return to the contemplation of brute fact, and it was based on a recoil from the inflexible rationality of medieval thought."

So, I associate rationalism with the Inquisition and other intellectual edifices built on self-serving sands. Logical positivism, on the other hand, is closer to what I see as the prevailing intellectual level. When you describe this level as "SOM/Rationality/Science" our disagreement vanishes.

As for the MOQ representing a new esthetic level growing out of intellect, I'm still of that mind and am trying to build a persuasive case for it. Any help you can offer would be much appreciated.

Intellect as Rationality [January 1998]

Ant:

I am unhappy with the replacement of "intellect" with "rationality." Firstly, "rationalism" is the philosophical theory of a priori ideas, that truth and knowledge are attainable primarily through reason rather than through experience. Unfortunately, I think its usage within the MOQ could become confusing especially as the MOQ is an empirical theory opposed to rationality. Maybe the term "reasoning" could be put in its place but even with this term, there are problems. [94]

Bodvar:

Gentlemen! I must hasten to say that "rationality" wasn't meant to replace static patterns of intellect as the official name in the MOQ. The reason for introducing the term stems from a thread in the early days of TLS when the evasiveness of this value dimension dawned upon us. At first, it was pinned down as thinking, mental activity, consciousness, "mind" for short, but this really screws things up. The MOQ rejects mind/matter as the fundamental division of reality so defining intellect as mind means lapsing back to the SOM.

I long stuck to "Symbolic Language" (and still think it's a good definition), but someone caught the idea that intellect can be seen as rational thinking. Long before the Lila Squad days, it had puzzled me greatly that Subject/Object metaphysics may be viewed as the intellectual level of MOQ! I even raised the question in a letter to Pirsig, but he did not respond. [95]

Ant:

One of the main ideas of ZMM (which was carried through to Lila) is that the dominance of rationality over the imaginative and artistic fields in Western thinking has fragmented the human intellect. Pirsig basically says we have a two-tier system where rationality (or reasoning) is seen above rhetoric, art, etc. As everyone knows, this goes back to Plato and his example of the charioteer and the two wild horses that need reigning in. One of the aims of Pirsig's work is to correct Plato's error and put the arts on an equal footing with the sciences again. I therefore feel that the term "rationality" (especially with the use of the term representing a philosophical theory antagonistic towards the arts) should not be used within the MOQ.

Bodvar:

Yes, exactly, but intellect isn't (all of) the MOQ. Pirsig is critical to the intellectual level which has come to dominate the scene completely, and I found it just within a hair's breadth to draw the conclusion that intellect has usurped metaphysics as well and claims to be reality itself (as Subject/Object thinking which is rationality/science). What you say is correct, but it confirms the "rationality" definition. Quality put art, imagination, rhetoric back on equal footing, perhaps even into the charioteer seat!

Platt! You once suggested the idea of MOQ as a new "artistic" static level growing out of intellect, i.e., as freedom from intellect's tyranny. Added to the "Intellect as SOM/Rationality/Science," it completed a circle that I still find attractive, but I may have gone off on a blind alley of my own. Anyway, I am open for criticism.

Ken:

Reading the posts convinces me that there are about as many conceptions of the Dynamic Quality idea as there are Squad members. It is confusing to me to try to sort out the approach that a particular person is taking to Dynamic Quality. Lila leaves a good bit of room for interpretation, particularly with regard to the pre sentient/post sentient areas.

What would you think of the idea of asking each member to write a short statement defining what Dynamic Quality means to them, not with the idea of coming up with a universally accepted definition, I doubt if we could do that, but to give everybody an idea of the range of DQs that we are dealing with. It would probably start a fierce debate but that is not bad and it would certainly help my state of confusion. [96]

Field Being [January 1998]

Martin:

Fear not old friend, for I suspect many of us have had trouble over this concept. At least I know I did. Recently I've been looking into a philosophy called Field Being (FB), based on A. N. Whitehead's writings and some contemporary philosophers.

A friend of mine at Fairfield University (CT), who is a student of the foremost FB philosopher, Dr. Lik Kueng Tong, sent me several essays that he has written about it (he has already decided to make FB the center of his graduate studies and wants to "pioneer" this "new" philosophy, so I treat his essays with authority). He said that FB is an attempt to reconcile eastern thinking with Western thinking.

Now, this immediately caught my eye since it is exactly what Pirsig wanted to do forty years ago. He explained that Western thinking envisions Being as "| |" separate and distinct entities, while eastern thinking envisions Being as "O" which is to say, all part of an intricate whole, the metaphysical one-ness of Zen. Field Being says that individuality is not real; we are all together—that individuality is just man's rationalization so he can simplify the world and deal with it on logical terms (sort of like it's too difficult to consider each part as being connected to and effecting all other parts). At the same time, Field Being says that Zen one-ness is an individuality of its own. We are just one big individual. Field Being makes a compromise and provides a solution by saying

Being is like a "U" many beings all united yet still distinct (sounds paradoxical eh?).

Well, from the MOQ perspective it doesn't have to be paradoxical, only within a SOM context it is. Each individual perceived value, which is to say each static value, is distinct in itself. However, prior to intellectualization, all values exist as a Dynamic whole, the Dynamic whole of the Quality event/Dynamic Quality. I put them together because they are one and the same, in my opinion. At least, that's the best way to make sense of them. ZMM's "Quality event" is Lila's "Dynamic Quality." Both are the pre-intellectual cutting edge that gives us the values with which we construct our reality. Where does static quality fit in? Well, remember the "analogues" that Pirsig speaks of in ZMM? These analogues that Pirsig says, "...are our reality, ever last bit." These are static quality.

Now back to Field Being. The most fundamental view that FB takes on is its non- substantialism. If any of you are familiar with Whitehead, you already know what I mean. FB posits that there are no independent, continuous beings, no individuals that last through time. FB sees reality as nothing but process. In other words, there are no nouns, only verbs. Static entities are again just mental constructions that make it easier to deal with our world. It's like that old paradox, "What happens to my fist when I open my hand?" We've hidden an action as a noun. "To fist" would be more accurate than to say, "To make a fist." I stopped fisting. That's why it disappeared.

Does this sound weird to you? I hope it doesn't because the MOQ can account for this too, with Dynamic Quality, the Quality event. What we're talking about is events, process, dynamics, and action. I like to think of DQ/QE as "nowness," the infinitesimally small fragment of time that constitutes Now. That infinitesimally small unit of time that is all that exists. Everything in the past is a memory; everything in the future is a hope. Now is all that exists. Now is the Quality event. It is Dynamic Quality (Now is always new). Now is also preintellectual because it takes a split second to

277

recognize it and think about it (remember that old game, Simon, where you try to hit one of four colored buttons as soon as they light up? That whole game is based on the fact that we are always a little behind true reality, caught up in our own intellectualized realities).

Field Being has helped me understand and reaffirm some very basic tenets of the MOQ. Reality is all action because it is DQ/QE, which is a Dynamic event. Static patterns don't exist in themselves because the world is all process. Static patterns are mental constructs because we rationalize to simplify our world so we can understand it. Our understanding of it is that intellectual (or post intellectual) level of awareness.

Does this mean that all these static patterns are unreal? We just live in a hologram or dream? Well, our intellectualized versions of the tree value or wife value or whatever are our own values, they are close to but not the real thing. But they are all we have. They are our construction of our reality and so they must be assumed to be as real as anything (as Bodvar pointed out in the quote from ZMM, the Quality event prompts us to create subjects and objects).

You might object, but things really do stay the same at least for a short time. So aren't they real static objects at least for that amount of time? My friend Dave Kovach from Fairfield University answers that actually their atoms are constantly vibrating, so each second they are (technically) a completely different entity from the second before (since their atoms are never in the exact same positions). It's just too hard to think of all these trillions and trillions of atoms, each moving in a different direction. It's much easier to think of the object as a static whole (and besides, we can't see the atoms).

Field Being is becoming a very popular philosophy, especially in the East. Dr. Tong has a network of six hundred professors in China who espouse his beliefs. It is very close to the MOQ, but it fails to have the utility that the MOQ has.

Ken:

Thanks for your attempt to clear up my muddled thinking. You gave the clearest exposition of the MOQ that I have seen in one essay. One of the problems I had for a while was that Pirsig had to deal with each step of the MOQ more or less in isolation because he was presenting a new idea and had to separate its components for clarity and this caused me to view the process in this fashion.

The understanding you have given me is that we humans are living in a sea of awareness, the basic components of which are the same for all. Individually we have different life and intellectual histories and thus interpret this sea of awareness individually which results in our perceived separateness. The picture you have now completed for me is that individually we are living in a constantly changing cloud of virtual awareness, which results in a constantly ongoing sense of reality as determined by the instantaneous contents of our static patterns of value. There is no reality that we can grab onto and say—this is it. We can, of course, grab an instant and try to describe reality but it will be a reality that is no longer valid. I can also see why one could say that humanity is one state of being because we are linked to the same underlying process, and thus dip into the same pool of awareness.

I would have to take issue with the Field Being idea when it states that there are no independent continuous beings. It is true that there are no material beings that persist through time, but there are beings whose ideas persist through time and those ideas contribute to the ongoing sense of reality for some of us. In fact, I think that this is probably universally true regardless of the quality of those ideas. We all influence and are influenced by some people whether their ideas are good or bad. Back in the forties or fifties, a group of people were discovered in New Guinea who had no contact with any other people of any kind within their memory. Their MOQ must have operated the same as ours.

This brings me to another problem I have with the MOQ. We and most everybody in the Lila Squad discuss the MOQ solely in relation to the human race. In this context, all of this makes sense. It makes sense until we begin to talk about the operation of

Dynamic Quality before sentience. The static patterns of value start with the inorganic level. This implies that the MOQ existed before sentience. [97] Pirsig himself talks about time being a static intellectual concept that is one of the very first to emerge from Dynamic Quality. Did he mean that the universe was imbued with intellectuality from the start or did he mean that the MOQ began with humanity? Does this mean that the Big Bang was Dynamic Quality or did Dynamic Quality cause the Big Bang? If so, what does that make Dynamic Quality—God?

It is said that the MOQ has been in existence always. How do we define morality and good in terms of the universe and/or the Earth except as a force for interrupting the flow of entropy toward randomness? I have to assume that this is so because entropy is the force that produced evolution and us. How does inorganic MOQ fit in with sentient MOQ? What becomes morality and good then? Is it what is good for the human race or is it what is good for the Earth? If the two MOQs exist in the sentient static patterns of values separately which takes precedence? If they are one then what is the definition of goodness and morality in those levels? My understanding was that morality and goodness was defined in terms of the universe but I continually see the terms used as if they applied only to humans.

I hope that you can see the problems I am having and I hope that you have answers that will clear up my confusion or can show me where my thinking went wrong.

Martin:

Well, I've struggled with it myself. Mark and Bo helped me out a lot, along with several philosophies outside of the MOQ: phenomenology, Field Being, empiricism, etc. We all know that Pirsig's books are jigsaw puzzles. You go along and find a few pieces and put them together, but then you get some pieces that belong somewhere completely different, and later you get another piece that fits with your first set, and so on. I'm not proposing that what I said was absolutely "right," but by putting together the pieces, it is the best way I have been able to understand Quality, in so far as it can be understood.

As someone pointed out, time is a static pattern (if it is the fourth dimension, then it is a physical static pattern like the other dimensions and matter and energy). However, when I say "now," I mean an infinitesimally small amount of time, which is to say "No Time" at all, just a point. It's just the moment of awareness, a continually evolving event that gives us our sense of time, space, and all the other values and value judgments we make.

I won't profess to be completely right since everyone will have a slightly different interpretation of Pirsig's work (I mean it's not exactly a pure syllogism). So, let this be a warning to you Lila Squad; don't let the differences stop us!

I don't know what you mean by "virtual" awareness. What you are saying sounds a lot like Kant. He said that our knowledge is a continuous synthesis of sense experience and a priori knowledge/memory. It may be true, but don't fall back into Kant's SOM thinking. Pirsig knew he couldn't defeat Kant, he just said that we must thank Kant for leading a certain line of thought to its necessary conclusion, but we're past due for a big paradigm shift. As long as we maintain that our knowledge is a synthesis of static and Dynamic values, and not a synthesis of object experience and subject memory, we'll remain within the MOQ.

You made a good objection to Field Being. I also pointed out to my friend that FB comes into contradiction with phenomenology, which says that there is an underlying "essence" that doesn't change over time, and there are methods (called Eidetic and Phenomenological Reductions) to discovering it. He just responded, "Yeah, but phenomenology is old and stale. Field Being hasn't been pioneered yet." And when you're going to become a professional philosopher, it's good to espouse new beliefs. Hey, the MOQ is pretty new! :-)

Hmmm. "The MOQ existed before sentience." No, the MOQ is a static intellectual pattern. It could only have been around as long as intelligence was around, and we know that actually it has only been around for perhaps twenty years. But that does not mean there was no reality. The MOQ is not reality; it is a set of lenses by which we interpret reality. The SOM lenses are old and scratchy; they no longer provide a clear view. Quality is reality. It is Dynamic and static, physical, biological, cultural, and intellectual. It has been around for as long as anything that has existed, although specific parts haven't. I don't see where the problem is.

As for the Big Bang, I discussed this a few months ago. It's really hard to tell since we don't know what existed before, if anything. In any case, the Big Bang was a physical event. You could say it was the first Dynamic value from which all static values cascaded (but not the last Dynamic value). But both Dynamic and static are components of Quality, which simply means everything, all values. Is Quality God? You could call it that if you want. I don't but Mark does.

That's one of the great things about the MOQ, how all encompassing it is. After Pirsig describes evolution, he addresses the teleologists (Is there meaning?) and points out that both are accommodated. There could very well be a meaning, although it would reside somewhere along or before the leading edge of experience (Dynamic Quality), and so even if there were a meaning, we wouldn't know what it was. If there was a certain plan that Dynamic Quality was unfolding for us, there's no way to find out. And, there also might not be a meaning except for the meaning we give it anyway. So whether or not there is an intelligent God goes either way, but certainly the MOQ doesn't favor old mythologies about angry or merciful Supermen who threw out exactly Ten Laws that must be followed to the letter, lest you burn in eternal hellfire. I think we've outgrown children's stories, agnosticism, deism, pantheism, and eastern conceptions of God—these are just as valid as atheism.

You keep using the term MOQ as a synonym for reality. I agree it is a philosophy about reality, but not reality itself. It's just a metaphysics. Let's get right to the heart of the matter—is it Good for the human race or is it what is Good for the Earth? Both! Pirsig

282

points out that morality applies to everything within its own context and in the great scheme of evolution. It is perfectly moral for a virus to kill a human—to the virus. That's all it can do—lie dormant or take over host cells. It is perfectly moral for one social more to overthrow an older one, if it is better. And of course, we have to take into account the grand scheme of evolution and the static levels (literally the levels of Goodness). Pirsig says that since a human is more evolved than a virus, it is more moral for a human to kill a virus than vice versa. It is very immoral for social values to dominate intellectual values. Well, you get the idea.

That does not give humans free reign to kill and maim and destroy everything just because they are more evolved. Remember, no set of values can exist without the ones below to support it. If we trash our planet, even though it is just physical, biological, and a little social value, then we'll die too. There is no dichotomy between inorganic MOQ (actually Quality) and sentient MOQ. That almost sounds like a body/mind split again!

Annotations by Robert M. Pirsig

89. If we could say where Dynamic Quality came from it wouldn't be Dynamic.

90. Eugenics: The study of hereditary improvement of the human race by controlled selective breeding. —American Heritage Dictionary

The MOQ does clearly support eugenics, since it is a way of modifying biology for social benefit. Because society is at a higher level, it takes moral precedence. After all, our marriage customs are a form of eugenics. I believe I have read that severely mentally retarded people are not permitted to marry under law.

91. The problem here is with the term, "absolute." It has been used by Western philosophers for years to describe the central reality of mysticism.

"The Absolute" means the same as "Dynamic Quality" and the "nothingness" of Buddhism, but it's a poor term because of its connotations. To me it connotes something cold, dead, empty of content and rigid. The term, "Dynamic Quality," has opposite connotations. It suggests warmth, life, fullness and flexibility. They are the same, but when the term, "Absolute," is dropped, the problem mentioned here goes away. Dynamic Quality is not dominated by context but it is not separate from context either.

92. I think the MOQ would say that society has a moral right to control biology. The danger is in that in controlling biology society creates customs that injure society itself. Clearly the cost of caring for biologically defective people is a burden on society, but the question is, if society sanctions the murder of a defective fetus, what other kinds of murder is it going to sanction? Think of the money that could be saved by executing all criminals, all mentally ill people, all people with an IQ below 100, all old people, all people with poor DNA patterns, all people who can't do 40 pushups, and so on. The question is—where do you cut it off? I personally am pro-choice, but I understand the moral integrity of those who are not. It is a matter for society through its mechanisms

of politics to decide and keep deciding as it evolves toward a better world.

93. This strikes me as so general it destroys the meaning of society for MOQ purposes. I think it is better just to keep it as the subjective customs of groups of people.

94. Good point.

95. I don't remember not responding, so it must have been an oversight. I don't think the subject-object level is identical with intellect. Intellect is simply thinking, and one can think without involving the subject-object relationship. Computer language is not primarily structured into subjects and objects. Algebra has no subjects and objects.

96. It would also violate the MOQ principle of leaving Quality undefined.

97. Within the MOQ, the idea that static patterns of value start with the inorganic level is considered to be a good idea. But the MOQ itself doesn't start before sentience. The MOQ, like science, starts with human experience. Remember the early talk in ZMM about Newton's Law of Gravity? Scientific laws without people to write them are a scientific impossibility.

Chapter 10

Every thoughtful person who hopes for the creation of a contemporary culture knows that this hinges on one central problem: to find a coherent relationship between science and the humanities. —Jacob Bronowski

Death [December 1997]

Dave:

My bottom line question about MOQ that I cannot yet resolve yet, though I believe it is of paramount importance to the adoption of MOQ, though I don't know why, is this—if I die, or all humans die, what does MOQ say about what's left? Is there anything or is there nothing? In a response to my recent post on quantum theory, it was suggested this question in quantum theory context was a mu or meaningless question. But for me this is an essential question that any metaphysics and it is one the SOM has been struggling with forever.

Any ideas? [98]

Mark:

Your question is paramount. It is perhaps the oldest of a culture that has separated reality into Me and Not Me. It is a cultural notion to consider a human as a local point of awareness, self contained, free from any connections. It is quite natural for this human to wonder what happens upon death. Not only can we toss out the Me/Not Me dichotomy (SOM) but we really don't need to dichotomize at all. Analysis only removes us from the ultimate reality that we, you, me, and the universe, are One thing. The common response to this is, "Yes, yes, One thing, right." We are all one thing, okay. But that doesn't help me in a universe that for all intents and purposes appears to be full of lots of things, all different. So, I agree with you on a "mystical" level, but operationally, I need more resolution; I can't think without breaking the universe up somehow.

Instead of calling you a sinner, the MOQ says, fine. It presents you with tools, which carve up reality better than SOM. It affords new insights, eliminates paradoxes, and better satisfies Mr. Occam. All good, by the way, exciting too, but look where these new insights are pointing—to the mystical premise that we are One thing, Quality, Good, God.

We don't really need to intellectualize the answers to paramount questions. We don't need to dice up reality in order to stand under it. I believe the process of searching is important, but one does not need an education to know Quality. The answers are in our heart, not our head. MOQ can give you an answer, but if you don't feel that mystical premise, it will lack real meaning. So, if you believe we are all one thing, then you already have your answer. Look for it within.

If you dismiss this premise (and I believe many do by intellectually acknowledging it without taking it to heart) then you are back to dicing up reality in a search for clues, and if you use SOM tools, then you have to carve up reality all the way down to the quantum level before a really nasty paradox slaps us upside the head. The power of the MOQ is that it offers the One answer for those that accept on faith, and better tools for discovering the One answer for the more rationally minded. It has something for everyone I think.

One fear I have is that we become so caught up in the wonders of these intellectual insights that we lose sight of their mystical origins. Understanding Nature on a quantum level is fine, but you are infinitely more important, more moral. Adopting the MOQ may make for more understandable science, but that pales in comparison to the human implications. If we are all One, then treating others as we would have others treat us not only feels right, it makes "sense."

Dave:

Under the MOQ, if all men were to disappear from Earth tomorrow it would not be a "healthier" place because it would have lost one of its highest levels of freedom. But the Earth and the

Universe would go blithely along most probably evolving some other sentient being here in a billion years or so. So, from my perspective not all ecological movements are about hugging trees or warm fuzzy bunnies but pure and simple self-interest.

That being said I do not think the current, or any, political, economic, or other social and intellectual value systems can or will make significant progress in the area of ecology until such time as their is complete rethinking and adoption of a new metaphysical/philosophical base. In my opinion the Metaphysics of Quality could well be that new base.

Platt:

Why is Dynamic Quality more moral than static quality? Why are the levels at a higher stage of evolution more moral than levels below? What standard are we using to make these assertions about what is "more moral"? Why does Pirsig say some things are more moral than others are?

I submit the standard is freedom. In Chapter 29, Pirsig speaks of Dynamic Quality: "Its only perceived good is freedom and its only perceived evil is static quality itself…any pattern of one sided fixed values that tries to contain and kill the ongoing free force of life." In Chapter 11 he says, "All life is a migration of static patterns of quality toward Dynamic Quality." In Chapter 29 he says, "They're fighting for some kind of Dynamic freedom from the static patterns. But the Dynamic freedom they're fighting for is a kind of morality too. And it's a highly important part of the overall moral process. It's often confused with degeneracy, but it's actually a form of moral regeneration. Without its continual refreshment static patterns would simple die of old age."

If life is "migration toward Dynamic Quality," and if the "only perceived good" of Dynamic Quality is freedom, it follows that life is a migration toward freedom. Without this migration propelled by the energy of the "free force of life," static patterns "simply die of old age."

Ken:

You have raised the points that have been bothering me about Pirsig's concept of Quality as it relates to the human situation on Earth and our responsibilities to our fellow species. I think that I understand Pirsig's concepts even though I have not yet mastered the ability to express myself in those terms consistently. If you are not familiar with Lovelock and Lynn Margulis' proposal concerning the Gaia Hypothesis, just take a quick look and there is a good amount of material on the net.

Your question of "why" is the question that we humans have been asking throughout the known history of the human race. I think we are making progress but not very much. That question is also bothering me. I agree with your statement that ecology is pure self-interest. I think that fits the case exactly. I think that self-interest is why we should try to think coherently about our situation here and try to come to some resolution of the problem. I also think that many, if not most, of the ecology "nuts" out there are barking up the wrong tree.

Pirsig's question about the "why" of evolution (why the fittest survive) is easily answered in the study of biology. They survive because they possess qualities or traits that enable them to exploit the ecological niche in which they find themselves better than their rivals, or that allow them to fit comfortably alongside their rivals. But that still does not answer the larger question of "Why?"

I think that this is one of the weak points of Pirsig's concept. He did not understand or did not give enough thought to this larger question. He himself stated to the Lila Squad that he had not mined all of the possibilities of the Quality principle. I think that this is an area that cries out for us to attempt to pin down or at least advance a little further. I do not think that it is enough to say that Quality is responsible for us being here. I am also a little uneasy about that aspect of the MOQ idea. We have taken the moral and truth idea of Quality a little too literally. I feel that it gives us a good tool and a good direction in which to work but, as I say, I am a little uneasy about calling it God or the Ultimate Truth and Morality. If we did this then the "many Truths" concept will lead us into a quagmire.

I have to go help a neighbor fix a leaky water line. This is all just off the top of my head. I will think about it. I think that you have raised the correct questions. If you are interested let's pursue them a little further. I agree with Pirsig as far as he goes. I just think he needs extension. He will agree with that I think.

Magnus:

Pirsig wrote: "All life is a migration of static patterns of quality toward Dynamic Quality," not: "Life is migration toward Dynamic Quality." It is the static patterns that are migrating. Without them, there will be no migration toward anything.

Platt:

To say: "The highest good is the correct balance of Dynamic and static" is to imply that the highest good is some sort of static condition.

Magnus:

No! Any Dynamic intervention gives a non-static condition.

Platt:

The objection raised about pure freedom being pure chaos doesn't hold up because chaos is simply a word we use to describe experience we cannot comprehend.

Magnus:

Let me describe what I mean with chaos. It's quite simple really. Every static pattern we've ever known will disintegrate and become nothing as in "no thing." The physical way to describe it is that every atom will fall apart and become indistinguishable from each other and the rest of the nothingness. Every Quality event will be completely unpredictable and nothing will be the same from "moment" to "moment," not that any "moments" as such would exist anyway. That's what freedom from all static patterns means; that's what chaos is to me. Please share what it is to you.

Platt:

If all concepts are static patterns, and if "nothing" is a concept, then "nothing" is a static pattern. If the "nothing" static pattern disintegrates into a "no thing" static pattern, what's the difference? The logic escapes me. Anyway, aren't the so-called particles that make up electrons and such "no things" just necessary figments of mathematical equations?

Magnus:

Of course, "nothing" is a concept. It's quite useless to invent words that don't denote anything. The "nothing," atom and other words I used were used because they were the only words I could come up with to try to describe my view of chaos.

Platt:

Chaos means to me—I have no idea; a situation I sometimes value for it spurs me to learn more, i.e., lay some static patterns onto the mysteries of life. Quantum physics, for example, was pretty much chaos for me until Doug and others took the time to patiently explain its fundamental patterns. This kind of chaos is a pure source of inspiration, I agree. "Don't throw away those Mu answers...They're the ones you grow on!" But it's not freedom from all static patterns. You're still around, Doug is there, the laws of Nature are as static as ever and so on. When scientists talk about chaos, it seems to me they're talking about phenomena they can't explain—a patternless pattern. And isn't that what Pirsig is talking about, too? [99] Only Pirsig says scientists are looking in all the wrong places for an explanation, or rather, they really don't have to look because, to paraphrase Pogo, "They are it." Quality.

Magnus:

Chaos as in "chaos theory" is also, I agree, a state that we don't understand, so we call it chaos until we do understand it. But it's still not freedom from all static patterns. The laws of Nature are quite intact. In fact, the scientists use the laws of Nature in their efforts to understand the state. So, we have at least three different kinds of chaos. Let's map them to the levels and see what we get.

Freedom from intellectual patterns—this would be your kind of chaos; I'd call it inspirational chaos, freedom from social patterns (and above)—some kind of revolution maybe: hippies, the French revolution. Now, freedom from biological patterns (and above)—this is the kind of chaos scientists talk about in chaos theory. (Actually, this is not quite true. I believe there is more than one discipline here. When talking weather, this is it. But I also think that chaos theory is used when describing the intricate patterns on, i.e., oak leaves.) Freedom from inorganic patterns (and above)— now, that's my kind of chaos. We're talking pre-Big Bang, non-existence chaos, big time.

Am I rationalizing too much?

Platt:

Thanks for a great MOQ based explanation of chaos. You've shown how to use the MOQ to "map" an abstract concept to different levels with resulting different meanings. Added to Bo's analysis of the social moral question and Doug's numerous examples, the Squad now has another classic model of how to apply the MOQ intellectual tool to specific problems.

I assume your pre-Big Bang non-existence chaos is pure freedom (DQ without sq), which we mortals can never hope to see in our DQ/sq reality, but can only have a "dim apprehension of." Do you ascribe beauty to this non-existent realm as I do? Do you think beauty plays a role in scientific theories about the pre-Big Bang? I read somewhere where that super string theory has been challenged by some on the grounds that the math involved is too complex and "inelegant."

Magnus:

Ouch! I hope you didn't expect a yes or no answer to that one. :-) Yes, I ascribe beauty to the limitless potential of this realm. On the other hand, potential is all it is. I think it is immoral to wish for such a state. It's four steps down the static ladder. It would be like disqualifying our universe as hopeless and start all over again hoping for a better set of initial conditions. I ascribe infinitely more beauty to our current universe. (Have you thought about the contradiction here? By going down the static ladder, you're supposed to lose freedom with each step. That works down to the inorganic level, but below that, you suddenly find all the freedom in the world, literally!)

And I don't think such a state can be reached by climbing up the static ladder. Sometimes I get the impression that this is what

292

you want to accomplish by adding new levels above the intellectual. Don't get me wrong; I respect your quest for more levels. I would be quite immoral doing otherwise and it doesn't really contradict the merrygo-round idea in my classicist essay.

However, more levels can only add freedom, but never reach the absolute freedom of the pre- Big Bang realm. I'm even more ignorant about the super string theory than relativity, if that's possible, so I can't comment on that specifically. But generally, if one theory predicts reality more accurate than another, I don't mind inelegance. That is the case with Einstein's relativity vs. Newton's absolute laws.

Doug:

I want to share a view of the Earth's life and death process. Let's do the SOM context versus MOQ context comparison again. Let's ask a SOM-ite and a MOQite the same question and compare their answers.

Question: Are you alive or are you dead?

SOM-ite answer: I am alive!

MOQite answer: Yes.

From the SOM perspective there is only alpha and omega—

beginning and end. That is why I have been saying that SOM-ites are "one life centric." From the MOQ perspective, as Bo says, a human is a composite of all four static levels. In DQ, those levels evolve continuously. Practically speaking and from a biological perspective the cells of which the biological level are made continuously die and new ones are born. Every 172 days you get a whole new you. You just are not aware at the largest system level (you) that these sub processes are happening.

My metaphor of the dance of lila is the same metaphor scaled to the universe. Some MOQites see individual life forms (and galaxies) as cells, continuously dying and new ones being born. This is the DQ/sq lila dance. It is beautiful. There is a provocative duality twixt the MOQ metaphor of life and the quantum physics metaphor. DQ is something like superposition. Sq is something like realized wave functions or what we earlier called quantum systems.

I do not know at this point in my personal evolution how to say this any better. Perhaps in a few years. Or the next iteration.

Magnus:

I think the answer lies in the confusion about what is considered to be a valid observer. For example, the Schrödinger's cat paradox, as described in The Mind's I (Thanks for the tip Doug), does not consider the cat to be a valid observer, since it might be dead. In the SOM world, the subject is mostly the part of the QE that "has the mind," i.e., a live cat or a human. This leads to the assumption that the cat must be in a superposition of live/dead until a valid subject observes it.

But in the MOQ, both parts of the QE are subjects from its point of view. [100] I think that quantum theory needs to acknowledge this. Sometimes, the instrument used to observe is considered to be a valid subject. At other times, there seems to be a need for a more valid observer. All static patterns of value are valid observers!

Doug:

You make us proud! What a breakthrough! What insight! Your conclusion is (in my view) correct. If you read all of the quantum material on this subject, the underlying assumption is always a SOM assumption that there is a Subject and an Object. In actuality, all quantum systems are Quantum systems. Therefore, a quantum system being observed is a quantum system observing the observer. Thus, just as MOQ predicted, we have co-observation.

To me this is evidence that the quantum connections are fact. We are all quantum connected!

Magnus what you have found is profound! You have my personal admiration, and I hope that of TLS. I cannot tell you how large a QE this is for me. Much as large as the ones Bo has shared, I am sure.

Bodvar:

The MOQ has liberated us from despair over such disturbing concepts as nothingness, being, everything, etc. According to it, language, concepts, ideas, including the above, are relevant only at the intellectual level. On that level they are as real as real comes and don't contradict direct experience (Dynamic Quality) any more than other stable levels' values They are static all right, but subject to change. For example, does our time's "nothingness" bear no resemblance to the "vacuum" of medieval ages? May I add that the Shakespearean non-being (to be or not to be) that has terrorized Western mind for so long is also nullified by the MOQ. Language that has hypnotized us for so long into believing that "death" is a state (that it is possible to be dead), is relegated to one value plane. The highest admittedly, but nonetheless subject to change and/or expansion. Even, as in our most ambitious endeavour, if we regard the intellectual level as subject/object thinking itself (reason), it may be transcended by a new level.

Pirsig on Space and Time [January 1998]

Ken:

Platt, sitting here and studying the Principles of Quality by studying the mail, I came to the realization that I had not attempted to answer your question to me about time. Time is not a logical absurdity. It is the consequence of the action of gravity on energy.

Ant:

MOQ and time is not discussed (at any great depth anyway) in Lila. I think they are related in the following ways: firstly, as the MOQ is meant to be an analysis of all reality, time can't be outside it. This may sound tautological but it is not logical to say that time, being an aspect of reality, lies outside this reality. Modern physics certainly thinks time is an integral part of the universe and the problem lies in working out how it relates to the rest of reality.

As with many entities, there are two aspects of time in the MOQ: the Dynamic and the static. The Dynamic aspect is what Northrop would say is a "concept of intuition," that is to say, the immediately sensed perception that events in our experience happen in succession.

The static aspect of time is what Northrop would say is a "concept of postulation." This is the intellectual construction (theoretical) of time, which is why I mention Kant, Einstein, and the quantum theorists together when discussing it. The most recent intellectual theories about time perceive it as having an external and independent aspect as well as an internal one. This is where Kant went wrong with his a priori theory and is what such people as Feynman and Hawking class now as "space time."

Previous intellectual constructions of time up to the 20th century were absolute, that is to say, people thought that when bodies moved or forces acted there was no affect on space or time. Einstein's theory of general relativity showed this wasn't true and that time did in fact have an independent existence, as Hawking says on page 38 of A Brief History of Time: "...In general relativity it became meaningless to talk about space and time as being outside the limits of the universe."

The MOQ says all of reality flows from Dynamic Quality and that everything we perceive is some type of (temporary) static pattern. This means that space-time evolved as an early static inorganic pattern along with the laws of physics and the particles they produced. This means that space-time itself is a static pattern that will one day dissolve back into Dynamic Quality. This is consistent with the Big Bang view of the evolution of the universe because this view states that space-time was created by the Big Bang and evolved as the structure of space and time that we now experience everyday.

Pirsig had the following to say on the above (in a letter addressed to me on October 6th 1997). It is especially important to note where he points out the part where I mention in my paper that the Dynamic aspect of time as being a "concept of intuition" is not strictly correct.

He says: "What Northrop says is correct but I wouldn't call it a Dynamic aspect. It's important to keep all 'concepts' out of Dynamic Quality. Concepts are always static. Once they get into Dynamic Quality they'll overrun it and try to present it as some kind of a concept itself. I think it's better to say that time is a static intellectual concept that is one of the very first to emerge from Dynamic Quality. That keeps Dynamic Quality concept free.

"The MOQ really has no problem with time. The MOQ starts with the source of undifferentiated perception itself as the ultimate reality. The very first differentiation is probably 'change.' The second one may be 'before and after.' From this sense of 'before and after' emerge more complex concepts of time.

"Time is only a problem for the SOM people because if time has none of the properties of an object then it must be subjective. And if time is subjective, that means Newton's laws of acceleration and many other laws of physics are subjective. Nobody in the scientific world wants to allow that.

"All this points to a huge fundamental metaphysical difference between the MOQ and classical science: the MOQ is truly empirical. Science is not. Classical science starts with a concept of the objective world, atoms, and molecules, as the ultimate reality. This concept is certainly supported by empirical observation but it is not the empirical observation itself.

"Poincaré's paradox occurs because concepts are the most ephemeral static patterns of all. If you mistakenly call one of these concepts 'ultimate reality,' then ultimate reality becomes ephemeral too. Thus classical scientific reality keeps changing all the time as scientists keep discovering new conceptual explanations." (From Robert Pirsig's letter to Ant.)

Well, I hope the above will be helpful to you, Ken. I look forward to hearing your (or anyone else's in the Lila Squad for that matter) comments on this; especially any ideas you may have on the related subject of "space."

Magnus:

Lots'a cool stuff here Anthony. It really puts another perspective on the "absoluteness" of the speed of light. Time is a derived concept through two or more stages; this makes speed an even more complicated concept. It depends not only on time, but on space also. The only thing accomplished by putting the speed of light as the absolute truth is to hardwire space to time.

Makes me wonder if it is possible to take time or space as the absolute instead and derive the rest from that. Or maybe we could find other more basic concepts instead of space, time, and speed that would closer reflect the ultimate reality. Or perhaps we are bound to use them but must remember that they are just derived concepts.

Bodvar:

I knew Anthony had an extensive Pirsig file, but this is just amazing, and very helpful. What Pirsig says here has a bearing on much of what we have been discussing lately.

Time and space? I have often pondered what the MOQ stance on these classical riddles would be. This much has however been clear to me—space as an absolute a priori entity as treated by Kant (built upon Euclid's postulates, especially the famous fifth one) is gone, and so is absolute time as perceived by Newtonian physics. And as the MOQ is a relativity of metaphysics, it must have some pretty radical views on space and time too.

And radical it was. Once I saw Pirsig's answer, I understood my unease about the matter. For instance, I had criticized Lars for wanting to find out "what's really objective," but to ask what time and space really are, was my way of objectivizing these things. Pirsig says that they are static intellectual patterns of value—and what else? Everything treated by us theoretically, mathematically, philosophically, abstractedly for short, is SInPOV. That could be the only MOQ answer. But that does not mean that we can't say anything about time and space; it only puts them in their correct slot. Pirsig goes on to say: "If you mistakenly call one of these concepts 'ultimate reality,' then ultimate reality becomes ephemeral too. Thus classical scientific reality keeps changing all the time as scientists keep discovering new conceptual explanations."

Yes, reality keeps changing because our concepts of reality, including space and time, is subject to Dynamic change. If anyone says that this makes the MOQ too conceptual and prone to change, I don't think Pirsig would object.

Ant:

Glad you liked all the Pirsig stuff. Magnus, I think your comment that velocity is even a more complicated concept than time is correct. If you could explain why an absolute speed of light "hardwires" space and time together that would be helpful (I guess it has something to do with general relativity but I'm not sure of the exact relationships here).

Magnus:

Standard disclaimer: relativity is by no means native to me so don't take this too literally.

Check the formula for speed, $v = s/t$ (velocity equals stretch divided by time). At relativistic speeds, s and t are affected, but they are affected equally much so that v is kept constant. Well, constant is maybe the wrong term. It's rather the only variable in the equation we are able to control.

By setting c as the absolute constant v at which light travels, you have determined (hardwired) the relationship between s and t. Maybe the speed of light isn't an absolute as previously thought and I'd definitely go along with Bodvar's extension (of Pirsig's comment on time) that everything that is an abstraction such as velocity or space is a static intellectual pattern of value trying to explain (or predict) aspects of reality.

I'd say that these abstractions are intellectual patterns of value enabling us to make an internal universe modeling the inorganic patterns of value of our external universe. It's almost what you just said. I'm just trying to avoid the word "reality." It seems to mean a lot of different things to different people.

Quality, Value, and Morals [January 1998]

Dave:

I will make an assertion that those elements of reality we now call "objects" in MOQ all will have aspects of their total reality that lie in each of the four static levels.

Maggie:

This makes sense to me. There are many "things" that we are unconscious of, that people have never noticed. Any of them would have aspects in other levels but not intellectual. They are not objects. They have not been observed. But, there is no intellectual pattern that is independent of lower levels. Any high level pattern has mediated and reordered lower patterns or it doesn't exist. And, if it mediates even one level of patterns, that automatically mediates sets of lower level patterns, with the chain effect going all the way to the inorganic. So, there's no pattern that exists in only the upper levels but there are patterns that exist only in lower. [101]

Hugo:

Dave, I can see your point that "objects," being intellectual constructs, will be part of the intellectual level, and us, being inherently biological and social too. They "have aspects of their total reality that lie in each of the four static levels." But this does not mean that there is, or was, nothing just inorganic, something nonintellectual, before we formed our view of the world.

I would say that we couldn't do without this naturalistic or realistic or evolutionary view of the world. But your idea goes straight to the heart of the idealistic worldview.

Dave:

I re-read Pirsig's Brüssels paper and may have some more insight into this. In discussing the relationship between Bohr's philosophy and the MOQ, Pirsig developed some diagrams of Bohr's system which place reality as a construct which was first developed in the mind of Observer A and then unambiguously communicated to Observer B. When Observer B or any Observers B concurs with the observation, you have a static pattern for that particular reality.

He seems to agree with this but takes exception with Bohr in that, from what I can tell from this brief overview, Bohr failed to clearly state that the input to his experiment was real also. Pirsig goes on to relate this real input to the experiment as Dynamic Quality. I take this, combined with other things Pirsig has said, to

300

mean that he agrees with the materialists inasmuch as there is a large group of stuff which is external to the mind which has reality whether the mind is present or not. And then goes on and agrees with the idealists that man's reality is a construct of the mind which is unique to the individual but that we can and do come to agreement as a society about a group of static patterns, which are mental, that we call reality. So, in one sense the mind/body split has some validity in that we have both a mental construct of reality in the mind and we have a physical reality of the body. But since we can't clearly say where one start and the other leaves off, we would should treat them as one.

Bodvar:

If what the quantum physicists observe, or put another way, if the physical has some reality beyond being inorganic value, i.e., approaches the "objectivity" of SOM, and mind influences it, we are solidly back in mind/matter metaphysics. This I think Pirsig saw and is the reason he did not follow it up. Perhaps it is a showstopper, but Quality is a universe different from SOM's. Remember the relativity analogue?

Dave:

I'm out of my element here in seeing the consequences. I understand the relatively analogue and agree that Quality is the mother of all relativity, but don't see why Pirsig would bring up Bohr and try to relate his work to Bohr's if he was uncomfortable with where that comparison could or would lead. I also don't see the threat to the MOQ. [102]

I know basically nothing about quantum mechanics but I've heard that the biggie is that the very act of observing quanta seems to have an affect on whether they appear or not. So, the observer is actually affecting the data. Is this not analogous to what naturalists have known about observations of wild animals? Is this not what Pirsig says about anthropologists and Indians? I thought one of the points of MOQ was just that—that every individual's observation is relative to the static patterns that the observer brings with him. Scientists cannot claim pure "objectivity" in so much as they bring "subjectivity" to the table every time. But in the MOQ, those paradoxes disappear because all there is are these four static levels of values, which interact with each other by this set of rules, and the potential that patterns can evolve by interaction with Dynamic Quality.

By using the Quality map we can develop an understanding of reality that surpasses or subsumes "objective" reality in so much as it acknowledges that every reality has, by our old map, a potentially "subjective" component. That old "subjective" component is every bit as real as the old "objective," so much so it makes that division meaningless. Proof of this is that the mere act of observing a quanta or a wolf can affect the data. So, we must subsume this old pattern into this new four level pattern, which acknowledges both components are a potential part of any reality and must be treated under a new set of rules to be understood.

Hugo:

I personally dislike the lumping together of quality, value, and moral. To me, Quality is a monad, a firstness, in Leibniz' or Peirce's sense, value is a dyad, a secondness, and moral is a triad, a thirdness. Value is "quality for some other (someone, something, some…)," and moral is "quality for some other, evaluated by some third," or simply "value for some third." (This view follows Peirce's triadic structures of logic, semiotics. I may diverge from Peirce in using them in an ontological/metaphysical analysis.)

Maybe my marriage of Pirsig and Peirce isn't a happy one. I believe I can make it work, but perhaps Pirsig and the Squad will withdraw after the first really intimate meeting. In my eyes, this concerns the same issue as my saying that relations are primary to objects, not the other way around.

My use of the term "evaluation" was not the ordinary; I was in need of a term for the becoming of a value, and my choice of evaluation was probably a mistake. If we stick to the idea that value is (nearly?) the same as relation, and work with dyadic and triadic relations, the term evaluation can go. I took your wording in the value principle, "Value encompasses what are usually known as causation and substance," as an indication that you might agree somewhat on the connection between the concepts of value and relation, but maybe I was wrong on that. I have been thinking along this line for a long time (meaning I am pretty hooked on it) and if we do not agree on this (value/relation) connection, then it might be the source of some disagreement.

I should say that I am still not at all clear on Pirsig's term moral, and I put it in a Peircean dress in an attempt to understand Pirsig's use. I was trying to get to what one may mean by a morality that is not the result of moral judgment, an ontological moral so to speak, and it occurred to me that the difference I sense between the concepts of Quality, value and moral, could be shown in a Peircean structure, value being dyadic quality (or a Quality relation) and moral being triadic quality (the special relation where the relation between two [the value] is for some third). This may off course turn out not to be a good move.

By the way, is "Quality event" a term for the becoming of value and moral relations?

Bodvar:

I admire your effort to "marry" Pirsig and Peirce and as I too have spoken about Peirce, allow me a go at a comparison.

What dissatisfied Charles Peirce was the dyadic logic (read: metaphysics) prevalent in his time. He did not call it subject/object metaphysics, but I see no hindrance to draw a parallel between these two. SOM is dyadism itself. His alternative was the triadic logic of semiosis (Greek sign, semeion).

My reference is Jesper Hoffmeyer's book (Livets Tegn, En Snegl paa Vejen, in Danish. I believe it is translated to English as Minding Nature). If you have it, look at page 29 and the diagram B which is to depict the semiotic tripod. For those who don't have the book, visualize a big Y. The down spoke is Interpreter, the right is Object, and the left is Primary Sign. To give a hint of what it is all about there is a similar diagram A where the down spoke is Doctor, the right is Measles, and the left is Red Spots. For the Doctor the Red Spots are sign of Measles, for the mother merely signs of something wrong with her child. They are nothing in themselves; there is always a relationship, a context. This is what you refer to as a contextualism (Dewey and Bateson, for instance?). At this point Peirce is at the same stage as Phædrus of ZMM when he reached the "trinity" conclusion:

Peirce: Interpreter-Object-Primary sign.

Pirsig: Subject-Object-Quality.

Phædrus did not stop there. He went on to discard the subject and object spokes and only Quality was left as the primary reality.

When Phædrus reappears in Lila, he has constructed another "figure," which is neither monadic, dyadic, nor triadic. The mystic quality is a Dynamic "ocean" in which the various static wave/patterns have formed. The patterns are not different from the ocean except for being patterns.

If Peirce had undergone the same development the Primary Sign spoke of his tripod should have taken on the same overwhelming importance. After all, it is clear that the "illness" of the child is more primary than the "doctor" or the "diagnosis." Then Peirce would have returned with a Metaphysics of Signs, the MOS (Even better because it is SOM backwards!). He would have postulated a Primary (Dynamic) Sign out of which four (static) Sign levels have crystallized: inorganic signs, biological signs, social signs, and intellectual signs. But Peirce could not go that far. In the 1960's it was madness to give up the subject/object division (and Phædrus suffered accordingly), but in the 1860's it wasn't conceivable at all and Peirce was stuck with the impossible situation of a dyadic mind/matter universe in which a triadic logic reigned, a problem that several Squad members still struggle with.

Thus spaketh Bodvar.

Hugo:

Peirce did in fact provide what we would call a "metaphysics," but he despised the closed philosophical systems of the past and preferred to provide "bricks and mortar for a metaphysics" (not sure of the exact words). This is the title of a translation into Danish of a series of articles in The Monist 1891-1893, made by

Peder Voetman Christiansen. These articles provide an outline of Peirce's metaphysics, and it has recently been re-issued in Denmark (I don't have the exact reference handy). I have not yet really understood what Peirce is saying, but the key bricks are an evolutionary cosmology, which perhaps is entailed in his synechism (continuity or connectedness as a basic), and a tychism (indeterminism), but the tychastic (by chance) process is countered by anancastic (mechanic— probably again entailed by his synechism) and agapastic (determined by love) processes in evolution. The latter idea might be found in Pirsig too, in his aesthetics, a movement towards the good, but it is certainly not part of the neo-Darwinian theory of evolution. I think a closer analysis of this "harmonic," or Gaia-like, aspect of evolution is called for.

Anyway, there is a tension in Peirce between an anti-metaphysical stance and some obviously metaphysical work, but this might be due to the chaotic nature of the heritage of Peirce's works; he did plenty and perhaps we should not wonder why he did not do more. And, in fact, I am not sure how far Peirce did progress on the connection between his evolutionary metaphysics and his triadic logic (semiotics). But this is the direction I want to move, and where Pirsig's metaphysics might provide another perspective.

So, the reason I keep pursuing Peirce's ideas in connection with MOQ is: 1) that we do need some sort of logical structure. This goes counter to the Zen way, and Pirsig in some places, but pursuing a metaphysics is a pursuit of such a logical structure—a way of defining the indefinable. Pirsig saw that it is not possible to get an absolute hold of reality, and his going for it anyway is the sort of pragmatic view, that we do need some handle on reality. Or perhaps this is just a choice between two ways of living, between Zen and the intellectual life. And given the intellectual life, we must pursue a better handle on reality.

2) The problem with the established dyadic logic is that it does not allow room for the subject/object divide. The divide is left

outside the logical structure, with all the problems following the neglect of the divide, which Pirsig pointed out.

3) As I have tried to indicate, the subject/object divide can be included in the triadic logical structure. It can be made explicit (this being part of a Peirce/Pirsig marriage). And this allows, first of all, for contextualism, the "many truths from different viewpoints," which is badly needed in a society torn between absolutism and relativism. And it will allow for the reconnection of logic and metaphysics—and hence of science and Nature—because it allows for a coherent view of us as being in and of our world.

Such a coherent view has not really been possible for a long while, what with a dyadic logic as foundation for philosophy and science, and before that with religion as the foundation of philosophy. Of course, there have been all sorts of efforts towards a unified view and we are all depending on these efforts, but the transgression, which we are in the beginning or the middle of now requires the letting go of parts of our foundation and trashing what seemed to hold us floating in the aspiration to make some better vessel.

Annotations by Robert M. Pirsig

98. There has been an essay about Chris's death at the end of ZMM since 1985 that goes into this. What most people mean by death is simply a breakdown of biological patterns, but there are worse deaths, where whole societies are destroyed and where valuable knowledge is lost forever. I think this is why books such as the Bible and Koran and Gita have been held to be far more important than any individual life. They have preserved the intellectual patterns that have saved whole cultures from degeneration into savagery. Similarly, it was the rediscovery of lost Greek patterns of intellect that is usually credited for the Renaissance.

99. Dynamic Quality and chaos are both patternless, and so it would seem they have a lot in common, particularly the fact that you can't say anything about them without getting into static patterns. But if you do, you can say that Dynamic Quality is good and precedes static improvement. It is the source of experience. Chaos, by contrast is the condition of total destruction. You can't call it either good or bad. It is not the source of anything.

100. Both are patterns of value. But as the diagram in SODV shows, subjective knowledge (social and intellectual patterns) is different from objects (biological and inorganic patterns). Their unity occurs only in the Dynamic Quality that precedes all patterns. Confusion is generated on this matter when it is forgotten that all scientific knowledge, including knowledge of objects, is subjective knowledge. This knowledge is confirmed by experience in such a way as to allow the scientist to generate a supremely high quality intellectual belief that external objects exist. But that belief itself is still subjective.

101. A materialist would say yes. An idealist would say no.

102. I see today more clearly than when I wrote the SODV paper that the key to integrating the MOQ with science is through philosophic idealism, which says that objects grow out of ideas, not the other way around. Since at the most primary level the observed and the observer are both intellectual assumptions, the

paradoxes of quantum theory have to be conflicts of intellectual assumption, not just conflicts of what is observed. Except in the case of Dynamic Quality, what is observed always involves an interaction with ideas that have been previously assumed. So the problem is not, "How can observed nature be so screwy?" but can also be, "What is wrong with our most primitive assumptions that our set of ideas called 'nature' are turning out to be this screwy?" Getting back to physics, this question becomes, "Why should we assume that the slit experiment should perform differently than it does?" I think that if researched it would be found that buried in the data of the slit experiment is an assumption that light exists and follows consistent laws independently of any human experience. If so, the MOQ would say that although in the past this seems to have been the highest quality assumption one can make about light, there may be a higher quality one that contradicts it. This is pretty much what the physicists are saying but the MOQ provides a sound metaphysical structure within which they can say it.

Chapter 11

"Why is the reality most acceptable to science one that no small child can be expected to understand?" —Henri Poincaré; Lila, page 118 Bantam paperback

What's Wrong with SOM [February 1998]

Magnus:

A common response to the MOQ is that expressed by Galen Strawson in the forum [http://www.moq.org/forum/strawson.html] (hmmm, Galen means "mad" in Swedish). Anyway, he doesn't think he's submerged in SOM-land in the first place. He doesn't really state which land he belongs to, but according to the Oxford web page, he's teaching Kant, and I really can't say if Kant went outside the SOM borderline. Anyone?

Then there are the people who don't even think that they are using a metaphysics at all. They are convinced that science is pure and totally free of presumptions.

Martin:

Kant practically defined the SOM! He "saved" objectivity, as Pirsig put it, when he proposed that there is a priori (in the mind, the subject side) knowledge that we automatically have, which we use to filter and integrate sense experience (object side). While we're at it, I'd like some ideas on why SOM is so bad. I remember someone saying that it's hard to explain the MOQ without explaining SOM first.

Keith:

This is my first post, so I'm apologizing in advance for making any newbie mistakes. Don't hesitate to point them out. The path to quality is through feedback and correction.

Pirsig mentions a lot of these problems in both ZMM and Lila. He has to, of course, otherwise he wouldn't have any reason to knock down SOM and try to replace it with MOQ. (That's why the assertion on needing to talk about SOM when explaining MOQ is often true. In modern culture, most of SOM is "common sense."

One must poke some major holes in this framework before anybody will want to give it up.)

In this task, Pirsig has the advantage of a semi-fictional universe under his command, many well-written chapters of persuasive prose, and years of rhetoric training. He brings all of these to bear on poking holes in SOM and in building up his MOQ. I think it's far more difficult to try to directly convince a person of the deficiencies of SOM without these tools. Examples are the way to do it, of course, but even so, the examples offered to an individual must be personally meaningful to them otherwise s/he will likely shrug it off with "so what?" That's merely an argument for having a lot of examples, I guess. But we're not arguing whether we need examples or not, just looking for some, so here's a start:

1. Values are subjective in SOM

This is, of course, the MOQ's primary differentiating characteristic. For some, of course, this is not a problem. Tell the true believers in SOM, the cultural and moral relativists, that SOM says there's no right and no wrong "except thinking makes it so," and they'll agree with you. They are happy with this situation, so getting them to see this as a problem will take additional work. Perhaps asking them if they think that the atrocities of the Holocaust (or some similar abomination) should have gone unchecked would do the trick. They'll be forced to concede that there's some "external" value system by which actions should be judged or else be caught in the contradiction inherent within the relativist framework of judging another group's actions by your standards.

Most people, however, don't operate strictly within the SOM and have beliefs about values that fall outside its boundaries. They either believe in a God who lays down moral rules or believe in some kind of human rights, perhaps based on some natural law theory. Arguing that SOM makes values purely subjective (therefore arbitrary and subject to human caprice) won't faze them since they don't strictly believe in SOM and think they already have a viable, universally valid value system to guide human actions. These points must be challenged on different grounds. Given this fact, the usefulness of this "hole" in SOM in explaining MOQ is questionable.

2. Subjects are "less real" than objects in SOM

A metaphysics of substance leads to over-reductionism, where all phenomena are explained by drawing causal relations between the phenomenon in question and the lowest, most fundamental level of reality, usually the physical world. Pirsig talks about this tendency in Lila where he goes on about explaining the behavior of the chemistry Professor in terms of his/her chemical properties in Chapter 12. A more reasonable approach allowed by MOQ is to explain/predict phenomena in terms of the evolutionary level on which it occurs, and then explain the connection between that level and the next lower level.

This is dangerous business, however. SOM's seeming insistence on explaining phenomenon in terms of physical properties has been fantastically successful over the past five hundred years or so (as Pirsig notes on page 7 of his Subjects, Objects, Data and Values paper, presented at the 1995 Einstein Meets Magrïtte conference in Brüssels). Grounding our theories in physical reality keeps us from flights of fancy, from continually inventing imaginary objects like aether and phlogiston (or ESP, or the ethereal plane). When the evidence procedures for science are followed, though, it seems reasonable to relax the implied requirements that everything be explained in terms of hard physical realities and allow ourselves to explore (with rigor) the static laws that govern the interactions within and between the "subjective" value patterns, opening up all sorts of interesting paths in the social science fields (Lila, Chapter 8).

If we don't keep these strict scientific evidence procedures, however, our imaginations produce all kinds of wild stories with no assured correspondence to the patterns we're trying to explain, so all we end up doing is making new myths for ourselves. I don't know how useful an example this is in persuading another to look at MOQ, however. Most people aren't scientists and those who are don't generally bother much with metaphysics. I came to a fuller appreciation of Pirsig's works through some systems science courses I took in college, so this example speaks to me, but perhaps not to many. I also fear I have not explained it very well.

3. Hume says it's wrong

Pirsig goes on for some time in Chapter 11 of ZMM on Hume's attacks on causality in the metaphysics of substance and Kant's reply to that and how Quality overcomes that problem. Similar stuff may be found in Chapter 8 of Lila. The trouble is, who cares? Only a very few philosophologists would be willing to carry on a casual conversation on these lines.

4. MOQ explains problem of "goallessness" in evolution and of "causality" in quantum mechanics. I'm not sure I completely understand all of Pirsig's arguments here, but in Chapter 11 of Lila, he talks a lot about all the problems in science that can be eliminated by SOM. Again, not too useful when taken as individual persuasive techniques (see #2 above).

Whew! Okay, after looking at the SOM problems Pirsig points out, I can't say that any of them alone make very good examples to use in explaining MOQ. It's all of these little things taken together that make the case. For me three things persuade me to value the MOQ above SOM:

1) The overall explanatory force of the MOQ appears stronger than SOM (which is still a pretty damn good way to divide up the universe; look at the practical utility of common sense and the science and technology that have sprung from this world view). Even so, MOQ unifies many separate fields into an overarching theory.

2) The core tenet of MOQ, that of Dynamic Quality, tells us that the static tenets of MOQ are just another intellectual construction of the undefinable DQ, perhaps superior to SOM, but still ultimately limited and flawed. Gotta like a theory that admits its own limitations.

3) Related to #1, values are placed in the primary position in the system, freeing morality from religious doctrine and giving it a rational basis that's integrated with everything else.

This last point, a sort of Nietzschean "transvaluation" as I heard someone on Usenet call it, is most important to me. It provides a fresh framework within which one may analyze moral questions.

Bodvar:

Greetings Keith, and welcome to the Squad!

The arguments you bring contra-SOM and pro-MOQ are just right on and show that you have a firm grasp of the problem. I can only affirm what you write about most people being oblivious to the fundamental weakness that (fail to) underpin the Subject/Object universe. They simply don't see any problem or if they do, believe it to be some built-in riddle to thwart the human "hubris." (In the old days when everything was seen in a biblical context, it was the proof for God's wisdom.)

Only a "maniac" like Phædrus would charge head on into the monstrous task of unmasking the foggy monster, and then, help me God, present an alternative! The Quality idea is just exasperating. It is megalomaniac to the hilt, but simultaneously it does away with the SOM paradoxes as if by magic. I try to check my tendency to heroworship Pirsig; there are other great thinkers (Hugo and I have spoken about Charles Peirce who was a kind of Quality forerunner) but Pirsig's simple yet genial stroke is unique in the history of philosophy. Remember the passage in Lila where Pirsig cites Poincaré's question why so few understand "reality"? Here lies the key to the resistance.

Ant:

Bodvar has previously explained to me why the subject/object universe does not work. I liked his explanation so much I used it for my MOQ presentation on the 12th. I quote the relevant section for everyone else on the Lila Squad:

So why introduce a new metaphysics?

This is probably explained best by my Norwegian friend Bodvar and the quality/quantity paradox in subjective/objective thinking:

"In the objective world there are no qualities, only quantities: sight/colours are various wavelengths of the electromagnetic spectrum; sound/music are air pressure waves; smell/odours are molecular configurations, as is taste, and touches are pressure sensation. Nowhere out there is quality (or values) to be found. The impacts on our sense organs are transmitted into electrochemical impulses traveling to the brain where it is translated back into our subjective perception. There is no direct connection between the two realms. If you start with the subjective/objective metaphysics (or the mind/matter idea if that sounds less 'metaphysical') subjectiveness is subjectiveness from here to eternity as is objectiveness; nowhere do the two overlap." (Email from Bodvar Skutvik to Ant, September 30th, 1997)

As can be seen from the diagram on SOM, quality is on one side of a metaphysical chasm and quantity is on the other. Quantity is perceived as inhering in substance; qualities are perceived as being non-substances. They are mutually exclusive and should therefore not be able to have an effect on each other. However, the fact that your mind can decide to move your little finger (a physical object) and a few pints of beer (a physical substance), which can alter your mind, totally dispels this idea. There is a serious metaphysical problem here.

I think the above should make it very clear to anyone why SOM doesn't work.

Three Shots in the Night [February 1998]

Donny:

Hello, all; I'm glad I could join you. I'm going to start by throwing out some responses to what's been said here—first, the daunting "so what?" question. Now, if you know Joseph Campbell, you know he was a brilliant scholar who dedicated his life to the study of myth. Once asked, "Why are myths important? Why should we care?" He responded along the lines of, "I don't believe in studying something because people say it's important. If you can get along without this stuff, fine. That's wonderful, go live

314

your life and be happy. If you're exposed to it and it catches you, just as well. If it doesn't catch you, don't bother with it; that's someone else's path. "

Now, that works for me. I have an unfinished second major in philosophy and I don't feel the need to dedicate my time to philosophical apologetics. I'm not a missionary—okay?—so that might not work for everyone. If that doesn't cure your woes then let me recommend a broadening of the question—why is philosophy important?

That's the same as asking—why do you study it? What's the pay off? Now reflect on that. My most influential professor here at the University of Tennessee (always start where you are) has been a great Hegel scholar (now retired) and a personal friend named Dwight. He said once: "People ask me what I do for a living and I tell them, 'I'm a metaphysician.' 'What's that?' they say, and I tell them, 'we pursue the question, "What really exists," and if that doesn't make one feel like a goof ball I don't know what would.'"

The pay off of science is clear—better things for better living. The pay off in medicine is clear, but what do you hope to get out of philosophy? In other words, once you start, how do you know when to stop? Someone said, "I've got the great answer here, and people ask, 'What was the question?'" Well, how the heck does the question, "what really exists?" arise naturally out on the street, in real life? Does it? I will have far more to say about that later, but I want to get out my initial responses first.

Martin suggests that Kant "practically defined SOM." I'm no Kant scholar, but my understanding is that beyond us and the thing for us (object, by the way, literally means "that which stands over against") he posited a thing in itself which was unknowable but presumably a transcendent unity that could be called God or Tao or Quality [103] (if it is transcendent then really to name it anything is to go off track because that's to knife it; it's X as opposed to everything not X). So, Pirsig is what Kant would have been if he studied the Tao Te Ching and could write as well as Mark Twain.

SOM (in "modern times") starts with Descartes (about a hundred years before Kant). He talked in terms of "mind" and "body," and left open the question of what is the link between the two. How can one know the other? And that is what Kant answered. Now broadly speaking there are three types of metaphysics: monism, all is one; dualism, everything is either one of two things; and pluralism. SOM is a clear dualism, but it's quite false to say (as Magnus said) that all metaphysics between Aristotle and Pirsig have been dualistic. The most important guy in here that's overlooked is Hegel.

Hegel came along about twenty five years after Kant and demonstrated that Kant's system still had a few flaws. Hegel cleaned them up and collapsed Descartes' duality into a very imposing and impressive monism. This is starting to run long, and I just wanted to open with a quick volley before dropping the bomb, but a brief final point. Magnus asked about demonstrating how science employs a set of presumptions. There are numerous ways to do this but what I find most interesting is this next question.

We know what it means to say F=ma is true, or for E=mc² to be true. We know what it means to say that all vertebrates have backbones. But what does it mean to say science is true? [104] We know what it is for something to be scientifically true, but in what way is science true? Or (another approach) if you disagree on the truth of X, you employ a proof in order to settle the question. So (upon reflection) the one thing that X cannot be is a method of proof itself. Two teams oppose one another in a baseball game; one wins. But if the game of baseball opposes the game of basketball....

Now I'll tell you this, science is true; it's just not scientifically true. It's true how? What's the truth, not in the game of baseball, but of the game of baseball? So there are three quick shots in the night (whether that's gunfire or whiskey I leave up to you). Once again, I'm happy to be aboard, and I'm looking forward to your thoughts.

Hugo:

Hi Donny, and welcome to the Lila Squad! I am all for critical analysis of the MOQ and this is not an immune reaction. If I have understood you correctly, Donny, you say Pirsig conflates (whether deliberately or not) the Mind/Body dualism (MBd) with the subject/object dichotomy (SOM). Alas, I cannot give any references to Pirsig, as I have not had time to re-read his books in detail for the last couple of years; I have had my hands full with the rest of philosophy. (For your information I am an "Aristotle, Bateson, Bohr, Peirce, Pirsig, Popper, etc. " kind of guy, just getting acquainted with John Dewey.)

My take on this question—MBd versus SOM—is A): that there is a difference; these two oppositions are not analogous, and B): I find your iterative approach towards analysing their meaning very interesting. On A: given there is a difference, what is the relation between MBd and SOM? In short, I think the MBd is mostly an ontological, and SOM mostly a logical, distinction. But we have to dig deeper. Mind/Body dualism has been a well established and out in the open worldview since antiquity. It is related to various transcendental views that there is something beyond our ordinary world, commonly connected with Plato's distinction between an ideal and an ordinary world and most evident in the Christian philosophy and similar religious world views, including, I believe, much New Age philosophy.

But perhaps we should distinguish between transcendental MBd and a more Cartesian form of MBd (that we literally are dual beings, made up of matter/flesh/body and mind/spirit/soul). At least I am not quite clear on the relation between these two. I see transcendental MBd as basically an absolute stance, the stance that there is something out of this world that we will never be able to know because it is by definition "out of this world." This is a kind of view that can never be rationally or empirically rejected, and probably the majority view in the world today. I suppose the more Cartesian MBd will be resolved into either a pure transcendental stance, or a pragmatic distinction between levels of reality similar to Pirsig's levels, but others may have a different view on this.

The Subject/Object Metaphysics has lived a more concealed life, though it has its roots in antiquity too. I take the subject object distinction to be a logical distinction, but one which has only been tacitly assumed, not openly expressed (and criticized) until quite recently, as far as I know. As such, the distinction is not something that can be rejected as false. It is an analytical tool, which may be used in an appropriate way.

Perhaps I should pause to explain how I use the words "logic" and "ontology," touching upon B above. Logic is basically the necessities in our knowledge, and ontology is our basic view of the world. The interesting point is that they are interdependent, or, more precisely, interplaying in an evolutionary process (I call this evolutionary metaphysics). One way of putting it is that there is no absolute stance. (This is not relativism, but evolutionism or contextualism, in "ism" terms; Peirce and Dewey are important players here.) Another way of putting it is that talking about words and talking about logic is talking about the world, at least hypothetically, in terms of the possible. (And this goes against the transcendental dualist view, the Platonistic view, which is quite common among mathematicians, for instance.)

Returning to Pirsig, he was the one who made me aware of this tacit assumption (the S/O distinction) in our basic logic (and, speaking of speaking of words, language and metaphysics are mutually interwoven). Knowing that many other gifted philosophers have worked intensely with these issues, I dare not say that Pirsig was the first to make it explicit; I have met upon related views in many others. But he did make it explicit that SOM is an assumption, which can be circumscribed, that we can go behind it, so to speak. And this is of course where his basic term—Quality—enters, and his suggestion of another basic dichotomy: Dynamic/static.

My view of his suggestions, the MOQ, is that they are part in an evolutionary process and furthermore I consider them very valuable parts, which I foresee will eventually gain more influence. And from the point of view of evolutionary metaphysics, showing that SOM is no absolute stance, that we can move behind it, is but one (maybe a crucial one) step in a long process of revealing absolute stances as not really absolute; we could call it a contextualization of rationality.

So, SOM is not a position held by anyone but a hidden assumption, an absolute stance. And the reactions towards unveiling this assumption, circumscribing the stance, are not considered as addressing anyone's position. Either one is willing and able to take part in this unveiling (and thank Pirsig or whoever for this eye opener) or one is not willing or able to see that there is any unveiling to be done, and looks upon Pirsig or whoever as a pain in the ass (or not quite sane).

Unlike the transcendental MBd however, I do believe that SOM can be addressed through open inquiry. Because SOM, or those parts of philosophy and science which tacitly assumes SOM, are already part of the rational project, they live by open inquiry and cannot hide outside of it, as transcendental MBd can. I am looking forward to more on Kant, whom I know too little of, considering his philosophical importance.

Ant:

The Mind/body problem is an old one. What is impressive about Pirsig's MOQ is that it avoids both the mind and/or body options. At the end of Part Two of ZMM, the narrator mentions Phædrus' Copernican Revolution with the example of Kant's fitting of the "objective" world with our sensory capabilities and not the other way round as previously attempted (and as you've also recently mentioned). What Pirsig does, of course, is to put subjects and objects in terms of values and not the other way round (as many, if not all, philosophers have been doing). Whether Pirsig's Copernican Revolution is as great as Kant's is a debatable point though I think it will become more appreciated as time goes on.

Magnus:

319

Hi Donny and welcome to the Lila Squad. Your answer demonstrates very well what I was trying to say. We on TLS, at least I, do lump most metaphysics between Aristotle and Pirsig into the same SOM bag. From a classical philosopher's point of view, that must seem quite unfair. You said that SOM is a clear dualism, but I think materialism is SOM too because it's trying to deduce subjects using objects. The same goes for idealism but the other way around; it's trying to deduce objects using subjects. In both cases, there's a presumption that both subjects and objects must be explained using the metaphysics.

I suppose that the words subject and object might not be used in monisms, but I don't think it's very hard to find their synonyms. As you might suspect, I'm not very well read in these matters. We're not into philosophology on TLS, but perhaps we should be more than we are. As Jason put it quite some time ago, "One has no right to take issue with an opposing position until he is able to restate his understanding of that position sufficiently enough to receive the other's approval." I don't think many materialists, idealists, or dualists approve of our description of their points of view. You might be the person to help us do that.

Donny:

Pretend all of you that you are the head of a University Philosophy Department (a fate I wouldn't wish upon my worst enemy), and the Dean comes in and says, "I'm real sorry Professor Knows-a-Lot, but we've got these terrible budget problems and I'm going to have to get rid of the entire philosophy program." And you say, "But Dean Tightwad, we need to study philosophy!" And Dean Tightwad says, "Well, perhaps you can help me. See, I was a business major, and I've never really understood what you do here." Now, how are you going to respond? This guy wants to know, bottom line, what's the pay off, and your job depends upon your answer. What are you going to say?

Magnus:

The day my interest in philosophy is dependent on budget, I hope I have the sense to quit. Another thing, budgets are social patterns are value. The sciences, including philosophy, are intellectual patterns of value. So, according to the MOQ, it is immoral for budget to inhibit science. Of course, I realize that much of science today is dependent on budget but it is nevertheless immoral. A disturbing thing here is the emotional detachment that is very common among philosophers. They live with the illusion that all different philosophies can be "objectively" compared and ordered. That is not the case. It would mean that "objective" would be a definition made in some kind of meta-philosophy. I'm not really sure, but if that is what Kant did with his a priori idea, then his philosophy is resting on itself, just as much as any other.

Donny:

Okay, we have two possibilities about what counts as understanding in philosophy: (1) seeing where it all fits in relation to itself. Somebody once said, "Philosophy is the study of its own history," and in the University it, by and large, is; and (2) what I call the "machine idea," that a philosophical system is like a machine that, if you've understood it, you can climb inside and make it run for you.

Magnus:

Philosophers don't dare to get emotionally involved because then their so-called "objectiveness" gets polluted by their personal likes and dislikes, what we call value. And value is something that is totally forbidden in all "objective" science. That's why philosophers say that "philosophy is the study of its own history." They're trapped in the Church of Reason and can't get out.

Donny:

If you understand the MOQ then you can, say, explain chaos theory in MOQ terms. Can anybody name other tests of understanding?

Magnus:

Not really, just that (1) is what we call philosophology and (2) is what we call philosophy. Pirsig uses those terms and we tend to follow him in these matters.

Donny:

See this fascinates me because philosophers can't agree on what philosophy is. If you give a friend a copy of ZMM to read and they ask: "Why should I?" what will you say? [105] In medicine what counts as understanding, bottom line is that you can heal the sick. What counts as understanding in philosophy? I'd like to keep this as a running side bar to our walk through German Idealism/MOQ, if that's cool. When we get to Hegel on the far side of Kant he'll say that philosophy has no content, and has no form either. (?)

Magnus:

This is not that strange really. Remember that philosophy is a meta-science; it's on a different level of understanding than, i.e., medicine. What Pirsig counts as understanding in philosophy, in my opinion, is that you can heal science.

Donny:

Before I press on to Kant, I'll first re-emphasize my subject/object vs. mind/body point. In the Anglo-American tradition, we're infected with Descartes and tend to interpret subject/object as insubstantial/substantial. "Quality can not be independently derived from either mind or matter." (Robert M. Pirsig, Subjects, Objects, Data and Values, page 12)

But if you read the German Idealists this way then you'll misrepresent them. So, there, when you see "subject" and "object" you can substitute "knower" and "known."

Magnus:

I substitute subject with knower, mind, subjective, insubstantial, etc. I substitute object with known, matter, objective, body, substantial, etc. I sense that you might not; please elaborate.

Donny:

Certainly. Pirsig makes the same equation you do without thinking about it and that's what I'm trying to show (or else my discussion of Kant will seem meaningless). Well, understanding Kant is a worthy goal in itself, but it wouldn't seem especially connected to the MOQ. The difference is, as I said earlier, an idea is not a body; it's not spatially extended. But it is a Gegenstand (an

322

object). [106] Put this tool in your philosophical toolbox: whenever you have a dichotomistic distinction (everything is either A or B), iterate it, that is, apply it to itself, and see where it falls. [107]

So, Mind/Body distinction (MBd) is clearly a thought or system of thought. It is not spatially extended; MBd has no body. It's an element of Mind. But what about SOM (knower/known)? It's obviously not a knowing consciousness; it's something (namely an idea) we know/are aware of. SOM is an object, a Gegenstand (literally "stands over against" consciousness). So, I hope now that it's clear that SOM and MBd are different. Pirsig missed that little point. [108]

Magnus:

I don't get what that was intended to prove exactly. The toolbox tool you gave us is, by our vocabulary, a philosophical tool, not a philosophy. But that's not the point. The point, which I was trying to make last week, is that Pirsig did not miss that difference. What he did was to wrap 'em all up in the same bag and call all of them SOM. I can imagine that there are more of these tools around but I doubt if any of them are able to grasp the MOQ. It would be like trying to explain the taste of chocolate with numbers, a good old example.

Donny:

If you want to make that distinction, okay. The point is that it's a real handy tool that will serve you well if you remember it. (Did anybody think to iterate the subjective/objective dichotomy? When I decide that, "That cloud is shaped like a rabbit," is subjective and "I'm wearing a brown shirt," is objective, is that decision subjective, or is it a brute fact?) [109] If subjective and Mind are the same, and objective and Body are the same, then I'd agree.

What I was trying to get at through all that cloud watching is— they are not. Pirsig was held captive by a picture and we all fall into the same "hypnosis" as he when we read him. But "objective" means "brute fact." Objective/subjective are types of truth, not types of things. So, I don't say Pirsig wants to make Quality an (known) object or a Body. I'm saying he wants to give it the truth status of a brute fact. He himself says that this is how it all got started. How do you assign grades in a rhetoric class? Is it subjective? Doesn't he clearly react against that? Doesn't he outright say he wants Quality to be absolute?

Magnus:

No again, he said that it was neither subjective nor objective. He avoided both horns of his faculty's dilemma by saying that subjective and objective are both derived from Quality, not that Quality was objective! The Church of Reason says that if a truth is not objective, it is subjective. That's what SOM is all about. All philosophies in the SOM bag defines one and only one truth based on a certain mix of objectivity and subjectivity. You should really read some of Doug's posts about many truths; they're brilliant.

And about the "brute fact" part—history, relativity, and most of all, quantum mechanics should be enough to show that there's no such truth as a brute fact truth. Pirsig snapped out of that hypnosis, not into another. I think this is the time for a—

Many truths to you Donny (and that's a good :-) thing). [110]

Vocabulary [February 1998]

Donny:

I didn't say there are brute facts. I said that is what we mean when we say that something is "objective." I've made no metaphysical claims. I'm just watching the language. Whether you believe me or not, my friends, I've said very little about my own belief about metaphysics (which should surprise you, but that's neither here nor there). I'm trying to raise a question, not lay down an answer.

Here's another handy tool: whenever you get a "what is X question," the first thought you should have is, "It's an English word. As such it means what we (collectively) use it to mean."

I showed that Mind (insubstantial) doesn't mean the same as "(knowing) subject" (what was likened to the Catholic idea of the soul) and neither does it mean the same as "subjective" (a proposition which is less than a brute fact, subject to interpretation). Now I'm talking about the words here. That's why

I called this "vocabulary." This is, by pure virtue of how the words are used, nothing metaphysical.

Body (spatially extended) doesn't mean the same as "(known) object" (you can know an idea, for example) and neither means the same as "objective" (a brute fact). Does everyone agree that far?

Now clearly Pirsig does collapse these words under Subject and Object. If I drew a distinction between plant and animal, and then drew a distinction between vertebrate and invertebrate and said that both of these could still be characterized as a plant/animal distinction, you'd find that odd, right? Where "plant" meant plant and invertebrate, and "animal" meant animal and vertebrate, you'd say, "But these are different things!" He makes this move without offering any justification or explanation for it, and that is why I assume (of course I can't know, nobody does but he himself) that he just didn't catch it. If anyone knows a place where he's clear that he's doing this, and explains why, please enlighten me.

And a further point is that it's not inconsequential. It makes a difference whether he's attacking a metaphysics built on Mind/Body (which is what I think he primarily has in mind) or on knower/known. So there's my point of view. Magnus disagrees. But rather than trading blows, or pressing on with Kant (unless of course you want to see the rest of Kant) I think I'll shut up long enough to hear what the rest of you think.

Peter:

First off, I think I knew a Donny from Science Olympiad when I attended Hixson High School. If you are he then hello again, if not, then never mind. (If you are him, then to jog your memory, I am the kid that everyone threw into the pool at the 1993 Nationals.) Hmmm. Isn't it possible to understand a particular philosophy by investigating and studying its tenets, without necessarily investigating the development leading up to it? Philosophies are usually entirely self-contained worldviews that don't necessarily need history to justify their statements, right?

Donny:

I want to say in my defense that before throwing Peter into the pool we asked him if he wanted to take off his watch and take out his wallet first. We were considerate thugs.

What counts as understanding in philosophy? It was suggested (and reasonably so, for this is what most academic philosophers do) that you understand X (MOQ, for instance) if you can see his or its position in relation to what goes before in the history of philosophy, and maybe see the impact X had on what followed. That's not the only (or best) approach but it is a start. (For a lot of philosophy professors this is the only move they can make, which makes them really literary scholars, not necessarily philosophers.)

Peter:

What counts as understanding in anything? For me, understanding is achieved upon the completion of internal mental structures, so that the philosophic system I am trying to understand can be applied to various questions and issues. I guess the Platonic argument of Truth in knowledge comes in here, so we must assume that the knowledge (generating the internal mental structures) is correct and complete.

It seems to me (from what I've seen of various aspects of our University) that the growing trend, in many departments, is to move away from deep fundamental questions and towards doing research on little detailed things. Which is not so bad, except that people seem to lose focus and tend to see research on the minor things to be on a par with research on the deep fundamental things. This happens in physics, sociology, biology, biochemistry...you name it. Where there is a need to look at details, there are always fifty year old Ph.D's who have looked at details their entire lives and disdain the thirty year old Postdoc that has ideas about the fundamentals.

This also seems to happen in philosophy. When such a major shift of world view occurs (as Pirsig is proposing), when someone comes along and looks at the deep fundamental questions (that could destroy the lifetime of looking at details that many academics have done), then there is naturally antagonism.

Donny:

I'll try and help you see why the academics don't much care for Pirsig, but keep in mind that I'm not really an academic philosopher myself. I've been around the University block enough to see that scene is in pretty sorry shape though. Keep grooving on these questions: What is Philosophy? What's the pay off here? What counts for understanding? Really their issue with Pirsig has to do with the whole direction philosophy has taken since the death of Hegel in 1831.

Descartes came up with this idea of Mind and Body. Under Body he put anything that is spatially extended (my chair, my PC, etc.); under Mind he placed anything that is not spatially extended (thoughts, ideas, the laws of physics). Descartes said everything is either one or the other, a less than bold statement, really— "Everything is either embodied or not." Well obviously! It becomes a metaphysics only when you go on to say that both of those "really exist." Does everyone see that?

Peter:

Perhaps this is an issue of semantics, but once you say "everything" is either embodied or not, isn't that already implying existence?

Donny:

"Subject" means "knowing subject," and "object" means "known object." [111] This terminology really comes in to play with the Germans, and the German etymology is much clearer. The German Gegenstand (object) makes clear that an object is was steht entgegen, "what stands over against" a knowing subject (sometimes our language does the thinking for us). So in (what should I call it?) grammatically correct subject/object talk (?) an idea is an object (although admittedly an object of an odd type). A thought, a mental picture, is something that stands over against the knower, "held before the mind's eye," so to speak. Now, again, just having subject/object talk doesn't make a metaphysics. What makes a SOM is saying, "Both S and O exist, and everything is one or the other." Now which does Pirsig talk about? It seems to me (I'll leave to you to confirm or deny) that he's thinking about something more a kin to Cartesian Mind/Body dualism, as is more the style of thought in the AngloAmerican world (call it MBd if you want).

Peter:

I think that for me, the power of the Metaphysics of Quality lies not just in what it says about what is real and not real—in the standard Subject/Object Metaphysics, things like ideas, thoughts, emotions, etc., are very real—but the relationship between things.

It is easy to say that "stories" exist and transistors exist. It is somewhat more difficult to determine what really exists when the stories reside in the organization of transistors. Even though Subject/Object Metaphysics acknowledges that pattern is the key to existence of anything, it doesn't really say much about the interactions between the various patterns, and it leaves us totally in the dark when the patterns are superimposed on top of each other. The beauty of the Metaphysics of Quality, at least for me, lays not so much in its definition of the levels of static Quality but rather in its description of the interactions of the different levels of Quality.

Donny:

Let me say on a personal note so you know where I'm coming from that I really distrust these broad categories—as a rule they carry little explanatory force. Generally, what happens is people pick some word ending in "ism" and turn it into some sort of battle cry. If one feels the need to bow down, well there are worse churches to do it in than the church of Robert M. Pirsig, but, personally, I find this partisanship unphilosophical and frankly undignified. Let's not worry just now about who's right or wrong, or who wins the game. One first wants to ask, "What game are we playing?" (A restating of "what's philosophy?") Instead, just look at what Mr. Pirsig tried to do, how, and why. As Wittgenstein said (or if he didn't he should have), "It's more important to be clear than correct."

Peter:

Well, this is a valid point, but I think that in a sense the Lila Squad is doing exactly this. From what I've seen people are trying to put together a coherent statement of the Quality of Metaphysics, and is Quality Metaphysics not what Pirsig tried to do? I don't know about the "Why?" question, but the "How?" question is detailed to a certain extent in Lila and ZMM themselves.

I agree that, in general, it is better to determine exactly what a philosopher said before arguing the validity and correctness of his points. But in a sense, we cannot do the former without doing the latter at the same time, especially when the Metaphysics of Quality was inspired by the shortcomings of the Subject/Object Metaphysics.

Maggie:

I just wanted to note something. I think the common sense, average person in the street position would be that "concrete" means dependable, touchable, and while it may have a history, the aspect that is being referred to is the unchangeable aspect. From this point of view, "abstract" is undependable, subjective, whatever you think, ephemeral.

I don't mean to interrupt your conversation, but it really struck me that to you, operating in the intellectual/social mode, abstract is changeless and concrete changeable, while to someone operating in the social/biological mode the opposite seems more true.

Magnus:

I liked Maggie's note about concrete/abstract. And of course, you may interrupt Maggie, that's the point of mailing lists. In the MOQ, abstract things are intellectual patterns of value and concrete things are inorganic patterns of value. This means that abstract things are ultimately dependent on concrete things.

Another thing, do you think it's possible to define a logic independent of a metaphysics? I see that you make a clear distinction between logical distinction and metaphysical claims and I can't say I do. I think a metaphysics is the discourse where logical distinctions are made.

Platt:

Donny tossed out some off-the-cuff questions. Here are my offthe-cuff answers.

Q. What is philosophy?

A. The search for underlying assumptions.

Q. What's the pay off?

A. Fun.

Q. What counts for understanding?

A. Whatever enhances your intellectual/social/biological life.

My question for Donny is—why ask these questions?

Breakneck Kant [February 1998]

Donny:

This is where the fun starts (or restarts). On a more objective level, it's been said that all philosophy since 1780 can be mapped onto Kant somewhere, depending on what's emphasized and what's downplayed, so don't underestimate his influence.

Kant's chief work is The Critique of Pure Reason (CoPR). He spent ten years working it out and published it in 1780. The general question of the CoPR is—what makes synthetic a priori knowledge possible? A "proposition" is the meaning of a declarative sentence. Of propositions, we can say that there are two reasons why they are true or false (T or F), and two ways we know they are T or F.

The Why: analytic propositions are T (or F) merely because of the words: Calvin Coolidge once said: "When a great many people are out of work, unemployment results." Synthetic propositions are T because of the way the world is: "The male cardinal has red plumage." How do we know? Empirical means you use your senses, often some inductive method. A priori is "other"—no observation needed.

An empirical/analytic statement is an oxymoron; there's no such thing. All you need to know to know the truth of an analytic proposition is what the words mean, but you don't need to observe anything. An a priori analytic statement is a logical truth. An empirical/synthetic statement is the routine truth of science and common sense. (A personal aside—the implication is that what the man on the street is doing is like what the scientist does in the lab only the scientist does it better. I hope that when that move is pointed out we can see it's nonsense.)

Before Kant, no one believed in the synthetic a priori. But Kant said that mathematics is based on this kind of truth. Previously it was argued that 9=3x3 was analytic, a statement of identity (Like Mark Twain is Samuel Clemens). Kant's not convinced. Okay, the year is 1581 and young Galileo is in church. Above him are these big chandeliers. Now, they light these things by hooking them and drawing them over to the balcony, lighting them and letting them loose to swing back and forth.

Now, Galileo, being a pious lad, is looking up toward heaven (the ceiling) when he notices that the duration of the swing of the chandelier stays the same even as the length of the swing decreases— it slows down in proportion. (This really is a true story.) So being a mathematical genius he comes up with the law of simple harmonic motion right there on the spot, that the time of the swing is equal to the square root of the length divided by the gravitational constant, right in his head. So he thinks, "I'd better test this. I'd time them with a stopwatch but the stopwatch hasn't been invented yet. I know! I'll use the rhythm of my pulse."

Now back off; forget everything you know and ask yourself, "What did he miss?" He made the assumption that time is mathematically intelligible—that the flow, or rhythm, or beat of time is mathematically consistent, like a point moving along a line at a constant speed. This isn't natural to human beings! It's not built into our biology. You can't do it until you have the math. The cave man couldn't think this way. And, in fact, an account of history shows that people haven't always thought like this. For the Greeks there were one set of rules of "physics" below the orbit of the moon and another above it. And in Christian theology, there's one type of world before the Fall, another after, and a third type will come after the Judgment. Science presupposes the continuity of space and especially time. This advent of a new concept of time makes the modern age.

Concept of time? If you mistake a badger for a skunk then I would say you've got the wrong concept of a badger. In what way can you get the wrong concept of time? I've apparently side tracked onto this with good reason—time is the key to metaphysics! Empirical science proceeds this way: Event A happens at Time A' in place A". Event B happens at Time B' in place B". Event C happens at Time C' in place B", etc. In other words, in science, you observe in space/time, but you can't look at space/time (Kant will say why). A "What is X?" question asks, "How do you pick it out?" Given a ground, can you identify the figure? So, the one thing X can't be is the ground itself. (Where does that leave metaphysics?)

Kant thought that the applicability of math to experience posed a problem and therefore was a synthetic discipline. Hume (a British sceptic) had said that the scientific method was an a priori synthetic discipline and since such a thing was impossible— science yields no truth. In plainer words, can you have knowledge of (the world of) experience prior to experience? Hume says no, Kant says yes, Hegel gives a strenuous no and Pirsig says yes. [112]

Magnus:

I wish you'd stop misquoting Pirsig in each and every post. I guess you're referring to Quality with this "knowledge prior to experience." But there's nothing certain about Quality at all. Kant's a priori knowledge is something that is true; Pirsig's Quality is something that is good.

I know that "good" in SOM-ese is very fuzzy and subjective. The Church of Reason scorns good and acknowledges only truth. But if you follow the truth trail to the end, you discover that all truths are axioms resting on nothing but themselves, valid in no other context but within themselves. This goes for metaphysics too. I really like Platt's answer to "What is philosophy?" Applied to truths it becomes, "Give me a truth and I'll find the underlying assumptions."

Good is more real than truth.

Donny:

Good is more real than truth. (And ain't that the truth?)

Magnus:

It's a good truth, not the truth.

Donny:

Ah, so there are different kinds of truth? Now we're coming back around to something I said way back in "Three Shots in the Night." Wittgenstein asked, "Does philosophy need a technical language?" No, he decided, because "There are no special experiences in philosophy." There is no equivalent to the scientist in his lab, or more importantly, at the laboratory door. The most important science goes on at the door. Suppose Dr. Lab Rat meets his colleagues at the lab door one morning and he's drunk as a skunk.

His colleagues tell him he can't go in. He's in no condition to be objective, to do science. Or suppose Lab Rat is in the lab doing tests with Gorgeous Gloria his blond bombshell of a lab assistant. (Ladies I apologize for this illustration in advance.) Lab Rat is supposed to be watching this meter, but he's really checking out Gloria while she operates whatever it is they're running. Now she catches him and says, "Lab Rat, you're supposed to be watching that meter. You've invalidated all our data with your sloppy readings."

In the lab, you have a moral/social imperative to be objective, that is, to maintain a certain posture, a pose. Objectivity is a role! You can put it on and take it off, assume it and drop it. All these people talking about "Is objectivity possible?" miss the bloody point. That's really secondary and not as important. (And Pirsig didn't catch this himself, which is why I bring up: what is SOM?)

So, objectivity is a pose that Dr. Science strikes while in the lab but philosophy draws from the every day experiences of life on the street (no special experiences). This is one place where Kant goofed. He assumed that experience meant "scientific" empirical experience, where what we do on the street is the same as what the scientist does in his lab but he just does it better. (Think of

Sherlock Holmes. He asks Watson, "How many steps up to the door at 221B Baker St.?" And Watson can't tell him and he says, "That is because you don't observe!")

This is nonsense. Lab Rat's objectivity is dependent upon nothing more than Gloria and everyone else's ability to recognize him as being objective, and their objectivity is likewise reciprocally recognized. This reciprocity is what Hegel means by Geist. (I can have good manners only because I can recognize good manners in others.) So, philosophers (lacking a lab door) don't have the same kind of regimented objectivity as scientists. (Heck, Don Juan does philosophy while high on peyote.)

Instead, in philosophy, there is an appeal to reason: "Be Reasonable, Bob!" What that means is, follow the rules of proof. The difference between philosophy and poetry is philosophy proves something. So, what's a proof? A proof is the most morally/socially acceptable way to settle an argument. If you and I disagree on something, there are a number of ways I can get you to agree with me. I can send Knuckles and Rocko over to "persuade" you. I can blackmail you, or withhold money. But we all agree there is some best, most sociably acceptable way to do this, to offer a proof! (And this is an assumption for how would one prove it?)

Magnus, it seems to me that you're so busy hunting this demon objective philosophy (or subjective philosophy) that you neglected to pause and reflect what does it mean to say someone is being objective. And, what is philosophy? (Which also asks: what's the pay off? And what counts as understanding?)

Magnus:

Not really, I'm not hunting objective or subjective philosophy. I'm hunting the presumption that if something isn't objective, it must be subjective. I'm not really interested in what it means to be objective, because the search for pure objectiveness leads only to infinite regression. I thought I answered the other questions one or two weeks ago.

Donny:

You did. But (as a rule of thumb) you could say that Donny doesn't value answers. We're programmed by schools (and I teach in one, I know) to take a question as a blank to be filled in. Rather I try to take questions as questions, something that begins a movement of thought. Answers stop thought. We've gotten used to seeing a question as a test and not as an opportunity or an invitation.

That's why (as other pointers, or tools) I have question questions—what is that like asking? Analogies like "What is time?" is like "When is time?" or, "Where is space?" or, "What is experience?" are like, "How do you know when you've had an experience?" (As opposed to what?) Or "What is Quality?" What's that like asking? Is that like, "What's a dog?" No, clearly not. Quality is property something might have the way a building might have "bigness." "What is big?" How does it arise naturally, in actual discourse, not as a classroom abstraction from life, but in life?

Why is it questionable and not screamingly obvious? If something is a real question (and not a rhetorical or school question) then it means something is hidden, and there are numerous ways information can be hidden. And so on.

Quality is reality is a truth but not the truth. As I said in my first email to the Lila Squad, we know what it means for "F=ma" to be true. We know what it means for something to be scientifically true. What does it mean to say "Science is True"? And it is true. That proposition is only nonsense if we take "true" to mean "scientifically true." There are rules for winning a game just as there are rules for proof. But how would you prove the truth between two rival systems of proof? The creation/evolution debate will never be resolved (as such) because one side looks to Biblical proof, and the other looks to scientific proof. It's like a football team playing a basketball team and nobody can agree on which game is being played. The debate is meaningless!

Look, is the distinction between subjectivity and objectivity itself subjective or objective? If it's subjective then that means we can disagree over whether Dr. Lab Rat is being objective or not, right? If not, then what? One's objectivity is a brute fact? Recognizable by all? But what if there are no objective people around? What if we're all drunk as skunks in the lab? Isn't it objective people who have to decide whether I am objective or not? Isn't that like asking—are good table manners objective or subjective? Wouldn't that mean that objectivity exists only reciprocally? How long will Donny keep talking in interrogatives?

Or (and here's the one that gets me going) is the abstract concrete distinction itself abstract or concrete? An abstraction is something timeless or universal, like 1+1=2. Something that is concrete has a history, it exists in time, it changes—it "lives," one might say. (Now this is a logical distinction, not a metaphysical claim.) Walter Neely's got a book, The History of Logic that's written like a history of math. Joe discovered "X." Like it was already there somehow. Can you imagine someone discovering the abstract concrete distinction? Bottom line—logical distinctions exist in discourse the way the rules of a game exist in the game's execution. Nobody discovered baseball.

Was that way too much at once, or way too tangential? Sorry. What I meant to say was, Magnus, the iteration of a distinction is a nice tool, but don't take at as anything more than that, and if you don't like it or you think it's part of some evil plot, don't use it. There are no philosophical laws, only pointers. Philosophy is an art, not a science. (That too is worth reflecting on.)

Magnus:

Why does art and science have to be separated? One of Pirsig's major goals with ZMM and Lila was to join them.

Donny:

Well, what I had in mind is not Art proper and Science proper, but like when we say: "John's got cooking down to a science," or "He's raised cooking to an art form." (It's fundamentally a metaphor.) The distinction is that in "a science" there is supposed to be a system, a formula, a recipe that you grind stuff through the same way or with very little variation. "An art" plays fast and loose. There are no systems, no procedures, and no recipes, just guidelines, rules of thumb, and pointers (and these can get pretty darn flexible). I guess you could say science values systems and art values free play, but I wouldn't get too caught up in chasing metaphors. (Language is fast and loose and fundamentally metaphorical.)

Magnus:

I'm beginning to doubt if you really read ZMM and Lila. All I said above is there, but much clearer than my ramblings. But if you're also trapped in the Church of Reason, I can understand your reasoning. There's no way to fit the MOQ within the Church of Reason.

Peter:

Actually, I have very little doubt that Donny has read ZMM and Lila. He has perhaps read it with greater skepticism, which should be applauded by all of us as more a virtue than a sin. :)

Hugo:

Peter made some good points on "objectivity" which I think we should notice carefully. The "meta-philosophical ideal of objectivity," as Peter calls it, has to do with truth, and is part of the very idea of doing philosophy and science. If this is disregarded, then we are entering another project, call it art, or life, not to be deranged but neither to be confused with the project of open inquiry.

The point to note is that the Subject/Object distinction does not have to do with the (misused) ideal of "objectivity" in any straightforward way. It has been used in such a way in "objectivist" science, this is true, but objectivist science is not equal to the project of open inquiry as such.

I find two things especially important. One is that "objectivism" in science, "taking what can be agreed upon by the community of inquirers in the long run" (Peirce's terminology) as that which can be true, and taking anything else to be "subjective," is severely delimiting our rational powers; it is the same as saying that we cannot use reason on what matters most in our lives. If this concept of objectivity is taken as a delimiting criterion for what we can find any truth about, this has a range of bad effects. It gives an absolutist understanding of science; that which is within the limit cannot be doubted.

Since all science tries to find a place within the limit, this means that much science fails to express the contextual limits of their conclusions, because this would make it less "objective." Hence we live in a society where what's rational is taken in an absolute sense— science says it has been scientifically proven, so we know (stated unconditionally). We live with a dichotomy between the "objective" and the "not objective," placing too much belief in the "objective," and too little in the "not objective." And furthermore this established concept of objectivity has hindered due concern for any better criteria or concept of truth based on the very process of open inquiry. This is really bad. :-(

The other important aspect in this is the positive angle on the subject/object distinction. The possibility of making a more contextual science, where one can utilize multiple complementary truths to depend on according to the point of view. Where the idea in objectivist science is that we can remove the subject all together, a contextual science will give up this impossible ideal and stress the necessity of making clear the particular situation of inquiry, conveying the kind of "subject" involved (goals, values, methods, etc.), and how this relates to the "object" of inquiry, to the knowledge and the non-knowledge obtained. (Non-knowledge is that which is hidden in/by any particular context.) It is past urgent to reform the project of science.

Anyway, thanks for your mail, Peter!

Annotations by Robert M. Pirsig

103. Quality in the MOQ is monistic and thus is not the same as Kant's "thing in itself" which is the object of a dualism.

104. In the MOQ, and in William James' pragmatism, truth is described as high quality intellectual patterns.

105. I think you can answer, "There is a possibility it will make you a better person." If the next question is, "What do you mean by better?" The answer should be, "You'll have to read ZMM and Lila to find out."

106. Not in the MOQ.

107. This has been done. The MOQ is an idea.

108. No, both the SOM and MBd are sets of ideas, and there is no reason to make a big distinction between them on this basis.

I think the confusion here is between the "object" of a sentence (Gegenstand) and a physical object. When you call ideas "objects" you destroy the normal meaning of those terms and introduce confusion.

109. In the MOQ, "brute facts" are also subjective.

110. This is one of those responses that give me the warm fuzzy feeling.

111.

Object: n.

1. Something perceptible by one or more of the senses, especially by vision or touch; a material thing.

2. A focus of attention, feeling, thought, or action.

3. The purpose, aim, or goal of a specific action or effort.

4. Abbr. obj. Grammar. a. A noun or substantive that receives or is affected by the action of a verb within a sentence. b. A noun or substantive following and governed by a preposition.

5. Philosophy. Something intelligible or perceptible by the mind.

(American Heritage Dictionary)

The "objects" in the MOQ refer to Definition #1. Objects are biological patterns and inorganic patterns, not thoughts or social patterns. The "objects" Donny refers to seem to be in Definition

#5. It seems to me that in Definition #5 subjects can also be objects. Thus any distinction between them is meaningless.

112. Pirsig says no.

Chapter 12

Every time you discover for the first time that something is better than something else, that is where Dynamic Quality exists. There is no fixed static location for it.—Robert Pirsig, Letter to Ant, February 23, 1998.

Romantic vs. Classical [February 1998]

Ciona:

It seems like the posts have been tapering off recently. I suppose I'll have to take some of the blame, having played a completely passive role so far (although according to quantum theory there is no such thing as a non-participating observer, so it can't be too bad). Anyway, I'm going to use this lull in the mailing list to bring up a few of my own observations/concerns. They're nowhere near the level of thought that's been culminating recently, but maybe with the input of the rest of the Squad hopefully they'll be able to develop somewhat.

Going back to ZMM, does anyone else think that there seems to be a predominance of classic rather than romantic thinkers on the Lila Squad? Most of the postings seem to be evolving in an extremely classical direction, and as a classicist myself, I would be interested in hearing from someone who had a more romantic perspective. I'm not sure if this is a result of romantic avoiding the Internet, or the idea of the Lila Squad, or merely being reluctant to participate in the more recent threads.

Maggie:

It seems like our conversations run that way. I find myself skimming a lot of the physics stuff. It's interesting to watch it being hashed out. I'm watching Doug and Magnus and Bo and everyone else closely, because I'm very interested in the divisions and breakpoints they come up with. It's the parallels and extensions to the social level that are my interest. And there are parallels.

Doug:

I am really curious about your observations: most of TLS being classicists vs. romanticists. Could you say more about how you distinguish the two classes of folk, e.g., topics, language, culture, etc.? For me this is a real problem. In the USA, we are embedded in a SOM culture with all the accouterments and baggage. Personally, when I try to talk with MOQ language people drift away. Notably the SOM language is simpler and faster. It is more efficient, short term, than MOQ. But it is less accurate and tends toward inconsistent generalizations.

Our TLS mates mostly use SOM language to discuss and describe MOQ. Do you? Is this what you refer to as classicist? Anthony has attempted to use MOQ speak. I have tried it a few times, but others seem to ignore it or be unaware of what we are attempting to do.

Martin:

Good observation. Pirsig admitted to being on the classical side (he studied biochemistry originally) and this probably gave him an incessant need to find out, "What is Quality? What the hell is it?" The romanticist would have just left it alone. The Zen master would have said, "you're thinking too much." But I think the point of the whole thing is the integration of the two. Where would we be if no one had bothered to analyze Quality? Rationalism is just as important as empiricism, but not more.

Ciona:

I've found the threads on quantum theory and physics to be fascinating. Right now, I'm reading The Dancing Wu Li Masters, which seems to relate nicely to what the Squad has been discussing. I would like to pose the question of how art relates to MOQ, however. (Hopefully, this could raise a more romantic side of the list.) What is the moral value of art? Would anyone be interested in pursuing this?

Doug:

Ciona, as you have read, Maggie, Platt, et al., make frequent attempts to pull TLS onto the romantic road via art, poetry, music, etc. Perhaps it is time for the likes of me to shut up about physics and the technical aspects of MOQ. Let's try that for a while. What MOQ aspects of art, etc., do you want to talk about?

Ciona:

I found a copy of Guidebook to Zen and the Art of Motorcycle Maintenance at the library recently. Has anyone else come into contact with this book? I've just started reading it, so I haven't had a chance to formulate much of an opinion on it, but it seems to be an interesting companion to ZMM. Unfortunately, it was published before Lila was, so it's definitely missing a substantial section of Pirsig's philosophy.

My apologies if any of these topics have been brought up before. I haven't been part of the list from the beginning. Thank you all for a wonderful association; the postings from this group have made checking my mail a far more interesting experience.

Do you say "lee la" or "lie la?"

Maggie:

I say "lie la." How about the rest of you?

I skimmed The Guidebook to Zen in the bookstore once and found it interesting and disturbing. My slant on Pirsig was not the same as the author's, as I remember. There are also a lot of portions that were cut from ZMM. I read them, and decided that they were left out for a reason. However, if I could get hold of it now, I'd read it again.

I have another name question—was anyone else disturbed by the protagonist of Lila being called Phædrus? I stumbled over that name every time I read it, and I still do. It's almost as if Pirsig had taken the actual name of the person, I don't know who, and at the last minute, used the computer to substitute Phædrus. Phædrus was the original, separate, pre-hospital personality. The narrator of ZMM was someone else. By the end of the book, they had made peace with each other. A rhetorical question.

Doug:

About The Guidebook to Zen and the Art of Motorcycle Maintenance, I have that and consider it good. Lots of anecdotal information from lots of resources. Also the early part on Zen instruction and the phases is fun and allows a SOM-ite to make comparisons to another world. I like to imagine that people in the middle of the next millennium will easily move twixt a Zen-like focused meditative behavior and MOQ-like defocused gregarious behavior. One without the other seems empty or incomplete. Also, the two states appear to me complementary.

I say, "Leye Lah."

Magnus:

It's a good thing this isn't an oral discussion or nobody would understand anybody else when saying Lila. I say, "Li" as in "lie" "la." I'm not quite sure, but I think the name Lila is mentioned in the movie Four Weddings and a Funeral at some outdoor reception after the first or second wedding.

Keith:

Like most, I think, I say Lila with a long "i," "Lie-luh," as that's how I've heard the female name pronounced. However, since reading Frijof Capra's The Tao of Physics, I've assumed that Pirsig picked this name because in Hindu mythology "lila" means "the play of God," "the creative activity of the Divine," (Capra, 87), a "rhythmic play which goes on in endless cycles, the One becoming the many and the many returning to the One," (Capra, 1998). This seems to be what Pirsig alludes to on page 6, when he writes, "There is Lila, this single private person who slept beside him now, who was born and now lived and tossed in her dreams and will soon enough die and there is someone else, call her lila, who is immortal, who inhabits Lila for a while and then moves on." Lila Blewitt of Rochester, New York is a transient player with a bit part in this grand divine play, but through her performance, we may discover something of the meaning of the play and perhaps of the playwright, as well. I'm afraid I don't know how to pronounce the Hindu lila, if that connection were valid. (Has anyone asked Pirsig if it is?)

Bodvar:

I asked Pirsig about it shortly after publication and he said it was like "lilac," and that, "it was the unsubtlety of the lilac odour and the hardiness of the bush that helped suggest her name to me." Does this sound like your phonetic "lie-luh?" Somewhere I have read that he did not know about the lila of Hindu mythology, but it's quite a coincidence when one reads the passage you cite. [113]

Reality is Quality [March 1998]

Keith:

I would take issue with the assertion that Dynamic Quality is just whatever seems better to us. I find this statement misleading. For example, I have a friend for whom eating cheeseburgers "seems better" than exercising regularly. Occasionally, I agree with her. However, I don't think that either of those activities qualifies as Dynamic Quality. [114]

A synonym for Dynamic Quality that Pirsig introduced in Subjects, Objects, Data and Values (page 17) may be of use here. Pirsig calls Dynamic Quality the Conceptually Unknown. I like this term. It loses some of the meanings of Dynamic (changing, patternless) Quality (good, valuable) but it cuts to another of its significant characteristics, that of being unknown to our intellect. To me, this is the essence of Pirsig's Dynamic Quality.

The key to understanding Dynamic Quality as the Conceptually Unknown lies with the realization that reality cannot be fully captured by language (i.e., understood intellectually). The reason for this is merely that language is part of the whole of reality, and by definition, a part of something cannot be greater than the whole. So, the process of intellectual abstraction necessarily leaves out aspects of that which it describes.

These left out parts are, therefore, Conceptually Unknown— Pirsig's Dynamic Quality. Now in one sense, the Conceptually Unknown Pirsig talks about in SODV is merely the current Conceptually Unknown. That is, after the experiment, it will be known through some static scientific formula or another and become static quality in his terminology. But in a larger sense, for the reasons laid out in the previous paragraph, there will always be parts of reality left out of our intellectual constructions of it and those parts will be what we call Dynamic Quality. Those parts that do fit in our intellectual constructions of things—that can/have been be captured in static patterns—are called static quality.

As an aside, it seems that in an even larger sense, everything can be considered Dynamic Quality before we have "sliced it up" into intellectual categories. In ZMM, Chapter 19, Pirsig talks about "the Quality event," an early notion, later formalized in Chapter 9 of Lila as Dynamic Quality, as being "preintellectual cutting edge of reality."

With this understanding of Dynamic Quality, we see that it becomes synonymous with the Sophist's idea of aretê, the Good. As Pirsig says in ZMM, Chapter 29: "The Good was not a form of reality. It was reality itself, ever changing, ultimately unknowable in any kind of fixed, rigid way." Pirsig makes the same connection between Dynamic Quality and the Tao of eastern thought in Chapter 20 of ZMM where he substitutes his term "Quality " for "Tao" in the Tao Te Ching. As Alan Watts writes on page 15 of The Way of Zen, the Tao (Dynamic Quality) is "the indefinable, concrete 'process' of the world."

So, what you can say about Dynamic Quality is really very limited, since it is by definition that which cannot be expressed intellectually, that which is left out of our models of the world. It is reality in its totality, not reality as we conceptualize it. To my thinking, the notion of Dynamic Quality is an epistemological distinction, an assertion about the limits of intellectual understanding. Perhaps it is also the same as Die Ding an Sich— the thing in itself in Kant's terminology.

Bodvar:

What you have written up to the last line of this paragraph is just great, and this is no major criticism. I just swoop down when parallels are drawn between Kant and Pirsig. Kant was the epitome of the subject/object paradigm and brought it to its ultimate refinement, so that its inherent weakness/absurdity was revealed. His Ding an Sich concept bears no resemblance to the Dynamic Quality as I see it. It was the ephemeral objective reality that was left when all subjective qualities were removed, while Dynamic Quality is the reality before any static patterns are formed. [115]

Keith:

An important corollary to the proposition that language cannot fully capture reality is that there is no single correct intellectual construction of the world, no single right answer (which is not the same as there being no wrong answer). Since there's no way for intellect to abstract the process of the world in a way that expresses its totality, there will always be multiple competing truths. We select among these truths by noting how well they correspond to our experience of reality (empiricism).

But back to the original issue of Dynamic Quality itself—the description I've given above left out one important aspect, of course. One way in which Pirsig's Dynamic Quality differs from Die Ding an Sich and the Tao is that "it," as the name suggests, is Quality, value, goodness—that is, morality. Pirsig arrives at this conclusion during his famous "between the horns" response to the dilemma of whether quality is subjective or objective, as described in Chapter 19 of ZMM. I believe this is an ontological assertion—a statement about the nature of reality itself.

It's probably this aspect of Dynamic Quality that is being responded to when it is said, "Dynamic Quality is just betterness." That's true enough as far as it goes. Dynamic Quality is betterness in Pirsig's system. It's the good, but not in a conventional sense. It's not Good as in Good vs. Bad or Good vs. Evil because Dynamic Quality encompasses all the "things" that might qualify to wear those distinctions. It's Good in a mystic sense, one that goes beyond our conceptual categories. What that might mean, I don't know, because I've not had an enlightenment experience that would open me up to the sort of non-intellectual understanding or apprehension of reality that seems to be required to intuit the Good in this fashion. (I'm still too much caught up in intellectual understanding to fully appreciate what Pirsig means by "direct experience" of reality.) I believe, however, that this is what Pirsig is talking about when he uses the term Dynamic Quality.

Well, I hope I haven't confused the issue any more by engaging in this "degenerate" (Chapter 5, Lila) activity of trying to box in Dynamic Quality epistemologically and ontologically. I wrote this post primarily for my own understanding and really being challenged by coming up with a personally satisfying understanding of it (which I have yet to do). Thanks to all who participate in this forum. The reading and thinking I've done since joining has been very rewarding.

Bodvar:

No confusion at all. During the short life of TLS, we have arrived at certain conclusions not explicitly mentioned by Pirsig, but still natural MOQ fallouts. For example, one discussion thread started by asking what value level this thing and that thing belongs to. A chair is obviously made of inorganic matter, but formed as a throne it is for showing off social status. It threatened to become absurd, but we finally agreed that from each value level point of view everything in the world is its own high or low value. When we focus on biology, everything is good or bad for our bodily cravings. When on the social plane everything is pro or con the cause we identify with, and finally when on the high intellectual perch everything is well or not so well formulated ideas. We, through this mailing list, definitely operate from intellect. So, feel free to work out better ideas, formulations, and definitions. You have the qualities to become a true MOQ scholar. Also feel free to criticize my bombastic assertions.

Keith:

To be accurate, we should say nothing at all.

Lao-tzu: The Tao that can be told is not the eternal Tao (Line 1, Tao Te Ching).

A monk asked Ma-tsu: Why do you teach Mind is Buddha?

Ma-tsu said: To stop a baby from crying.

The monk said: When the crying has stopped, what then?

Ma-tsu said: Then I teach, Not mind, not Buddha.

The monk said: How about someone who isn't attached to either?

Ma-tsu said: I would tell him, Not beings.

The monk said: And what if you met a man unattached to all things? What would you tell him?

Ma-tsu said: I would just let him experience the great Tao.

(Notes on Tao Te Ching, Stephen Mitchell translation)

No one has jumped on any of the statements in my original post concerning the identification of Dynamic Quality with value. As a result, I haven't had the opportunity to explore that aspect of Dynamic Quality as I did with the epistemology of Dynamic Quality. Since I personally have a more difficult time seeing the justification for this identification than with the justification for the limits of intellectual knowledge, I'd like to spend a little time on it.

To my understanding of MOQ, Pirsig makes exactly one ontological assertion: Reality is Quality—that is, value. See the diagram, Chapter 20, ZMM, or the concluding paragraph of Lila, Chapter 7: "Quality is morality. Make no mistake about it. They're identical. And if Quality is the primary reality of the world then that means morality is also the primary reality of the world. The world is primarily a moral order."

My question: what is our justification for accepting this? [116] In Lila, Pirsig starts by merely asserting reality equals Quality as fact. He does, of course, provide many examples that seem to support his contention. In Chapter 5 of Lila, for example, Pirsig discusses the example of the hot stove: "Value is more immediate, more directly sensed than any self or any object." Chapter 8 of Lila is devoted to showing how a value-centered metaphysics dissolves the platypus of a Subject/Object Metaphysics. Likewise, in following chapters, especially Chapter 12, examples of other dilemmas resolved by MOQ are discussed.

However, all of the many examples throughout Lila seem to beg the question of whether reality equals Quality. Assuming the premise may be a fine rhetorical strategy, but it does not make for a strong logical argument. The only place I've found something of a positive case for the identity is in Chapter 19 of ZMM, where Pirsig takes us through Phædrus' reasoning in rejecting each of the two horns of the subject/object dilemma. In capsule form, a proof version of Pirsig's reasoning in Chapter 19 goes something like this—if something exists, it is either objective or subjective or reality itself. Quality exists. Therefore, Quality is either objective or subjective or reality itself.

Let's consider the case where Quality is objective. Now, if quality is objective, then x, y, z follow. Ah, but it's not the case that x, y, z obtain. Therefore, Quality is not objective. So, let's take the case that Quality is subjective. If quality is subjective, then p, q, r. Ah, but again, not p, q, r. Therefore, Quality is not subjective. Therefore, Quality is not subjective or objective. Therefore, Quality is reality itself. (This formulation of the argument in Chapter 19 has my own spin on it. Pirsig's actual argument only concerns whether Quality is objective or subjective, not whether it's reality itself. I added that assumption because I think it's implicit in Pirsig's reasoning and it's clearly needed to make the identity statement true.) [117]

Now this is all sound reasoning and we've got a good case for reality equals Quality, assuming the reasons for rejecting both subjectivity and objectivity (p, q, r and x, y, z) are really not the case. In my estimation, though, Pirsig glosses over p, q, r and x, y, z. To be sure, I need to perform a closer analysis of his arguments in Chapter 19 than the scope of this post allows. I think it's clear, however, that the arguments Pirsig makes here are essential to justify the belief that reality equals quality, assuming I'm correct that this is the only place a real argument is given. [118]

I want to close this section by asking the group what justification you have for believing Pirsig's identity Quality equals reality? Do you find the reasons Pirsig gives for rejecting subjectivity and objectivity in Chapter 19 compelling? Are there arguments (even beyond Pirsig's works) that don't beg the question other than the one identified in Chapter 19? More broadly, do you think proper justification requires dialectic precision or is a rhetorical argument sufficient? Is this point a matter of faith? (Are we really building a Church of MOQ?) On a side note, is the reality equals Quality identity at odds in any way with the epistemological consideration that reality is not completely knowable intellectually? [119]

Ken:

Keith, I don't think hamburgers were what Pirsig had in mind when he said that Dynamic Quality may be simply betterness, although we could certainly start with a hamburger, or for that matter any of it ingredients, and wind up with a discussion of the limits of our knowledge of the universe. I know that I should wait until I have re-read ZMM and Lila in the light of your comments before I enter the fray but that wouldn't be any fun.

I am not sure that all of this talk about not being able to understand reality because we are a part of it is right. I would be interested to hear your explanation of why that is so. Just saying it doesn't make it so. I can see a somewhat weak analogy in the case of the computers we are using. I feel sure, if it hasn't already been done, that a computer could be programmed to understand itself, to repair itself (medicine), and even build baby computers. It could also develop a whole worldview of computers including, or maybe beginning, with the original Greek computer group and working up the line of computer philosophy to the present understanding of the position of computers in the universe.

You can say that computers have an overriding intelligence that is capable of programming this information in them, but so do we. We have Dynamic Quality, which continually pushes us in the direction of greater understanding. It should be obvious, whether we accept all of the science or not, that there is a force in the evolution of the universe that continually nudges the physical world in the direction of greater information content. This force is what I look upon as Dynamic Quality. If we simply look upon Dynamic Quality as a synonym for Eastern Mysticism, or the Way, then we have not made any advance with the concept of the Metaphysics of Quality.

I agree that the Conceptually Unknown probably cannot be fully captured by language, but I believe that it can be by a combination of language and symbols when the riddle of the universe is finally fully unraveled. You can object that we will never be able to understand the beginning and perhaps the end but I say that it is premature to make such a statement. At our present level of ignorance, we are not in a position to make a firm statement about many things, and certainly not about that. If, at this level of understanding, mysticism soothes our anxieties, then well and good.

It may well be that that is where we will wind up but as of now I am not prepared to accept it. There are many mysteries out there, but many mysteries have been explained in the last hundred years and I expect many more will be explained in the next hundred. As of now the two-slit experiment looks like the hand of God but so did many things previously that are commonplace now. Quantum Electrodynamics opened up many vistas to us as well as Chaos Theory. I feel sure that Quantum Chromodynamics will become less mysterious in the next hundred years.

My interpretation of the MOQ is simply the pressure of the evolution of the universe on our subconscious minds (among many other somewhat ephemeral things) that causes us to select from our field of awareness those things that are compatible. In my view, everyone experiences the MOQ at their level of capability and always have. This is what accounts for the Many Truths idea.

It is getting late and I have a cold and my drink is empty and the bed is looking better all the time so I am going to knock off this fun and allow my Dynamic Quality to function unimpeded. You sound like a thoughtful person. I am just literal minded and can't help it.

Keith:

Quite right that just saying so doesn't make it so. However, I do believe there are justifiable reasons for believing this is the case. First, a clarification: it's only in an intellectual sense that we can't understand reality. What I said in my post was that, "reality can not be fully captured by language, i.e., understood intellectually." We can apprehend reality through direct experience (more later), but we cannot know it fully through our intellectual models.

Don't take this as a rejection of rationality or science. It's simply an acknowledgment of the limitations of intellectual understanding, which Pirsig believed amounted to an "expansion of reason." (ZMM Chapter 14) What is this limitation in our intellectual knowledge? Does it mean we'll never move beyond our present stumbling blocks in scientific understanding?

No, emphatically no. You are completely right to say that, "at our present level of ignorance we are not in a position to make a firm statement about many things." While I do think that prospects for moving beyond the seeming fundamental limitations imposed on knowledge by the particular cases of the Uncertainty Principle and Chaos theory are limited, many more intelligent than me have thought we were at the limits of knowledge in one field or another in the past and been proved completely wrong. I have no disagreement whatsoever with your general assertion that things that appear mysterious now will be understood in the future. I even hold out hope, along with you and Stephen Hawking, that we may one day find a Grand Theory of Everything, which unifies all of physics.

However, that isn't the same as asserting that through a "combination of language and symbol" we will find that "the riddle of the universe is finally fully unraveled." Such a unified theory of the universe would be an explanation of reality only at the physical level. Surely, it would unify all of physics into a coherent system. Would it do the same for psychology? For art? Even for biology? No. In MOQ speak, it would be merely a complete intellectual description of the inorganic level of quality. But what of the rest? Aren't they equally part of reality? How is it that this so called Theory of Everything misses them?

The problem such a theory (and more generally, any intellectual description) is that in its striving to be a universally applicable objective description of reality, it will by necessity completely miss the subjective nature of experience.

Platt:

Keith! To take up your challenge—what justification (do) you have for believing Pirsig's identity Quality equals reality? —I offer the following rationalizations that are, as you say, necessary to getting what are essentially mystic ideas across to someone.

The Gotcha Proof:

You can't deny that reality is value without asserting a value. Example: did I hear you say bull when I claimed reality is value? Do you think you're right? Do you think being right is good? Gotcha.

The Living Proof:

You can't deny that to live (maintain reality) requires assumptions about what is good. You have to act to live. Action presupposes choice, choice presupposes purpose, and purpose presupposes value. Examples: it's good to keep your eyes on the road while driving. It's better to chew gum than smoke.

The Something from Nothing Proof:

The basic question for philosophy is: Why is there something rather than nothing? I know of only three rational options, each based on an unprovable premise: 1) God 2) Accident and 3) Ethical requirement. God is the religious premise, accident the scientific premise, and ethical requirement the MOQ premise.

No need to elaborate on the God premise—God as the First Cause. Literature is full of that argument. The accident premise fails by self-contradiction: events fall into causation patterns for no cause whatsoever. The ethical requirement premise has at least something going for it. It's good to be alive. A good universe creates life. To cause such a universe to be, an ethical cause can be assumed. (In MOQ speak, the universe prefers precondition Good.)

At this point, all rationalizations end and infinite regress takes over. Who made God? Who set accidents in motion? Who created the ethical cause? All logical truth eventually winds up here, at infinity. The American novelist, John Steinbeck, said it best: "The lies we tell about our duty and our purposes, the meaningless words of science and philosophy, are walls that topple before a bewildered little Why?"

So we come to my Final Proof:

Ultimately, the only thing that stops infinite regress and answers the question, "what's true?" is one's own innate sense of Quality. It stops when an individual (whether cleric, scientist or philosopher) decides for himself for whatever reason (explanatory power, simplicity, elegance, coherence, correspondence, consensus), that's a good truth.

To explain, allow me to turn to Robert Burns, the 16th century Scottish poet who you should like, for he wrote:

"I'm truly sorry man's dominion, Has broken Nature's social union."

Here's the relevant quote:

"Oh wad some power the giftie gie us, To see ourselves as others see us."

Just as you cannot step outside yourself to see yourself as others see you, we cannot step outside our reality to see it as someone outside our reality would see it. We tried. Lord knows we tried. Science took us all the way down to the reality of the subatomic world, and there we lost it. We found we could not observe reality at that level without disturbing it. There we discovered that the object could never be completely separated from the subject, and suddenly the whole world of subjects and objects—the world of me in here and you out there—came tumbling down. The assumption that reality (or information) exists independently of us blew up in our faces, leaving our entire subject-object worldview in shambles.

Few have come to terms with reality as discovered by quantum mechanics except for physicists like Eddington:

"Something unknown is doing we don't know what—that is what our theory amounts to." Or Heisenberg: "The common division of the world into subject and object, inner world and outer world, body and soul, is no longer adequate and leads us into difficulties." Or Schroedinger: "Subject and object are only one."

Or the philosopher Robert Pirsig: "(Subjects and objects) can be used as long as it is remembered they're terms for patterns (of values) and not some independent reality of their own."

The assumption that there exists an objective reality independent of subjects is no longer tenable. We have met Quality, the fundamental ground-stuff of the world, and it is us.

Ken:

As far as not being able to see ourselves as others see us, if we wanted to go to the trouble we could monitor ourselves with camera equipment long enough and in enough situations to get as good an idea as anyone else has.

Platt:

Seeing you as a camera sees you is not exactly what Robert Burns had in mind. If you kiss the camera on its lens, I doubt it will have much of a reaction. But hopefully your kiss will have some effect on a human kissee who will see you as something more than an electronically encoded apparition. The point is you can never know what it's like to be kissed by you, any more than a physicist can know both the exact position and velocity of an electron

Despite your faith in ultimate knowledge, there are some intellectual "never knows" built into the structure of the universe. Or so Gödel's Theorem and Heisenberg's Uncertainty Principle say.

But, all is not lost. Perhaps a form of understanding beyond the scientifically intellectual: the Mu understanding, thinking without thought, the aesthetic experience of Dynamic Quality, beyond words but real.

Have you experienced such an understanding? Need I ask?

Keith:

This is the problem of qualia. Qualia is a term used in the philosophy of mind. The idea is that some mental states have "qualitative characters," something that it's like to be in that mental state. As Sydney Shoemaker explains in Functionalism and Qualia: "Functionalism (or behaviorism, or materialism, or 'causal' theories of mind, the objection has been made against all of these) cannot account for the 'raw feel' component of mental states for their 'internal,' or 'phenomenological,' character." (Philosophical Studies XXVII, May 1975, 292-315)

In a nutshell, the problem is that a description of mental states as physical states of the brain doesn't tell us anything about the subjective experience of being in that state. How does an increase in serotonin levels explain what it is to feel euphoric?

Thomas Nagel believes that the inability of an objective (separated from a particular viewpoint) conception of the functioning of mind (such as reductive physicalism) to account for the subjective content of experience points to a limitation in intellectual understanding: "If we try to understand experience from an objective viewpoint that is distinct from that of the subject of the experience, then even if we continue to credit its perspectival nature, we will not be able to grasp its most specific qualities unless we can imagine them subjectively. We will not know exactly how scrambled eggs taste to a cockroach even if we develop a detailed objective phenomenology of the cockroach sense of taste. When it comes to values, goals, and forms of life, the gulf may be even more profound. Since this is so, no objective conception of the mental world can include it all." (The View From Nowhere, Thomas Nagel, 1986, page 25)

No intellectual account of the universe will be able to explain what scrambled eggs taste like to a cockroach, what it's like to be kissed by you, or what it's like to be a bat (see Thomas Nagel, What's It Like to Be a Bat? The Philosophical Review LXXXIII, October 1974.) But all of those things exist, don't they? They are part of the reality we're hoping to explain, aren't they? I certainly can't deny that there is something it's like to be kissed by my girlfriend. But in what sense does the description of me and my girlfriend as quantum wave functions capture that experience? In what sense does a description of us as complex aggregates of various carbon compounds explain it? In what sense does the idea that we're vertebrate mammals of the species Homo sapiens explain that feeling? How does the idea that love is an innate psychological need for humans elucidate the nature of the experience?

In short, by stripping off the Lockean secondary qualities of sense experience to apprehend the world in terms of primary qualities, we lose the ability to make sense of our experience of reality, which is, of course, purely in terms of secondary qualities. When we go purely for Classical Quality, we trade in Romantic Quality.

Well, that was maybe a long way to go for that point. It's not the only way to go, either. I think the elucidation of the qualia problem is apropos of my original post and especially of Platt's response. There are certainly other ways of arriving at the conclusion that reality is ultimately not completely knowable through intellectual understanding—from Descartes' meditations on whether he can trust sense experience or whether a devil is actively deceiving him, to Kant's nomena, unknowable in itself, to the modern scientific determinist paradox of a world governed by causal relationships but specifiable only with probabilistic mathematics (doesn't that imply there's something missing from the scientific description that we're summarizing with probability factors?) to, as Platt alluded, Gödel's Incompleteness Theorems (thought I really don't know the math meta-theory to tell whether his work is extensible to language at large)—following any of these leads may well bring us to the same conclusion about the limits of knowledge.

Now, as I implied at the beginning, I don't think we have any real argument on this point. I never meant to say that reality is completely unknowable by intellect. That wouldn't be true. I do, however (for some of the reasons laid out above), believe it is the case that reality is not completely knowable by intellect, a somewhat different proposition. I also believe that we cannot say that any of our concepts represent reality in an absolute sense, but are merely models that to a greater or lesser degree explain the data we gather through observation.

Since value is Quality is reality, this is an especially difficult concept to explain to someone! All of the discussion above should inform the answer to this problem. First, there's the epistemological consideration that would lead you to explain that value/reality is not ultimately explicable in intellectual terms, partly because it includes the subjective character of experience, which is irreducible to a rational description. Taking this view to the extreme, however, would lead you to say simply, value is (or to say nothing at all), as your response to Ken on understanding reality suggests. This mystic approach is not very useful in getting the idea across to someone, though.

Second, the ontological consideration that identifies value with reality would lead you to explain value in the same way you'd explain reality to someone—well, I conceive of it as divided into four ethicoevolutionary levels: the Inorganic, the Biological, the Social, the Intellectual. Value (reality) that can be conceived of through these fixed concepts is static value. The sum total of these patterns and that which does not fit into these categories is the totality of reality, or Dynamic value.

People will look at you strangely.

Probably the only way you can describe what you mean by value is by guiding the listener through some of the considerations that brought Pirsig (and presumably you) to the conclusion that reality is nothing but value. What do you think value is? Is it in an objective fact about the universe? Are some things actually better than others are? Are values just things in our minds, just individual preferences and beliefs? Or is value not subjective or objective but something on its own?

The concept of value really is a conundrum for a believer in MOQ because it's at once the undefinable flux of direct experience, which is also understood through all the concepts of individual things and events, and static levels that we use both in everyday life and in MOQ speak. It is all of the stuff in the world, but it only makes sense when we start, as Pirsig did, by saying that it's not (just) value in the traditional religious edict or social order or individual preference sense, but it's reality itself, whatever that is, and then go about explaining how we can conceptualize a chair as a collection of dharmas (Chapter 30, Lila) and how that might help us overcome some problems in causality and then saying that it also manifests itself as biological drives, and elaborating on how that conception might help us fix some holes in evolutionary theory. And on and on. Hmmm. Might as well just hand them the books.

Looking back on this response, I have the feeling that I shouldn't have gone down this path and instead should've simply stopped with the questions in the first section, as I don't think I've added any clarity to the situation with my answer. Ah well, it's late, enough weekend philosophizing.

Ken:

I had an epiphany last night that kept me awake for a while. I was going to construct my personal interpretation of the MOQ but I think it would be more fun if I threw out an idea and see if it attracted any interest. One of the problems I have been having without realizing it was that I have been concentrating on Lila and ignoring ZMM. Last night I went back to ZMM and skimmed through some of it.

On page 245 of the paperback Bantam edition Pirsig writes: "In our highly complex organic state we advanced organisms respond to our environment with an invention of many marvelous analogues." A little farther on: "Quality is the continuing stimulus which our environment puts upon us to create the world in which we live. All of it. Every last bit of it."

On the next page, he relates Quality to the Tao in the Tao Te Ching of Lao Tzu. Substituting Quality, he reads:

"The quality that can be defined is not the Absolute Quality.

The names that can be given it are not Absolute names.

It is the origin of heaven and earth.

When named it is the mother of all things."

At that point, he is speaking of Romantic Quality, later Dynamic Quality. I tried a similar substitution using "Force for

360

Greater Information Content" and found that it worked just as well and made more sense to me. It should be obvious to all of us that there is a force in the universe that is acting to oppose entropy and store a greater content of information in the universe. It is evident in the formation of galaxies, stars, evolution, and eventually us. It is continuing to act in the processes of our minds.

Without negentropy (hang-ups in the flow of the universe toward complete randomness) the universe could not have developed in the way that it did. The formation of most of the stars from Hydrogen represents negentropy in that it greatly extends the lifetimes of the stars and allows time for all else to happen. After the depletion of Hydrogen and the explosion of some stars, energy was provided for the formation of iron and the remainder of the heavier elements. From this debris happened earth.

When we get to the evolution of life, every possible combination of the available elements was tried in accordance with local environmental conditions. Those combinations that exhibited the greatest negentropy persisted and gave a platform for still greater information content. This process, happening randomly and always latching the greatest negentropy, eventually resulted in us. When we get to us, we can see the same process happening intellectually. History makes obvious (despite the Greeks) that there is a pressure toward higher morality in this whole process including the workings of our minds.

To my mind, this view of morality encompasses all of the inorganic processes in the universe as well as the continually growing morality of our species. If we call this process the Tao, or Dynamic Quality, or The Force for Greater Information Content (Morality) makes no difference. This process is not definable because of its complete randomness. The only thing we can say is that Quality has always worked and we hope it always will.

Of course, the whole universal process is probably heading toward complete randomness but in the meantime Dynamic Quality rules. Does any of this make any sense? At the moment, it does to me and I'm sticking to it. Keith, your email address seems to indicate Texas. As one who was raised on the banks of Red River in Oklahoma, I am wondering why you have not taken this opportunity to say a few words about Texas. :-) Isn't it fun?

Keith:

While I was indeed born in Texas and find myself living here happily once again, I grew up in Wisconsin, less than an hour's drive from the Minnesota cities mentioned in ZMM and Lila. As a result of this upbringing, I've been inculcated with the fine values of the Midwest. The sort of self-aggrandizement evident in "Don't Mess With Texas" bumper stickers is quite foreign to me. You'll get no praise of Texas from me other than that I like the weather and find Austin to be a fine city.

On the whole, I see Greater Information Content as a very serviceable, alternative description of Dynamic Quality. At the same time, isn't there something missing from this description? Where is morality under this description? When we identify the ultimate reality as Quality, the ethical component of MOQ follows directly. If we identify the ultimate reality as Information Content, how do we include moral judgments in the schema? Like the synonym Conceptually Unknown, the descriptor The Force For Greater Information Content seems to only capture part of what we mean when we say Quality; both miss the moral component. I suppose one could argue that Dynamic Quality doesn't capture the mystical (Conceptually Unknown) aspect very well, but I think the moral force is the primary identification and that the name we give it should reflect that.

No real argument with your view, though, Ken. I think it's a valuable aid in attempting to understand the fundamental process of the universe.

Bodvar:

Keith! Your question is what Lila was written to answer! The real problem is that so few understand how fundamental a break the MOQ is with what has preceded it. Allow me a silly metaphor. Before the Apollo program, there were a great many suggestions what the moon was made of (cheese one of the more outlandish).

But it was never doubted that it would be a substance. Now, if the space exploration had revealed it to be a hole in a sphere with a universal light behind it (like the Medieval concept) it would have been a fundamental break!

Keith:

Indeed. My problem is that the examples Pirsig uses in Lila beg the question of whether reality equals Quality. I'm not arguing that MOQ doesn't have great explanatory power or that the reasons Pirsig gives aren't intuitively compelling. I guess the real underlying question is—what grounds should justify our beliefs? While persuasive, I don't think the types of arguments Pirsig gives us in Lila (look, it explains x, y, z better) are sufficient justification. [120]

Bodvar:

The same applies to the philosophical suggestions of the consistency of reality. The old Greek philosophers ended an ancient tradition of reality is good and their quest for a true reality was a break at the time it occurred, but time has sedimented into our seemingly unassailable Subject/Object Metaphysics. There has been an endless row of suggestions of the finer structure of this reality, but never since the Sophists has the basic S/O been questioned.

I hear protests. Did not my favourite philosopher suggest such and such a reality which is a break with everything previous thought? I do not know all philosophical systems within Western tradition, but I doubt if there is one that takes leave of the S/O blueprint. There has been those who have suggested a pure materialist or a pure idealist view, i.e., that matter is really mind or vice versa, but never to scrap the mind/matter notion wholesalely. Tell me if you have a candidate.

Breaks of this magnitude face the troubles of not being provable from the system they left. Einstein's relativity was a break with several tenets of classical physics, and only Bertram Russell, besides Einstein himself, claimed that he understood it. Quantum physics is still worse. It is a break with reason so to say, and not even the founders professed to understand their own assertions. What is the justification for accepting these theories?

Keith:

They make claims that are empirically verifiable. [121] Both relativity and quantum mechanics make precise predictions which can be tested to disprove the respective theories. To me, that's convincing justification for believing the theories, as I find empirical proof of this sort sufficient justification for the belief in question. What justifies that belief is harder to say!

Bodvar:

There is no known proof for relativity and quantum mechanics that a classic physicist would accept. It is only that they work! Faultlessly and infallible. Admittedly, Newton physics calculation brings space shots to wherever; but inside the atom, at speeds approaching that of light and in strong gravitational fields, it fails. Only relativity and quantum calculations count at the extreme conditions.

The MOQ is a metaphysical equivalent. It works, it explains experience marvelously well, and solves the mind/matter riddles, but a proof that the SOM can accept is impossible. I have called it the mother of all relativity. (Doug would possibly call it the Schrödinger Cat of metaphysics?) Some of us have drawn the parallel to Gödel's Theorem: no all-embracing system can prove itself. Really Keith, what is the proof for the Mind/Matter metaphysics, or the justification for accepting it? No mocking or scorn—I see your point and would like to hear your opinion.

Finally, I have cautioned against using ZMM in the MOQ discussions. It's a splendid book and shows Phædrus' thorny way toward Quality, but at the stage that you refer to (the horn dilemma) he had reached a trinity of Subject/Object Quality, and that is not what he presents in Lila. The MOQ is a dualism too, but the dividing line is between Dynamic and static quality. The basic claim that there is only Quality and that art is how to divide it, is, as said, not provable.

Keith:

I'm not arguing there is a proof for Mind/Matter metaphysics. It's accepted as a given by the majority in our culture right now, though. That fact doesn't make it true but it does make it uncontroversial in most circles, and therefore excuses it from explicit justification. MOQ does not have the same luxury. It's not a majority held opinion. Therefore, it needs some justification for its assertions for it to gain a foothold. [122] I'd prefer if at least some of the justifications given didn't assume the conclusion. [123] Also, I question the analogy between the scientific theories of relativity and quantum mechanics and the metaphysical theories of Mind/Matter and MOQ. As I stated above, it seems that the former theories have verifiable consequences that follow from their (unproved) assumptions. That is, they are falsifiable. Does the Metaphysics of Quality follow the same pattern? I'm not sure. I want to explore this a bit more. [124]

Doug:

Like SOM, MOQ has an unknown/indefinable that it calls Dynamic Quality. DQ is just like mass, length, and time. We can describe it: the Quality event, the edge of now, direct experience, archetypal change, surprise, etc. But damn it, we cannot define it! And SOM classical science denies its existence!

Hugo:

I can agree with most of what you say on the epistemic aspects of Dynamic Quality, Keith; thanks for your very valuable contributions! As for the ontological aspects, they concern something I have been working with for a while. In fact, I, like many others on the Squad I guess, have adapted this view of reality in a way, which make it difficult to actually argue for it in a way which would be convincing for those with another view. I tend to think of it in terms of something like a Kuhnian paradigmatic revolution, though I would insist that communication across paradigms is possible.

Anyway, as for the arguments for Quality is reality, they are to me deeply connected with a process view or an evolutionary view. How do things arise? How can we understand becoming? This is the question that started my personal philosophical quest. There is a Dane, Simo Koeppe (Danish: Køppe), whom I may have mentioned before, who wrote a book on the levels of reality a few years back.

There are many issues which I like in that book, and the levels are the well known four levels (not inspired by Pirsig, it is after all a quite common view), though the social and psychological level (he is a psychologist by education) are parallel. But he has a distinct materialist view, and I recall an argument which went something like this, in terms of systems theory: any system consists of interrelated subsystems, and these subsystems of further interrelated subsystems, and so on. But, he argued, at some level there has to be indivisible atoms (or quarks or whatever), because if not, then everything would consist of nothing. It would be infinitely reducible to a mere vacuum or nothingness. And, given these atoms, everything could in principle be explained from their dynamics. Of course, this is only in principle, he said. In practice, we have to use the idea of systems and levels.

This struck me as immensely reductionistic, and I wondered about why he considered the interrelations as not really real. Since then, I have seen how relations, or values, kind of disappear in the common view of things. The "thingish" worldview makes us unable to see certain aspects of the world. Seeing this blindness once, it is to be found everywhere. One way of putting it is that the "thingish" worldview is blind to emergence; it is blind to the creative aspects of the world. In the "thingish" view, emergence is not really the becoming of new; it is merely the workings of lower level dynamics. [125]

But, and here I am approaching the question of the nature of reality, this just doesn't work. As Bo says, we cannot prove the MOQ, but we can show it works better. If we think about the present conjecture on a scientific worldview (meaning, a world view open to inquiry), everything arose out of nothing, or at least out of something that was fairly homogeneous, which had very few degrees of freedom. Now we see a world with an enormous complexity, with very many degrees of freedom. The Theory of Everything, which the physicists are searching for, may say something appropriate on the beginning of the universe, and our emulation of this beginning, but that's it. It will have very little to say on the present world just as the theory of gravity has little to say on the lives of birds.

If our ideas of explanation by reduction do not work on this grand scale, how can we believe they work on lesser scales? If the fundamental physics has very little to say on our world, why do we believe that explanation from below captures every aspect of the nature of reality? And if we do not believe that, if we ask what explanations from lower levels we miss out on, then we are back with the reality of relations, values, etc. And if relations or values are what makes complex reality something new, something real, apart and above from the remains after dissection, is this not the same as saying that value or relations are the fundamental part of (complex) reality?

If we can agree this far, then the rest of the argument will be to follow this down to the bottom, as Koeppe did, and in the end ask to the becoming of the elementary particles. Are they special or do they too consist of (arise out of) value, relation, Quality? If we ask the physicists, their answer will be something like energy and symmetry breaks.

And if they are forced, they either retreat to transcendentalism and the hand of God, or they say something that is very close to Pirsig: the fundamental reality is value (using other words, perhaps). To the open mind (in my particular case Pirsig was the prime eye opener), there really is no stance from which an entirely "thingish" worldview makes sense. And I think our best alternative is something like Pirsig's, leaving many open questions, of course. If we keep at it, it should take no more than a few decades or centuries before we can make a good case for it.

I personally think we are doing OK.

Identity of Quality and Reality [March 1998]

Keith:

367

I found Doug's exposition of the role of Dynamic Quality within MOQ being the same as the role of mass, length, time within physics very compelling. Having read it and understanding the problem in those terms, I have suspicion that Bodvar, Hugo, et al., were trying to tell me this very same thing in their replies to my post—that the identity of Quality with reality must be accepted as a given in the formal system of MOQ. Part of me can see this, but part of me still looks for some further justification, preferably the possibility of empirical verification on either the original premise of reality equals Quality or on some consequence of that premise within the MOQ.

Last time I argued that the only place I could find Pirsig making a positive argument for reality equals Quality was in "the between the horns" section of ZMM. Since then, I've found another argument for the identity. In Chapter 5 of Lila (pages 75-76 of the Bantam paperback edition), Pirsig takes on the logical positivists by arguing that it is an empirically verifiable fact that value equals experience, using the hot stove example. Pirsig seems to think that the identification of experience with value is empirically verifiable. If this holds true, I think my personal criteria for justifying the belief will have been fulfilled.

However, I've always had a hard time wrapping my mind around this example. What's to keep us from reverting to the traditional understanding of the hot stove example where the oaths the person on the hot stove utters come from their subjective valuation of pain, not from the primary empirical reality? [126] I'm hoping someone can explain this passage to me in a way that shows how this latter interpretation isn't plausible.

Donny has repeatedly asked questions along the lines of: what does it mean to say, "Science is True?" As Donny's indicated, I think my line of questioning touches on something similar. I probably need to back up and ask the question: what counts as justification (proof) of a belief? [127] By what criteria should beliefs be justified? Anybody have thoughts to share?

Thanks to Bo, Hugo, Platt, Doug, et al., for helping me along in my understanding.

Jason:

Bodvar, I greatly enjoyed your recent response to Keith's pointed inquiry. It's fundamental questions and responses like this that really move our discussion forward. One tangential comment from my side, though.

I definitely don't claim anything approaching a comprehensive understanding of all the subtleties and nuances of Western thought, but I have stumbled upon several interesting non-S/O philosophical systems over the past year or so. Two in particular stand out as candidates for your inquiry: the phenomenology of Edmund Husserl and the existential phenomenology of Maurice Merleau-Ponty. Both of these men exhibit a complex (and sometimes obfuscated) writing style that is challenging to say the least. However, after wading through a few of their most noted works, I'm convinced that they were both on to something akin to Pirsig's MOQ. If anyone is interested, I would be happy to share my limited understanding of these two thinkers. More likely, however, someone else on the list (i.e., Donald, Ant, etc.) with formal training in metaphysics would be in a better position to affirm or deny my intuitions.

Bodvar:

"The occult" has not been broached on the Lila Squad forum, and I wonder if anyone has an opinion of the Quality approach to this super-sensitive subject. Pirsig calls it "the empirical trash-heap of SOM," (Lila, page 363) but doesn't treat it specifically—except in the passage about "the Dharmakaya light" (El Greco's paintings) starting on page 344. But I am interested primarily in your Husserl and Merleau-Ponty mention, Jason.

Maarten:

For several months now I've been following the various discussions, and all of the regular contributors to the mailing list have been a great help in enhancing my understanding of Pirsig's work. Forgive me for being a "lurker" for so long, but I simply didn't/don't know enough to contribute much to the various threads. However, the postings of the last couple of days are touching on some subjects that I find particularly interesting.

The word "occult" is overused very much and has come to stand for a wide variety of meanings. I assume that you used it in the sense of "supernatural," and I would like to comment on the notion of the Dharmakaya light being supernatural.

The passage you mention (Chapter 26, page 393 in my Corgi paperback) is short but I think Pirsig makes clear which place the Dharmakaya light has in the MOQ. First, he says "it is a huge area of human experience cut off by cultural filtering," and after that he states that it is not some sort of supernatural occurrence. After the notes on El Greco is the following:

"In a Metaphysics of Quality, however, this light is important because it often appears associated with undefined auspiciousness, that is, with Dynamic Quality."

The Dharmakaya light is closely linked with Dynamic Quality! I like that.

For me this is one of the most important passages of Lila. It is a point where the MOQ, I think, seems to be in accordance with something that is at the heart of Buddhism. Now Pirsig doesn't say that Dynamic Quality and the Dharmakaya light are the same, but I find the following, taken from a book by a Tibetan Buddhist master, very interesting:

"Could this possibly suggest that the role of meaning…is somehow analogous to the Dharmakaya, that endlessly fertile, unconditioned totality from which all things rise?"

(Taken from The Tibetan book of Living and Dying from contemporary master Sogyal Rinpoche.)

The lines above are from a paragraph where he discusses similarities between Tibetan Buddhism and the theories of physicist David Bohm. I have not yet had a chance to read works of Bohm however.

In Buddhism, the Dharmakaya is the dimension of unconditioned truth, into which any kind of concept has never entered. It is the ground of all, from which subjects and objects emerge. To summarize this point, I think that Dynamic Quality and the Dharmakaya, while not necessarily identical, do convey much the same meaning. Dharmakaya therefore should have nothing to do with occultism.

Bodvar:

Maarten, how did you manage to stay in the wings for so long with such well founded and well formulated opinions? Anyway, welcome to the Lila Squad. Yes, I agree to the occult being a very loose term; it was really the supernatural I had in mind. I also admit that Phædrus of Lila denies that the Dharmakaya Light is something magical. If the occult is the trash heap of subject/objectivism, then the miraculous is its Unassimilated tray. I once participated at a discussion forum on Colin Wilson (who is an authority in this field) but it ended in a frustrating impasse. Everyone there was unfamiliar with Quality so it was SOM's two trenches: either you believe everything or everything is rejected offhandedly.

I will not tire you by describing the line of argument, but when I tried to introduce the Quality twist to it, I soon understood that it is the Greek paradoxes all over again. They wanted it explained on the subject/object premises, and that's not possible. SOM is the creator of the impossibilities! There simply is no supernatural in the MOQ scheme.

This may mistakenly be received as if the Quality has no room for mystery, that it is cold and super rational, sterile, but nothing is more wrong. This much said, what phenomenon do I classify as mysterious? Facetiously, everything in a SOM context, but that will not do. I shall be more specific, but first a digression. I feel that my reputation as a pillar of rationality at the Lila Squad is at stake by wallowing into such a minefield, and yet the MOQ cannot refuse to be applied. Everything is transformed by it so why not the paranormal?

I will not bring in UFOs or X-Files—that is not my great interest—but there are phenomenon so well documented that one

371

must be willfully blind to refuse its presence: the so called poltergeist effect, for instance—a young person's uncanny ability to wreck havoc on their surroundings. There are many conspicuous examples, but it's no use piling up "facts." Again, everything is really supernatural in the SOM universe. Moving my body by mental willpower is a major magical act. No one has ever explained how mind interacts with matter, but people only react when the more sensational "action at a distance" is involved.

Let me have a go at Keith's hot stove example:

This demonstration is the absolute first of the MOQ introduction, even before the equation, if a thing can't be distinguished from anything else, etc. Pirsig must see it as a crucial one. One can almost hear him grit his teeth over the effort to convey an insight (selfevident as insights are to the beholder) to the reader.

The first thing that comes to mind is the autonomous nerve system's reflexes; you touch something hot and the limb retracts automatically, and you wonder why this explains that value is between the object you touch and your subjective sensation of pain. Yes, even if you admit that the reaction occurs before the pain, you still don't see where value enters the picture. It's the way the human organism is hardwired. Full stop!

But however far you go back through the train of events you will never find the point where objective heat turns into subjective reaction. Either the subject goes right into the stove, or the stove becomes the subject. What it amounts to is that the subject smears itself onto its surroundings and/or the object invades the subject. Pirsig's conclusion is that if the subject/object division is artificial, some third agent is primary to, and mediates, even creates, subject and object. He goes on to call it value because this term straddles both S and O (in the SOM context), and has been troubling it from back when?

The value in this particular example I would call biology, common to all organisms. Remember the amoebae near the acid drop simile in ZMM? But value is the creator/mediator of reality at all static levels. To start at the inorganic dimension it mediates the chaos/inorganic order relationship (or moral code), at the biology level it creates the inorganic/organic order one, at the social plane it creates organic order/social order relationship and, finally, at the intellectual level, makes this seeming dualism into an eternal truth, the ubiquitous SOM, which is (just) another value mediation. Perhaps we may call it the social order/cultural order code. Remember that he structures the various levels sediments, from bottom up: Matter, Life, Society are plain enough, but the top structure Pirsig only vaguely calls Culture.

Annotations by Robert M. Pirsig

113. I did know about the lila of Hindu mythology and have attended Ram Lila celebrations in India, but I never consciously connected it with the Lila of the book.

114. Eating cheeseburgers is biological quality.

115. This is very good.

116. The harmony (i.e. Quality) it produces among the elements of our existing understanding.

117. The statement that Quality is reality itself does not follow logically from the statements that quality is not subjective or objective. That is why Pirsig never said this.

118. No, as stated in ZMM, the belief that Quality equals reality came much later and was arrived at by a more complex process. There was an intermediate period where Phædrus thought reality was three-termed, with subject, object and value—a "blessed trinity" he called it. This does follow logically from the conclusion that quality is neither subject nor object, since previously subject and object have been considered the totality of everything. Later Phædrus felt that three-termed realities are rather unwieldy (low quality) and rare in metaphysics, and tried to collapse them into one. He saw that if you collapsed them into the object you got a materialist metaphysics. If you collapsed them into the subject, you got an idealist metaphysics. But who had ever collapsed them into value? He tried it and saw that it could be done. As time went on, he saw that not only could it be done, but that it solved huge philosophic problems that had dogged metaphysics for centuries. It produced harmony where there had been disharmony. It had high intellectual quality.

119. Not as long as Quality is not completely defined.

120. The "(look it explains x, y, z better)" is the basis of all scientific theory, and in fact, all knowledge. The key word is "better." It is betterness, quality, that justifies all our beliefs. I find it impossible to imagine what more Keith can possibly want. (I'll bet he wants something better :-))

121. The MOQ makes claims that are empirically verifiable, such as that sitting on a hot stove has negative value. Most of our lives are spent empirically verifying that something has higher value than something else.

122. Truth is not supposed to be determined by social popularity, but if it were, ZMM is in good shape, since it has continued to sell very well year after year for 27 years now.

123. The hot stove experiment doesn't assume the conclusion. There can be a million more experiments like it, which predict that something is valuable or not valuable and the result can only be determined by the experiment. In fact, most scientific experiments, particularly those in applied research, are aimed at showing that something is valuable or not valuable.

124. It looks as though Keith is looking for something he can see. And he thinks values are not something he can see and therefore are not empirical. But if you think values are not empirical, try removing every trace of them from the world as we understand it and see what is left. You can't even get out of bed in the morning without making a value judgment that it is better to do so. The question is, "Why can't some people see that a value judgment is in operation?" Or, to put it better, "Why do they see it but insist that they do not see it?" This was the question that haunted Phædrus in his English classes in Bozeman.

125. This superbly answers the question raised in my previous note.

126. When you examine pain closely you see that it is not in the mind. Pain that is subjective, i.e. has no medical origin, is not considered to be real pain, but a hallucination, a symptom of mental illness. "Subjective valuation" of pain is a form of insanity. But you see that pain is not out of the mind either. When a medical patient is unconscious, i.e., whose mind is absent, there are no objective traces of the pain to be found. Once can possibly find the causes of the pain with scientific instruments but one cannot find the pain itself. So if pain isn't in the mind and it isn't in the external world where is it? The answer provided by the MOQ is

that pain, like hearing and vision and smell and touch, is part of the empirical threshold that reveals to us what the rest of the world is like. At the moment pain is first experienced it is not even "pain," it is just negative quality, a third category, outside of subjects and objects, whose definitions have not yet come in.

127. By their quality.

Chapter 13

"For years I have felt a lot of social pressure to write more, but that has been in conflict with a lot of Zen pressure not to write more. A third book weakens Lila by making it seem like a middle member of a series rather than a final statement. Also I do not know of anything to say that is more important than what was in Lila, so the third book would of necessity be weaker. That would give all the critics who do not like the Metaphysics of Quality a chance to say: 'See it's worthless after all.' When they sense weakness in an artist they are like sharks smelling blood. They will not stop until they feel they have torn him and his reputation to pieces to complete their own egotistic satisfaction. J.D. Salinger avoided them by stopping writing just in time. Ernest Hemmingway did not. But during the ride back from Mexico it became apparent to me that the third book actually is being written. It is called the Lila Squad."—Robert Pirsig's letter to Bodvar

ALife [March 1998]

Horse:

Hi. My name's Horse, I live in the Cambridge area in the UK and I've been affected by Pirsig and his work for about the last 8 years. I first came across ZMM in 1976 but at the time I was more interested in motorbikes than Zen or Quality. I discovered it again in 1990 when I returned to university to do a degree in Artificial Intelligence. I read the book in 24 hours straight through and wondered why I didn't get it the first time around. Still, such is life. I found Lila in the University bookshop some time later and read it looking for the same feeling that I got from ZMM, but it wasn't there. A couple of years later I read it again and realized that I had made a mistake in the first reading as this was a more interesting book than ZMM but still I didn't fully realize the fundamental difference between ZMM and Lila.

In 1996, whilst at an Open University summer school studying Ethics, I was reading Lila and it was as if someone had hit me in the back of the head with a mallet. Discussions at the summer school were, coincidentally about the meaning of life (sounds corny I know) and its problems within the subject/object view of the universe. I couldn't stop talking. I had suddenly realized the importance of the Metaphysics of Quality. I've read Lila and ZMM several times since and never fail to be fascinated by the insight, clarity, and intellectual beauty of the Metaphysics of Quality. There are a couple of things that concern me regarding the means by which the MOQ may be disseminated to the world at large.

The first is that it does not become some form of ideological or dogmatic mantra and the second is that it is not hijacked for political purposes. I think that this has been the case a number of times in the past, Darwin's theory of evolution being a case in point. Having said that and having looked through the Lila Squad site and read the most recent postings, I think this will be unlikely, at least from this group, as there seems to be an intelligent and considered view of the MOQ. I also think it is important that the MOQ is shown to be capable of supporting and strengthening many of the ideas that exist today but which may have previously been rejected as non-scientific/subjective, and thus by implication meaningless, but which may now be shown to be valid in a different context. Some examples may be Ethical systems, some of the Social Sciences and the Arts in general. Some of these have been dealt with by Pirsig but I think that many of the areas where the MOQ will throw new light will be regarded with suspicion by those with vested interests both within these fields and without.

A couple of points about the MOQ itself—I feel that there is a strong connection between fuzzy or multi-valued logic, chaos, and the Metaphysics of Quality. I'm currently working on this (sporadically as I have a young boy and a brand new pair of twins who all require regular attention, not to mention my partner). I also think that there is a great deal of scope for incorporating at least some of Pirsig's ideas into my main interest, that of Artificial Life. Still this is for the future, although hopefully not too distant.

Finally, in Lila, Pirsig mentions the battle that has been raging for centuries between intellect and society. In the past, the means of distributing the products of the intellect (ideas, beliefs etc.) have been owned or controlled by those with the greatest interest in ensuring that society is stronger of the two. Now, for the first time in history, there is a tool that provides the means for the intellect to fight back against control and subjugation by society. It is a tool that, ironically, has been provided by those forces that exert the strongest control over society—the Internet. It seems pretty obvious and probably most of you in the Lila Squad have already seen this but I just thought I'd mention it anyway, just in case.

Bodvar:

Back then we had a plunge into this field. I am not sure what conclusion we reached and cannot summarize the argumentation, but I have a hunch that the number crunching Deep Blue isn't the road ahead. I recently read that that kind of approach is impotent when playing the game "GO."

Horse:

As far as I can see this is basically correct, especially the bit about "GO." I started to learn this "game" a few years ago but had to drop out due to other pressures. I think the biggest mistake that artificial intelligence theorists made, quite understandably given the knowledge and paradigm within which this field started, was to take a reductionist approach to "intelligence." By making the assumption that any system is no more than the sum of its parts, the various means of collecting and outputting sense data were studied and an attempt made to reproduce them, mainly in isolation from each other. This is a bit over-simplified but a fairly reasonable description. The one thing that they appeared to forget was that human intelligence had several million years to evolve in the way it did with all of the various individual physical attributes interacting with each other within systems that involved interaction with other humans in an extremely hostile environment.

In recent years, changes in direction have produced some more interesting results with the introduction of connectionist systems, evolvable programs, and fuzzy logic. Artificial Intelligence is really a "top down" approach to machine intelligence, whilst Artificial Life is a "bottom up" approach to life. Both seem to be learning from each other and hopefully they may achieve some form of "middle out" solution.

Bodvar:

And yet, the human brain is a kind of computer, so unless we introduce "mind" as something transcending "matter" there is a connection between the gray matter and intelligence. Give us an input.

Horse:

This is where I think that MOQ comes in. I also mentioned in my biography "I feel that there is a strong connection between fuzzy or multi valued logic, chaos, and the Metaphysics of Quality."

Within SOM (which is basically dualistic, mind/matter, subject/object, etc.) are the extremes whilst the bits in between seem to be forgotten. This is where the fuzzy approach seems to meet with MOQ, or at least there appears to be some sort of conjunction. Everything in between the extremes is of varying value with regard to the extremes and is a combination of those extremes. When a person is asked if they are male of female they can, generally, say that they fall into one category or another. When asked if they are happy the answer will be fuzzy: sometimes, often, occasionally, etc. They are making a value judgment and the perception of that value is fuzzy. This breaks away from the discrete system of a or not a and becomes a and not a.

I think that this may possibly apply to the value hierarchy that Pirsig describes in Lila and be at the root of some of the arguments I've been reading in TLS. Are static patterns of value really fuzzy SPoVs? In the divisions between inorganic, biological, social, and intellect, where does one start and the other finish. [128] This may also reflect some sort of chaotic/fractal value. As I said in my biography, I'm not sure yet. These are just initial thoughts and need a lot more serious contemplation. As these nascent ideas start to become more coherent I shall throw them into the Lila Squad pot and see what sort of reaction they get. Hopefully I shan't get too badly scorched.

A possible approach to Artificial Life may then come out of some of these ideas, as the degree to which something possesses life, is autonomous, is intelligent, etc., is, in my opinion, fuzzy. How does artificial life exist in the MOQ universe? To what degree in an artificial life form do static and Dynamic Quality contribute to this type of creature? I can feel that I'm painting myself into a corner at the moment so I shall rest for now and think a bit (lot) more.

Magnus:

Hi Horse and Squad. I really liked your Artificial Intelligence post the other day. It's a subject I terrorized the rest of the Squad with this fall. I'd love to have another go at it. Just one point—you said: "In the divisions between inorganic, biological, social and intellect, where does one start and the other finish."

I must stress that the division between the levels is not onedimensional. When deciding in which level something belongs, you shouldn't think: hmmm, is it biological or inorganic? In that case it's probably both. Bo's multi-dimensional analogy is much better. If something is biological, it must have inorganic values also. In the analogy, it is two-dimensional. Every thing that has values at a certain level also has values at all levels below it, (the dependency principle). A cell has senses (biological value), so it must also have inorganic value, for example mass.

There's nothing fuzzy about the level division, it's crystal clear.

I Get It [March 1998]

Peter:

I've been lurking due to large amounts of schoolwork, but I had an epiphany today: patterns are all that exist! Any thing is just a configuration of other patterns. This is what I've known all along but didn't really internalize! Sorry to sound so childish, but this is really a great, fun revelation for me.

Maggie:

Yes! It is great. I remember when it happened to me, but I got it directly from reading Lila. I can almost see the page in front of me. If you don't mind my asking, do you know what triggered this for you? I'm curious about what it takes to make the shift.

Bodvar:

Hi Peter and Maggie. Firstly, educate me on the "epiphany" term. My dictionary only gives "commemoration of the magi" (The three wise men arriving in Bethlehem for the birth of Jesus), but you natives use it in a revelation or insight sense.

Peter, your insight reminded me so of my own "mind at the end" epiphany back in the early sixties. It was shortly that all of reality was language. It was immensely strong and convincing, but simultaneously going against reason and this bothered (a very weak description—driving me mad is more like it) me greatly for more than ten years, until I came across ZMM. I join Maggie in her request that you try to unravel your line of thought.

Doug:

Congratulations Peter! You are halfway there. Patterns are the static part of MOQ! They commingle and interpenetrate the Dynamic part of MOQ. Patterns resist change, and Dynamic Quality imposes change on them. This unending circle of static and Dynamic is the MOQ.

Donny:

Bo, the term "epiphany," used to mean a "revelation," comes from James Joyce. He grooved on the fact that what's taken to be the most important revelation, the revealing of Christ, took place in an ordinary stable in a fairly insignificant town. The term is used to refer to a major (mystical or psychological transforming) revelation that comes out of a common everyday experience or activity. Zen has a comparable idea in "satori." Sudden enlightenment, no meditation or philosophical study required—you're just doing your laundry and "Bang!" Joyce felt that all our daily activities had a mystical/mythological significance.

Horse:

Hi Bo and Squad. I thought I'd make a bit of time to reply to some of your comments in your welcome post before the Ethics thread flares up again. Not that I mind the Ethics thread continuing—I don't, as it is something that has interested me for some time. You asked: "In your introduction you hinted to a MOQ angle to Artificial Life. Is that AI, by the way?"

Not exactly. ALife (Artificial Life) is a response to the often rigid patterns that developed within AI (artificial intelligence). ALife covers a lot of areas of thought and experimentation but the part that I'm interested in is to do with a school of thought developed by Rodney Brooks at M.I.T. some years back. It uses a system called subsumption architecture, which, in a nutshell, is a layered system of actions wherein higher (more complex) levels build on lower levels. Its rules are extremely simple (move, stop, turn, etc.) but from these rules, complex behaviour develops. Its complexity develops in response to its environment. It also has a great slogan: "Fast, Cheap and Out of Control."

Bodvar:

On the AL/AI issue, Magnus said that he pestered us with it, but many of us were eagerly flaunting our various understandings of the Turing test and other theorems. However, your mentioning the slogan, "Fast, Cheap and Out of Control," evoked a memory of a book by Kevin Kelly, Out of Control, which I read in 1995. I found my copy and saw that I had underlined various passages with references to the MOQ.

This book must be written from the "subsumption architecture" idea. Look at this passage:

"Powerful computers birthed the fantasy of a pure disembodied intelligence. We know the formula: a mind inhabiting a brain submerged in a vat. If science would assist me, the contemporary human says, I could live as a brain without a body. And since we are big brains, I could live in a computer's mind."

This classical, umm, SOM approach, the free-floating mind that looks upon objective reality, is what the MOQ so fervently opposes. First an aside: throughout the entire life of TLS, the definition of intellect has troubled us. The obvious—intellect as mind (of SOM) or consciousness or awareness or "ability to think"—has surfaced again and again and just as often have I rejected it. The intellect of Quality is none of this: it has grown out of the social level! "Mind as such" has no place in the MOQ! This is a horribly important point to understand the Quality idea, but back to Out of Control.

The book contains an approach to the mind, or intelligence problem, which at first resembles the Quality one, but after life it jumps to intellect, missing the social dimension altogether, and is soon just as lost as the Matter/Mind approach. For example, it refers to the Black Room experiments (once a big thing to Colin Wilson, do you know him?) where people being deprived of sense impulses soon loose their ability to concentrate and goes into thought loops or start to hallucinate. If body was the creator of intellect, it should be as snug in a black room as elsewhere. The body/brain connections are not severed, only the ones to the environment! And not to the material environment, but to social reality.

These are subtle distinctions, but still crucial. The only feasible thing is to regard mind as Mind/Matter thinking, making both intellectual value patterns. What this means for the AI/AL I haven't yet probed, but I feel there is an opening here.

SOM as MOQ Intellect Level [March 1998]
Platt:
From the beginning of the Lila Squad, Bo has maintained that the intellectual level is SOM (rationality, language, science). [129] It's gradually seeped into my mind that Bo is right about this. SOM is the current mental framework and means of communication in which we operate from day to day, enabling us to "make a living" and enjoy "the good life."

That this level has accomplished wondrous things no one can doubt. One need only point to the technology supporting the Internet and the consequent emergence of the Lila Squad to bow humbly before the power of subject/object intellect. It's inconceivable to me that at one time in human history the subject/object concept of "me in here and you out there" simply didn't exist. Yet, from what we can garner from the unwritten past, such seems to be the case. During that prehistoric period, everything was "we," ruled by invisible gods who roamed the environment dispensing good and evil as per their whim. The concept of "I" as an individual person with some control, however meager, over one's own destiny was nowhere to be found. I wonder who was the person who first broached the idea of "I," and what horrible punishment the all-powerful group and their accompanying gods bestowed on her for such heresy.

The history of man since then could be summarized as the struggle of the I [130] against the We, the Intellect against Society, a mighty struggle that continues to this day. Whether it's ethnic conflict in Bosnia or political correctness in the U.S, the siren call of social quality (now heralded as equality) lures individuals back into the SOM rejecting social level of We. (Witness the academic attacks on rationalism and those bad white European males.)

Far from condemning SOM, the Metaphysics of Quality holds it to be the highest level yet achieved. [131] It is the SOM, the intellectual Level, which distinguishes between me in here and the mob out there and has bestowed on me the inalienable right to life, liberty, and the pursuit of happiness. Thank you SOM for granting me freedom from social approval, from group think, from the evils of Churchism, Statism and the growing appeal of Oneworldism.

I also thank SOM for containing within itself the power to see its own weaknesses, whether it be recognition of its self-contradictions or its discovery of the quantum world where subject and object is no longer a viable dichotomy. It is these chinks in the otherwise admirable fortress of the SOM that raise the issues addressed in the MOQ.

It is not the purpose of the MOQ to poke away at these chinks in hopes of toppling the SOM edifice but rather to fill them in so one can understand himself and the world more fully and clearly. The largest chink is, of course, values. SOM explains a lot, but doesn't explain them. Unless that hole is filled, SOM risks erosion and eventual dissolution, with humanity falling back into the killing fields of the social level with its churches, cults, and sacrifice of self for the sake of an invisible God of the Public Good.

To fill the hole may require a new level above SOM. I'm not sure about this. After all, the MOQ is an SOM document based on SOM reasoning. [132] Yet it points to an attitude that's different from SOM, an attitude of: "Push on until you capture the beauty of the thing, because if it isn't beautiful, you really haven't got it yet." Great scientists, dedicated SOM-ers, have this attitude. They understand its importance. They may even realize that without this element of Quality (the "unconditioned," as Ant put it), their endeavors within the SOM structure and the structure itself may ultimately fail.

So, I fully agree with Bo's insight that the SOM and the intellectual level are one and the same. To support it, to protect it, to avoid losing it and sinking back to "anything goes" irrationalism or a "because God says so" mentality, we need to recognize its vulnerability to attacks from academic philosophers, social dogooders, spiritual evangelists, and its own internal paradoxes. To that end, the MOQ is the best S/O answer I've found yet. [133]

Maggie:

One "record" of the memory (a perceptive acknowledgment of this event) is found in Genesis, in the description of Original sin, when the serpent tempted Eve to tempt Adam to "eat of the tree of the knowledge of good and evil." (Julian Jaynes deals with this concept of the emergence of this human ability in his book, The Origin of Consciousness in the Breakdown of the Bicameral Mind that we've mentioned here before. If you haven't read it, you'd probably like to.)

The "punishment" is that people are no longer able to simply exist naturally in a natural world, comfortable in their unthinking action, doing as their parents did, never making conscious choices, never knowing that the choices could be made (being driven out of the Garden of Eden). The "punishment" in making intellectual choices is having to live with the results of choices. The "punishment" is having a desire to control even more than we can control, and being disappointed in being unable to control (to "have") all that we desire.

I think that the level you're referring to, the social level, with its churches, cults, etc., is the instance in which certain individuals participate in the intellectual level, but their effect on the social patterns is through leadership, i.e., one person has an insight, and others are affected by this insight because they follow through social/biological mechanisms such as loyalty, imitation, perception of coercion.

I think there are different sets of social/intellectual structures, in which whole groups of people can rise to participate in the intellectual level. Through the acceptance of these structures— such social practices as science, inquiry, and willingness to explore, to be aware of as much information as possible—have come "new" intellectually mediated social structures. But that is not the same as a new level. It's more like a social pattern that has put down new roots and reformed the biological and inorganic in such a way that higher awareness and participation is possible on more of the levels.

It might require a smaller quantity of support (as the amount of land needed to support a person, which has decreased) but it does not, however, negate the supporting role of lower levels (consider the number of third world workers who support one American) or the need of an army, an entity prepared to interact in social/biological ways to protect the social/intellectual existence of the people of a nation. If the underlying support is lost, for whatever reason, even if it is through the "enlightenment" of the people who formerly maintained that support, the whole system collapses, being unable to reform itself with its center of gravity in lower levels. (Witness political correctness that follows after the original enlightenment of experience with diversity.)

I don't think we need a new level to explain them, though there still might be a new level coming into being. I just don't think it's needed here.

Bodvar:

To say that I appreciated Platt's support would be an understatement. He has had the same puzzlement and doubts as myself, but then takes off in a flight of thought that lands him smack on. I was a bit doubtful at one point where he wrote: "After all, the MOQ is an SOM document based on SOM reasoning," but soon I saw what Platt meant. Any outgrowth from a static level starts at the parent level's terms. (How can it be otherwise?)

Pirsig hammers on this in the intellect/society relationship. Intellect is no free floating view from nowhere (as Hugo says). In its infancy, it was very much a social prop—language upheld the common myth—as ideas were all about the tribal survival. Only much later as intellect had helped human societies rise to civilizational proportions (Greece) did it take over. Reality became intellectual, i.e., subject/object metaphysics.

The "fall myth" is still with us and will always be. In his Up from Eden, Ken Wilber brings a view which is very like Pirsig's, except for one crucial point—awareness is seen as the traditional objective light dawning after darkness, but that is not the intellect of the MOQ. Intellect is no "God's eye view"! It was merely awareness (of the value) of individual self as different from other (or subject/object consciousness!). No small feat though, it is a new moral dimension!

I know Julian Jaynes work (from Colin Wilson's preoccupation with the split brain theory) and after reading Lila for the first time I wrote to Pirsig to ask if the emergence of intellect (of MOQ) could be seen in such a context, and he replied:

"I haven't read Julian Jaynes' book but what I heard of it seems to match the Metaphysics of Quality exactly." (From Robert Pirsig's letter to Bodvar)

Like Platt I admit that it's difficult to visualise a time when the concept of self was weak or lacking, but Jaynes entertains this idea and Maggie will know that his claim is that pre-conscious experience was no Cartesian "I think therefore I am," but "voices from the gods." About this Pirsig said in the same letter:

"I don't know if they were more in touch with Dynamic Quality, but certainly they were less in touch with the modern intellectual pattern that declare those voices to be illegal. It is the easiest thing in the world to call a thought a 'voice.' I think this is what the ancients did and this is in fact done in the last chapter of Lila. But Phædrus is aware that the doll's voice is not vibrating any air molecules around his ears, and this distinction I think it's best not to blur, if only to keep the psychiatrists away." (From Robert Pirsig's letter to Bodvar)

The "bicameral" bit is the brain's two halves communicating by a giant nerve bundle which when severed (as in surgery to cure epilepsy) causes a person to become two: one intellectual and one artist! The first one dominating awareness, but the second marking its existence through bodily reactions.

I agree Maggie. No (manifested) new moral level is needed to see SOM as intellect, but I would like to keep Platt's idea on Red Alert. It is still Dynamic forces trying to evade the laws of intellect (as SOM!). Platt once wrote about art having always been around; cave paintings no less artistic than the modern expressions. The Dynamism that made them paint such masterpieces (whatever the purpose) was no more stone age than computer age.

Finally, look to this passage in the same letter from Pirsig: "The emergence of the intellectual level is most closely associated in my mind with the ancient Greek philosophers and particularly Socrates who continually pitted truth seeking against social conformity. This seems why they killed him." (From Robert Pirsig's letter to Bodvar)

Isn't this also the emergence of subject/object metaphysics?

Maggie:

Sorry to have to ask. I'm lost and can't seem to catch up. Now that you seem to have worked to a plateau, can you state this SOM as Intellect of MOQ idea in twenty words or less?

Bodvar:

Hi Maggie. I heard your request above the din. A twenty-word summary of the SAIOM idea? Impossible, but take it in steps. Remember our initial attempts to define the intellectual value level? The lower levels seemed pretty self-evident, but the top one evaded us. The first and most obvious as mind (of SOM's mind/matter) raises serious trouble.

For long, I held that language (linguistic symbol manipulation) was the solution, then we went over to rationality, math, scientific method even. From my Lila copy I see that I have jotted down a note dated 1993 about the correlation between the events that ZMM describes (the birth of subject/object thinking in the early Greek culture) and the emergence of the intellectual level in Lila. So finally, I launched the SAIOM idea—the Intellect of MOQ is subject/object metaphysics itself!

The benefits are: 1) it once and for all brings the wrong, but ineradicable SOM-lag, "intellect as mind" out in the open. Now intellect is seen as thinking in a particular way—the subject/object way. 2) SO (the M dropped) is brought inside the MOQ fold, no longer a competing metaphysics lurking outside in a metametaphysical realm. It has a satisfying closed circle effect on me, but no more rhetoric!

This was the shortest I could manage, hope you get the gist of it.

Ant:

From what I understand about the MOQ and the SOM is that the MOQ contains (what the Buddhists call) the unconditioned (Dynamic Quality) and the conditioned (static quality) while SOM only contains the conditioned. Pirsig says (especially in ZMM though he doesn't use this Buddhist terminology) that the conditioned can be divided many ways (e.g. classic/romantic, hip/square,   subject/object,   or inorganic/biological/social/intellectual).

The difference therefore between the MOQ and SOM is that the latter does not "contain" the (mystic) unconditioned (Dynamic

Quality, Tao, Dharma) and that even in the division of the conditioned (which is done for pragmatic reasons in the MOQ and not because of some ultimate truth which is supposedly out there) the MOQ and SOM differ. In SOM, more or less, the inorganic/biological patterns are reduced to objects and the social/intellectual patterns are reduced to subjects.

I think what you are getting at is that as the conditioned (static quality patterns) is the conceptualised, so in a sense, all our concepts of the universe are intellectual. However, the social, biological, and inorganic patterns still have an independent existence from the intellect, so to say the SOM equates with the static intellectual quality level in the MOQ seems to be incorrect from a static point of view.

Maybe I've missed something here so I would be interested in hearing anyone else's opinion on whether or not SOM equals the intellectual level of the MOQ. Please state the exact problem here— i.e., why does (the Western notion of) mind as intellect raise serious trouble? What about the intellectual level in Eastern thinking? That isn't SOM is it? I don't think intellect is necessarily thinking in the subject/object way.

SOM has inherent metaphysical defects in it (e.g., mind/matter). Aren't we in danger of re-introducing these if we introduce SOM into MOQ? Why isn't it better just to move on and concentrate on the problems that might arise solely with the MOQ and forget SOM all together?

Bodvar:

The problem occurs if subjectivism (S of SOM) is imported into the MOQ as its intellectual level! The Western notion of mind is the whole "mental abstract spiritual what's not material realm" and if MOQ adapts SOM's mind as its own intellectual level, where is SOM's matter to be placed? As the inorganic level! But that leaves biology and society without foundation. However, if Mind/Matter collectively is seen as intellect it cleans it all up. Another consequence of mind as intellect is that the MOQ's assertion of the higher level's moral preponderance leads to another problem—each mental quirk becomes highly moral. A man with a gun who has an impulse to kill is justified because he "thinks" of doing so, and intellectual patterns are highest good. This is clearly absurd.

As far as I understand it, Eastern thinking is not an identical twin of the MOQ. The common arch Quality that the old Greeks changed to subject/object metaphysics survived as Eastern tradition and because it hasn't been through the SOM phase, it needs no transformation back again. It is the original intuitive version! They probably don't understand the SOM point of view and don't call anything mind, or matter, for that sake; only "undifferentiated and differentiated," which is DQ/SQ. This means that the Eastern intellectual level (seen through MOQ) did not become mind/matterish, but took on another hue (Dharma perhaps).

And yet I think Western tradition has an advantage for its SOM detour. If/when the MOQ comes of age it has the benefit of seeing both sides. Perhaps the East has done so all the time? That issue is enough to fill another year's discussion.

Thanks Anthony, for posing these fine honed questions. Strike back if this still sounds unclear.

Doug:

Anthony and TLS—Yes! Yes! Yes!

It delights me that you still have the energy to pursue this. Hugo, can you simplify this whole thing?

We did not discard SOM, we subsumed its rearrangement and reclassification, but we did not nor do we wish (opinion) to adopt SOM as MOQ's intellect. Ant makes a key point—how is MOQ's intellect different from SOM as intellect of MOQ (SAIOM)? The answer for me is that SOM rejects/denies Value. MOQ embraces/creates Value.

So if we make SOM the intellect of MOQ what changes in SAIOM that enlightens it to Value? Explain how all of a sudden SOM knows how to classify value where prior it did not!?

Pirsig on Mind [March 1998]

Ant:

Well, to be fair to Bodvar and the MOQ, I think the SAIOM issue has to be sorted out either way. The problem I have in evaluating this idea is that I'm still not totally clear in my own head what Bodvar is getting at, hence the number of questions to him in my last email. Last night I found a phrase (which I meant to paste to the Lila Squad before) where Pirsig mentions mind. Pirsig states:

"The word 'mind' is freighted with all sorts of historic philosophical disputation. Buddhists use it much differently than Western idealists who use it much differently than Western materialists. Like the term 'God,' it's best avoided. To prevent confusion, the MOQ treats 'mind' as the exact equivalent of 'static intellectual patterns' and avoids use of the term when possible." (From Pirsig's letter to Ant, January 2nd 1998)

Is that any help to anyone? Does it reduce the confusion? For me the word "subject" denotes mind and society while "object" denotes chemicals and biology. In light of the above statement, to put subjects and objects (together) as equivalent to the MOQ intellectual level seems contrary to Pirsig's thinking. [134]

An additional point to Doug is that the four static levels of value (Inorganic, Biological, Social, Intellectual) are all a practical device in the form of static intellectual patterns of value (or mind), while in SOM, subjects and objects are seen as the representations of reality (i.e., literal truths). I therefore cannot see how you can substitute SOM as a whole for intellectual value patterns. The two terminologies seem very different; one is provisional and accepts many truths (the MOQ) and one thinks it's giving us the one and only truth (SOM). As Pirsig says in Lila, the pencil (e.g., MOQ) is mightier than the pen (e.g., SOM).

I cannot therefore see how you can paste SOM within the MOQ system. I'm sure Bodvar will have a number of things to say about the above (and my previous questions) so I'll give him a chance to reply before rambling on any further.

Doug:

This is what we MOQites know about MOQ, viscerally, intellectually, and spiritually! Pirsig was so harmed by his quasiintellectual persecutors that he shows extreme negative attitudes towards their SOM doctrine, with SOM's tiny mindset, and SOM's plethora of platypian paradice.

Bodvar:

I fully understand Doug's need to "avenge" Pirsig (Pirsig himself is also harsh at times towards SOM), but Phædrus of Lila is not so zealous. Somewhere he says something to the effect that it is not the intention of the MOQ to trash all of subject/object metaphysics, but how can SOM avoid being trashed if it competes with the Quality of being reality? [135]

Doug:

I am not so much avenging Pirsig as I am trying to show that SOM-ites did the same thing to Pirsig by erasing his mind with electro-shock as the (SOM) Church did to Galileo and others when their intellectual static patterns of value evolved and began to gain power.

I agree with you that Pirsig tells us that we cannot throw SOM away. It is an imperative part of our legacy...static quality. But it is not adequate for the new thinking we need for progress in Millennium III. So, MOQ, or a new philosophy like MOQ, must subsume SOM.

Donny:

Let's be careful about who does what to whom. It was the psychologist who "zapped" Phædrus. Today, Doc Shrink'em is the most powerful force or morality—or at least moral enforcement. (What a ghastly claim, akin to the Pope of Galileo's heyday!) There are certain social/moral conventions that one must adhere to in order to be granted "personhood" (to paraphrase Erving Goffman). People are things we talk to, while objects (be it the Greenland ice cap or a mental patient) are things we talk about. Hegel calls these moral norms the "ethical substance" because the point is that it is both ethical and substantial—that is, the solid world of stuff is the same as the social world of normalization and personhood.

Hegel does say the world (social and natural alike) is constructed of ethics/morals/values. But as for Doc Shrink'em, consider when Billy Bomber blows up a building and kills innocent people—a hundred years ago we would have called in the priest to explain, "Why did God allow this to happen?" Now we call in the shrinks to tell us, "What made Billy do it?" The point for now is that Phædrus didn't get zapped for taking issue with SOM; he got zapped because he stopped responding to the outside world, sat in a room and pissed on himself. His sin wasn't against SOM (or any other "intellectual theory") but against society—social value.

Doug:

I want to use a Pirsig quote here in response to your words: "Years later, after he was certified as 'sane,' he read 'objective' medical descriptions of what he had experienced, and he was shocked at how slanderous they were. They were like descriptions of a religious sect written by a different, hostile religious sect. The psychiatric treatment was not a search for truth but the promulgation of a dogma. Psychiatrists seemed to fear the taint of insanity much as inquisitors once feared succumbing to the devil. Psychiatrists were not allowed to practice psychiatry if they were insane. It was required that they literally did not know what they were talking about." (Page 328 of 410 in the Lila Bantam hardbound edition.)

Focus especially on the last sentence in the quote!

I think Pirsig is showing us unambiguously that those powerful "Doc Shrink'ems" are intrinsically incompetent, as was any professor at Bozeman at the time Phædrus was there who felt s/he "objectively" taught "quality."

In SOM legacy, we of TLS know, Aristotelian substance/body/matter/property (the objective) reigns over the insubstantial/mind/immaterial/value (the subjective). We hear the

SOM-ites preach, "Be objective. Your subjectivity is of low utility."

Donny:

Actually, Phædrus didn't have a good understanding of Aristotle—and frankly neither did the goof ball "Aristotle expert" teaching the course in ZMM—so the "Aristotelian" label is a tad out of whack. I still object to this "object" equaling "objective," "subject" equaling "subjective" move. Somebody said that they are like two different shades of green, but still essentially the same thing. No, no, no. Let's look at the words how they are really used: "Be objective. Your subjectivity is of low utility." Is that supposed to the "SOM-ite" (oh boy) moral imperative or something? Now, that is a straw man.

Doug:

Yeah, unfortunately that's exactly what many of us have to deal with in today's work-a-day world. I just spent three dreadful years as a director of a large, global corporation where those ubiquitous words made my ears ring. For your edification, that same corporation worships at the font of one of the most SOM Ivy League Universities.

It is ingrained, Donny, regardless whether you see it as a "strawman." It's no sham! It is pure, Aristotelian, substance legacy with all of its objective isolability and separability. It's a "Hold still while I measure your objective properties" legacy.

Donny:

I work in an art department. I'm now pursuing a BFA in fine art. When you "read" a good piece, it's not unlike "reading" cloud shapes. Everyone has his or her own subjective little angle. But that's not attacked! That's part of what art is. Art has no (or little) problem with subjectivity. (Of interpretation—but of quality? When it comes time to hand out grades....)

Now return with me to Lab Rat and Gloria in the lab. In the lab, there is a moral imperative to be objective—well, of course! That's what science is. But the point is that objectivity and subjectivity aren't "things" on to themselves; they're roles—a posture one

396

assumes, takes up, and drops at appropriate moments. ("Damn it Lab Rat, be objective!" The idea [or ideal?] of Sherlock Holmes being the objective observer every waking hour is silly stuff.)

Doug:

OK, let's play the classical SOM science role of objectivity. What happens when we do that? In general, we get the wrong answers!

Why? Because classical SOM science assumes, objectively, that an object may be isolated from its environment. Why does it assume that? Because of the SOM presumption (which Hugo so elegantly showed us) that a schism exists twixt Aristotelian S and O. That schism is a major piece of the SOM legacy.

MOQ shows us that Static Patterns of Value (SPoVs) are cowithin Dynamic Quality. SPoVs are inseparable from: DQ and other SPoVs in DQ. SOM-ites denigrate this MOQ axiom.

So the SOM presumption that an observer may objectively observe an object in isolation, in general, is wrong. The SOM mythos is wrong on one of its most closely held assertions.

The new science, quantum science, affirms necessity for a more MOQ-like mythos as foundation philosophy. It decries the inadequacies of SOM science as a general tool of science.

(Note: SOM science works well but only approximately in the super-atomic realm. It does not work in the subatomic realm. Further, since the Inorganic SPoVs of MOQ were invented by Quantum SPoVs at the [unmentionable] level below (Pirsig's chaos), here is another piece of evidence that SOM deserves its proper diminished role—subsumed within the MOQ.)

Bodvar:

In the quoted passage Doug says, "Science assumes objectivity, that an object may be isolated," etc., but it also assumes a subject observing things and events. If the SOM as Intellect connection is made things fall in place. Humans focus (mostly) at the intellectual level and (seen as SOM) it's no wonder we can't avoid the subject and object—the division is intellect.

Doug:

I'm going to just blurt this out and see what happens. This is my impulse (without heavy thought) response to your words.

To me, you show here the problem with SAIOM. To quote from your paragraph above, "...it also assumes 'A' subject observing [isolated, separable] things and events." I emphasized the article "A." A subject is just another isolated, separable thing in classical SOM science. And worse, classical SOM science denigrates subjects as unverifiable and unclassifiable value.

SOM may not be the intellect of MOQ because it always separates and isolates SOM things (MOQ SPoVs). (See note.)

SOM may be an intellectual tool in the MOQ intellectual toolbox, but not the whole toolbox.

MOQ does not "...assume A [separate, isolated] subject...." It assumes All SPoVs in complementary interrelationships with DQ and with all other SPoVs in DQ. (Sorry for the repetition/tautology of prior posts.)

Again, this is how I see it. If we make SOM the intellect of MOQ, we are back in SOM. Don't go there. This is SOM attempting to survive, and we see its tack again as low value via its forewarned means: deception.

Also, I see this as a test of the MOQ. Consider it a major test! If MOQ cannot resolve this unambiguously for all, then is it a good metaphysics for all?

Bo, you, in my opinion, have given MOQ its largest challenge to date. Thank you for this potent MOQ Test worthy of both you and Pirsig.

I hope we can place this in the annals of TLS as "MOQ Test 1— SAIOM."

I am enjoying this immensely!

Mtty Bo and TLS!

Note: and MOQites must develop the skills to move readily twixt MOQ and SOM just as we must move readily twixt the intellect (more SQ proximate) and meditation (more DQ proximate).

Bodvar:

But this is not reintroducing SOM. It is degrading it from status as reality itself to another MOQ value "dimension." A windfall value is that it once and for all defines the intellectual level (I have the impression that we gave it up). SOM is safe under the MOQ's greater umbrella, and needn't be fought off as an enemy (while we still use its terms). Remember the slash and burn of the competing anthropological theories in Lila? This prevents MOQ from doing away with SOM—it becomes a prominent, but "dreamed" part of the MOQ. Enough for now.

Hugo:

As I have said before, I believe the proper definition or characterization of the intellectual level is by its self-reflective nature, and I have shown how all the four levels can be seen as levels of representation or reflection. The inorganic is the pre-representational level (in Peircean terms) sporting only monadic (quality) and dyadic relations, but not the triadic relations of representation. The biological level (which is not necessarily bio-logical) is characterized by the autonomy of entities representing their world, and the social level is characterized by the mutuality of autonomous entities representing each other. The intellectual level is characterized by autonomous entities representing themselves. Niels Bohr liked to give the example (from a Danish philosopher called Poul Moeller) of a student sitting at the table, thinking of himself sitting at the table, thinking of himself sitting at the table, and so on ad infinitum.

Magnus:

The way I see it, the only level doing any representation at all is the intellectual. On the other hand, that is all it does. The moment something is represented, it is an intellectual representation. Of course, this intellectual representation is dependent on inorganic patterns of value, so ideally, a representation is an isomorphism between the represented inorganic patterns of value and the representing static patterns of value, which in turn confuses things as to which static pattern of value is representing which.

But that was not what I intended to say. To say that SOM is the intellectual level of MOQ raises the question—what do you mean with SOM? I said the other day that it's easy to mix up the law of gravity with gravity and I think it's equally easy to mix up the intellectual idea of SOM and the actual metaphysics of SOM.

Last week, I found yet another way to look at your SAIOM idea. What SOM value is the same as the intellectual value of the MOQ? I'll drag up the old example of Phædrus in the chemistry lab. The scientific method (SOM) urged him to formulate new hypotheses as experiments were tested. There was no way of knowing which hypotheses should be tested, but it was also impossible to test all. What happens here is that SOM uses the big Q to choose. SOM doesn't recognize this, but it does it anyway. Until recently, it's been possible for SOM to close its eyes to this valuing process constantly used. But it'll soon be plain for everyone to see, thanks to Quality Metaphysics.

Hugo:

I think it is crucial to become more clear on the SOM/MOQ relationship, and here follows some reflections on the latest contributions from Bo and Doug. Bo poses the question—where is SOM to be found in MOQ? But this is not the right question, I think. Subject Object Metaphysics is Pirsig's term for the traditional frame of thinking, which takes "the subject/object divide" as an unquestionable foundation. His MOQ moves beyond that, by putting this divide into question. There are two main views available within SOM.

One is "the view from without," or "the view from nowhere," the idea that the observer is somewhere outside of what is observed, and the idea that all that can be known for certain is that which can be viewed from without. (The observer which is implied in this view is usually neglected precisely because it is outside; it is idealized away by the combination of a subject/object divide and the idea that the knowable, the "objective reality," is all that matters.)

The other main view is "the view from within," or "the blind subject," the idea that the observed is always part of the observer, and that all that can be known of this view from within is the subject's view of itself. This is of course, as is also Pirsig's explication (a huge simplification). Logical empiricism, or positivism, for instance, combines a strong empiricism with a focus on the "objective." It may be seen as a sort of "collective subject" view, stating that we can know no thing beyond our experience, but also that we can have "objective knowledge."

There have been all sorts of efforts towards avoiding the bad implications of the hidden SOM presumption, making the philosophical landscape a lot more complicated than can be handled in one book, let alone in a few emails. But in order to address the really fundamental questions, such a coarse explication can be necessary. In the long run, however, a more detailed analysis will be needed. Here I am concerned with the fundamental question of the relation between SOM and MOQ.

Both oppositions above are logically strong, within their own presumptions. Pirsig's genius (and it was a stroke of genius, what ever predecessors there may have been) was to see that the presumptions were common for these two opposites. What is presumed, metaphysically presumed, that is, unquestionable from within these stances, is the subject/object split. (And this is where we have to be very careful and thorough.) The subject/object split is not something that is part of SOM, it is presumed by SOM. It is the very foundation upon which SOM is build; but not a known foundation, not something that can be looked upon and criticised within SOM.

And this is the only justification for Pirsig to attack "SOM" as one common position—that it rests on a common foundation. Those who cannot see that do not feel as part of one "SOM position," and they are right. There is no such recognized position. No one could hold the "SOM position," because to see it as a unity one has to be aware of the common presumption, and being aware of the common presumption, one is already halfway into MOQ or some similar larger metaphysical frame. This is what these philosophers, whom we have seen as predecessors or relatives of Pirsig, have in common. They have sensed—and explicated, more or less—a larger metaphysical frame which could do more than argue one of the two (big sweeps here) oppositions, which could point to a third path that threw light on both the oppositions as to what they were: reductio ad absurdum's of one and the same wrong presumption of which they were insufficiently aware.

We should not ridicule this inability to see the metaphysical foundation. The path towards awareness of one self, including one's foundation for living, for feeling, and for thinking, is a long and difficult journey and it is a journey never ended. We ourselves are only on our way, we have not and cannot reach a goal, a place of complete awareness, any more than there is an end to the mirror views of one mirror in another.

So, in my view the MOQ is a step further beyond SOM on a path towards greater awareness—greater intellectual awareness—because it is only on the intellectual level that we can be aware of our selves. This is indeed what makes the intellectual level distinct.

What does this mean for the relationship between MOQ and SOM? SOM is not the intellectual level of MOQ—they are both intellectual phenomenon, both specific ways of looking upon our selves and our world. And SOM is not simply subsumed as a part of MOQ, because SOM arose from neglect of the presumed subject/object split, diverging because of this, and there is no ground for this diversion in MOQ or some similar metaphysics. Both of the extreme oppositions are no good, as anyone who succeeds in seeing their metaphysical roots will acknowledge. This does not mean that everything has to be dumped.

The oppositions were, and are, extremes. There are many intermediate positions, even some resembling Pirsig's. And the strength of any larger metaphysical frame, which makes clear where and how the subject/object split is at work, is exactly this: in such a frame we can use the subject/object split as a tool, being aware of what we are doing, instead of blindly presuming some subject-object split, the workings of which we are not aware of. Only in some frame like MOQ can we use the subject/object split as a tool, with skill. This could not be done within SOM.

This is why a MOQ-like metaphysics provides for a new concept of objectivity, something that will change science to some degree and our view of science to a large degree. As for a new concept of subjectivity, subjectivity and objectivity will merge into contextuality. And this is why our view of truth will change— whether from a relativistic position or/and the objectivistic position—with these views of truth merging into a complementary view of truth. The complementary view of truth is a truth that is contextual, and by being contextual, it leaves room for the good to rule. It is not objectivism, which has no place for the good, and it is not relativism, which has no place for truth.

Thanks to you all for pursuing this important issue.

Bodvar:

It was at the "they are both intellectual phenomenon, both specific ways of looking upon our selves and our world" point that I thought that you had me cornered, but then the obvious struck me. Does Hugo mean intellect (mind) of SOM or the intellectual level of the MOQ? It makes a world of difference. In the former, the MOQ is merely another subjective theory about objective reality. If it is the latter— yes, yes! The MOQ is an intellectual pattern of value (InPoV), and so are SOM and SAIOM. Everything is InPoV at that level, but Dynamic Quality is outside the static patterns and is now searching for ways to circumvent even intellect's constraints, and if SOM is seen as intellect...ipso facto! That's why the MOQ is born—to go beyond the intellect/SOM. To call it a new static value level is way too soon, but it is a meandering "sprout," searching for a foothold.

Hugo:

Yes, I did mean the intellectual level of MOQ. You seem to draw something like the following conclusion from this—since SOM is at the intellectual level of the MOQ, the MOQ must be beyond that, sprouting into some new level. And I, so far, disagree

403

with this conclusion. This has to do with my considering all metaphysics selfreflective; metaphysics is the intellectual (still speaking from some MOQ-like stance) endeavour towards understanding our selves and our world. And any such endeavour is necessarily self-reflective. Selfreflectiveness is dizzying and avoided by most rationally inclined people, but there is no path toward greater awareness if we try to avoid this self-reflective nature of intellectual understanding.

Anyway, acknowledging the intellectual level as necessarily selfreflective, and seeing that this self-reflection is not an "all or nothing," but an awareness which can be furthered, there is no need for a MOQ moving towards some new level. There is only the growing awareness of the intellectual level, moving from vague suspicions to mythology and metaphysics. The Metaphysics of Quality is (I believe) a step towards greater awareness, but not a step towards another level.

Bodvar:

Again, I believe that the SAIOM idea is the only way to meet your requirements for recognition of the merits of the subject/object division. Earlier I have attacked awareness (and still do if it implies the "view from nowhere") as foreign to the MOQ, but perhaps SOM is "awareness" of subjective self as different from non-self (objects)? Such a view merges ZMM's "SOM replacing ancient Quality" with Lila's "Intellect out of Society." It rounds everything off in a closed circle fashion. Aesthetically, as Platt would have it put.

From my point of view, I am not swayed, but then you will probably say the same. Only the master himself can settle this, but it's wrong for me to write to ask—as if a favour—so if anyone more "neutral" has a letter to Pirsig in progress…please!

Hugo:

No need to call in the cavalry yet, Bo. We are still talking, aren't we?

Thanks for your detailed response, and let me know if I have missed something you consider important.

Loyola Presentation [March 1998]

Bodvar:

Hi Doug. I just finished your Loyola University report. Great! I bet you gave them a QM (Quantum Mechanics/Quality Metaphysics) tour de force. You have probably done more for the Quality cause here that all our postings put together. I am proud of you, and think that goes for all of us.

Doug:

Thanks for the kind words. They mean much coming from you, our esteemed beholder of The Quality Event. Actually, I used QM gently to make the keen point that QM is a very high quality benchmark for MOQ (QM is a Quality benchmark for Reality). Near the beginning of the talk, I used the following points:

A. Pirsig's SODV paper presentation at Brüssels in May 1995,

B. My coincidental query to him re: QM interrelationship with MOQ, and

C. Pirsig's subsequent snail mail to me of the SODV paper, as the initial QM connection.

Then near the end of the talk, I used my own intense study of QM (MOQ II) as it relates to MOQ (MOQ I) to qualify my personal conjectures. (Metaphysics of Quality and Mechanics of Quanta)

In my view the most effective points of the talk were: 1. Comparison of Ignatius Loyola's intellectual pattern experience with the Church and the Church's social pattern immune system coming to within a hair's breadth of thrashing him. (A movie is available.) That story is much like the brujo in Lila, but the brujo was tortured. In both cases intellectual static patterns of value won.

2. A nearly identical story most of you are familiar with regarding the Church's inquisition (one hundred years after the Loyola inquisition) and punishment of Galileo. By comparison to #1 above, this is a case where, in the short term, the intellectual static patterns of value lost their battle with the social SPoVs. (Perhaps most remarkable, to me, is the every day nature of this.

405

All of us to a greater or lesser extent experience this DQ change ultimatum among the change resistant layers of the SPoVs with which we (knowingly and unknowingly) have complementary interrelationships.)

3. And this one I love most, constructed of an assemblage of Hugo's, Platt's, my own, and other Squad mates' words: "The House of MOQ has many truths all ruled by Good. The House of SOM has one Truth which rules and demotes the good. The House of Cultural Relativism has no truth and therein chaos reigns." That came at the end of the last question at the end of the presentation.

4. I compared Robert M. Pirsig's efforts on behalf of MOQ to W. Edward Deming's efforts on behalf of SQC (Statistical Quality Control). Deming attempted to get USA corporations and governments to use his new intellectual patterns of value at the middle of the 20th century. He was ignored, told that he was insane, and to go away because US corporations and governments knew what they were doing and did not need Deming's new ideas. They, in essence, chanted: Status Quo is the Way to Go. Deming took his ideas to Japan where they were nurtured with open arms, adopted, and practiced. The Japanese established the Deming Prize. We know the outcome! The Japanese machine, Japan, Inc., kicked the USA's butt! The same thing is happening now, as we speak regarding Pirsig's New Philosophy. Eastern countries are adopting and installing it now. The USA will enter Millennium III at an extreme disadvantage, in my opinion.

Sad, how we resist change, and how devastating it can be. As Pirsig told us so brilliantly, "Static quality patterns are dead when they are exclusive, when they demand blind obedience and suppress Dynamic change." See page 121 of the Bantam 410 page hardbound edition.

Again, thanks Bo!

Finally, Lila Squad, I am sincere when I say that I could not have done the talk at Loyola without the training, education, and experience provided by The Lila Squad site and its capable teammates. This forum is absolutely crucial to the future of MOQ as the New Philosophy for Millennium III. I know we all look forward to being part of fulfilling Pirsig's dream as practitioners and adherents of the MOQ.

And Mr. Pirsig, if you are reading this, every one of us here in TLS thank you for your Brilliance, your Wisdom. Sir, you sparkle with the artistic aretê of enlightenment!

By the way, Loyola (St. Ignatius Loyola a.k.a. Inigo de /Onez y Loyola) was persecuted by the Church for his intellectual SPoV revolutionary ideas, which threatened Church social SPoV dogma/doctrine. Just prior to his thrashing, he was saved by an enlightened Church authority and the intellectual Jesuit Order was established. Pirsig refers to Loyola in his work. Loyola's story is almost a mirror of Pirsig's story about the Züni brujo. This is a good example of an enlightened authority recognizing intuitively the Value of an intellectual idea in its potential to make the Church dogma and doctrine "better." All of this transpired in the first half of the 16th century (Jesuit Order founded in 1534, Pope Paul III recognizes the Jesuit Order in 1540). But they did not learn the general lesson. About 100 years later, they persecuted Galileo (1633) and forced him to recant his affirmation of Copernicus' ideas. I think the difference here is Loyola was an insider and Galileo was a scientist viewed as outside the Church.

In Pirsig's letter to me about this he said, "Dear Doug, "I don't know if this interests you or not, but it's a valuable connection for the advancement of the MOQ. If the honors students are interested, the teachers will pay attention. If the teachers pay attention, the whole Jesuit order may take some interest. And if the Jesuit order takes interest it could in time actually budge the whole Catholic Church since they are historically known as its most intellectual members. A good line of discussion would be the constant conflict between those Dynamic ones who want to move the Catholic Church forward into new patterns and those who feel that these new patterns are dangerous. The MOQ actually supports both views and shows why they must always coexist even though they are eternally opposed.

"Best regards,

"Robert M. Pirsig."

Any words directly from him are so precious to us; I thought you would want to see these.

Annotations by Robert M. Pirsig

128. I would agree that valuation can be intense or weak and that this scale is without sharp divisions. However, I think the MOQ will be better if the divisions between levels are sharp rather than fuzzy. An analogy could be made to the law, which is a set of intellectual rules for social quality. The justice which the law serves can vary in intensity without sharp distinction, but the laws themselves must make sharp distinctions or they become ineffective.

129. I've always thought this is incorrect because many forms of intellect do not have a subject-object construction. These include logic itself, mathematics, computer programming languages, and, I believe some primitive languages (although I can't remember what they are).

130. The word "I" like the word "self" is one of the trickiest words in any metaphysics. Sometimes it is an object, a human body; sometimes it is a subject, a human mind. I believe there are number of philosophic systems, notably Ayn Rand's "Objectivism," that call the "I" or "individual" the central reality. Buddhists say it is an illusion. So do scientists. The MOQ says it is a collection of static patterns capable of apprehending Dynamic Quality. I think that if you identify the "I" with the intellect and nothing else you are taking an unusual position that may need some defending.

131. Within the intellectual level, mathematics, especially quantum mechanics, seems higher to me.

132. It employs SOM reasoning the way SOM reasoning employs social structures such as courts and journals and learned societies to make itself known. SOM reasoning is not subordinate to these social structures, and the MOQ is not subordinate to the SOM structures it employs. Remember that the central reality of the MOQ is not an object or a subject or anything else. It is understood by direct experience only and not by reasoning of any kind. Therefore to say that the MOQ is based on SOM reasoning is as useful as saying that the Ten Commandments are based on SOM

reasoning. It doesn't tell us anything about the essence of the Ten Commandments and it doesn't tell us anything about the essence of the MOQ.

133. I think this conclusion undermines the MOQ, although that is obviously not Platt's intention. It is like saying that science is really a form of religion. There is some truth to that, but it has the effect dismissing science as really not very important. The MOQ is in opposition to subjectobject metaphysics. To say that it is a part of that system which it opposes sounds like a dismissal. I have read that the MOQ is the same as Plato, Aristotle, Plotinus, Hegel, James, Peirce, Nieztsche, Bergson, and many others even though these people are not held to be saying the same as each other. This kind of comparison is what I have meant by the term, "philosophology." It is done by people who are not seeking to understand what is written but only to classify it so that they don't have to see it as anything new. God knows the MOQ has never had two better friends than Bo and Platt, so this is no criticism of their otherwise brilliant thinking. It's just that I see a lowering of the quality of the MOQ itself if you follow this path of subordinating it to that which it opposes.

134. True.

135. As far as I know the MOQ does not trash the SOM. It contains the SOM within a larger system. The only thing it trashes is the SOM assertion that values are unreal.

Chapter 14

There is nothing more difficult to take in hand, more perilous to conduct, or more uncertain of success than to take a lead in the introduction of a new order of things, because the innovations has for enemies all those who have done well under the old conditions and lukewarm defenders in those who may do well under the new.—Machiavelli, The Prince

Quality without Morality [March 1998]

Struan:

I first read Zen and the Art of Motorcycle Maintenance in 1987 whilst on a motorcycle trip across Europe and Africa which lasted almost a year, wore a tent to shreds, and generally changed the life of a young man trying to make sense of the world. I read Lila in 1993 and for the last few years it has sat on my shelf being regarded with detached curiosity. I never actually got round to really thinking about what it was proposing until recently. To my utter disappointment, I have come to the conclusions expanded in my essay below.

It pained me to write it and I sincerely hope that some kind person out there can convince me I'm wrong. Believe me, this essay was not written as a final denunciation. Instead, its purpose is more to allow others the opportunity to point out why I've missed the point and to put me right. Equally, whatever conclusions I finally arrive at with regards to the Metaphysics of Quality, as works of fiction both these books will remain for me an exceptional achievement.

Lila; Quality without Morality

A few weeks ago, I revisited Pirsig's books in an attempt to understand how the Metaphysics of Quality might be applied to practical moral dilemmas. I thought that the best way of testing it as a theory would be to look at its practical consequences for mankind. After all this is the system which for Doug [http://www.quantonics.com/LilaReview.html] is a "profound

411

discovery" which "I see world legal structures eventually adopting." Such a grandiose claim needed looking into and so look into it I did.

It soon became clear that this was simply emotivism in disguise. Pirsig cleverly picks and chooses which level of evolution to apply in which context and in doing so exposes the complete futility of his quest for a new ethic. There is nothing here beyond the "boo/hurrah" of his own feelings, the discarding of a dualist metaphysics and determinism, both of which were abandoned long ago by modern scientific philosophy, and lastly, the complete misunderstanding of modern physics itself.

Pirsig repeatedly says things like, "If one adheres to the traditional scientific metaphysics of substance, the philosophy of determinism is an inescapable corollary." The problem here is that nobody does adhere to this. The whole point of Heisenberg's Uncertainty Principle was the complete destruction of any deterministic theory of the universe and so Pirsig is attempting to navigate a problem that simply does not exist and has not existed for over half a century. He makes comments such as, "…if the determinists let go of their position it would seem to deny the truth of science," and yet we know that in fact the very opposite is true. The determinist had to, and did, let go of that position because the truth of science required them to do so.

But as Pirsig himself points out, the MOQ has much more to say about ethics. Or does it? In the context of the American civil war Pirsig claims that "an evolutionary morality argues the North was right in pursuing that war because a nation is a higher form of evolution than a human body," and so the hundreds of thousands of lives were justifiably lost because the higher level of evolution (society) prevailed over the lower level (biology).

In the next paragraph and in the context of capital punishment, Pirsig goes on to claim that in the case of a criminal who does not threaten the "established social structure," it is plain that "what makes killing him immoral is that a criminal is not just a biological

412

organism. He is not even just a defective unit in society. Whenever you kill a human being you are killing a source of thought too."

What seems to utterly evade Pirsig is the fact that the hundreds of thousands who died in that civil war were also a "source of thought too," and that therefore by his own criteria the war was morally wrong because the ideas lost through these deaths were at a higher evolutionary plane than the nation they were sacrificed for. And here the philosophy becomes even more muddled because it would be possible to argue (as Pirsig hints at) that the ideas of equality that drove the war on were morally superior to the nation and the ideas of those who defended it. But by what criteria do we decide which ideas take precedence? The MOQ has nothing to say on this matter and yet this is one huge part of ethics. Perhaps this is why "real philosophers" have little to say about the MOQ and it simply boils down to the fact that the MOQ has little to say about them or their subject. [136]

Far from being in a position where it is possible to say, "I see world legal structures eventually adopting this ethical system," we are looking at a structureless mish mash of nonsense. In practical terms, how could we possibly advocate a system which could allow the killing of a mental retard to provide organs for a genius who would die without them, simply because the genius appears to be on a higher evolutionary level? [137] Or the destruction of millions of Jews by the Nazi party because their biological bodies and possibly even their (static) society and traditions were dominated by the Dynamic intellectual idea of a super race. [138] This is utterly bizarre and surely no system of ethics can work on such an arbitrary criteria.

The fact is that Pirsig is using an ethical system based upon pure emotivism to pick and choose which value layers he chooses to read into any given context, in a vain attempt to give rational credibility to his emotional urges and it is by this method that he is able to fit "all the moral conflicts of the world (into) this kind of framework."

413

The objections raised here (and they are by no means exhaustive) are thus two fold. First, the MOQ seeks its credibility by trying to be at least as credible as a determinist theory of Nature and in doing so measures itself against a discredited worldview. It succeeds but only in the sense that it becomes equally incredible.

Second, the MOQ utterly ignores the relationship of ideas in ethics and the presence of each value layer in the human being, to the extent that it has almost nothing to say about morality. If person A kills person B then the MOQ might say that person A was justified in killing person B because person A did it to protect his nation state, which is of more value that the biological entity of person B. Alternatively, it might say that person A was wrong to kill person B because the source of ideas that constitutes person B was of more value than (for example) the nation state person A was defending. I'm sure we could all come up with a whole host of other scenarios within this context and we can have no way of choosing one over the other within the framework given.

For these reasons alone, the Metaphysics of Quality is of no concern to anyone seeking an ethical framework.

Wrong but sort of Right [March 1998]

Kevin:

In response to your mini-essay, I must say you are wrong, but in a right sort of way. All in all, you have some points, which need to be used to question MOQ, but not reject it.

Four points:

1). On Emotivism:

Everything is emotivism yet it is not a criterion for deciding the veracity of a claim (MOQ included). Don't accuse Pirsig of having emotional motivation to say something truthful, just argue that what he says is false.

2). On Determinism:

A). Even though determinism has been discarded, no one knows why. The Uncertainty Principle left the science and philosophy worlds metaphysically hanging. We know the facts— we cannot determine the path of an electron. Yet, the question of

414

what that means to metaphysics was left unanswered. Quality gives us the alternative paradigm needed (as you probably already have read enough of to understand).

B). The MOQ is more set against the subject-object metaphysics than determinism.

C). Not everyone has caught up with the new age of uncertainty (e.g., Christians). Don't blame Pirsig for beating what you think is a dead horse when others think the horse is still running the plains created by God.

D). Neo-determinism still has grounds for resurrection. Perhaps things are uncertain only because we are not precise enough to discover them. And if we live in Newton's world, and Newton's laws still work, perhaps we are still governed by Newton's determinism. Besides, uncertainty does not necessarily mean free will.

3). On Ethics:

A). Ethics is obviously an evolving debate in the Lila Squad. You're like the person who catches a person changing their mind and say, "Everything you say is wrong!" Ethics has always been a difficult subject for philosopher to tread with the roaring debate between modernity and post modernity in the background. The MOQ is a work in progress, so let it progress...don't pull the cord just yet.

B). MOQ has given us a new paradigm to discuss ethics, an evolutionary paradigm moving towards Dynamic quality and measured with static quality. It is the terminology needed to discuss the new metaphysics of the age. MOQ is a paradigm shift and, even though the landscape has not change much, the lens through which we view that landscape has changed dramatically. Every time you put on a new pair of glasses, you must reexamine everything known. That is what Lila did (and the Lila Squad is still doing) with the superior lens of quality.

4). On Pirsig:

A). MOQ is bigger than Pirsig. Although he made the original revolution, he is not the god of Quality and he is bound to make mistakes like all us mortals.

B). I believe you have caught Pirsig in a contradiction, but I will let him defend himself. [139]

Struan:

Firstly, everything is plainly not emotivism (in the philosophical sense) unless you are a convinced emotivist and if you are then what possible use can you have for the MOQ? The MOQ is setting itself up as something different and this is why it is quite proper for me to point out the underlying morality of Pirsig's position. Under an emotivist framework, I could quite rightly state that inorganic matter has a right to dominate humankind because I feel that this is the moral order of things. The only way you can argue that I am wrong is to forward a different, non-emotivist framework which you can show works better. This is precisely what the MOQ seeks to do and precisely where it fails to convince.

Emotivism is by definition the dismissal of metaphysics from the field of ethics and it seems quite extraordinary that you should claim that everything is emotivism. If you really believe that then how can you forward any metaphysics at all, let alone the MOQ? I really don't know what else to say to that point. It is truly bizarre.

Second, on Determinism:

A). Lots of people would claim to know why because it is a false supposition. What else do you need? If anything, this knowledge has reconciled many of the problems between science and religion, especially in the field of ethics.

B). It is clearly set against both.

C). The point of science and philosophy is surely to posit the most probable hypothesis. If I were to argue that the world is supported on the back of a turtle and justify it by saying that it is no less preposterous than the prevailing theory that the world is hanging by huge invisible threads, you would quite rightly point out that while this may be the case it is hardly going to influence anyone who knows what they are talking about and that I can't expect to be taken seriously. This is precisely what Pirsig does when he talks about chemistry professors near the end of Chapter 12 in Lila and he surely cannot be expected to be taken seriously if he wants to describe a new metaphysics. Your comment about Christians may apply to the ones you know, but I know many who have caught up with this new age and one in particular who is involved in pushing the barriers further as an astronomy research fellow.

D). There is no real difference between the two positions here quoted except in some a priori sense. One might just as well postulate that my cat created Jupiter, though you are right that uncertainty does not necessarily mean free will. I would add that determinism does not pre-suppose a lack of free will either.

Thirdly, on Ethics:

Pardon? A nice PR spiel (?) but you aren't saying anything substantial beyond the statement that ethics is a difficult subject and you think you have found a way forward. Prove it.

Your discussions on ethics are futile unless you can lay out some ground rules with which to approach them. It is simply not good enough to decide that Ghandi was better than Hitler was then proceed desperately to seek (and fail to find) a way in which the MOQ can be forced to concur. The only possible course (which sticks within the bounds of reason) is to start from a neutral morality and show how the MOQ forces you to take one position or the other. Your process is equivalent to taking the sum $2+2 = 5$ and realising that it doesn't add up, you conclude that the answer must be 5 (i.e., Ghandi is better than Hitler) because that is how you feel about it, so you adjust the $2+2$ until it becomes $2.5+2.5 = 5$ and, "hey presto," the MOQ works again. Again, your ethics are emotive and as such deny the MOQ before you even start.

Lila was after all an inquiry into morals. If it had been an inquiry into emotivism Pirsig could have chucked out the metaphysics and saved a lot of effort.

And finally on Pirsig:

A. Fine with me. I only care for the argument, not the personality.

B. I believe so too, but I actually think that this is a fundamental flaw which anyone who supports the MOQ needs to be able to reconcile. I hope someone can.

Kevin:

I confounded the definition of emotivism. I apologize for my stupidity. I have no ground rules for an ethics debate with MOQ except to say that at the end of a moral action we should be closer to Dynamic quality than before the moral action. The way of determining that is still up in the air, with me anyway.

Struan:

Not stupidity at all—I was using it in the technical sense and you were not. I apologize for assuming you were. I have homed in on ethics because if the MOQ is not about ethics then what practical use is it? Lila was an "inquiry into morals," after all, and I fail to see the point of all this unless we can apply it to practical situations.

I admire your honesty but come back to my conviction that until you have an ethical framework, you having nothing of substance whatsoever. I believe that this problem is of the utmost importance and it must be answered if the MOQ is to be taken seriously, which I believe is what the Squad wants. Whatever some on this forum may think of academia—and I consider their rejection of it to be little more than intellectual cowardice—you must be able to show intelligent minds precisely why the MOQ is important and of what practical use it can be to mankind. If the Squad cannot do this, then it will inevitably lose those members with integrity and become a slightly bizarre cult with impossibly weird beliefs and bitter advocates.

I hope this does not happen.

Two Contradictory Statements [March 1998]

Magnus:

Hi Struan. You wrote: "Firstly everything is plainly not emotivism (in the philosophical sense) unless you are a convinced emotivist and if you are then what possible use can you have for the MOQ? The MOQ is setting itself up as something different and this is why it is quite proper for me to point out the underlying morality of Pirsig's position. Under an emotivist framework, I could quite rightly state that inorganic matter has a right to dominate humankind because I feel that this is the moral order of things. The only way you can argue that I am wrong is to forward a different, non-emotivist framework which you can show works better. This is precisely what the MOQ seeks to do and precisely where it fails to convince."

You continue with: "Emotivism is by definition the dismissal of metaphysics from the field of ethics...."

But earlier in your essay, you stated that: "It soon became clear that this was simply emotivism in disguise." These are two very contradictory statements. The MOQ provides a connection between metaphysics and ethics. Not only a connection, they are simply the same thing. You can't judge a metaphysics, any metaphysics, through the eyes of another metaphysics, which I think you're doing. For that, you would need a meta-metaphysics.

Struan:

No, they are not contradictory in the sense that I am not contradicting myself. I am pointing out the contradiction, not indulging in it. It is not my contradiction if the MOQ has nothing to do with metaphysics. Metaphysics is the mask, emotivism the face, and all I have done is point this out. Equally, I am not judging one metaphysics through the eyes of another; I am (in this instance) judging it through the eyes of an elimination of metaphysics so your objection is invalid.

Magnus:

Further, on in your essay you argue that "modern scientific philosophy" has abandoned dualist metaphysics and determinism. So, what is this "modern scientific philosophy"? Does it explain modern physical observations better than the MOQ?

You say that Pirsig completely misunderstands modern physics. To be polite, let's just say that everything about modern physics supports the MOQ.

You claimed to be pained by writing your essay. We're quite willing to ease that pain if you let us.

Struan:

The simple answer to the first part of the question is quantum mechanics and the second, yes. But also: existentialism and logical positivism. Although they do have their problems, they are nowhere near as intractable as the problems I have pointed out for the MOQ.

To be polite back, let's just say that it obviously doesn't. Well that was a constructive dialogue, wasn't it? Hmmm.

N. Peat—"The professor on the drums"—great drummer, great band.

Magnus:

So, you're one of those guys that think that it's possible to eliminate metaphysics. I'm not. I think that either you put your cards on the table and state a metaphysics, or you don't but presume one anyway. The only difference is that while we're aware of the MOQ, you're not aware of the metaphysics you're using. Platt said the other week that philosophy is the search for underlying assumptions. In your case, I guess you'd find SOM.

Struan:

No I'm not. A very odd conclusion. You are reducing the author to the argument. I am only too aware of the underlying assumptions of my beliefs but as I considered this to be a forum for argument rather than a personal ad, I prefer to let the argument speak.

Magnus:

But your argument that the MOQ is emotivism means nothing to us since emotivism (the doctrine that moral evaluations ultimately represent nothing more than expressions of personal preference, attitude, or feeling) is a philosophy near the S on the one-dimensional SOM scale. On the other hand, you refer to logical positivism when you want to be near the O on the SOM scale. The question is—how do you decide which philosophy to apply to which problem? Is quantum mechanics a philosophy?

Struan:

Are you joking here? Of course it is a philosophy. All investigation into the fundamental assumptions that govern our understandings is philosophy and if that doesn't include quantum mechanics then I don't know what does. How strange.

Magnus:

Yeah, we're a strange bunch. Are physics, chemistry, and medicine philosophies too? Make up your mind.

Struan:

Even more strange. How can I make up my mind? They are additional to each other. When you are in a supermarket and your wife says, "We need bread, milk, and coffee," do you say, "Make up your mind"? Hmmm.

Magnus:

We think that rationality has its limits. To be "not rational" doesn't always mean irrational as in bad. If everyone were being rational all the time, nothing really new would ever happen. We'd be a world of totally predictable robots.

And exactly how is quantum mechanics rational? Nobody has a rational explanation for it. Being rational means (to me) "to conform to currently accepted theories." We need to expand our theories to make quantum mechanics rational, and expanding a theory is a nonrational step. The MOQ makes room for this.

Struan:

I have never said that it does mean bad. I simply point out that if you are going to be "not rational" then it is bizarre to try to rationalise your irrationality. There is no value judgment here whatsoever. I love being irrational, but I obviously can't rationalise it. The whole concept of even attempting to do so is absurd.

Yes, I can see the problem if that is how you view rationality. I would suspect that to most people rational means "based upon reason." If we find that current theories are not based upon reason

421

because we find new evidence that refutes them, then we reject them and formulate a new theory that conforms better to reason and so becomes more probable. In this way, any good new theory is totally reasonable and entirely rational.

Magnus:

The keywords here are "formulate" and "good." How do you know if a newly formulated theory is good? You can't use the old theory that was just abandoned. And the new one is based on old theories and the new evidence. But given the old theories and the new evidence there are an infinite number of new theories that explain reality. It doesn't matter how many experiments you perform to narrow the new theories down to a minimum. There are still an infinite number of them. Which one do you choose? There is no rational means to do it. Phædrus discovered this in the chemistry lab in ZMM. Take a look, it's much more fun to read than my ramblings.

You say: "There's no value judgment here whatsoever." So you have obviously not yet grasped what the MOQ is about which makes your arguments even less worth.

Struan:

I think our "argument" should end here. Comments like this really are just plain stupid. [140] Perhaps we see the birth here of "MOQ Fundamentalism." Sorry to intrude on your "religion."

Grounding of Ethics [March 1998]

Hugo:

Welcome to the Squad, Struan! What an entry—reminds me of my brother when he comes visiting—charging the premises in a loving manner. I am sorry to be brief in the following—I am pressed for time—but I thought a quick answer was better than none. However, if you have some other grounding of ethics in stock, even if only the inklings of a hope, please share it with us; we need all the help we can get on this one.

Struan:

Nice one. I like it. There is nothing I enjoy more than a good debate with intelligent people. I can be arrogant, opinionated, and brutally honest, but I would buy each one of you a drink at the bar and delight in your company. Of course, you may not want to reciprocate in kind.;-)

My expertise (?) and interest is in the ethical dimension so most of what I say relates to that, but obviously they are all inter-related and probably contingent. If the MOQ is naturalistic then it falls to the naturalistic fallacy as pointed out by G. Moore in his Principa Ethica of 1903; namely, that it is fallacious to define good in terms of a natural object. As with all the following, the authors can do a much better job of explanation than I can and so I will not bore you here by repetition.

The work of Isaiah Berlin is another "hope," again the primary source is better than my ramblings so I shall refrain. A. MacIntyre is probably the foremost ethicist of recent years and I challenge anyone reasonable to read his works and still subscribe to the MOQ. (Short History of Ethics RKP, 1967—After Virtue Duckworth, 1981—Whose Justice? Which Rationality? Duckworth, 1988)

Hugo:

I would request that we do not consider this discussion of ethics as some sort of test of the Metaphysics of Quality. I believe there is much to the MOQ besides ethics—first of all a metaphysics. And our discussion of whether we can construct a coherent and plausible system of ethics on the grounds of the MOQ, here and now, can hardly be taken as a critical test of the MOQ as such. Rather, it is part of an ongoing probing and development and as you say, the ethical dimension is related to the rest.

Struan:

I think that the MOQ has to have practical value if it is to be worth anything and the only possible practical value I can see for it is in the field of ethics. If there is some other area where it might be useful other than as an intellectual exercise, then I would be very happy to hear about it.

Hugo:

I absolutely agree that the Metaphysics of Quality, or any other would-be metaphysics, has to have practical value to be worth anything. And I agree with you on the ethical issue (if this is your view) that there is a gap to be filled before the MOQ can be said to be a working ethical system, whatever that is. I do have hopes that the MOQ can contribute to ethics, and this hope is what makes me, and will make me, pursue this issue as long as I still have hope.

On the more practical side, I myself find Pirsig's metaphysical ideas valuable as that, a metaphysics. A metaphysics is what unites knowledge and as such, it plays its part between and around fields of knowledge. I use Pirsig's, and similar, ideas in the philosophy and methodology of science with the practical aim of doing research which has a say on sustainable development, inquiring into the interaction of man and Nature, especially concerning agriculture in its broadest sense.

Well, I had rather hoped you would bore me with a short summary of your view. I find it difficult to discuss whether to wear my Quality trousers today. If they are the only ones I have, I would hate if I found them not good enough to wear.

Seriously, I hope you would be kind enough to indicate which sort of ground you base your ethics on. I am not familiar with the latter two writers you refer to, neither do I have any easy access to their works, and I am sure some others on the Squad are in the same situation.

Struan:

With the greatest respect, I'm not really sure my personal view is relevant to this forum. I have merely endeavoured to point out flaws in the MOQ and to explain what I see as its true motivation. I would equally respectfully suggest that most good book shops will be able to get you the books I have suggested and that you would find them a most worthwhile investment as they directly relate to your views as you have put them here. This sounds a bit like a cop out, but I don't want to turn myself into a spokesman for Berlin or MacIntyre, not least because I am not capable of doing them justice and the primary sources are there for all to see. I hope you will allow me to continue merely to analyse the MOQ rather than postulate an entirely separate ethical system.

Having said that, the basic position of Berlin seems to be that there is no objectivity in morals, that people are the best judges of themselves. But he emphasises pluralism, empathy, understanding and respect, historical context, and the use of reason.

MacIntyre is more difficult in the sense that he almost takes an outsider's view of ethics and rarely gives value judgments. I think that summing him up in a few sentences here really is not a sensible thing to do. His aim (I think) is partly to attempt a bridge between the emotivist Aristotelian Thomists, and the rationalists. He is engaged in pointing out the flaws of all of these traditions in the hope that they recognise their own limitations.

In the context of the MOQ, I would suggest that the limitation is that it is irrational. On this forum, we have the odd situation of people agreeing that it is irrational yet trying to argue that it is still rational in a fundamental way. This is surely a contradiction.

Hugo:

I do not see this contradiction. But I agree that the role of rationality—how we reconcile ourselves with our powers of reason— is a very basic question, perhaps the most basic question in philosophy. Here on the Lila Squad we are generally aware of the limits of reason. This is part of why we are here, because Pirsig's philosophical books highlight the limits of reason. Yet, reason is what philosophy is about. Is it a contradiction to rationally discuss the limits of rationality? I don't think so. This is after all the very distinctive feature of intellect and self-awareness.

The question is not really whether we should use our "feeling." We cannot do otherwise. We cannot live by reason alone. But I do not find this an argument against better reason. Quite contrary, I find that the dominating rationality today leaves much to better, the most essential being a partial blindness to its own limits. We have to acknowledge that, although reason is our common means of finding our way forward, reason is always limited.

I take the Metaphysics of Quality, and its relatives, to be a step forward towards greater self-awareness, towards a reason that is more aware of its own limits. Yet, the proper role of reason remains a pivotal philosophical and existential question.

On the question of naturalism—naturalism is a dangerous concept to use, and I must take the responsibility for bringing it up. Naturalism has been used in different ways through history, in concordance with the development of natural science. The way I use naturalism takes the fallible nature of our theories of the world into consideration, (only) stating that there is some connection between how the world is and what we ought to do, between the true and the good. In this perspective, the MOQ is a radical form of naturalism, stating that the true is (but) a kind of good.

Moore said that any philosophy which seeks to define good (for instance the idea that the established natural science can decide on what is good) commits the naturalistic fallacy—talking of, I believe, Hume's questioning of how any propositions on what ought to be (values) can be deduced from propositions on what is (facts). Moore did not consider good the kind of property that could be decided upon through experience (science, for example). Later on, the naturalistic fallacy has been taken (by R.M. Hare, I believe) to be the confusion of the distinction between the description and the evaluation of a thing.

Pirsig takes the opposite route of Moore and Hare. He says that value is basic in experience, that the distinction between description and evaluation is a secondary distinction. In a way, we might say that Pirsig agrees with Moore that the good cannot be defined by way of a descriptive theory, because the good is primary to any description, primary to the distinction between knower and known. Pirsig agrees with Moore that the good is not a kind of property that can be found by way of observation; the good is not something inherent in objects. But Pirsig furthermore says that the good is not something imposed by (the emotion of) the observer. The good is primary to the distinction between subject and object. This observation, which comes from the basis of

Pirsig's metaphysics, makes for the view of ethics entailed by MOQ.

We might consider Pirsig's philosophy a resolution of an ethical paradox as coined in Moore's naturalistic fallacy: "If there is no path from what is, to what ought to be, no path from the true to the good, then where the h... does good come from?"

Struan:

Beautifully put. But Pirsig is forwarding a resolution that has no empirical evidence to substantiate it. Is not altogether more "reasonable" to take a non-cognitivistic resolution and simply say that ethical language is not descriptive and indeed that ethics itself is not a form of knowledge? Of course, if we are wanting to be unreasonable then that is fine with me, so long as we realise that we are being unreasonable.

Hugo:

I do not consider the probing of Pirsig's ideas completed; the probing has barely started. As I said above, I do not find it "reasonable" to abandon reason, nor to have blind faith in reason. And I definitely find ethics to be a form of knowledge, the kind of knowledge we call wisdom, perhaps. There is something like a knowledge of the good life, a knowledge that has little if anything to do with intelligence. This, I believe, is what Pirsig was after and this is what I am pursuing. I am using my powers of reason, and I am using my feeling and empathy. However limited they are, both have their part to play.

Credibility of Non-Rationality [March 1998]

Andy:

Struan, friend, you asked us in a recent email to point out why "I've missed the point and to put me right." Gladly. Let me preface this by saying I've only read Lila one and a half times and have not looked back at the specific passages you cite, although I am reading it again now, and will look at this book through the lens you suggest and get back to you at a later date about that.

Struan:

I shall look forward to it although the word "friend" has made me wonder what's coming.

Andy:

World legal, economic, and political structures already utilize Quality. Quality, for me, isn't a type of religion or dogma that has proponents and detractors. It is what guides the choice of an employer in selecting a new hire from a pool of applicants. It is institutions that give grants (i.e., National Science Foundation, National Institutes of Health, IBM, etc.) use to guide their process. Quality is not new, it is not unique to Pirsig, and he certainly can take little credit for its use. It is a term Pirsig uses to describe what exists in natural processes.

Struan:

If you replace the word "Quality" with "emotivism," I will agree with you. What is needed is a differentiation between the two; otherwise, quality simply becomes what you subjectively feel is good. As yet, nobody has even come close to resolving this, at least not to my knowledge. Again, we see emotivism in disguise. [141]

Andy:

I agree that Pirsig misunderstands this issue of reconciling killing (murder) and evolution. I would submit to you that there are no moderate schools of thought on this issue that are completely consistent.

Struan:

There are. Emotivism is the first example that springs to mind. I should point out that I am not a convinced emotivist (far from it) but emotivism as espoused by the likes of A.J. Ayer is totally consistent and eminently moderate.

Andy:

I don't follow your civil war argument. How do you conclude that the ideas lost were at a higher evolutionary level than the country? I don't see any way of knowing at what evolutionary level their ideas were, apart from the observation that they thought

428

to get a gun and risk their lives to defend their families and country. This seems to indicate the opposite of what you state.

Struan:

I'm glad you don't follow. This is precisely my point. I don't follow either. This is not my conclusion, as I pointed out to Magnus earlier. I am merely pointing out the inconsistency of Pirsig's position, not trying to posit my own. I am showing that this is inconsistent and so am pleased that you agree. The contradiction is not mine; I merely point it out. [142]

Andy:

There is no way to give rational credibility to something nonrational. This is Pirsig's basic problem that he went insane trying to resolve (ZMM). To try to resolve it in the complex, multi-variable field of ethics confuses things further. It is a very difficult question. I find it helpful to frame it thus: how do we give a social system a human characteristic (like conscience or Quality) that cannot be defined? The answer is: we can't. It is an impossibility. Quality is not, to me (and again others, including Pirsig, may disagree), too useful for institutional ethics. It is like aesthetics in the sense that it is personal and individual. So, the way around the impasse in my question is to educate and develop individual conscience, to nurture our own perceptions of that feeling or essence which Pirsig calls Quality, and apply them from the bottom up, not from the top down. I believe this may be the source of some of the problems you raise.

Struan:

The first sentence sums it up. This is not a rational position. It is irrational and nonsensical. I seek a rational argument and you cannot give it. We are (at first sight) on two entirely different wavelengths, yours irrational, and mine rational (by your own admission). But wait, you say that, "that it is personal and individual." Pure emotivism from your own mouth (fingers). If this is the case why not discard the metaphysics and make your life a lot simpler. You are using reason to argue that your position is unreasonable which strikes me as a very odd thing to do.

Andy:

I disagree with the conclusion of your essay. It is you, and not "we," and most definitely not I, who are looking at "mish-mash." If you are going to give your interpretation or opinion on this, express it as such, not as "our" opinion. You don't know what I'm looking at. If you are looking at a mish-mash of nonsense, fine. But what I am looking at, right now, is the words of a man (you) who is struggling to understand the words from another man's (Pirsig) struggle to understand something that cannot be defined or subject to conventional methods of analysis. So please, use "we" only in a speculative or conditional sense (e.g., we can see, or we may be looking). The way you use it here is not only inaccurate, it puts words in my mouth.

Struan:

On the contrary, I maintain that "we" are looking at a mish mash of nonsense. That is what I meant and that is what I stand by. Whether you realise its lack of validity or not is not remotely relevant. I'm not putting words in your mouth at all. You can say what you like, but it remains nonsense.

Andy:

Don't tell me what is or isn't my concern in my search to understand ethics. I will be the judge of this, not you or anybody else. The minute you start telling people what is and isn't of their concern, you're telling them how to think, and that's when all the trouble really starts. If you want to state your opinion, fine—if it challenges people to think deeply about their personal convictions, even better. But in stating your opinion, or an argument, state it as such, not as a selfevident fact.

Struan:

I would never tell anybody how to think. For example, it is no concern of yours whether I am having lobster for supper tonight, but you are welcome to think about it. The MOQ is irrelevant to anyone seeking an ethical framework and yet if you want to think about it then that is fine by me. But this may be a cultural thing. I am English/Scottish and the accepted practice in academia here is to state what you believe to be correct, it being accepted that the reader will realise that everything you write is your opinion. After all science is the study of the most probable, not of a priori fact. If Einstein had written: "I think $E=mc^2$," then most people over here would suggest the "I think" was superfluous or even tautologous. I don't know which country you are from, but if your conventions are different to ours (and I've yet to find any that are) then I hope I have cleared that up.

Andy:

I would love to hear your opinion on what would be of concern to an ethicist who has escaped, but certainly not discarded, rational thought. I believe that any ethics that cannot be guided by an individual, and thus in part by emotion, is irrelevant to our society.

Struan:

Clearly emotivism is your only refuge, either that or prephilosophical conviction and superstition. I'm not saying there is anything wrong with either of these positions but the latter is by definition unreasonable and so to try and reason it out is pointless, since while the consistency may be valid, it is the inference that is suspect, and it is the inference that irrational thought cannot substantiate.

Once again I would put it to you that if you have "escaped" rational thought, then valid though your superstition might be, it is pointless for you to use the tools of reason to show that you are being reasonable. What you have is an "ad hoc" hypothesis that is irrational at the core but dressed in the veil of rationality. But a good argument cannot be stronger than its modally weakest premise and so to base an empirical conclusion upon an a priori premise is simply poor logic, as Kant pointed out in his brilliant destruction of the ontological argument.

If you have no intention to be logical then that is fine, but there endeth reasonable debate. If you have intentions of being logical then you must be consistent. I'm not making any value judgment here as to the validity of your position and if people want to indulge in irrational debate then I can see it might still have meaning for them, but for me personally I see little point as all it boils down to is a series of boos and hurrahs.

Andy:

I think we misunderstand each other at a deeper, simpler level than I first thought.

Struan:

I agree.

Andy:

The world is not exclusively rational. The world is not exclusively non-rational. Do you agree?

Struan:

Yes.

Andy:

The search for an ethical system is a search to create a rational form of judging the ethical value of all phenomena. Yet, not all phenomena fit into rational or non-rational categories. So, we are left with a dilemma of epic proportions, which is how to judge spontaneous actions (which are not always rational) by non-rational criteria. Do you agree?

Struan:

No. All phenomena do fit into rational or non-rational categories. The term non-rational includes all that is not rational and so taken as a pair they are by definition exclusive. Note that this is not the same as saying that mind and matter taken together are exclusive but it would be the same as saying mind and non-mind taken together are exclusive. Also an ethical system does not have to be rational.

Andy:

Therefore, in the attempt to create this system, we can see how both rational and non-rational factors can be useful. Do you agree?

Struan:

No, because I disagree with your premise as I have said above.

Andy:

Do you believe in the phenomena that Christians call God? I realize this is a difficult question, but do you believe the entire universe can be explained in rational terms?

Struan:

No and no. Those are two entirely separate questions.

Andy:

Do you believe that everything is rational and reducible to a system of thought that we, at the end of the 20th century, can understand? Or do you believe that there are some things that escape our intellect and escape rationality and we cannot explain away simply and clearly?

Struan:

The latter.

Andy:

As for your rhetoric, I am from America, but I went to school here and also for six months at the University of Sussex, in Brighton. I studied 20th century social and economic British history. If you are stating what you believe is correct, then use the appropriate pronoun I, not we. For the MOQ very much concerns my ethical search, and therefore your assertion in your first email is incorrect.

Struan:

We must agree to disagree. I will continue to use the appropriate pronoun in all arguments, however I will not use in reply to you if you find it offensive. I fail to see why you view it as such, but out of respect, I will refrain.

Andy:

I welcome your intellectual challenge to the Lila Squad. Discussion of these issues is good. To reduce all of these issues to rational human language is inaccurate. If this is the purpose of the discussion you initiated, I will no longer participate. I am looking for a more inclusive answer.

Struan:

But the reduction to rational human language is precisely what you are trying to do and precisely what I am pointing out that you

433

are doing and precisely the root of my objection. This is a forum that only allows communication by language. All I have done is point out that you are being non-rational at which point you try to rationalise your irrationality as if you take my observation as an insult. But you clearly state yourself that, "To reduce all of these issues to rational human language is inaccurate." So why do you attempt to do so?

I hope I'm being clear here but maybe I'm not, so I shall put it another way. Be proud of your irrationality. If I say that your position is unreasonable, then say, "Thank you very much, I'm glad you understand," rather than launching into a pseudo reasoned argument against me. We agree that rationality isn't everything and we both see the value of irrationality, where we differ is that I think your attempt to rationalise irrational things is doomed to failure.

Andy:

I hope I haven't created any feelings of personal animosity. That was most certainly not my intention. But I will continue to resist that which I perceive to not be true.

Struan:

None whatsoever. I enjoy nothing more (well few things more) than a good debate with intelligent people and am enjoying this immensely.

Negative and Positive Reflections [March 1998]

Horse:

Good to see you took the plunge and posted to the Squad, Struan. I read your essay with great interest as I think that it is a good thing that there are negative as well as positive reflections on the MOQ. This is the only way that the MOQ is likely to progress from an interesting set of initial observations and thoughts into a properly thought out metaphysics. If in the process it fails—well that's life. I don't think that this will be the case, but maybe that's because I'm a natural optimist.

As a general comment I would say that in your comments you are being overly harsh towards the MOQ, considering that it is in its infancy. It may not currently have the answers which you want, or state them as you wish to see them, but Pirsig has provided a framework within which it is possible to build a more coherent metaphysics than has currently been available. As far as I am aware, no previous metaphysics has been either consistent or complete. In fact, I am not sure that this is possible given that which makes people what they are and our current state of knowledge.

Struan:

I merely say what I see. If that is harsh then so be it, it is not my fault. If the MOQ has anything to offer it will survive the attacks of people like myself and even come out stronger because of them. I often worry that people don't put things forcefully enough for fear of giving offense and that cannot be good for progress. I have strong beliefs, but if I am proved wrong to my satisfaction, I will be the first to admit it.

Horse:

Your initial words are to point out that Lila "is simply emotivism in disguise." A fair point. Many people approach the world from the perspective of that which they care about. The state of caring is in itself an emotional state. Where we are talking about ethics and ethical behaviour I think that emotion is a part of the reasoning process as it stems from human belief systems. This does not mean that it is the whole of the process, just one part. A workable ethical system is one that can be adopted by people, who are inherently emotional. If we propose a system by transcending emotion and being purely rational then the system itself is likely to be rejected and ultimately worthless. Again, this does not mean that an ethical system must appeal purely to the emotional side of those who are to adopt it, but there must be common ground.

The construction of formal ethical systems in the past have, in the main, been academic exercises and most have attempted to utilize the rational nature in humans. How many have produced an ethical/moral code that most people can understand, let alone adopt? For that matter, which of the major ethical systems have failed to be abused in one way or another? Ethical systems within the framework of MOQ, with the emphasis on Quality, may produce a system that is not only coherent and workable but is appealing enough for people to want to accept. Pirsig's examples may seem to lack coherence in some ways if they are considered purely from within a Subject/Object framework.

Struan:

Again, we come to the crux of the matter. If I am right, that this is emotivism in disguise (and you say it is a fair point) then that is an end to all reasonable discussion. You seem to be espousing the pluralistic approach of MacIntyre in that last paragraph which is fine, but that is already a well established approach to ethics (probably the most important of our time) and so it seems odd that you should want to trudge through problems that are already resolved. If it is a case of finding a system that people will find attractive and want to work with then you have a point. A good sprinkling of new age mysticism onto an emotivist or libertarian core may be just the job. Not of great interest to me and rather disingenuous, but I can see the attraction in a practical sense. Perhaps I think intellectual honesty has more quality than social effects. Having said that, I don't think many people will be influenced by the analysis of any ethicist as realistically people have always just done what they feel is right and always will do so. How interested parties rationalise this is of little consequence.

Horse:

You say that nobody adheres to the idea of a Subject/Object or Substance based Metaphysics. I do not believe that this is so. The course on Ethics that I finished eighteen months ago was littered with references to "the subject/object metaphysics." In fact it was as a result of this that I realised that Pirsig not only had something valid to say about our current framework of belief but that the MOQ was a possible way out of the apparent paradoxes contained within SOM. Within physics, there still exist schools of thought that are sceptical (sometimes downright scathing) about the quantum view of existence.

The initial furor of quantum physics emerged at the beginning of this century and it wasn't until after the middle of this century that Popper produced his idea of the 3rd world of Objective contents of Subjective thoughts. This from the man that single-handedly changed the way we perceive the scientific method and flew in the face of his former colleagues in the school of Logical Positivism. Whilst many people reject determinism and adhere to the idea of "free will," this is nothing to do with any knowledge of Heisenberg or quantum physics.

Heisenberg's destruction of determinism neither supports nor undermines the notion of free will, if anything it confuses the issue. If there is no such thing as cause and effect at a quantum level then how can it exist at any higher level? And if everything is indeterminate (statistical probability) then how does this imply free will or any grounds upon which to base a libertarian system? Pirsig's explanation from different evolutionary levels at least provides (for me) provisional solid ground from which to examine this and other ideas. It may fail but it will not be for lack of trying.

Struan:

I disagree with you here but this is beside the point anyway. I don't subscribe to it and neither do any of my peers or any of the foremost names in ethics today, and not one of us needed the MOQ to come to this conclusion. So, in that respect there seems little point in arguing that this is still a current worldview. It may be amongst the masses, but so what?

Again, this business of free will comes up and you are quite right in what you say. It seems clear that free will is consistent with either a deterministic system or a non-deterministic system and equally there is no logical incoherence in proposing free will as absent from either system. I fail to see how the MOQ has any bearing upon this matter as, conceptually, there is no problem to resolve.

Horse:

I'll have a go at a couple of points in your essay. I may get fairly wide of the mark but this is an initial stab at it. I'm on fairly shaky ground when it comes to American history but I was under the (possibly naive) impression that part of the reason for the Civil war was to do with abolishing slavery in the south. This was, I assume, where Pirsig referred to John Brown. Seen from this perspective the war was justified, as it was an attempt by an intellectual system, that of human rights, to assert itself over a flawed social system based on treating human beings as objects. In the process, a great number of people were killed. I think that the intellectual system that supported a social system where all people are treated fairly is superior to the intellectual system that supports a social system where some are treated badly due to the idea that they are property. Emotivism, I hear you say; this is only Horse saying that he likes one system and dislikes another. Not at all.

From the MOQ point of view the former system is more capable of producing a greater number of individuals who will progress to an intellectual level and whose ideas may provide for change within that level. In the latter system, any attempt by some of its components (slaves) to progress to a level beyond biology/utility will be suppressed on the grounds that they are a commodity/resource for the society to consume. I think that Human Rights, as a system of ethical beliefs, can be placed mainly within the intellectual level of MOQ, so any fight to protect human rights over social utility is justifiable. This is the raison d`etre of groups such as Amnesty International.

Struan:

Forgive me if I get this wrong but it seems to me that you are saying a number of odd things here. Slaves surely are already progressed beyond the level of biology. One only has to listen to Blues music to know this. Some of the greatest works of art and science have emerged from severely oppressed people and methinks you are on very dangerous ground here. I would venture to suggest that the slaves were already a Dynamic intellectual force for change within the Southern States and so your example seems to fall to the ground. You could just as well argue that bringing slaves over from Africa was morally just in that they were placed in a context that heightened their Dynamic potential. You have nothing but emotivism to help you decide which line to take. It can be twisted whichever way you like and this is why the MOQ has nothing to say about ethics. These are just the sorts of arguments that are futile unless we have a consistent framework, already in place, with which to approach them (more on this later). This hierarchical view is not consistent in any a posteriori sense and so is useless in the field of ethics.

Horse:

You next go on to capital punishment and the apparent contradiction in Pirsig's views. My own thoughts may be different to Pirsig's in that the MOQ would show that it is wrong for any society to punish any individual by killing them even if that individual threatens the established social structure. The only way that an individual can threaten the established social structure would be through ideas and the MOQ states quite plainly that for society to threaten or suppress an idea is immoral. There is a difference here between the threat by the growth of an idea and the threat by violence in support of that idea. The former is moral according to the MOQ in that it is an idea and thus of a higher evolutionary state than society. The latter is immoral in that it is biology attempting to overpower society. In addition it is immoral for society to kill a human being as it has other resources that it can bring to bear to contain any biological threat to itself and where it has an alternative that enables it to refrain from damaging one of its constituents these should be considered first.

Phew!

Struan:

But again, we see the same inconsistency. If we apply what you wrote in your previous paragraph, I could well argue that the society in question may be such that it is extraordinarily successful at producing people with new ideas. If one person (or group of people) with one idea destroys that society and with it a whole series of other ideas, is that not morally wrong? Again I am not indulging in the inconsistency, I am merely pointing it out. Under this framework, you can pick and choose which level to focus on and so it all seems to fit, but it only fits because it is so blurred that anything goes.

For almost every moral situation you put forward and resolve under this framework, I will be able to demonstrate the opposite resolution with equal consistency and equal force using precisely the same criteria. What sort of a moral framework is that? The only way you will consider that I am wrong is by recourse to emotivism. The only possible course which sticks within the bounds of reason is to start from a neutral morality and show how the MOQ forces you to take one position or the other.

Horse:

I think this is a case of putting the cart before the horse. What is a neutral morality? Surely a system of moral values is something which allows people to evaluate what is a right course of action or which is a wrong course of action or if there is a degree of both within the choice to be made. If an ethical system is neutral then none of the above is possible and so there is neither right nor wrong nor anything in between. Neutral morality implies no morality. I think MOQ itself supplies the necessary ground rules with which to approach an ethical system. Ethical systems are value systems and as the MOQ is founded on value, it would make sense to utilize this. MOQ is not value free; it is the opposite, but in the same way that Darwinian evolution is "neutral" within Nature at a biological level, so MOQ is neutral within a metaphysical sense. It is necessary to find some way of determining which course of action/choice is of greater positive value than another action/choice.

Maybe we could start by examining the current major ethical systems and see if there is some scope for incorporating them within the MOQ. I'm thinking here of deontology, Utilitarianism, virtue, communitarianism, and rights. I wouldn't necessarily consider communitarianism within this system as I think it is, at the moment, highly confused and confusing, but you may think differently.

Struan:

No, my apologies, you have the wrong end of the stick and I have not made myself clear. I shall try again. I am talking about the methodological process of examining the veracity of the MOQ. What I mean is that instead of agreeing that Hitler was worse than Ghandi, for example, and then trying to work the MOQ round this fact, what we need to do is take Hitler and Ghandi with no preconceptions and apply the MOQ which, if it has value, will force us to come to one conclusion to the exclusion of others, i.e., that Ghandi was good or bad relative to Hitler.

All the discussions I have read so far on this forum take the former approach and so it will hardly be surprising if they finally come to the conclusion they set out with. In fact, it would be extraordinary if they didn't. This is not a pedantic point. It is utterly crucial to the validity of the process and would save a considerable amount of effort if implemented. The problem is that I fear it cannot be implemented here because if we take away the emotive premise there may be nothing left to implement a good methodology upon.

Ant:

Struan, in the "moral situation" mentioned below about vegetarianism could you please demonstrate the opposite resolution of this situation "with equal consistency and equal force using precisely the same criteria," i.e., by using the MOQ, show why it is more moral to eat animals than vegetables.

"Is it moral, as the Hindus and Buddhists claim, to eat the flesh of animals? Our current morality would say it's immoral only if you're a Hindu or a Buddhist. Otherwise it's OK, since morality is nothing more than social convention.

"An evolutionary morality, on the other hand, would say it's scientifically immoral for everyone because animals are at a higher level of evolution, that is, more Dynamic than are grains and fruits and vegetables. But it would add that this moral principle holds only where there is an abundance of grains and fruit and vegetables. It would be immoral for Hindus not to eat their cows in

441

a time of famine, since they would then be killing human beings in favor of a lower organism."

(Robert Pirsig, Lila, Black Swan, 1991, reprinted 1994, page190/191)

I look forward to your answer with interest.

Struan:

The simple answer is I can't. My only defense would be to claim that I did only say "most," not "all," but a more honest answer would be to admit I exaggerated.

Determinism [March 1998]

Ken:

Perhaps you would explain to me why you consider determinism to be a false supposition. I think it is your reason for believing this that has caused these misunderstandings. Also, my forty year old Random House unabridged dictionary does not define Emotivism and I am not sure what it is. Could you give me a brief definition?

Struan:

Gladly. The uncertainty principle is also known as the indeterminacy principle and so there you have it. Although I realise that in an a priori sense this does not obviate determinism, to all rational purposes of mankind it does, if we are to be reasonable about it (if you will forgive the tautology). I should say again that I have nothing against being unreasonable and indeed enjoy it on many an occasion. I should point out before I make the following definition of emotivism that, summed up in such a short space, it is relatively straightforward to pick holes in it. For a more comprehensive thesis I urge those interested to look at: Warnock, G., Contemporary Moral Philosophy, MacMillan, 1967 or Ayer, A.J., Language Truth and Logic, 1946. I should also point out that this is not necessarily my position.

Anyway, Emotivism came from empiricism which, as I'm sure you are aware, divided all meaning into two categories: logic/analytic (a priori), that which is true by definition, i.e., an unmarried man is a bachelor; and empirical (a posteriori) knowledge which is the field of scientific endeavour and includes everything that comes to us via our senses. The central thesis of Ayer and the emotivists is that ethics does not fall into either category of meaning so we cannot make sense of it. When people use ethical language, they are doing no more than conveying emotion.

As I say, this is what I believe adherents to the MOQ are doing. Pirsig decides on an emotional level that the Northern States were right to go to war then seeks to justify this using the MOQ. Others on this forum decide on emotional grounds that Ghandi was better than Hitler was and then proceed to justify this position using the MOQ. Both fail purely because the MOQ cannot supply a rational basis for their emotions.

Again, I repeat, as some think I casting negativity over them by saying the above; there is nothing necessarily wrong with relying on emotions. They are just as valid as rationality, but to take an emotive standpoint and justify it rationally is simply futile. The rationality, because of what it is, will fail. The MOQ may be valid, but it is not and can never be rational.

Ken:

On the Determinism question—in my mind the quantum theory has nothing to do with Determinism. It operated at the quantum level upon which the universe is constructed. As Horse said, we cannot have a predictive system sitting on top of a purely random system. I think we just need more information.

Struan:

I see no reason why we can't have a predictive system sitting on top of a random system. If evolution is the replacement of disorder with order then it seems inevitable that the former will replace the latter. A very crude example would be two shipwreck survivors swimming randomly about in the ocean, one with a raft, the other with water. They happen to meet and combine their possessions with the result that both survive longer than their less fortunate shipmates. Very crude yes, but a demonstration of how order can result from disorder and also of how it can prevail.

Ken:

In my view the universe began in a purely Deterministic way which was later modified by the theory of Deterministic Disorder (Chaos) resulting in a universe which is guided by Dynamic Quality (Evolution) in which the force for greater information content (the operation of evolution) resulted in a continually increasing level of betterness (morality, value?). In this view, Dynamic Quality has been operating since the beginning. In my opinion the Universe is a moral order which is not deterministic except that there is a pressure for continually increasing morality or value which is the result of random latching of value which result from the initial conditions set by the Big Bang.

Struan:

This strikes me as pure conjecture. Do you have any evidence for this whatsoever? Also, you have described here how chaos came out of pure determinism. Does this not strike you as just as odd as a predictive system coming out of chaos? You reject one in favour of the other, but if you accept that one is conceptually possible then you surely must accept the other is too.

Ken:

It seems to me that the first thing you and I have to do is come to some agreement on quantum theory and the Theory of Deterministic Disorder before we can progress any further. You say that quantum theory is a purely random system and that you see no reason that we cannot have a deterministic (predictive) system sitting on top of a random system. I say that the atom, the molecular world, the universe, and life are composed of quantum electrodynamics and quantum chromodynamic functions, which are currently considered to be the basic physical actions.

This means that quantum theory did not just give the larger universe a start and then subside and go its own way. These quantum functions are an intimate and basic part of every atom and molecule and element that makes up the totality of the universe. If there were not predictability in these functions then there is no way that the remainder of the universe could be predictable. Since the universe appears the same to us and to astronomers night after night, year after year, and century after century, then any change in function at the electrodynamic and chromodynamic levels must either be nonexistent or very slow indeed.

Obviously, the same actions happen over and over in similar functions to produce predictable results. To reiterate, we cannot separate quantum action from atomic and molecular action, therefore I conclude that the action at the quantum level must be predictable even though we have no explanation for it at the moment. To my mind, the universe was deterministic at the beginning because a coherent physical process can be built up from the end of the Planck time (I think about 10 to the minus 43 seconds after the Big Bang) up to now.

Even so, the numbers of physical processes in the universe that change linearly with time and are thus solvable with linear differential equations are a very, very small portion of the totality of physical processes in the universe. What was needed was an approach that would make possible the extraction of meaningful information from nonlinear processes and thus make possible a much deeper penetration of the dynamical systems of the universe.

That approach was found in Chaos Theory or Deterministic Disorder. This theory allowed people to understand that many simple processes in Nature could generate great complexity without randomness. An extract from the book Chaos by James Gleick:

"In non-linearity and feedback lay all of the tools for encoding and then unfolding structures as rich as the human brain. Chaos shows how a purposeless flow of energy can wash life and consciousness into the world. Creation takes place at the edges where growth occurs, and because the laws of growth are purely deterministic, they maintain a near perfect symmetry. A snowflake is a record of the history of all of the changing weather conditions it has experienced. Evolution is Chaos with feedback. Dissipation is an agent of order. God does play dice with the universe, but they are loaded dice."

445

The point of the above is to bring into the discussion the fact that, from a purely deterministic beginning, there is a way to introduce non-linearity into the physical processes of the universe, which will give us a way to escape pure determinism and restore effective free will—all of this without a complete departure from determinism.

In my previous posting, I made the remark that in my opinion the universe was a moral order that was not deterministic. By this, I mean that the universe is not predictable in a practical sense because of the complexity involved. Again, in my view, evolution is a purely physical process that progresses because of the fact that for a given physical environment every possible combination of processes will occur given enough time. Those processes that latch will supply a platform for further advances in complexity.

Given enough time those processes will supply a chain of possibilities that can produce the best (in Pirsig's terms, most moral) possible outcome. This is the deterministic process, as modified by deterministic disorder, which I maintain produced the current conditions and us. In Dynamic Quality and Pirsig's terms, this is a moral (in the physical sense) process. In my view, this process is not pure conjecture because much of it can be verified experimentally and more can be made plausible theoretically.

Keep in mind that the term "chaos" is an unfortunate choice of terms that does not convey the true functioning of the process. Deterministic Disorder is a better choice of terms although still not quite satisfactory in my mind. I think that this picture is not the same and is much more plausible than your idea of determinism coming out of the purely indeterministic (according to you) quantum process.

It seems clear to me that the above process that I have laid out is supported by observation, empiricism, and believable theory and is in no sense prodded by pure emotion. When we get to the sentient (human) level, I think that we begin to encounter a few, but not insurmountable, problems between purely physical Dynamic Quality and Dynamic Quality from the human viewpoint.

Struan:

Thank you very much for this, Ken. I need some considerable time to think about it and will respond later when I have digested it properly and formulated my response.

Great Lila Squad Shoot-out [March 1998]

Bodvar:

Hi, Horse! I have been labouring on a response to Struan, but after having read your piece, I let it drop into the wastebasket. Magnus', Hugo's, and Andy's responses were good, but this is just splendid. Everything shows a deep understanding of what the Quality idea is about, but particularly the point about "neutral morals" (I can't see that Struan answered it) reveals the crux of the matter. But I shall not argue by proxy; there will be time enough to meet Struan personally.

Dear Struan...

It "pained" you to write (good old emotions), but you are "brutally honest" and decided to tell us the truth, huh. Oh well, we have read reviews by Strawson and have had strawmen visiting before so I guess we will survive. You bait us heavily. From this ingratiating and innocent opening it sounds as if you basically adhere to the Quality idea, just having a few minor objections to Pirsig's interpretation of such and such events, but from the following messages a different picture emerges; it looks like you don't buy anything of the MOQ.

So for an opening let me ask—do you accept the first quality postulate, about there being nothing but value and that the division is between Dynamic and static value (or quality or moral)? This is not self evident or provable, that much I know already.

If this is utter nonsense to you, well, there are those who find this very sensible because the logical steps following from this basic assertion seems to produce a better model than the so-called subject/object one. If it is at this early stage that your objections stem nothing that a "kind person" will say can "put you right."

Your cure-all "Emotivism" (a contraction of emotion and motive?) is in a way the primary thesis of Quality. Emotions are

447

values and Quality is reality, the only motivation. What about love? No minor factor? But there are levels of value starting with matter, as you possibly know. Emotions are, in my humble opinion, social value, or "representation," as Hugo would say.

Struan:

If emotivism is the primary thesis of quality then great, I was hoping it wasn't as I'm not an emotivist and feel that such an approach has fundamental flaws both conceptually and practically. It is not my "cure all." On the contrary, it is just what I didn't want to hear. This shows that my point has been utterly lost (possibly my fault for not being clear enough).

Bodvar:

Another point that made me doubtful of your grasp of the Quality idea was this paragraph in your reply to Andy:

"If you replace the word 'Quality' with 'emotivism' I will agree with you. What is needed is a differentiation between the two; otherwise, quality simply becomes what you subjectively feel is good. As yet, nobody has even come close to resolving this, at least not to my knowledge. Again we see emotivism in disguise."

Struan:

On the contrary, it shows I know more than I first thought about what Quality is all about. Quality is not the rejection of subjectivity, per se; it is the conclusion that mind is contained in static inorganic patterns while matter is contained in static intellectual patterns, with the reconciliation being that they can contain each other without contradiction. This is a completely different thing to saying that what you subjectively feel, as a term, carries no meaning and this is what you attempt to do. Quality merely blurs the boundaries; it does not dispose of personal identity. The doubtful grasp is yours. Whilst you have both hands firmly on the bells and whistles, the core is tucked away so tightly you can't see past the pretty colours and beautiful sounds.

Bodvar:

Subjective is the negative SOM indicating what is not to trust, and your emotivism is clearly synonymous with subjectivism.

However the chief Quality tenet is that the division is not between subject and object (mind/matter) so the accusation of "what you subjectively feel" or its twin, "only in your mind," doesn't carry weight in the Quality reality. If you don't accept, or understand, this conclusion, okay, no hard feelings, but why tell us that? We are already, uhm "painfully" aware that 99.99 percent don't.

Struan:

Firstly, it is your emotivism, not mine. It is not me trying to escape subject/object metaphysics—it is you. I am already free, which is partly why the MOQ is meaningless to me. You are turning a onemile journey into a thousand mile epic, with blinkers on, unable to see the shortcuts. Secondly, I understand the conclusion but think you fail to appreciate the method by which you have arrived at it. I refuse to accept a conclusion that is arrived at by suspect methodology. I would even go further than that and put it to you that this is not your conclusion, it is in fact your premise.

Bodvar:

Another weak spot is your "neutral morals" that Horse referred to. I can't see that you did little more than put up a smoke screen in trying to escape from that dead end, but it demonstrated your subject/object roots.

Struan:

The point about neutral morals is completely misplaced. You can disagree with my suggested methodology, but to twist my words into something else is really quite foolish. I understand that I wasn't clear to Horse in the first place, but having clarified my position, I would be astonished if he didn't accept my explanation as valid.

This next point is starting to become farcical. I do not have subject/object roots. Again, you assume that anyone who disagrees with you has subject/object roots and again you are utterly and irredeemably wrong. Even viewed historically, the vast majority of scientists have seen mind as simply an extension of matter and hence fail to draw a distinction, when applied to the last few decades the rejection of this division is almost complete. The view that secretly we are anonymous dualists is quite outrageous.

Bodvar:

I see that you volunteer to elaborate, but it is superfluous, I've heard it exactly one billion times before. For centuries, the SOM has had the privilege of being "the obvious," demanding objectivity and heaping the burden of proof on another, but here at the Lila Squad we take the luxury of regarding Quality as obvious. At least that way the critics make an effort to understand.

Struan:

You hear from me what you want to hear and ignore what I say.

Bodvar:

Have another go at Lila and return when you know what it is about.

Struan:

I will certainly have another go at Lila, it is a great work of fiction, but confess that I never had much time for peaceful literary society-like groups, so perhaps it is best if I do withdraw and stop wasting everyone's time.

Bodvar:

Have another go at Reality and return when you know what it is about.;-)

Struan:

O.K., I concede that I am in entirely the wrong place. I assumed from the web site that the Lila Squad was something that it is not. My mistake. I thank you all for your insights some of which have been very useful (Hugo and Ken in particular though not exclusively).

I give you and everyone my sincere best wishes. I admire your pioneering spirit and quest for truth; the world has more quality because of it.

I shall continue to watch with interest.

Ken:

This situation is approaching the point of ridiculousness. I don't want to see a damper put on the discussions on the Squad, even if everybody is wrong except me. Struan, you are just like Pat Malone, an uncle of mine now dead. He too had an abrasive manner. He could p... you off while handing you a hundred dollar bill. He is now dead but I think he has been reincarnated in you. If you could just switch to a rubber mallet instead of using a sledgehammer in your discussions, I think we would all get along fine.

I am arriving at a position that is not the same as all or most of the rest of the Squad but we are still able to discuss and even criticize each other within the bounds of reasonable discussion. For instance, I think that all of the talk on the Squad about the uncertainty principle giving the boot to determinism shows a misunderstanding of the uncertainty principle. I think that the universe is still deterministic except that I think that deterministic disorder makes the process so complex that the universe is effectively not deterministic.

I also think that the operation of Dynamic Quality as it operated in the pre-sentient period (before humans) should be thoroughly threshed out and understood before we take up the question of human value and morality. I think that the human position in the universe demands that some biological concerns be placed ahead of perceived human concerns. I don't think that there is a conflict; I just think that the mass of humanity does not realize what is ultimately in their best interests.

I could go on but this is by way of demonstrating that I can still participate in Squad discussions and be an accepted member despite my contrary views. I don't think that any of us is in possession of the final answer. We are all on our separate paths. Witness Bo and Doug's differences.

Struan, for my part I wish you would reconsider and rejoin the Squad. Maybe this time you could use a rubber mallet instead of a sledgehammer. :+)

Annotations by Robert M. Pirsig

136. There's no inconsistency here. It's moral for a society to prevent a criminal from destroying it by killing him if that is necessary. But an imprisoned criminal is no longer a threat to society and it becomes arguably immoral to kill him because he is still capable of thought. The Confederates, who started the Civil War by shelling Fort Sumter in South Carolina, were out of prison and shooting and killing men of the United States Army. This is a criminal act. Lincoln made it very clear that although he abominated slavery that was not the cause of the Civil War. He told the Confederates that they did not take an oath of office to destroy the Government of America, but he did take an oath to preserve it. As long as they were attempting by force to destroy the elected government of the United States he had a right to stop them by whatever force was necessary. When they stopped shooting and began obeying the laws of the United States the right to kill them expired. At that point the US Government did stop killing them.

137. Both "the genius" and the mentally retarded person are at the social level. At the intellectual level would be the law that requires them to be treated equally.

138. Ideas are static in the MOQ. The idea that one culture is superior to another goes back to prehistoric times.

139. This has been done in the previous notes.

140. To say that a comment is "stupid" is to imply that the person who makes it is stupid. This is the ad hominem argument: meaning, "to the person." Logically it is irrelevant. If Joe says the sun is shining and you argue that Joe is insane, or Joe is a Nazi or Joe is stupid, what does this tell us about the condition of the sun?

That the ad hominem argument is irrelevant is usually all the logic texts say about it, but the MOQ allows one to go deeper and make what may be an original contribution. It says the ad hominem argument is a form of evil.

The MOQ divides the hominem, or "individual," into four parts: inorganic, biological, social and intellectual. Once this analysis is made, the ad hominem argument can be defined more clearly: it is an attempt to destroy the intellectual patterns of an individual by attacking his social status. In other words, a lower form of evolution is being used to destroy a higher form. That is evil.

However, the MOQ suggests that this only an intellectual evil. In politics, for example, to identify your political opponent as a former Nazi is not evil if he really was a Nazi, because politics is a dominantly social activity rather than an intellectual activity.

141. As I understand it the term "emotivism" is a way of reducing all value to biology, thus making it a part of the SOM universe. The MOQ sees emotions as a biological response to quality and not the same thing as quality. There are many cases, particularly in economic activity where values occur without any emotion.

142. Incorrectly, as a previous note explains.

Chapter 15

"In the sky there is no distinction of east and west; people create distinctions out of their own minds and then believe them to be true." —Buddha

Bells and Whistles [March 1998]

Donny:

I feel a need to comment on the Magnus/Bo/Struan war—I've said time and again that most people approach philosophy with this "we are saved; you are damned" attitude. Pick a position, choose a side, take your favorite "ism" word as a war cry, and set pikes to receive the charge. How many times do I have to say it—it is not only unphilosophical, it's undignified (in other words, some of us feel you're acting like children). Come on, that's Square One stuff and here we are, The Lila Squad! We're supposed to be on Square Three or Four.

Philosophy is not about reaching conclusions, finding the highest position, or uncovering the truth. I like what Wittgenstein said: "If you want to know the truth, go study science." Science pursues truth; philosophy pursues clarity. It's more important to be clear than to be correct!

Philosophy is about exploring the wider view (Hey, wait! What is really going on here?) and exploring alternative points of view, approaches, and thinking about good questions. I want to get a cultural immune system alert. A bell maybe? "Bing! Bing! Bing! Bing! Bing! Bing! Bing!" It goes off whenever this cultural immune system, this thinking about positions, kicks in.

Magnus, you're the High Priest of Pirsig—why don't you be in charge of that? :-7

Magnus:

But to be philosophical and dignified we have to have some common ground, right? I think that the common ground required to be what I think you mean by philosophical and dignified is objectivity. Objectivity makes it possible to rationally reason about different points of views. I'm not really sure exactly at which point we start to drift apart. Do you think that a common ground is required to be philosophical and dignified? Do you think that the common ground is objectivity?

I'll go on assuming "yes" on both of those questions. Whistle if you don't. Here comes the break. The MOQ has abandoned objectivity and has no common ground (with other points of views) on which to be philosophical and dignified. I think we have yet not learned to cope with this. Pirsig chose to write novels instead of lining up in front of the Church of Reason (oops, that triggered an immune system bell, right?) because it's impossible to be philosophical and dignified about the MOQ.

The MOQ agrees. Truth comes with a context, the context in which it is true. Mostly for Struan: the MOQ does not provide absolute answers to ethical dilemmas. It does however provide a framework with which to contextualize dilemmas. [143]

I think that this is what Pirsig has already done—the most viable approach he could come up with was the MOQ. The Lila Squad has also thought about some really interesting questions. Usually, the result of such a question is a little clearer view of some part of the MOQ. Granted, the MOQ is not a question, it's an answer. By the way, this "philosophy is not about getting answers, it's about thinking about good questions," is starting to bug me a little. I saw it in the local newspaper the other day too. Can't really tell why it's bugging me but I'll try keeping the immune system bell handy.

It seems like philosophers think it's a virtue to formulate questions without answers. On second thought, that should be "questions without objective answers." They think it's fun to watch poor students on Square One agonize over the implications of each answer followed by a carefully formulated answer. The philosophy professor however, knows that there is no objective answer to the question, so he can easily spot the flaw of the student's answer and yell: "Ha, you're being subjective!" You're doing exactly the same thing when you say that we're acting like children.

Don't get me wrong—questions are vital. Questions are Dynamic; they impose intellectual change. But they need answers, otherwise no change is achieved and nothing is gained. I usually think of objectively unanswerable questions as evidence of the limits of objectivity.

I'm looking for common grounds here; I hope it shows through. It's not objectivity but at least we're all talking English.

Hugo:

Here in Denmark, a few days ago, a right wing politician was attacked on the street in Copenhagen. This is not everyday stuff here. I can't recall a previous example. The attackers were a group of Autonomous, a radical left wing group of young people. The "reason" for the attack was that in the recent election immigrants and refugees in Denmark were a dominating theme, and this particular politician argued that we were heading towards a multi-ethnic society, and she argued against such a course. The arguments were pretty fierce. She got a good election, by the way.

So, apparently out of humanist concerns, these youngsters violently attacked a politician, a human individual. Politically, this was plain stupid. If they had done it just before the election, she would have had an even better election, and it did raise a lot of public support for her. Later, in a television show, some Autonomous argued that they were squarely against violence, but that the attack was understandable. They failed to say it was wrong.

And sure, the attack was understandable; but that did not make it less wrong, or less stupid. Why am I telling you this local news story? Because it shows a common trap of opposition, by fighting the opposition, you become more and more like the opposition. Gregory Bateson described this process as Schismogenesis, applying it on the cold war escalation, for instance.

I am sure this is a social level kind of process, and part of the driving force of evolution, creating swift antelopes and swift cheetahs in unison. But the intellectual level distinguishes itself by some degree of self-awareness. I hope the Autonomous in

456

Copenhagen can see how stupid and wrong their actions were, upon a little reflection. And I hope that we here at Lila Squad, and elsewhere, will learn to detect Schismogenesis in action, learn to distinguish the self-blind social building of opposing parties from the self-aware process of inquiry. In inquiry, we must hold our little hand mirror up in front of us, every now and then, and investigate our own stance.

Pirsig pointed this out. He offered his Subject Object Metaphysics as a hand mirror to the opposing parts of "subjectivists" and "objectivists," wanting to show them that they were holding their opposition in a mutual stance, like acrobats suspended from a common point. Look, this is how it looks from outside, from my Metaphysics of Quality point of view, he said. Neither of you can stand where you stand without the other—you are keeping each other apart! Nonsense some say—we are right and they are wrong—and they cannot move until they look in that mirror, firmly secured in their opposition as they are.

Let us not move into some other rigid stance of opposition. Let us all not forget to bring our hand mirror with us wherever we go.

A Rubber Mallet [March 1998]

Struan:

Donald was right in his "Bells and Whistles" posting and my reluctance to posit my own position within this forum was motivated in part by my desire to maintain the position he outlines, and thus (can I blame my relative youth?) I betrayed my own convictions. Thank you for helping me see this Donald and my apologies to all.

Thanks to those who have sent emails to me. I appreciate the words contained therein. Being misunderstood I can accept, but being misunderstood and misrepresented seems indicative of a deeper problem. If the general consensus coincides with the view of Bodvar that on this forum Quality must be taken as the "obvious" and is therefore, by extension (mine not his), the God of the Lila Squad then, like the agnostic who stands up in Church and says, "I don't accept your God," I am in the wrong place and I can understand the animosity and peoples' erection of oppositional boundaries in order to maintain group identity. Society is desperate to stifle new ideas, on this much we agree. If this is the case I apologise for the intrusion and perhaps those who want to continue a debate without the closed ideology will recommend to me that we do so in another, more suitable forum. It seems to me that any "handbook on reality" is doomed to failure and anyone who adheres to a hierarchical system of reality will undoubtedly place themselves on top (apart from their God of course). The MOQ is fundamentally anthropocentric and so the dangers are compounded.

Bodvar asked some questions and I failed to respond reasonably so I will do so now. Bodvar asked:

"So for an opening let me ask—do you accept the first quality postulate, about there being nothing but value and that the division is between Dynamic and static value (or quality or moral)? This is not self-evident or provable, that much I know already."

You say there is nothing but value, Bodvar, in other words value is everything. But what is everything? Value? Then all that you are saying is that everything is everything, which doesn't say anything. If it suits you linguistically to use the term "value" then that is fine with me. I prefer the more economical "everything" which doesn't require a tautology for clarification. Having said that I can go along with you so far.

Now, to the division of value (everything) between Dynamic and static value—if we agree there is an "everything" (value as you put it) and I suspect we do, then it would seem clear that we can divide this value in which ever way it suits us. The "everything" doesn't mind; it just carries on being everything. For example, I can divide my garden into a biological part of the whole and an inorganic part of the whole, I can divide it into vegetables, flowers and soil, or I can just say that it is a garden full stop. Alternatively, I can divide it into any other classification that I see fit. All of these boundaries are equally valid. Again, if you want to draw a boundary between these two aspects of "everything" than I am happy to go along with you.

So we agree. But what does this tell us? I don't see that you have said anything more than that the universe is a universe (one-whole) and that you want to place a dividing line between what you define as Dynamic and static value (or pure experience and filtered experience or however you feel most comfortable expressing it). Simply by making that division of one into two you entertain some form of dualism, but I can see why you want to do so.

I think your language is rather convoluted but I see no reason (or non-reason) not to accept this and indeed have thought for some time that it is self-evident.

I like Pirsig's mountain analogy and with far less literary skill would like to extend it. When you climb to the highest peaks, you have to be mighty careful that the path you forge is taking you in the right direction. If you stray in the lower regions there is always someone to call you back, but up in the rarefied heights you are out of reach of the voices of others below and so the wilderness threatens more than ever. One day the others might pass you, but by now you are so far into the wilderness you can't register their passing and their voices seem unreal. If only you had listened to that fool at the bottom who implored you to take a map, but of course you knew where you were going and God was on your side. What could possibly go wrong?

Donny:

I think a (I won't say "problem" but) complication here is that it seems to me that a third of the Lila Squad (a lot of the lurkers, I think) are fans who read Pirsig's books, think he's a cool guy and a kick-butt writer, and joined up out of admiration, in other words, for them the Lila Squad is like a fan club. And that's cool, but— another third are philosophically inclined types who think Pirsig has the answer in the MOQ and the Squad should be flushing out the MOQ and asking, "What does Pirsig mean by…" and "What would Pirsig say about...." This is the third that tends to get bent out of sorts by alien SOM—the enemy.

Then, Struan, there are some who, while also interested in philosophy, think: well, R.M. Pirsig didn't spend his career studying my philosophy; why should I spend my "career" in philosophy studying him? In other words, we're more interested in working out our own worldviews more or less in relation to Pirsig's MOQ, but not dependent upon it. As I said, this isn't a problem, just a complication. Different people come to the Lila Squad with a different agenda/approach/expectations. Maybe we should shoot for a happy— no, Quality—balance? A Dynamic balance?

Bodvar:

I don't know how to formulate myself not to sound convoluted, but I am glad to see you back. If you find me the pompous self appointed "ideologist" of the Lila Squad (my words entirely) you are possibly right, but once upon the time Pirsig's idea resolved a quandary that threatened my peace of mind (to say the least) and I cannot but try to repay my debt. About this, I am probably emotivistic and willing to overlook a few soft spots in Lila. I find Pirsig's achievement so enormous that it would be superhuman to get everything right at once. It is up to us to probe the various openings that the MOQ allows.

I accept your value/everything point. As I see it, Pirsig chose the term because it is the weak spot of, if you allow, the subject/object worldview. It is shunned like the plague, but impossible to get rid of. Also do I accept that the MOQ is dualistic and that also SOM is a division of everything. Pirsig even calls it a "Quality metaphysics," it only divides everything differently. Also that it was an exaggeration of me to call the Quality idea obvious within the Lila Squad; it obviously isn't.

If I now infuriate you by sounding so meek, I'll even comply with your Occam argument. The MOQ isn't more economical, but the next criterion of explanatory power it fulfills is light years ahead of the SOM. I know that, umm, SOM more than anything

460

else would like to see the Quality undivided—another Eastern mysticism. That's the hardheaded value. And emotionless rationalists could deem harmless New Age religious nonsense, but Phædrus put his knife upon the fault line of the mind/matter notion and it split open in a way that, like Humpty Dumpty, can't be put together again.

Ken:

Bo, I know how passionate you feel about the Metaphysics of Quality, and I know the amount of time and study and thought you have put into it but when one gets our ages passions cool and we can show forbearance toward the younger ones whose passions are more immediate and urgent. I can still remember when I knew everything. Even if it does not ultimately answer all of our questions, I think that the MOQ can help to make us more comfortable in the situation that we are caught in without a reasonable recourse.

Bodvar:

Sorry for sounding so Jesuitical, but I had to preempt the attack. If Struan had been given the right to choose the weapon/premises, I would have been easy prey. Anyway, he is back and that's fine. Otherwise, your good points are taken.

Existence of SOM [March 1998]

Horse:

Lila Squad, sorry for the delay in replying but I wanted to think about this carefully. There are a number of points raised, which I would like to address. Some of these points are addressed to Struan whilst others are general.

The points to cover are:

1) Existence of Subject Object Metaphysics [144]

2) Emotivism and MOQ

3) Rationality

4) MacIntyre and Communitarianism

It looks like a lot but obviously I'm not going to do an in depth analysis of everything. Some of the above will get mixed together at various stages, so please bear with me.

1) Existence of Subject Object Metaphysics

Sorry to labour the point but I think it is important. You may not subscribe to this view and you say that the foremost names in ethics today don't either. I presume that you mean, in addition to MacIntyre, Taylor, Sandel, Waltzer, etc., but would exclude Rawls, Nozick, and other liberalist/libertarian thinkers. Just a guess. There may be no direct reference to SOM as such but this is the underlying view of existence and the framework upon which "rational" thought is based. The rational thought that I am referring to is the framework upon which "Western" reality rests. This can be traced back to Aristotle and beyond, but is generally seen to have been formalised by Aristotle. From this tradition we have the dualist view of existence; subject/object, mind/matter, etc., further supported by Kant, Kierkegaard, Hume, etc.

This is, I believe, what is referred to as the subject/object metaphysics. In a general way it can be summed up as a or not a. That is to say, all things either are or are not. A very simple test to show that the dualistic method is at the heart of most western thinking is to ask a scientist or philosopher what they think of multi-valued or fuzzy logic. Of those that have heard of it the majority will say that it is nothing more than probability. Many others have stated that fuzzy logic is either false logic or simply refuse to discuss it. Prof. William Kahan of UCB described it as "the cocaine of science." The problems that have been encountered attempting to integrate something as simple, obvious, and intuitive as this have been enormous. It goes against the grain of bivalent logic, which is established Western logic. I agree with you, Struan, that better educated and less myopic individuals are gradually coming around to a multi-valued view of existence but the progress is slow. The MOQ is an example of the gradual shift. Chaos, fuzziness, and quantum mechanics are other examples. But as far as I am aware none of the others are encompassed by a complete metaphysics. They are, in the main, anomalies within SOM. You are definitely wrong in your view that the SOM is necessary as some sort of counterpoint to MOQ. Subject and Object are not rejected; they are just seen as opposite ends of a particular spectrum with an infinity of possibilities in between. This goes for other aspects of a dualist reality. The MOQ is purely a base from which to explore other aspects of reality. You have your way, we have ours. To say that we are wrong and you are right is pointless, elitist, and dualist.

2) Emotivism and MOQ

I think that with emotivism we need to look at the ideas of the philosophical school that produced this term, that of logical positivism. You can basically sum up their entire ethos in a single sentence: if the subject of a sentence cannot be measured and/or expressed mathematically then that sentence has no meaning. In other words if you can't poke it or formulate it, it doesn't exist— another classic dualist example, objective or subjective. The school of logical positivism (LP) was a response to the domination by the (mainly) Christian Church of established thought patterns and beliefs. It was an attempt by a number of individuals to place scientific thought and structure at the top of the belief system hierarchy. By displacing the church as the propagator of truth, science becomes the only way to express beliefs about the universe and reality in general. LP tried to reduce philosophy to no more than linguistic analysis.

If you disagreed with this system then you were an emotivist. A few hundred years prior to this, you would have been called a heretic and burnt at the stake. Logical positivism had one fatal flaw. It was wrong. The logical positivists had reduced science to an ideology of false consciousness. As I said in my previous post, one of LP's formulators, Karl Popper, realised as much and had the grace to admit it. So, logical positivism, as with so many traditions and belief systems, uses the ideas of conformance and exclusion in order to achieve and maintain its own importance. Either you are within the framework and one of the cognoscenti or you are not and thus are wrong, misguided, heretical, etc. LP by definition does not accept the validity of values, as they are neither measurable nor open to expression within mathematics. Values are

463

not objective and are consequently mere subjectivist ramblings. By definition then, the MOQ, which is based on values has no meaning and is thus irrelevant. A nice twist. This is very much the sort of orthodoxy that Pirsig came up against with anthropology and Boas.

3) Rationality

What exactly is this rationality then? (A good title for a book maybe!) It seems to be a relative term; relative to what is considered true at any given point in time. It is certainly not an absolute term as history shows. Starting from the pre-Socratic Greeks it has been redefined so many times that in some ways it has tended to lose any credibility that it may have once had. It is no more than another way of saying that if you are a right thinking person and you accept current dogma regarding reality then you are a rational person. To be rational is to be sane and to be irrational is to be insane. Again, right or wrong, rational or irrational. You used pretty much this dualist idea yourself. I suppose we could use the term non-rational to mean that one understands the position of rationality but feel that it is incorrect. At least this is less likely to get you carted off to the nut house. Again, we come to ideology and the idea that what is true is that which the majority believes. If you do not believe what you are supposed to believe, as the majority of people do, then you are not rational and must be re-adjusted until you once again align with rationality. Historical examples of rational thinking are that God exists, religious creationism, the Earth is flat, the Universe is geocentric, etc. This is a marvelous tool in the propagandist's toolbox; one that the social manipulators use mercilessly. But obviously, as I don't accept the rational point of view then what I say cannot have any meaning! So here's what we have so far—that the term Subject/Object Metaphysics refers to the dualistic school of thought which believes that things are or they are not; a or not a. That the term emotivism is a catch all rebuke to ensure that we don't stray outside the bounds of logical necessity. That rationality is no more than conformity to a commonly held belief.

4) MacIntyre and Communitarianism

This could be tricky. I came across MacIntyre about two years ago whilst reading The Principles of Biomedical Ethics, by Beauchamp and Childress. He was described as a Communitarian philosopher/ethicist, and having dug out a couple of books that refer to his framework of thought, I see no reason to dispute this. My apologies to yourself, Struan, and to MacIntyre, but I feel that MacIntyre and the rest of the Communitarian ethicists are so caught up with the idea that society is the pinnacle of evolution that I want to puke. This is not to say that I feel that society and social activities are unimportant, I just believe that some individual rights are of greater importance than the rights of society. This is probably the crux of our disagreement. At this point, you can call me irrational, emotivist, or whatever you like, but I have not seen any evidence so far, presented by either yourself, MacIntyre, or anyone else, to make me believe otherwise.

From this point on much my information regarding MacIntyre and Communitarianism is from:

The Principles of Biomedical Ethics (Beauchamp and Childress)

Liberals and Communitarians (Mulhall and Swift). (Horse's slightly blurred recollections of an Open University course on Ethics, Life, and Death.)

As I understand it, the basis of MacIntyre's ethical framework is based on Aristotelian virtue, or to be more accurate, it is a reconstruction of neo-Aristotelian virtue based ethics. He uses three central concepts; that of:

1) Practice
2) The Narrative Unity of a Human Life
3) Tradition

1) Practice

The concept of Practice revolves around any activity that is coherent and complex and part of some co-operative human activity. Internal goods are achieved through that Practice. Also, if an activity lacks internal goods it does not count as a Practice. This provides the basis for MacIntyre's first definition of the virtues:

"A virtue is an acquired human quality the possession and exercise of which tends to enable us to achieve those goods which are internal to practices and the lack of which effectively prevents us from achieving any such goods." (MacIntyre, After Virtue) So participation in practices is essential for possession and exercise of the virtues. This effectively forces any person that wishes to participate of virtuousness into social interaction. The one is only obtainable through the other. By entering into social interaction, rules pertaining to that social interaction will be inherited. Those rules will provide the basis for rational debate concerning the practice. An example of a practice is Chess. This is sufficiently coherent and complex, is a social activity, and involves rules that make debate about a chess match a rational exercise. As long as we stick to discussing chess within the framework of those rules, our debate is rational.

2) The Narrative Unity of a Human Life

With The Narrative Unity of a Human Life, MacIntyre looks at the intentions, desires, and goals of a person and relates them to the actions that take place in a person's life and the settings in which those actions take place. There are two types of intention—short term and long term—and a number of desires and goals. MacIntyre seeks to relate a person's history to the history of the settings within which actions take place. For an action to be intelligible, it must be seen as an episode in the history of a person's life. A person's life thus becomes a form of narrative—a biography—wherein each of his actions is seen as part of a greater whole. In addition, each narrative is part of a greater narrative and the relationships between individual narratives create complex social interactions. So there are both individual and shared narratives. MacIntyre refers to it thus: "If the narrative of our individual lives is to continue intelligibly, and either type of narrative may lapse into unintelligibility, it is always the case both that there are constraints on how the story can continue and that within those constraints there are indefinitely many ways in which it can continue." (MacIntyre, After Virtue) The framework of the Narrative form provides a person with the means of making a rational choice when different practices exert conflicting demands. A person must constantly ask, "How may I best live out the narrative of my life?" in their quest to achieve the good life. The quest and the constant reference to both the individual and the shared narrative educates the person about themselves and what they are seeking. MacIntyre now offers a revised definition of the virtues which is:

"...[They] are to be understood as those dispositions which not only sustain practices and enable us to achieve the goods internal to them, but will also sustain us in the relevant quest for the good by enabling us to overcome the harms, dangers, temptations, and distractions which we encounter, and which will furnish us with increasing self knowledge and increasing knowledge of the good." (MacIntyre, After Virtue)

3) Tradition

With the concept of Tradition, MacIntyre starts to relate Practice and Narratives into a historical framework:

"...As such I inherit from the past of my family, my city, my tribe, my nation, a variety of debts, inheritances, rightful expectations, and obligations." (MacIntyre, After Virtue)

So the possession of a historical and social identity coincide. Tradition thus becomes membership of a socially inherited set of Practices within a larger historical Narrative and with this MacIntyre moves toward a position that we are not solely responsible for the way in which our lives are formed or progress. Where people are understood as members of traditions, the history of their own life becomes part of the larger historical narrative with its consequent argument for an extension within the historical and current social framework. Rational decisions can be made against this background and determine the person's available resources as to how best to pursue the good life. All rational decisions will be made in terms of a tradition's best understanding of itself in relation to the practice of that tradition and by evaluating and criticizing alternatives within the overall historical and social framework.

The above is an extremely condensed explanation of the theory put forward by MacIntyre in After Virtue. It not a full or complete account but gives a general taste of the direction in which he is heading. There is more of the same in Whose Justice? Which Rationality? and Three Rival Versions of Moral Inquiry.

MacIntyre is generally seen as a militant or extreme Communitarian. The Communitarian view is that everything fundamental to moral principles derives from communal values, the common good, social goals, traditional practices, and co-operative virtues. Liberalism is rejected by militant communitarians as it does not allow the subsumption of individual belief and enterprise by the community. The more moderate form does, to an extent, try to accommodate some forms of liberal belief.

Militant communitarianism is extremely hostile to individual rights and sees the libertarian as antagonistic towards tradition. It aims to impose on individual's conceptions of virtue and the good life and limit or eradicate those rights conferred by liberal societies. Only by acceptance of Communitarian ethos can a person be seen as rational as the idea of rationality is defied by Communitarian and social principles.

So here, we have a system that is blatantly and exclusively social in its approach to morality. No account is taken of individuality except in the sense that there is an acknowledgment that people are constituents in a social system. The notion that individuals and their ideas are of any consequence is subsumed by the needs of the society. This is a philosophy for ants and termites. It is also the embodiment of the social/intellectual struggle, which Pirsig has pointed to in Lila. This whole debate in many ways is a re-enactment of the conflicts that Pirsig talks about. The objectification of a system of Moral Values parallels the Boas treatment of anthropology. Apparently, we are excluded from talking about values in any way other than through the so-called rational methods put forth by MacIntyre. If we do then we are being emotivist. (This also parallels nicely with the psychobabble expression "in denial.")

An edifice is being constructed which disallows any form of "irrational" values. Communitarianism and its proponents are a growing force in moral philosophy. They are building on the foundations of neo-Aristotelian virtue. As Boas and others succeeded in doing with anthropology, Communitarians are turning ethics in a science with the consequent exclusion of values. But values and value judgments are the very basis of ethical systems. This debate is, I suspect, the first of many that will be directed toward MOQ and those of us in the Lila Squad who wish to see MOQ succeed as the successor to SOM are going to have a fight on our hands. SOM has twenty five hundred years of momentum on its side. MOQ is barely out of the womb.

I'd better conclude at this point as this is getting overly long (I can almost hear some of you snoring). I would like to hear from others in the Lila Squad who feel that this is important and discuss ways in which future assaults can be dealt with.

Struan:

I will answer your points quite briefly at the moment as I still think you have the wrong end of the stick with regards to what I am trying to say.

Horse:

Entirely possible. A human failing from which I suffer sometimes.

Struan:

I have promised myself that I'm not going to distract myself into side issues that I have views upon, but are not relevant to my position. I hope that this is not ungracious of me and will answer any specific points you put to me.

I will take up your example of fuzzy logic: "Of those that have heard of it the majority will say that it is nothing more than probability."

I am interested to know how you came to this conclusion about scientists. Did you actually ask them and if so, how many? Or have you simply decided what you think they will say and written it here?

Horse:

I reached this conclusion due to my own experience, that of others that I have talked to, and a number of references which I have used in the past. But you are right, this is rank inductivism and I am guilty. Mea culpa! (We've got to get rid of some of these "ism's"!)

Struan:

It happens by coincidence that I was visiting Leicester DeMontford University a few weeks ago where there is a great deal of research going on into fuzzy logic and it seems clear to me from speaking to one chap who was involved in this research that they do not in any way see fuzzy logic as outside the bounds of science. What I was told was that fuzzy logic is a mathematical model for representing uncertainty. So for example, if I throw a tennis ball, conventional mathematics will find it impossible (due to the complexity of the action and context) to be certain where it will land. Fuzzy logic allows you to work within an area of uncertainty. The same chap was absolutely clear that this system is formal mathematics with membership grades being precise numbers. He left me in no doubt that this is a logic of fuzziness, not a logic that is in itself fuzzy. You are totally wrong in saying that it "goes against the grain of bivalent logic which is established Western logic." It does absolutely nothing of the sort and moreover as a mathematical model, it cannot go against established Western logic because it relies completely upon it. If it didn't accept mathematics, it wouldn't exist because that is all it is.

In fuzzy logic there is a principle known as the Extension Principle, which establishes quite categorically that crisp (traditional) subsets are fuzzy subsets and so there is no conflict whatsoever between fuzzy and crisp methodology. I'm afraid that you will have to do a lot better than point to fuzzy logic if you want to persuade me that modern science is steeped in SOM. You state yourself that this is very important, but why is it for you? I suggest MOQ needs SOM and I think you know it. You write:

"You are definitely wrong in your view that the SOM is necessary as some sort of counterpoint to MOQ. Subject and Object are not rejected, they are just seen as opposite ends of a particular spectrum with an infinity of possibilities in between."

Have a look at my Rubber Mallet posting for my view on this. I don't see SOM as a counterpoint to MOQ. I see the MOQ as evolving from SOM and thus being contingent upon it and upon refugees from it. And are you able to escape your own charge of being pointless, elitist, and dualist when you say I am wrong? And further, you say, "Logical positivism had one fatal flaw. It was wrong." You have your way, they have theirs. I only point this out because whenever I have said something like that, people tell me I'm stuck in a SOM pattern and can't be expected to understand. It's become akin to being accused of a pact with the devil.

I think you misunderstand Emotivism as rejecting anything that cannot be observed. On the contrary, it gives emotions absolute validity in ethical systems. It raises them to the highest possible level, recognises their value, and shows people that morality is not just a dry rational formula. Emotivism allows the construction of the MOQ and gives it a big thumbs up. You have it totally the other way round and are confusing the technical term "meaning" with the popular use of meaning. Emotivism is the affirmation of the value of emotions, not the rejection of the value. Your misperception is more common than you think and comes from popular analysis and (dare I say it) the Social Moral Values that our leaders want us to swallow. Yes, Emotivism came out of Logical Positivism but it gave a whole new slant that I invite you to explore. I really don't want to get into much further debate on this issue as I think it has been one of the major causes of friction

471

between others and myself. My way is not your way, so perhaps another approach is better.

I have no fundamental problems with your analysis of rationality. The only point I would make is firstly to state that if you think I am typing this message out using my eyelashes at sixty words per minute then you are being irrational. You may object to the semantics, but you know precisely what I mean just in the same way as Pirsig's students saw Quality in essays they were required to mark. You can't just simplistically write off the word as meaning sane or insane and you also have used the dualist idea of right and wrong. Thus, I repeat what I said in a personal email to a Squad member and say (and please forgive the expression) that there is a difference between being "irrational" and being "irrationally irrational." I have no problem with the Lila Squad or anyone else being irrational. My problems start when they become "irrationally irrational."

So I suggest that what we have so far is a series of misunderstandings of each of the points you rebuke me for. I'm not going to become a spokesman for MacIntyre as I have given lectures upon his flaws and upon his strengths and know them reasonably well. If you don't agree with his ethical system then that is fine with me as I have plenty of problems with it myself. I do think you fail to do him justice and suggest that the only reason he "makes you want to puke" is that you have set yourself up a rigid hierarchy which denies the importance of context in assessing value, but I'm not sure there is much point, in this context, of us getting deeper into it (unless you think otherwise?).

I'm sure you will have noticed my reticence to expand these ideas in past postings and my reticence continues simply because I'm not sure a general discussion of ethics is going to be of any direct use to the MOQ or this forum. If the positions of other ethicists becomes relevant as the "ethics based on MOQ" discussion continues then I'm sure they can be brought in as needs be. Please feel free to disagree, but I would suggest that ethical discussions here would be best served by having the MOQ at the centre rather than MacIntyre, Murdoch, Berlin, or anyone else. If you and others can start to construct a practical ethical system based on the MOQ then I would offer my oar from an outside perspective, which you can take or leave.

What do you think?

Horse:

To go quickly through some of the other points, as the main issue here is MOQ and not fuzzy logic, I would refer to Lofti Zadeh, who I believe first used the term "fuzzy logic" and is often referred to as the father of fuzzy logic:

"...Rather than regarding fuzzy theory as a single theory, we should regard the process of 'fuzzification' as a methodology to generalize any specific theory from a crisp (discrete) to a continuous (fuzzy) form...."

This ties in with what you say regarding the extension principle, which states:

"...That the classical results of Boolean logic are recovered from fuzzy logic operations when all fuzzy membership grades are restricted to the traditional set $\{0, 1\}$. This effectively establishes fuzzy subsets and logic as a true generalization of classical set theory and logic. In fact, by this reasoning all crisp (traditional) subsets are fuzzy subsets of this very special type; and there is no conflict between fuzzy and crisp methods."

This position, however, took years to establish and is in effect a triumph of reason over stubborn refusal to accept fuzzy logic as a superset that contained crisp logic in much the same way that MOQ contains SOM. This seems to be the position that Pirsig takes. Fuzzy methodology is now becoming established as valid thirty plus years after Zadeh challenged the mathematics of systems theory. I used fuzzy logic as an example, as MOQ fuzzy logic seem parallel in many ways, so when you say:

"...I see the MOQ as evolving from SOM and thus being contingent upon it and upon refugees from it..." this seems to imply that Subject/Object (substance) is prior to Quality. This is not the case from the point of view of MOQ whereby Quality (Dynamic) is prior to Subject and/or Object.

I didn't say that emotivism rejects anything that cannot be observed. This is the position of the more extreme logical positivist (LP) such as A.J. Ayer. To be more accurate Ayer talked of subjectivism rather than emotivism but the two terms are often used interchangeably. Here you misunderstand my point. The LP stance on emotivism is, I believe, that any moral argument is invalid as there are no empirical tests that can be performed on it and if we accept that ethical statements are not empirically valid judgments, then such propositions can't be controlled by observation, and must be seen as mere intuition.

I found the next bit on the net: "One problem with this argument is that logical positivism is self refuting. It claims any genuine truth claim must be able to be tested by sense experience. But this claim itself can't be tested by sense experience. So, by its own standard, logical positivism can't be a genuine truth claim." Which pretty much supports my claim that they are wrong, hoisted on their own petard. Personally, I have no problem with emotivism.

I didn't go further with MacIntyre as I didn't want my last post to turn into a book (which it was in danger of doing) so I only gave the outlines of his stance in After Virtue. The main reason that MacIntyre's position makes me feel ill is for a far better set of reasons than that I am set in a rigid hierarchy (I hope!). Some of these reasons are political, so I shall try to avoid them where possible. Others are ethical, or more accurately, objections to the ethical system of radical Communitarianism as it currently exists and the position that MacIntyre holds within that system.

Communitarianism, where it upholds the rights of a social system to protect itself from the biological excesses of its individual members can be acceptable. Where it attempts to destroy the intellectual rights of individuals over society (freedom of speech, etc.) I take issue. This is often the difference in belief between a moderate and a radical Communitarian. Another problem is that with much of Communitarianism, and MacIntyre in particular, this system is based on neo-Aristotelian Virtue theory. The big problem here is that this is a personal ethical system, which does nothing whatsoever to curb the excesses of the real social problem, the social institutions of government, church, and the multi-nationals.

Communitarianism plays right into their hands. No wonder these institutions advocate such a system. The proles get on with being nice people whilst the institutions get on with shafting us; this is repeated again and again throughout history and will continue whilst idiots like MacIntyre propound their particular brand of oppression. Oops! Sorry I'm getting political but hopefully you see the point I am making.

One final point about MacIntyre, et al., is similar to the above section on Logical Positivism. When a system of belief is designed with the intention of excluding other systems of belief with which it disagrees and which would damage it, and then states that the excluded systems are invalid due to the definition of the excluding system, something is terribly wrong. By defining rationality in terms of his own system and then calling other systems irrational is rank stupidity on MacIntyre's part. This is a dishonest system and more, it is immoral (unless one believes in a system which says that intellectual dishonesty is moral).

Personally, I would welcome your direct input with regard to constructing a practical ethical system based on the MOQ. I don't want to be presumptuous and speak for others though. I think this little bout has made some of us think carefully about MOQ and ethics and I'm really glad you have said what you have. So, waddaya say Struan. I know you're up to your neck in it at the moment but hopefully you could spare some time.

Struan:

Nice rhetoric Horse. Misplaced, but nice.

Horse:

Misplaced? Never! Rhetoric? I thank you as an admirer of Protagoras and all other Sophists, living, dead and somewhere in between.

SOM as Intellect [March 1998]

Bodvar:

Horse, your piece could have been twice as long. Never have I been more awake than when reading this. I subscribe to every point and can only add one thing—the Communitarianism movement has gone me completely by (since involving myself in the Lila Squad I haven't read a single book on contemporary culture/philosophy!) but if that is what Struan follows he may have all his wishes fulfilled within the MOQ framework. You will know that Pirsig is not blind to the needs of "society," not at all. Much of the hostile reactions to Lila from the liberals stems from this mostly misunderstood aspect of the MOQ.

I am looking forward to discussing these points of Lila with you in the future but for now, I feel that a bend is rounded in our way ahead. For a while, I thought that you and Struan had a hoax going (you two obviously knew each other from before) to wake us from our complacency, but this entry convinces me of your sincerity.

Struan: are we still talking? Well, I take the chance even after my "chairman" antics. You said that it was no new idea, and this I would have liked you to elaborate. I am all smiles if that can be shown.

The above about the MOQ evolving from SOM as a metaphysics I agree with fully. It is the SAIOM confirmed again. This notion of Subject/Object thinking as the Intellectual level of the MOQ mops everything up. No ostracizing of enemies, SOM is the highest moral, only subservient to Dynamic Quality itself.

Struan:

The day that I know everything is the day that I will stop talking to highly intelligent people such as yourself. I have no doubt that that day will never come, so talk away. I'm not so sure you will be all smiles at my answer. I am having difficulty in seeing Quality as anything other than Ultimate Reality, God, Allah, or whatever other name we wish to ascribe to that which we see as the font of all "things." If this is the case then many religions have taken the stance that the human mind and its expression as rationalism is the greatest good below their Ultimate Reality.

We can see this in Christianity where many claim that God is beyond reason and some consider it the height of anthropomorphic blasphemy to try to reduce Him to our level. When people claim that Quality is indefinable, the source (creator?) of everything, timeless, etc., then I find it difficult to draw any fundamental non-semantic distinction between the MOQ and mystical aspects of almost any religion. What am I missing here?

I would suspect that our disagreement on this point starts with my suspicion that MOQ not only evolved from SOM but also is contingent upon it. If I am right in thinking that SOM is dead and has been for a long time then the usefulness of the MOQ disappears along with it. I'm hoping that it can be shown that the MOQ does not need to be oppositional to SOM, but one only has to browse through this forum to see that most contributors are so busy deriding SOM they don't get onto constructing a coherent MOQ. This I feel is a shame, because a large number of intelligent people are going to look at the MOQ and conclude that it holds nothing of value for them because they never accepted SOM in the first place. Is it not time to lay off SOM and concentrate on MOQ?

Platt:

Why does Nature correspond to mathematics? Because Nature was created by the pattern-making power of mind, a transcendent mathematician if you will, seeking to recreate itself, just for the fun of it, a very high value in the pantheon of values.

Struan:

If I had said that, I would have been accused of being stuck in SOM and quite rightly too. Is this not simply restating the idealism that Pirsig so wanted to dispose of? (Chapter 12, Lila.) If, "Nature was created by the pattern making power of mind," then this would categorically place mind as fundamental to the universe with the physical brain merely being a detector of a transcendental mind. This view arose out of dualism, particularly when combined with Descartes personal view that mind is more immediate and certain than anything material and as such fails for the following reasons. I argue against it on its own terms here and will come to an MOQ interpretation later.

If mind is more fundamental than matter, then there must be at least one mind that is neither physical nor dependent on anything physical. For if every mind were physical or dependent on the physical, we would have to say that matter is more fundamental than mind. If a mind exists completely non-physically, then its existence must be subjective. This means that the mind's identity depends upon what some mind believes it is. By the law of excluded middle, the mind that its identity depends on must be either itself or another mind.

If it is another mind, then that mind must be either physical or non-physical. If it is physical, then matter is more fundamental then mind. Since that contradicts our original assumption, it must be nonphysical. It can't be true that each mind owes its existence to another mind, for something must exist before it can make something else exist. Therefore, idealism requires that there be at least one nonphysical mind that is responsible for its own existence and whose identity depends upon its own beliefs about itself. It is whatever it believes it is.

Consider now the strange theory of truth that arises from the existence of such a being. Instead of being correspondence to reality, truth is merely whatever the being believes about itself, and reality is merely correspondence with truth. Instead of having knowledge grounded in truth and truth grounded in reality, this theory has reality grounded in truth and truth grounded in knowledge. This is a complete reversal of the correspondence theory of truth.

Suppose, now, that the being chooses to believe that he is a physical being. Since believing something is what makes it true, such a being can truthfully believe that he is physical. Yet, it is because he is not physical that the reverse correspondence theory of truth is true for him. Thus, such a being who believes himself to be physical is both physical and non-physical. Since that is a contradiction (I stress that I am arguing against idealism on its own terms here), there can be no such thing as a non-physical mind whose identity depends upon its own beliefs about itself.

Since such a mind had to exist in order for there to be any nonphysical minds in an idealist universe, the universe is either an idealistic one without non-physical minds, or idealism is false. Since an idealist universe without non-physical minds is a contradiction, idealism must be false. Of course, you don't state explicitly whether you see this mind as being purely mental and in MOQ terms, I wouldn't expect you to think this to be the case. You do however draw the distinction between Nature and mind ("because Nature was created by the pattern making power of mind") so I take it you have some fundamental dualism there.

If you were to view this mind in MOQ terms as being of the same substance as Nature (i.e., Quality) [145] then you seem to be moving towards a "panpsychism" position where all physical things have a mental side and vice versa. I don't see that you do subscribe to this as you postulate a fully developed mind as primary while panpsychism postulates a primitive undeveloped form of mind within all matter that is developed into more complex forms by evolution. [146]

It strikes me that you are putting forward a good argument for the traditional God of Western religion—a great mind, which creates all of Nature. Is this not your "transcendental mathematician?" [147]

Pirsig on Space [April 1998]

Donny:

Something else that might interest you all is Process Philosophy. I don't know much about it, but the bottom line is that what really exists is not a thing but a process. The universe is flux, a movement (presumably towards something). I believe Alfred North Whitehead is the big guy in this camp (this "ism").

479

Ant:

I've never read Whitehead either, though from the times I've heard him mentioned in the Department, he seems to be on similar lines to Buddhist philosophy and Pirsig. He is also mentioned in Lila. From what you've written here it seems that the MOQ could be said to be a type of process philosophy in the sense that the universe is a flux and a movement towards something better. I will ask a few of the Department's tutors whether they've heard of it and come back to you if anyone has.

Donny:

We forget that Aristotle's Nichomacheian Ethics is Part One of a two-part work on Politics. For Aristotle the moral unit isn't the individual; it's the polis, the city-state. The "subject" here is most certainly not an internal psyche; it's a society.

Ant:

That's an interesting point I did not know before.

Donny:

Pirsig never escaped the Church. He just set up a new denomination. What the Church is, is this need to pick an "ism," make it a war cry, to select an enemy (the SOM-ites), and dig in to the trenches. I've said before, I find that mentality unphilosophical and undignified. It's the result of trying to force fit philosophy into an academic setting. More later.

Ant:

I see your point here Donny but the introduction of a mystic element in Pirsig's MOQ sets it outside the Church of Reason. You could say, uncharitably, that Pirsig has set up a new church, the Church of Reason and Intuition. However, I think this is uncharitable as Pirsig's MOQ seems to be aimed more towards individuals changing things (in their everyday lives) by using the MOQ rather than institutions employing it on a wider "political" level.

Donny:

Now that's where one might find "subjective" and "objective." What about this idea of the (knowing) subject and (known) object?

In ZMM, Pirsig is clear that experience is the result of the bumping together of subject and object.

Ant:

No! That is to fundamentally misunderstand ZMM. Experience creates subjects and objects. Subjects and objects are derivations from experience, not the other way round.

Pirsig (ZMM): out of Quality come forth subjects and objects (approximately meaning Mind/Body) and experience is the result of a subject and an object encountering one another. But Quality is not in experience, for it, after all, gives rise to experience (Lila). Quality is experience. Experience is Quality.

Donny:

Maybe, but as far as ZMM goes I seem to recall him saying something like: Quality creates experience—subjects and objects— and thus is not itself directly experienced. We never know Quality, as such, in itself, unless we do collapse that "I/other" distinction and zip on off to nirvana and/or the nut house) which is neither subject or object.

Now obviously you can't create yourself (experience creating experience). That's Quality in its role of the transcendental skyhook (the thing in itself).

Pirsig sheds his Eastern flavor and says what really exists is only Quality.

Ant:

Sorry to correct you again Donny but he certainly doesn't shed his Eastern flavour in Lila. In the latter part of this, he clearly states that Dharma is an Eastern term for Quality.

Donny:

Yes, I know. I'm saying his ontology is less Eastern. As he moves away from "out of the Tao," there come forth pairs of opposites, and out of the pairs of opposites come forth all experience. I could be wrong, but my impression is that in Lila he's always talking about what's in time, while ZMM resonates more with transcendental mysticism (talking about what's "beyond" time, the atemporal unity). Or these could just be shadows of different mindsets I was in when I first read each book (shrug).

Quality has two states (these are my own words): the potential and the realized (the in itself and the for itself in Hegelian lingo). As his diagram in the Einstein Magritte article shows (on the [http://www.moq.org] web page) he identifies inorganic and organic static patterns of value as "objects," and social and intellectual static patterns of value as "subjects," saying that these insubstantial things are a higher form of value evolution than the spatially extended, solid "stuff."

Ant:

Two points here: "space" is a SOM construct; it is simply a useful fiction. Secondly, subjects and objects are only analogous to the static patterns in the MOQ (for instance, there's no evolutionary link between subjects and objects and very often no recognition of continual change within the SOM theories). Moreover, as Bodvar has said to me previously, Pirsig only equated subjects and objects with static intellectual patterns for his Einstein Magritte paper so as not to alienate his audience in Belgium too much. He certainly does not believe they are literally equivalent.

Magnus:

Any static pattern of value can be subject or object in any experience, a Quality event.

Ant:

From the MOQ point of view, there are no such things as subjects or objects.

Magnus:

There must still be a subject in the Quality event of two colliding atoms. Both atoms are not objects. Both atoms are subjects from its point of view. On the other hand, when you hear a new idea (an intellectual pattern of value), you probably consider yourself to be the subject and the idea to be the object, right?

Ant:

Wrong. What you've written here Magnus is a very good example of looking at the MOQ from within the SOM prison. This is not to say it is easy for anyone, including myself, brought up using subjects and objects, to break out of it. In the above passage, from the MOQ point of view (and remember this is the system we are trying to establish here, not some type of SOM from which your comments are derived) the atoms, "you," and the new "idea" are the following:

1. Both the colliding atoms are inorganic static patterns of value.

2. "You" are a collection of inorganic, biological, social, and intellectual static patterns of value.

3. The "idea" is an intellectual static pattern of value. Moreover, keep in mind that there has to be another person, directly or indirectly, where this new idea comes from, it just doesn't appear in thin air out on its own.

Doug makes the related point: "In classical SOM science assumes, objectively, that an object may be isolated from its environment (while) MOQ shows us that static patterns of value (SPoVs) are cowithin Dynamic Quality. SPoVs are inseparable from: DQ and other SPoVs in DQ."

This is worth repeating in conjunction with what I've written above as the SOM myth (which you are perpetuating) that an observer may objectively observe an object in isolation has to be laid to rest before you can understand the MOQ properly.

Magnus:

I agree completely, but I can't repeat that in each and every post. Atoms, people, and ideas are, like subject and object, usable terms. We all know what these terms mean in MOQese. There's a difference between being submerged in SOM and using practical SOM terms. Another thing, it's really only inorganic patterns that are spatially extended. All other patterns are spatially extended only due to their inorganic representation, the dependency.

Ant:

As I said to Donny above, space can be a convenient intellectual construct; whether or not anything actually is extended will never be known.

Magnus:

I agree again, except the perpetuating part. I said that each atom is a subject from its point of view. That implies that each atom is an object from the other's point of view, hence not isolated.

Ant:

There is no direct correlation between subjects and objects with static value patterns. One of the main tenets of the MOQ is to replace SOM. There is no need to reintroduce subjects and objects within the MOQ and to do so will eventually lead to the reemergence of all those SOM problems Pirsig seeks to avoid/solve with his metaphysics in the first place.

Magnus:

Yes there is. Each Quality event is the origin of a subject and an object. Subject and object are synonymous with static patterns of value, except that being a subject also means that the observation is done from the subject's point of view. The only change we really need in the semantics of the words subject and object is that the subject can never be isolated from the observed object.

Donny:

When I talk about Subjects and Objects, I mean Knower and Known, and that should make it clear that they can only exist as a coupled unit (you can't have a knower who knows nothing, and you can't have something which is known that is not known by anything) and that this coupled unit is what we mean by "experience." After all, you've never experienced anything that didn't involve these two critters.

The point of a monism isn't to eliminate knower and known (unless you're prepared to pop on off to nirvana and none of us are), but to show that these two are aspects of the same thing: tat twam asi—that thou art—as it says in the Upanishads.

Ant:

I've never real given much thought to what the point of monism is; it seems to avoid the mind/matter problem, which appears to be its main use. I think it's just best to say Knower and Known are very useful concepts. This follows the Cittamatra tradition in Buddhism that asserts that entities exist within the flow of perceptions but not as independent subjects and objects. As Paul Williams confirms:

"(In)...the Cittamatra tradition...external objects are constituted by consciousness and do not exist apart from it. ...There is only a flow of perceptions." (Paul Williams, Mahayana Buddhism, Routledge, 1989, page 87).

And as Herbert Guenther adds:

"...Experience is the central theme of Buddhism, not theoretical postulation and deductive verification. Since no experience occurs more than once and all repeated experiences actually are only analogous occurrences, it follows that a thing or material substance can only be said to be a series of events interpreted as a thing, having no more substantiality than any other series of events we may arbitrarily single out. Thus the distinction between 'mental' and 'material' becomes irrelevant and it is a matter of taste to speak of physical objects. In other words, although we shall continue to speak about matter and mind, we must bear in mind that it is but a figure of speech as untrue as the statement that the sun rises or sets.

"...There is no reason to believe that the objective constituent of a perceptual situation is literally a spatio temporal part of a physical object, because the idea of a physical object can not be abstracted from the data of sense but is a hypothesis and is defined by postulates." (Herbert V. Guenther, Philosophy and Psychology in the Abhidharma, Random House, 1957, page 144/146).

Do you see the problem of taking the concepts of Knower and Known as literal truths yet?

The "problem" with ZMM is that Quality is not pinned down properly (note this may be deliberate) and in this book it is possible to find contradictory statements of what it is, is not, what it creates, etc. In light of SODV and Lila, I think the best interpretation of what Pirsig means by Quality is that it is the event of immediate experience.

At the end of Chapter 19 (of ZMM) where the narrator concludes that Quality "is an event," the terminology of subject and object is used (Quality is the point at which subject and object meet) but this is because the MOQ was not developed yet and there were no better concepts at the time. If there had been, the above sentence would have read something like this: Quality is the event from which inorganic, biological, social and intellectual patterns of reality are derived.

"Space" is an SOM construct.

Donny:

I'm amazed no one picked that up. If space is not real then consequently neither is time. The universe is an (shall I say "mere") illusion and what really exists is a transcendent unity, which is (by definition) non-spatial and atemporal. That's called transcendent mysticism. Eastern "philosophy" is saturated with it (I'm not saying that's bad) and German Idealism plays seriously close to it. Now is that Pirsig's position?

Ant:

Yes, I think it is, though I'm not too sure about the "illusion" part; "appearance" might be a better word. Anyway (in the context of the SODV paper), this is what Pirsig wrote to me about space:

"I have thought about Bell's theorem and what it might mean for the MOQ and so far have concluded that this theorem is just more of the same subject/object mess. 'Local' and 'non-local' presume a physical space. Physical space is a subjective intellectual pattern, which is presumed to correspond to an objective inorganic pattern. These patterns are so entrenched they are some of the last to disappear during the enlightenment process, but before pure Dynamic Quality is understood they must go. The 'nothingness' of Buddhism has nothing to do with the 'nothingness' of physical space. That's one of the advantages in calling it 'Quality' instead of 'nothingness.' It reduces the confusion." (Letter to Ant, June 1st 1996)

Donny:

If so, why waste all that paper on Lila? What's the point of talking about evolutionary levels if space and time don't really exist anyway? [148] Now we're back at Kant's time paradox. To create something, to cause something, to give birth to, requires time! First A, then A causes B, then B. Nothing can create time. That's where Kant said that the universe doesn't exist.

Ant:

Causation is another redundant SOM concept so I don't know how that would affect Kant's time paradox.

Donny:

This is where the Upanishads say that the world is illusory (and this is where metaphysics starts getting ugly). "Dynamic Quality and static quality come in after the unity, Quality, divides." Hmmm. Or another way to look at it is this: Dynamic Quality is the unity, the in itself, a mere theoretical potentiality that is necessarily unrealized, and static quality is the manifold of experience, time and space. All this confusion is what results from taking the question as a blank to be filled in. I shouldn't do that. Let me back off and start over again. See if the next mail is any clearer.

Ant:

Your comments here made me laugh Donny, as things can get very confusing at this level. I don't know if the following will be helpful to you but Pirsig has said numerous times that the MOQ is a pragmatic theory (i.e., for practical purposes it is useful to conceptualise things; to do so improves our lives immensely). The MOQ (as with every other theory) is not literally or ultimately true. At least Pirsig recognises the limitations of human conceptualising unlike numerous other writers. In Lila, for instance, the evolutionary levels were just the best way for Pirsig to conceptualise reality at that time.

487

And talking about time, Robert Harris (the physicist Bodvar introduced me to) said the "measurement" of "before and after" in units of time is analogous to measuring the depth of a river with a ruler. Time orders reality as much as the ruler orders the river (i.e., it is just a useful measuring tool). The difficulties arise when people start thinking time literally exists in its own right. It doesn't! Or do you think it's better to go along with Kant and say time exists but the universe doesn't? I know which theory I like better but I think it would be best for me to see that paradox of Kant's before totally dismissing it.

Do you see the problem of taking the concepts of "knower" and "known" as literal truths yet?

Donny:

Well duh. :) I think I said myself that the idea of Buddhism, transcendental mysticism, and (to some extent also) German Idealism, is to eliminate the I/That distinction and realize tat twam asi (that thou art). Hegel, for instance, sets out to prove that the knower and what it knows, what stands over against it, are one and the same. Kant sets out to unify the manifold (the "many-ness") of experience and collapse it into a single Being.

Ant:

Now, as I also indicated, our functioning is dependent on some I/that distinction. That's how we encounter the world (if you are Kant). If you are Pirsig, you start with immediate experience: you, I, It, time, space, etc., come afterwards.

I've never seen any conclusive psychological proof to support Kant that we come into the world with the a priori concepts of space and time already present. If you can cite any modern psychologists (with convincing evidence) who are certain that a newly born baby already has these concepts a priori, please do. Moreover, even if you can, this argument still seems to be sliding into SOM assumptions that there is a "real" physical space and time "out" there.

Donny:

Things come after things in time, in the realm of experience. Time doesn't come after anything. This is why Kant gave up his first formulation of the "nomena" as: "That which causes our phenomenal, time/space experience." See, Dynamic Quality doesn't cause (or precede) static quality since it's atemporal. The atemporal can't precede the temporal.

The way I think about this is— I've never experienced anything that wasn't spatially temporal (even having a thought, you have it at a particular time and place). You've never experienced anything that wasn't spatially temporal. So my conclusion is: the realm of experience is a spatially temporal phenomenon (necessarily). A transcendent unity (God, Tao, the moral self) is "outside" (metaphorically speaking) of our experience. Nirvana means, "to blow out," as in a candle.

That's the realm of maya, time/space. So, a "true" state of tat twam asi would zip us off to Nirvana and/or the funny farm. For example, you quoted Pirsig saying:

"I have thought about Bell's theorem and what it might mean for the MOQ and so far have concluded that this theorem is just more of the same subject-object mess. 'Local' and 'non local' presume a physical space. Physical space is a subjective intellectual pattern which is presumed to correspond to an objective inorganic pattern."

How the hell do you have a pattern without space/time? I mean think about that. A pattern is a rhythm, a repetition, either through time or across space. Come on, that's what the bloody word means.

Ant:

Again, Donny you are taking the SOM view that there is a real physical space and time "out" there. For my recent MOQ paper, I defined patterns as "repeated regular or logical forms of order," or "methodical and/or harmonious arrangements." I previously used the definition that a value pattern is a "repeated arrangement of an existing thing." Pirsig commented on this definition thus:

"The phrase 'repeated arrangement of an existing thing' tends to bring subject/object metaphysics into the picture. It suggests that the 'thing,' that is, the object, is producing the patterns of value rather than the patterns of value producing the thing. In the MOQ it is better to say a 'thing' is a repeated arrangement of a pattern of value." (Pirsig's letter to Ant, January 2, 1998)

These patterns are so entrenched they are some of the last to disappear during the enlightenment process, but before pure Dynamic Quality is understood they must go.

Donny:

Well that's what I've said, too. Static quality is concrete; it's in time/space. We speak of repeated regular or logical forms of order. Something is repeated in time or across space with methodological and/or harmonious arrangements. Things (even forms of order or value) are arranged in time or space. Patterns are patterns in time/space. That's the only way something can be a pattern, rhythm, or cycle. It repeats across time or space. Like I said, that's what pattern means.

Ant:

Remember, time and space are static intellectual patterns too.

Donny:

Dynamic Quality is not. That also means, however that it's not a thing; it's literally nothing at all, as Pirsig goes on to address below:

"The 'nothingness' of Buddhism has nothing to do with the 'nothingness' of physical space. That's one of the advantages in calling it 'Quality' instead of 'nothingness.' It reduces the confusion." (Letter to Ant, June 1, 1996)

Ant:

Donny, Pirsig does not think Dynamic Quality is literally nothing; hopefully this following quote shows you why:

"The Dynamic reality that goes beyond words is the constant focus of Zen teaching. Because of their habituation to a world of words, philosophers do not often understand Zen. When philosophers have trouble understanding the distinction between static and Dynamic Quality it can be because they are trying to include and subordinate all Quality to thought patterns. The

490

distinction between static and Dynamic Quality is intended to block this.

"'Patterned' and 'unpatterned' might work as well except that 'unpatterned' suggests that there is nothing there and all is quiet. There is nothing in the sense of no 'thing,' that is, 'no object,' and the Buddhists use nothingness in this way, but the term Dynamic is more in keeping within the quotation, 'Within nothingness there is a great working,' from the Zen master, Kategiri Roshi.

"The logical positivists fundamental error in my opinion is the assumption that because philosophy is about words it is therefore about words alone. This is the fallacy of 'devouring the menu instead of the meal.' Their common argumentative tactic is to say that anything they cannot feed through their little box of linguistic analysis is not philosophy. But if discussion about 'the good' (which is fundamentally beyond words) is not philosophy then Socrates was not a philosopher since that was his primary subject." (Robert Pirsig's letter to Ant, August 17, 1997)

The quote about Dynamic Quality from the Zen master, Kategiri Roshi, "Within nothingness there is a great working," seems to be the pertinent one here.

Donny:

There's no object or subject. Knower and known disappear. Time and space go away—we transcend them. This is what I mean by saying a transcendent unity is literally nothing. You could take it this way: what's the difference between everything and nothing? Answer: none, everything! The Whole has no relevant contrast, and the only way something is something is by being picked out/identified, and then contrasted with what it is not.

This is Buddhism. Being one with everything is the same as "blowing out" your flame. That's why they talk about anatman (no self) equaling Bramahan (the universe as a Self). This is also what Pirsig says in the argument that begins with, "A thing that can not be distinguished from anything else cannot exist...."

Perhaps I should expand upon that thought—first come inorganic patterns. They're rigid and confining and Quality is a movement from rigidity towards flexibility/freedom. So organic patterns of value develop, but they, too, quickly become rigid, so to escape those society evolves, and (in order to keep from flying apart) social norms, patterns, rules, etc., form. So, we go on to the intellectual realm, but in order to last, it must have some kind of rules (reason, objectivity, whatever) but that's too rigid so we go on to this direct, intuitive, post-intellectual, post-verbal hunch—Dynamic Quality?

Ant:

All the static patterns of quality are manifestations of Dynamic Quality so the above is not strictly accurate.

Donny:

Now, isn't it clear as Christmas that the above picture of the world is riddled with temporal lingo? "First, then, and so forth." They are evolutionary levels, and the point of calling something "evolutionary" is to say it improves over...(yes) time! So, on the one hand Pirsig affirms that reality is a transcendental unity (like the Upanishads and the Buddha). But then he turns around and gives an explanation of (scientific) time/space experience. Hmmm. What is going on here? Time fascinates me.

Ant:

Same here.

Donny:

It seems to me to be the ultimate explanadum (that which is to be explained) of metaphysics, for the one who gets to say what counts as a checkerboard, also gets to say what counts as a checker! We assume that time equals the mathematically intelligible time of science, but that is unprovable. After all, for a scientific proof to be any good that's what time has to be.

Ant:

That's a good point, Donny. However, time is not the foundation for the MOQ, Dynamic Quality is. Time is merely one intellectual concept over which Dynamic Quality has priority (as you were inferring with one of the above paragraphs).

You can not combine both evolution and Dynamic Quality within the same system of thought and show that they are contradictory. Dynamic Quality is outside any system of thought, including the MOQ. As the MOQ is an intellectual system, it can only recognise Dynamic Quality's existence; it cannot contain it. Evolution is an intellectual static pattern so Dynamic Quality is outside this as well.

Donny:

Not foundation—Explanadum. He who gets to say what counts as a checkerboard also gets to say what counts as a checker. So, if you delegate the authority to decide what time is to someone else...well, this is why analytic philosophy strikes me as so hollow. Or to say the same, that things exist in time. Things exist by getting into time and so to ask, "How does that chair exist?" is to ask, "How does that chair get figured into time?"

I'm influenced by Heidigger here. He said that metaphysicians make the mistake of looking at/for being(s) (what exists) when they should be looking at Being—the condition of existence. Quality isn't a being (it's not a "thing" as you say); it's a condition of being. Kant and Aristotle get a lot of flak around here, and I think they're both being misrepresented.

Ant:

Despite the above question, I do have a lot of time for Kant. For all his faults, he seems to be one of the first philosophers to ask how we perceive, which was a new way of looking at things. Generally, I don't like reading Aristotle but I thought his book on Rhetoric was a good read, especially his comments on the differences between young, middle aged and old men.

I suppose with any of these philosophers (Pirsig included) you've got to read them for yourself and then make your own mind up about them.

Donny:

Yeah, it's either that of find someone whose knowledge you trust and rely on what's said. Naturally, the former is best, but not always practical. The Lila Squad is supposed to be a forum for academics and laymen alike. We can expect everyone to read Pirsig's two books, but not to read every other title, author, and subject that comes up. Fair enough?

Bodvar:

Donny, no doubt Anthony will reply, but I just can't resist jumping in at this point. I think you put the finger at a sensitive spot here, something that perhaps will make Anthony see the significance of the "SOM/Intellect of MOQ" fusion. Anthony asserts that space and time are subject/object metaphysical constructs, which is correct enough—each and every concept is knower/known-ish—but if one then kicks the said SOM out of the MOQ reality...well, Houston, we have a problem!

Enter the SAIOM idea (after this the two are interchangeable). The knower and the known is what intellect is all about—every last bit—from a Subject/Object as metaphysics patterns of value. This is madness and what broke Phædrus of ZMM and made him find the Quality idea as a way out of the blind alley. In my opinion the SAIOM notion is implicated in his work, but he probably regarded it as too much for one helping so he left it dangling. The "mind" is left as the opposite of "matter" and this has kept messing up the issue. Anthony has an Eastern slant to his thinking which is valid enough, but a bit frustrating to you, Donny.

If for no other reason, the SAIOM idea accentuates the point where the Quality idea takes leave of every hitherto known philosophical system: if Intellect is seen as a "mere" value level and the mind/matter division equals intellect, then—and only then—is SOM "conquered" and we are forced to see that that dizzying chasm is, well, an evolutionary level, but not reality!

So now if you retort, hmmm, if every concept, theory, idea, etc., is an intellectual construct, doesn't that make the MOQ, and SAIOM, intellectual constructs too? It does, but now intellect isn't mind of SOM (as metaphysics) but as a static level of the MOQ, and the chief tenet of Quality Metaphysics is that all static levels in its time spawned the next. The Dynamism uses the last static latch as a springboard and necessarily its "values" as means for its development, so we will of necessity know and/or conceptualize our way to a greater view. This is the mind-blowing force of Pirsig's thinking. Perhaps Nietzsche was on to something similar but he did not recover from the first stage.

Finally, Ant wrote: "Moreover, Bodvar has said to me previously, that Pirsig only equated subjects & objects with static intellectual patterns for his Einstein Meets Magrïtte paper so as not to alienate his audience in Belgium too much. He certainly does not believe they are literally equivalent."

I just quote this passage to make a confession—Pirsig did not say so explicitly to me; it was only my impression after he had declined Tor Nörretranders' invitation to next years' conference in Copenhagen. What he said was this: "The MOQ isn't suited for that kind of exchange." However, I still maintain that I sensed a motive as you describe it.

Conversation with Andrew [April 1998]

Jason:

What follows is a collection of crude and unrefined thoughts extracted from a recent journal entry. You may find these interesting. You may find them funny. I find them meaningless....

April 7th, 8:23 PM

Nihilism in 90 Minutes.... (Rather, 90 seconds—0 seconds.)

Enlightenment is insanity. Insanity is the terra incognito of the rational. Nowhere to turn from here.... Everything closing in on nothing. Gravity always wins. (Meaningless)

Metaphor.

Silence...(ideas fall away).

Indifference...(relations fall away).

Darkness...(reality falls away).

Enlightenment....

I'm attracted to you because you believe. Honestly believe. Beauty.

Never again....

(By the way, not to worry, since nihilistic attraction, too, is meaningless.)

Existential angst? Far beyond that. Pure evil. Pure good.

Conversation with Andrew:

I write because I am not enlightened. True enlightenment would preclude (and prevent) all being.

The Tadpole:

Born, we live in a sea rich with meaning. We swim from here to there with little or no direction in mind. Eventually, we realize that our "direction" is to swim. We swim with previously unknown enthusiasm. Faster, faster.... Eventually, we realize that the water level is falling. Our choice of directions become fewer and fewer. Yet on we swim. Faster, faster.... Unaware, we settle into a gently flowing current, which only aids in propelling us on. Faster, faster.... Suddenly we are out of control, swimming faster and faster directly into the vortex of a whirlpool! Those that are lucky miss the deadly heart of the whirlpool (by some unknown twist of fate). What comes next is still unknown. Only time will tell. We may continue to swim, futilely denying the reality of our newly gained existential wisdom—a wisdom of non-wisdom. Or, we may embrace this wisdom and become one with the whirlpool, continuously swimming round and round in beautiful, perfect concentric orbits—always aware that the minute the illusion is abandoned, we will plunge into the nihilistic (unknown and unknowable) depths on the other side of the whirlpool. (We have to believe.)

The Downward Spiral:

Beginning at Ignorance, man slowly, but persistently sinks into the "lower" realm of Knowledge, all the time adamantly convincing himself that his is actually improving his position. It is only after passing through the veridical certainty of Knowledge and arriving at the ultimate untruth—nihilism—that one may realize true Enlightenment. (At which point, of course, it doesn't matter.)

Therefore, either struggle to secure your present (perceived) position or prepare to loose everything and gain yourself.

On the MOQ:

Ultimate "reality" is unreality, (i.e., Dynamic Quality).
Nothingness.

To exist (pragmatically) we must "project" a reality around ourselves, while at the same time "inserting" ourselves into the projection. Hence, the Quality event. A four level ontological framework (i.e., the MOQ) more practical, more valuable than others. It is self-consistent in the presence of inconsistency. Being and nothingness. Quality and irony.

On Prior Illusions Regarding Caring:

Previously, I have "subscribed" actively, with my "whole (miserably Cartesian) heart and mind," to Pirsig's philosophy of Caring.

Operating under the illusion that Caring was a condition that I and I alone (quasi-solipsism?) could impose on a situation, I struggled with all my intellectual and social might to truly "care." Arriving at work, I would sit, committed to "care" about the program I was writing. Others would drop by with a casual "hello" or a similar conventional gesture of good will and I would shrug them off, thinking to myself, "God, can't you see I'm sitting here trying to 'care' about something?" ("Quality knocks on the door and you say, 'Go away, I'm waiting for Quality.'")

Only after realizing the futility and meaninglessness of everyday life—everyday everything—can you "understand" and "know" true Caring. Caring is disinterested interest, being so indifferent about reality that its meaning is undeniable.

The Life as Art and Imagination:

The objective, absolute truth is—there is no objective, absolute truth. All is Maya. Illusion. Use your illusion. Create your illusion. Perfect your illusion, always bearing in mind that what you're working on is nothing but an illusion, a finite goal in an infinite game....

Inspired by the thought and life of Robert M. Pirsig, complemented by the life and thought of the author.

"It's going to get better now. You can sort of tell these things."

Annotations by Robert M. Pirsig

143. This is how I have always seen it. Just as two opposing sides can cite the Constitution as support for their case in the Supreme Court, so can two opposing sides cite the MOQ. "The Devil can quote scripture to his own choosing," but there is no reason to throw out the Bible, the U.S. Constitution or the MOQ as long as they can provide a larger context for understanding.

144. There has been no an academic category called "subject/object" metaphysics for the same reason that before Columbus discovered America there was no such geographical category as an "Old World." Columbus discovery created the "Old World" as that entity which Columbus left behind. In the same way the MOQ has "created" subject-object metaphysics as that system of thought which the MOQ has left behind.

145. Quality is not the same as Nature. Nature in the MOQ is the inorganic and biological levels.

146. Note that in this entire statement the words "quality" and "value" have vanished, except for a mistaken equivocation of Quality with Nature. He has missed Platt's question completely. He has given us the argument of SOM materialism against SOM idealism, both of which have been left behind by the MOQ.

147. And would that not damn it to a positivist hell forever? Some can see merit in a scientific understanding that is not incompatible with religion. Others fear it like the Devil itself.

148. They are high quality explanations of experience.

Epilogue

Once the initial enthusiasm and trepidation of uploading a rough draft of Lila's Child to a website had faded, I gave up working on the project for a variety of reasons. Then, quite unexpectedly, in September of 2000 I received a message from Bodvar that Robert M. Pirsig had written to him concerning the project. In his letter to Bodvar, Mr. Pirsig described how he stumbled across Lila's Child on the Internet and how impressed he was with it. Inspired by Mr. Pirsig's interest in the work, I took up the project again, hoping perhaps to finally see it in print.

In April of 2001, having had nearly completed a second draft, I wrote to Bodvar to let him know of the progress. Bodvar returned my letter with the suggestion that he write to Robert Pirsig inquiring if he would consider providing an introduction for Lila's Child. I agreed that this was an excellent idea. A week or so later I heard back from Bodvar with word from Mr. Pirsig that he would like to see the manuscript when it was complete. I asked Bodvar to please write Mr. Pirsig back and let him know it would be another month before the manuscript was ready.

When I first wrote to Bodvar, I assumed the manuscript was nearly complete, but now that I realized who was going to be looking at it, I suddenly knew that it wasn't even close to being done. What's more, it was clear I would need at least another year to polish the manuscript properly, not just a month. I couldn't help wondering to myself what possible motive Bodvar could have to think of involving me in this project in the first place, for it was obvious by now that not only was I completely incompetent, but I was in way over my head with a real chance of drowning. Nonetheless, after another month and a half of work I sent the newest version of Lila's Child to Mr. Pirsig, not without severe misgivings that the manuscript needed much more work.

A week or thereabouts after sending the manuscript off, one of the original contributors to the Lila Squad discussion group wrote withdrawing permission (obtained before starting the work) for the use of those posts in the print version of Lila's Child. Though it was one of the most difficult letters I have ever written, I immediately wrote to Mr. Pirsig informing him of the problems cropping up. I realized the Lila's Child manuscript would require a complete rewrite. I assured him that I was up to the challenge, but frankly, I was completely downhearted. Part of me hoped I could just get the manuscript back untouched and maybe I would be able to forget this whole Quality thing for the last time.

In July 2001, a package arrived from Mr. Pirsig containing the Lila's Child manuscript complete with an introduction and annotations. Several of those annotations are missing from the main body of the Lila's Child manuscript presented here, since in doing the rewrite those notes made little sense without the suddenly illegal posts that triggered them. Rather than leave those annotations on the cutting room floor, it seems better to present them here with short introductory questions of my own words.

The Missing RMP Annotations

Question:

Do Dusenberry's methods indicate that social patterns cannot be defined by intellectual patterns?

RMP annotation 149.

To answer this I'd say that Dusenberry really didn't have any methods. He opposed the static "objectivity" he saw in other anthropologists because it shut out a deeper intellectual understanding that came from his friendship with the Indians. He just wrote and said whatever he liked. I suppose this could be called "Dynamic intellectualism" though it is better not to invent new terms for such an ancient trait.

RMP annotation 150.

The fields of anthropology and sociology do define social patterns. Dusenberry's objection was that when they define societies using the rules of inorganic physics they leave out something.

Question:

Why the ambiguity on four or more levels?

RMP annotation 151.

The answer is that Pirsig doesn't like being unnecessarily arbitrary. If someone likes five levels, he can have them. It's still the MOQ, even though he personally prefers four levels.

Question:

Is art a social pattern?

RMP annotation 152.

This is interesting. I hadn't thought of it but it sounds right. It fits in with evolution since singing and dancing and painting can be considered prehistoric arts that occurred before intellect.

Question:

Or is art a biological pattern?

RMP annotation 153.

But note that art is never done by animals. That eliminates art as a biological activity.

Question:

How can art both describe and be part of static quality?

RMP annotation 154.

I think there is an equivocation between "arts" and "art."

Arts are specific static patterns, such as drawing or music. Art is a high quality endeavor that can apply to anything, even motorcycle maintenance.

Question:

Do atoms have social value?

RMP annotation 155.

This is why it is important not to extend the term "society" beyond its dictionary definition: "a group of human beings broadly distinguished from other groups by mutual interests, participation in characteristic relationships, shared institutions, and a common culture."

Question:

Do intellectual patterns of value have a physical reality?

RMP annotation 156.

Better to say "mental reality." Physical reality is inorganic or biological.

Question:

Since Pirsig says that only biological beings sense value...

RMP annotation 157.

If I had known in advance that this argument was coming up I would have said an "intellectual sense of value."

Question:

Then how did inorganic patterns evolve?

RMP annotation 158.

If I had known in advance that this argument was coming up I would have said an "inorganic sense of value." It is emphasized in Lila that inorganic values and intellectual values are different

Question:

Are organic patterns the senses, or do they value the senses?

RMP annotation 159.

I think the MOQ should say organic patterns are the senses plus the bodies that support them.

Question:

What does Pirsig mean by high and low quality?

RMP annotation 160.

I don't think you need to explain low and high quality in dialectical terms. When a baby cries, it tells you it is experiencing low quality. Everyone knows what that means. It can be speculated that high and low is the first of all static divisions of Dynamic Quality and without this differentiation no further differentiation would take place.

Question:

Does seeking a higher Dynamic freedom necessarily mean a static detour?

RMP annotation 161.

This parallels an historic argument among Buddhists over whether enlightenment can be spontaneous or whether you have to go to school first. Zen argues for spontaneity.

Questions and Answers

When I received the package with the annotated manuscript from Mr. Pirsig, a letter was enclosed in which he invited me to send back any questions or comments that might arise. I suppose the kid who grew up watching Michael Jordan play basketball and then one day discovered himself on the court playing in a game with the man himself would feel much like I did (and still do).

I think at first I tried too hard; my questions seemed wide of the mark somehow, though putting a finger on exactly how and where proved impossible no matter how many times I rewrote them. The delight of reading Mr. Pirsig's answers came to complement that feeling nicely, however. Reading over them now, it seems that the good questions aren't really my questions but everyone's. The experience of discussing Robert Pirsig's work with so many people over the last few years has proved invaluable to this stage of the project. Without all the input I received from others too numerous to mention here, I would have talked myself out of returning the manuscript.

Over the next few months, we sent the document back and forth several times. This exchange has helped my understanding of the MOQ immeasurably. I share it here on the chance it may be of value to others as well though I am aware there are certainly people more knowledgeable than I am who would ask different and better questions.

I pondered quite some time on how best to present this section, and then I realized Mr. Pirsig had already solved that problem for me by copying the annotations I had questioned at the bottom of the original document and adding his new notes to them. For ease of reference, I have numbered them as they appear in the main part of the book.

RMP Annotation 4

In the MOQ, all organisms are objective. They exist in the material world. All societies are subjective. They exist in the mental world. Again, the distinction is very sharp. For example, the "President of the U.S." is a social pattern. No objective scientific instrument can distinguish a President of the U.S. from anyone else.

DG:

I find this very simple and helpful. I would like to go back to some of your writings in order to ask you to please clarify your meaning on a couple points. First, from Lila:

"In a subject-object metaphysics morals and art are worlds apart, morals being concerned with the subject quality and art with the objective quality. But in the Metaphysics of Quality that division doesn't exist. They're the same. They both become much more intelligible when references to what is subjective and what is objective are completely thrown away and references to what is static and what is Dynamic are taken up instead." (Chapter 9, page 134, Bantam paperback)

From your SODV paper:

"When we get rid of the words 'subjective' and 'objective' completely often there is a great increase in the clarity of what is said."

These quotes seem to suggest that an entirely new way of viewing reality might be desired, one that "completely throws away" any reference to subjects and objects (Doug's Dynamic/static acronyms seem an effort in that direction).

You continue with this line of inquiry in Chapter 12 of Lila, page 177:

"A conventional subject-object metaphysics uses the same four static patterns as the Metaphysics of Quality, and divides them into two groups of two: inorganic-biological patterns called 'matter,' and social-intellectual patterns called 'mind.' But this division is the source of the problem. When a subject-object metaphysics regards matter and mind as eternally separate and eternally unalike, it creates a platypus bigger than the solar system.

"It has to make this fatal division because it gives top position in its structure to subjects and objects."

What I (and many contributors) seem to be having difficult reconciling (and your notes here have helped immensely, thank you!) is if the subject-object division is a "fatal division," shouldn't we avoid it? Now I see that the MOQ makes use of the SOM but does not give top position to those subject-object references. Still, it makes use of them. Doesn't that still mean any subject/object division is a fatal division nonetheless and one the MOQ should no longer have to make? Do we just make the division out of convenience now, to "wean" ourselves of the SOM? Or was the "fatal division" designation of SOM a bit harsh to begin with?

From Lila:

"The Metaphysics of Quality resolves the relationship between intellect and society, subject and object, mind and matter, by embedding all of them into a larger system of understanding. Objects are inorganic and biological values; subjects are social and intellectual values." (Page 344)

I interpret this to mean, like "truth is a species of good" (James quote, page 416 of Lila), subjects and objects are a species of the MOQ but no longer the top division of a presumed metaphysics.

The presumed metaphysics of Western culture (SOM) has now been embedded in a larger system (MOQ) with a much greater resulting clarity than could be obtained using either system of thought by itself.

RMP:

Yes, it's clear I've been of two minds on whether subjects and objects should be included in the MOQ. My earlier view, when I was concentrating on the confusion of subject-object thinking, was to get rid of them entirely to help clarify things. Later I began to see it's not necessary to get rid of them because the MOQ can encase them neatly within its structure—the upper two levels being subjective, and the lower two, objective. Still later I saw that the subject-object distinction is very useful for sharply distinguishing between biological and social levels.

If I had been more careful in my editing, I would have eliminated or modified the earlier statements to bring them into agreement with the latter ones. However I missed these and it's valuable that the Lila Squad has caught them. The main danger to the MOQ from subject/object thinking at present seems to be when it tries in a conventional way to encase values and declare them to be either objects or thoughts. That was the attempt of the professors in Bozeman in ZMM that started this whole MOQ.

At present, I don't see that the terms "subject" and "object" need to be dropped, as long as we remember they are just levels of value, not expressions of independent scientific reality.

DG:

I would like to ask for clarification on a quote from page 178 of Lila that also seems related to this: "So what the Metaphysics of Quality concludes is that all schools of thought are correct on the mind-matter question. Mind is contained in static inorganic patterns. Matter is contained in static intellectual patterns." The last two sentences here seem to contradict the earlier division of inorganic-biological as objective and the social-intellectual as subjective, although, now armed with the information of these notes, I sense it relates to philosophical idealism (ideas before matter)?

RMP:

Yes, the relationship of the MOQ to philosophic idealism is an important one that is not adequately spelled out in Lila. In a materialist system mind has no reality because it is not material. In an idealist system matter has no reality because it is just an idea. The acceptance of one meant the rejection of the other. In the MOQ, both mind and matter are levels of value. Materialist explanations and idealist explanations can coexist because they are descriptions of coexisting levels of a larger reality.

The MOQ does not deny the traditional scientific view of reality as composed of material substance and independent of us. It says it is an extremely high quality idea. We should follow it whenever it is practical to do so. But the MOQ, like philosophic idealism, says this scientific view of reality is still an idea. If it were not an idea, then that "independent scientific material reality" would not be able to change as new scientific discoveries come in.

DG:

The MOQ enlarges the context of the questions being asked as described in ZMM?

RMP:

Yes.

RMP Annotation 19

In Lila, societies are quite separate patterns that emerge from and are superimposed upon of organic bodies of people, but they are not combinations of these organic bodies of people.

DG:

The combination of biological bodies of people might be called a mob. A mob is not a social pattern any more than an ant colony.

RMP:

Although the word "mob" to me has a connotation of social destructiveness. Just "group" seems better.

DG:

Yes, I see what you mean. The connotation of social destructiveness occurred to me too but I put it off to the moral conflict between the biological and social level. Just "group" seems better to me too though.

RMP Annotation 25

This is okay. In Lila, I never defined the intellectual level of the MOQ, since everyone who is up to reading Lila already knows what "intellectual" means. For purposes of MOQ precision, let's say that the intellectual level is the same as mind. It is the collection and manipulation of symbols, created in the brain, that stand for patterns of experience.

DG:

I know very little of Zen (and of course I am seeing it from the perspective of Western culture) but from what I do understand, to still the internal discursive dialogue is to approach the essence of "knowing." Does the MOQ agree with this?

RMP:

In German there are two words for "know," kennen and wissen. The Zen approach reduces Wissenschaft (scholarly knowledge) and thereby improves Kenntnis (recognition without intellectual interposition).

DG:

In one sense, it seems ludicrous to believe the little voice inside our heads is doing anything more than chattering to itself. On the other hand, when that voice stops, the world stops, or so I have heard it said. Does the MOQ have anything to say about this little rational voice?

RMP:

It seems loudest when new things are happening that need explanation. Soto Zen meditation is a carefully contrived situation where as little as possible is happening and this rational voice tends to run down like an alarm clock that nobody is winding. When it stops completely enlightenment can happen.

DG:

For the longest time it seemed loudest when I tried to quiet it but now I sense that such quiet was something so new that it cried louder for explanation?

RMP:

I guess so. The voice is just static intellectual patterns reacting in fear of the Dynamic Quality that has been present all along.

DG:

Why do we fear affirmative Dynamic Quality?

RMP:

Because it threatens to destroy static patterns. As stated in Lila, static and Dynamic Quality are in opposition to each other. Radicals and liberals who are dissatisfied with static patterns will feel less threatened by Dynamic Quality. Conservatives and reactionaries will be more threatened by it.

RMP Annotation 29

The MOQ, as I understand it, denies any existence of a "self" that is independent of inorganic, biological, social or intellectual patterns. There is no "self" that contains these patterns. These patterns contain the self. This denial agrees with both religious mysticism and scientific knowledge. In Zen, there is reference to "big self" and "small self" Small self is the patterns. Big self is Dynamic Quality.

DG:

So the MOQ might say we invent the self and then believe in our own invention.

RMP:

Or better, the big self invents intellectual patterns that invent the small self and that collection of small selves known as "we."

DG:

Why?

RMP:

The question, "Why?" is always an intellectual question. It is always part of the static patterns of the small self. Any intellectual answer it gets will by necessity also be a part of the static patterns of the small self. Since the big self cannot be contained by small-self patterns, there is no intellectual, patterned answer to "Why?" A lot of the enigmatic unpatterned nature of Zen results from teachers trying to give non-intellectual, non-patterned answers to "Why?" That is, they are trying to give, as an answer, the big self itself, which surpasses all questions and is the only correct answer that can be given.

DG:

I recently heard an interview with a sculptor who claimed one of the criteria for what he considered to be real art would be that it is functionally useless. For instance, though buildings are frequently called works of art, they are functional and therefore not art at all. Real art is about the changing of perception, not functional conveniences like indoor plumbing and electricity. In other words, a "piece" of art is not limited to the functionality of the object in question but rather subject and object blur into each other. In Lila, Phædrus mentions something about "a fourth Dynamic morality which isn't a code. He supposed you could call it a code of art or something like that..." as if this Dynamic morality had no real function to speak of. Is "big self" functionally useless like art?

RMP:

I used to travel with art people who were always arguing matters of this sort. The MOQ says art is high quality conduct and leaves it at that. Since quality can be recognized but not defined there are no definitions of what is and what is not art, including functionality. Hence the title of ZMM.

RMP Annotation 30

I think the answer is that inorganic objects experience events but do not react to them biologically socially or intellectually. They react to these experiences inorganically, according to the laws of physics.

DG:

I guess I'm a little uncomfortable using the word "experience" in relation to the inorganic level. In Lila you wrote: "The question of whether an electron does a certain thing because it has to or

510

because it wants to is completely irrelevant to the data of what the electron does." (Page 181)

"Wants to" seems to imply experience though the MOQ seems to say since we are actually superimposing our intellectual values on the data, whether an electron experiences or not is completely irrelevant. Perhaps it depends upon which definition of experience we use:

1) The apprehension of an object, thought, or emotion through the senses or mind: a child's first experience of snow.

2) a. Active participation in events or activities, leading to the accumulation of knowledge or skill: a lesson taught by experience; a carpenter with experience in roof repair. b. The knowledge or skill so derived.

3) a. An event or a series of events participated in or lived through. b. The totality of such events in the past of an individual or group.

It seems to me the only way an inorganic electron or atom can experience is if there is "mind" involved.

RMP:

I think definition 3a works for electrons if you drop the word "lived." One usually thinks of mind in connection of experience, but there are plenty usages of "experience" where mind is not involved. An example would be a news story that begins, "The City of Los Angeles experienced minor earthquake tremors today." Nothing wrong with that. No editor would throw that sentence out as incorrect. The experience is inorganic. Los Angeles reacts to the experience inorganically by shaking a little.

DG:

So the forest experiences the sound of the tree falling even when no one is around?

RMP:

That's an interesting answer to the famous question used to argue against philosophic idealism. The idealist answer is, "What tree?" The questioner has posited a hypothetical tree and then asks, "What will this hypothetical tree do?" This is like asking, "If pigs

511

could fly how high would they go?" Who knows? Hypothetical trees and pigs can do almost anything.

DG:

It would seem while an editor might not find a problem with a sentence like "The City of Los Angeles experienced minor earthquake tremors today," the idealist would ask "what City of Los Angeles?"

That's why I felt a bit uncomfortable using the term "experience" in relation to the inorganic level but now I sense you are saying we can only talk hypothetically about experience (other than our own) in any case?

RMP:

When the term "experience" is used one automatically enters the subject-object way of thinking that there is an object that is experienced and a subject that experiences it. All sorts of tangles begin, including those here. The way all this got started was with Platt's statement that "As I understand it, the MOQ equates Quality with direct experience. In turn, experience creates static patterns of value. The problem is—how could inorganic static patterns be created unless inorganic entities like atoms were able to experience? If atoms don't experience, at what level did experience arise? And, how could experience arise from a lower level of no experience? This seems to be a subject/object platypus. Is there a MOQ solution?"

So Platt himself at the beginning sees that the problem is an SOM problem. The MOQ solution he asks for is given in Note 31.

RMP Annotation 31

Since experience is the starting point, it doesn't arise from a lower level of no experience. Logically speaking, a starting point that arises from something else is no longer a starting point.

DG:

It would seem that many researchers in the relatively new field of "cognitive science" are beginning to agree that "experience" is indeed a fundamental aspect of reality that defies further analysis.

RMP:

This is good if they don't think of this fundamental aspect of reality as an SOM object. I would guess, however, that they do.

DG:

Well perhaps. But it seems to me that it is implied in the acceptance of experience as a starting point that reality cannot be "objective" in the scientific sense of the word. Of course, I am not really qualified to say one way or the other so I should probably shut up before I make a fool of myself again.

RMP:

Chapter 1 of Anthony McWatt's doctoral thesis will go into this in more detail.

RMP Annotation 37

I don't think they are fuzzy.

DG:

But they are human specific.

RMP:

Anders is slipping into the materialist assumption that there is a huge world out there that has nothing to do with people. The MOQ says that is a high quality assumption, within limits. One of its limits is that without humans to make it that assumption cannot be made. It is a human specific assumption. Strictly speaking, Anders has never heard of or ever will hear of anything that isn't human specific.

DG:

So I take it philosophic idealism is a higher quality intellectual idea in this situation vs. the physicist working in the lab who would find materialism to be of higher value?

RMP:

That sounds right, although modern physics has produced laboratory paradoxes for materialists that do not exist for idealists. I think it is best to understand both systems, and shift from one to another as it becomes valuable to do so.

RMP Annotation 39

That is what is supposed to occur with these notes. The "Great Author" is a sarcasm used by Richard Rigel, not a term of respect.

DG:

Rigel seems representative of the negative quality that celebrity brings in its wake. I get the feeling that the character of Rigel was modeled after more than one person?

RMP:

No Rigel is just me, setting the stage for the MOQ. I tried to think of the best attack I could make and then put it in his mouth. One interviewer asked me, "Are you really Phædrus?" The answer was, "Yes I really am Phædrus. I also really am Richard Rigel. I also really am Lila. I also really am the boat."

DG:

I must confess I took the position during one discussion with the group that Phædrus and you were not the same person. I wrote that from reading the letters others in the group had shared from you I gathered you were warm and humorous but I found Phædrus to be somewhat cold and so dog-gone serious all the time. I wrote that Phædrus seemed to be a mask, like the masks we all wear, which seems related to our attempt at objectifying our inner values by creating idols (as you discuss on page 459 in Lila). It occurred to me since reading your notes on "big self" and "small self" that I've been considering the person as "small self" while you're using the context of "big self"?

RMP:

Yes, Phædrus is overwhelmingly intellectual. He is not a mask, really, just a literary character who is easy for me to write about because I share many of his static values a lot of the time. I don't think big self and small self are involved here. My editor wanted me to make him a warmer person in order to increase reader appeal. But making him warmer would have made him more social and weakened the contrasts between himself and Rigel and Lila that were intended to give strength to the story. The fact that everyone seemed to think that Phædrus was me came as an unpleasant surprise after the book was published. I had assumed that everyone would of course know that an author and a character in his book cannot possibly be the same person.

RMP Annotation 46

Not so you can tell someone about it in common language. However the taste of chocolate is a distinct chemical entity that can be defined with precision by flavor chemists. (I once wrote articles on this for General Mills Research Laboratories)

DG:

This is very interesting. I take it the flavor chemists use an uncommon language to describe flavors just as physicists use an uncommon language to describe the atomic system. What kind of articles did you write? (if you don't mind my asking.)

RMP:

It was just a company magazine for the laboratories, written in common language for stockholders and the general public. Interesting work though. I did one of the first stories ever on epoxy resin adhesives that General Mills developed, and got big jars of samples to take home with me.

RMP Annotation 56

The word "produced" implies that Dynamic quality is a part of a cause and effect system of the kind generated by scientific thinking. But Dynamic Quality cannot be part of any cause and effect system since all cause and effect systems are static patterns. All we can say is that these static patterns emerged and that they are better than physical nothingness.

A philosophic tradition of scientific value-neutrality would argue that you cannot say these value patterns are better than physical nothingness because scientifically speaking in the real world nothing is better than anything else. But if these patterns had not emerged there would be no life. And if life is not better than death and the science that life produces is not better than non-science, then this scientific tradition of value neutrality is no better than no words at all. That is, it has no merit.

DG:

So in a sense, science says we are here by chance while a metaphysics of value would say we here by Design? Or is even saying that much beyond what we can say of Dynamic Quality?

RMP:

Yes I think even saying that much is beyond what we can say of Dynamic Quality.

RMP Annotation 57

In the MOQ time is dependent on experience independently of matter. Matter is a deduction from experience.

DG:

Could you elaborate on what you mean by "independently of matter"? I can see that time is dependent on experience but am having a difficulty with the rest of your first sentence, especially in the context of your second sentence.

RMP:

I think the trouble is with the word, "experience." It can be used in at least three ways. It can be used as a relationship between an object and another object (as in Los Angeles experiencing earthquakes.) It is more commonly used as a subject-object relationship. This relationship is usually considered the basis of philosophic empiricism and experimental scientific knowledge.

In a subject-object metaphysics, this experience is between a preexisting object and subject, but in the MOQ, there is no pre-existing subject or object. Experience and Dynamic Quality become synonymous. Change is probably the first concept emerging from this Dynamic experience. Time is a primitive intellectual index of this change. Substance was postulated by Aristotle as that which does not change. Scientific "matter" is derived from the concept of substance. Subjects and objects are intellectual terms referring to matter and nonmatter. So in the MOQ experience comes first, everything else comes later. This is pure empiricism, as opposed to scientific empiricism, which, with its pre-existing subjects and objects, is not really so pure. I hope this explains what is said above, "In the MOQ time is dependent on experience independently of matter. Matter is a deduction from experience."

DG:

Yes, this does help, thank you. What bothers me slightly—I am sure I am not seeing it in the proper light yet—is how experience can be synonymous with Dynamic Quality? Isn't experience that which we define?

RMP:

Dynamic Quality is defined constantly by everyone. Consciousness can be described as a process of defining Dynamic Quality. But once the definitions emerge, they are static patterns and no longer apply to Dynamic Quality. So one can say correctly that Dynamic Quality is both infinitely definable and undefinable because definition never exhausts it.

RMP Annotation 61

It is the point at which static patterns emerge where there were no static patterns before. It is not a two-way street, and therefore the term "interaction" seems inappropriate.

DG:

I notice there is no reference whatsoever to Dynamic Quality in your definition of "Quality event" but it is implied indirectly through "emerge."

RMP:

The term "Quality Event" has created some problems. It was first used in ZMM to distinguish quality from a subject or an object. However many readers seemed to consider an event to be itself an object. This of course makes Quality one of a class of objects, and destroys the whole purpose of the MOQ. That is why you don't see the term "Quality Event" at all in Lila. (Or if you do, it's an overlooked bug.)

DG:

Right. You use the term in your first book but not in your second. "Quality event" is resurrected in your SODV paper however. Bodvar suggests this paper was written in an effort to cater to a primarily SOM audience. Do you agree? How would your approach to that audience differ today?

RMP:

Yes that was an effort to reach a primarily SOM audience. I haven't thought about them much recently. I think my approach to them today would be to leave them alone with their paradoxes. They are an extremely intelligent group but have a religious faith that this intelligence is the answer to everything. Whenever you talk about Quality you can almost see on their faces that an internal effort is being made to subordinate what you are saying to their existing intellectual understanding of things. To put it in the Zen metaphor, they have worked hard through the centuries to fill their cup of intellectual tea. The rewards of this effort are everywhere. They are not about to dump it out because some stranger says something else is better.

DG:

When you say "this intelligence," I am assuming you mean "wissen" since "kennen" is "recognition without intellectual interposition." If such knowledge is not intellectual, where does it fit into the MOQ?

RMP:

Yes, "wissen" is meant. "Kenntnis" would be the more primitive recognition of a repetitive pattern, such as a baby first recognizing its mother's face.

DG:

Would "kenntnis" be considered a primal biological pattern of value or more along the lines of a Dynamic process?

RMP:

More along the lines of an immediate Dynamic-to-intellectual process. As the baby grows up its static intellectual patterns grow more complex and dominating, and its Dynamic awareness tends to become weaker, unless corrected by some special effort, such as Zen training.

RMP Annotation 65

It seems close but I think it is really very far apart. In the Copenhagen Interpretation, and in all subject-object metaphysics, both the observed (the object) and the observer (the subject) are assumed to exist prior to the observation. In the MOQ, nothing exists prior to the observation. The observation creates the intellectual patterns called "observed" and "observer." Think about it. How could a subject and object exist in a world where there are no observations?

DG:

This is a tough one to wrap one's mind around. It must have given Bohr philosophical fits. I am not sure how different the Copenhagen Interpretation is to Bohr's own thinking but didn't he steadfastly refuse to speculate on this at all?

RMP:

I don't remember. It was several years ago that I did my reading of Bohr. At the Einstein Meets Magritte conference I was surprised to discover that the quantum physicists I talked to had a low opinion of Bohr. Werner Heisenberg and his successors were held in higher regard.

RMP Annotation 69

Good question. The "Gateless Gate" analogy of the Buddhists may be the answer. In this analogy, as one approaches the gate it seems to be a goal, but after one has passed through and looks back he sees there never was any gate.

Translating back into the MOQ, one can say that Dynamic Quality is a goal from a static point of view, but is the origin of all things from a Dynamic understanding.

DG:

Could you please clarify the meaning of "understanding" as in "a Dynamic understanding"? Can we use the term "understanding" in context of Dynamic Quality?

RMP:

"Awareness" can be substituted if that sounds better.

DG:

Awareness does have a different connotation to it though it is sometimes difficult to separate experience and awareness. Additionally, if awareness and experience are considered synonymous then I see a problem with note 30.

RMP:

I think you are looking for intellectual precision here about the nothingness of Nirvana. Static experience and static awareness are easily separated. Dynamic anything is not.

DG:

Perhaps I am still stuck in the mindset of experience as static quality. I am curious about one of the MOQ principles in Lila: "There's a principle in physics that if a thing cannot be distinguished from anything else it doesn't exist. To this the Metaphysics of Quality adds a second principle: if a thing has no value it isn't distinguished from anything else."

If "Dynamic anything" isn't easily separated from anything else, does it exist? Or is "easily" a key word here?

RMP:

Dynamic Quality is value and thus is very easily distinguished. When one creates a word for it and tries to distinguish this word from other words in a set of static intellectual patterns, confusion results. But the confusion is caused by the static patterns that seek to subordinate Dynamic Quality to themselves.

DG:

If I understand something, doesn't that make it static quality?

RMP:

If we understand it intellectually.

DG:

Of course, this is probably just what you mean by the "gateless gate."

RMP:

Yes.

DG:

After pondering this for some time, I looked to the dictionary for definitions of "understanding":

1. To perceive and comprehend the nature and significance of; grasp.

RMP:

This is good.

DG:

2. To know thoroughly by close contact or long experience with: that teacher understands children.

RMP:

This is very good.

DG:

3. To grasp or comprehend the meaning intended or expressed by (another): they have trouble with English, but I can understand them.

1. To comprehend the language, sounds, form, or symbols of.

2. To know and be tolerant or sympathetic toward: I can understand your point of view even though I disagree with it.

RMP:

This is good.

DG:

To learn indirectly, as by hearsay: I understand his departure was unexpected.

RMP:

Not good.

DG:

To infer: am I to understand you are staying the night?

RMP:

Very good.

DG:

To accept (something) as an agreed fact: it is understood that the fee will be 50 dollars.

RMP:

Okay.

DG:

To supply or add (words or a meaning, for example) mentally.

RMP:

Bad.

DG:

I take it you are using definition #1, and while it seems we are able to perceive the significance of Dynamic Quality, to comprehend it is another matter entirely. I am not entirely satisfied this is correct.

I thought perhaps you are using "understand" in a more philosophically oriented context so I picked up The Use and Misuse of Language (edited by S.I. Hayakawa) and looking in Chapter 1, "Why Discussions Go Awry," I found seven definitions of "understanding" pertaining to the multi-cultural sharing of ideas through discussion:

1. The following of directions
2. The making of predictions
3. The giving of verbal equivalents
4. The agreeing on programs
5. The solving of problems
6. The making of appropriate responses
7. The making of proper evaluations

RMP:

All seven are good.

DG:

All these seem static enterprises except possibly #6 and #7. If we understand a thing, we make an appropriate response to it. Yes, that seems close. I like #7 a great deal as well though the word "proper" seems very static and preconceived and might be better dropped and replaced with "better."

RMP:

Certainly a Dynamic understanding is not to be captured in all these static definitions. I would call it an understanding in which the "understander" is 100% gone. (Mind and body, cast away!) Poetic Zen literature calls it the mutual understanding of thieves who pass each other in the night. The Tao Te Ching says of it, "He who speaks does not know. He who knows does not speak." But since the Taoists are speaking here that means they don't know either.

RMP Annotation 75

Traditionally this is the meaning of free will. But the MOQ can argue that free will exists at all levels with increasing freedom to make choices as one ascends the levels. At the lowest inorganic level, the freedom is so small that it can be said that nature follows laws but the quantum theory shows that within the laws the freedom is still there. I remember a physicist telling me that according to quantum theory all the molecules of air in a room could of their own free will move to one side, suffocating someone standing on the other side, but the probability of this happening is so small no one need ever worry about it.

DG:

It sounds as if the physicist who told you that believes that there really are molecules "out there" floating around in the room. I guess if he didn't he wouldn't be much of a physicist though, right?

RMP:

I think he might have trouble in his professional organizations if he talked too much about it, and thus be disregarded professionally. However, physicists are the most open-minded people I have met with regard to metaphysics because their overall theoretical understanding has been is such a disarray since the 19th century. However, when you are working in the laboratory day after day, it's silly to have to remind yourself every minute that what you are working with are ideas. "Objects" are a great shorthand for stable collections of ideas, and reduce the mental workload.

RMP Annotation 86

Since in the MOQ all divisions of Quality are static, it follows that high and low are subdivisions of static quality. "Static" and "Dynamic" are also subdivisions of static quality, since the MOQ is itself a static intellectual pattern of Quality.

DG:

This seems related to your annotation concerning the "gateless gate" and my comments on whether a Dynamic understanding is possible. I interpret this to mean you tend to agree a Dynamic understanding really is a logical contradiction.

RMP:

From an intellectual point of view, Dynamic understanding is a logical contradiction. Logic does not control Dynamic understanding however and within it there is no contradiction.

DG:

As a boy, I loved science fiction novels and short stories. I remember reading a story of how men were genetically engineered to withstand the rigors of the environment on Jupiter in an effort to colonize the planet. The only problem was that the subjects of the experiment kept disappearing soon after being sent to Jupiter. The researchers suspected foul play, some unknown predator preying on them perhaps. The twist to the story was that the genetically altered men simply liked their new environment so much they had no thought of their previous life whatsoever; they were completely ambivalent. I have no way of knowing but it seems to me this might pertain to a Dynamic understanding too?

RMP:

The experience of freedom and the experience of Dynamic Quality are similar although it's important not to carry that analogy too far. Freedom always occurs as a negation of some static pattern. Dynamic Quality is affirmative.

DG:

If Dynamic Quality is synonymous with experience, and Dynamic Quality is affirmative, why is so much suffering experienced in life? So much so that one of Buddha's Four Noble Truths was life is suffering. In Lila, you say something about suffering being the negative face of Quality. Is Quality all a matter of how we perceive it to be? Are suffering and freedom somehow related?

RMP:

Yes. If you're not suffering from anything, there's no need to be free.

RMP Annotation 97

Within the MOQ, the idea that static patterns of value start with the inorganic level is considered to be a good idea. But the MOQ itself doesn't start before sentience. The MOQ, like science, starts with human experience. Remember the early talk in ZMM about Newton's Law of Gravity? Scientific laws without people to write them are a scientific impossibility.

DG:

This seems another area that philosophic idealism would help clarify?

RMP:

Definitely. I read somewhere that there are 21 competing and conflicting laws of gravity. What is poor earth to do?

DG:

Clearly "something" (RMP: object?) existed before we (RMP: subject?) became sentient.

RMP:

I think this statement leads down the primrose path of subjectobject metaphysics. The idea that "something existed before we became sentient" is an idea that did not exist before we came sentient. It's like the law of gravity in ZMM.

DG:

It seemed better to apply sentience to the individual rather than to humanity as a whole, so "before sentience" simply means before we (you, me, the reader) became sentient. After all, social and intellectual patterns of value are not about groups of people. So in that context it seemed to me Newton's law of gravity is an idea that existed before we (unless someone reading this is 300 years old) became sentient. Of course, now I see that since ideas do not pertain to groups but to the individual, that idea could not have existed before I became sentient. These ideas must coexist as value levels, but how?

RMP:

In the late 1800's the chicken-and-egg argument about whether ideas precede inorganic nature or inorganic nature precedes ideas was considered philosophically important. No one to my knowledge has ever shown that the idealists who considered ideas to come first have been wrong. The discussion has since died away.

It is important for an understanding of the MOQ to see that although "common sense" dictates that inorganic nature came first, actually "common sense" which is a set of ideas, has to come first. This "common sense" is arrived at through a huge web of socially approved evaluations of various alternatives. The key term here is "evaluation," i.e., quality decisions. The fundamental reality is not the common sense or the objects and laws approved of by common sense but the approval itself and the quality that leads to it.

DG:

In my reading of William James, I noticed he often used the term "agreement" in a similar fashion to how you're using the terms "approval" and "affirmative" so I took the time to look up each root word in the Practical Standard Dictionary:

Approve: to regard as worthy, proper, or right; commend; sanction; ratify; confirm.

Affirm: to declare or state positively; make (a statement) and maintain (it) to be true; maintain; assert; aver.

Agree: to come into or be in harmony; be of one mind; concur.

When you say Dynamic Quality is always affirmative, at first I took it to mean that DQ is always positive. By comparing all three terms, however, I sense a common thread of evaluation leading to confirmation, which is neither positive nor negative. Those terms come later, after further intellectualization. Is that your thinking too?

RMP:

Yes, my statement that Dynamic Quality is always affirmative was not a wise statement, since it constitutes a limitation or partial definition of Dynamic Quality. Whenever one talks about Dynamic Quality someone else can take whatever is said and make a static pattern out of it and then dialectically oppose that pattern. The best answer to the question, "What is Dynamic Quality?" is the ancient Vedic one——"Not this, not that."

DG:

It seems common sense to believe that the "something" which existed before our awareness equates with what we call history.

Still, there is no possibility of our ever knowing with certainty what took place before our experience of the world arose.

Laws, on the other hand, seem eternal, if we do indeed assume that "something" exists apart from our experience (though we can never say with certainty what that something is). A law is the same each time we encounter it. Confusion seems to arise in assuming a law and the idea of a law to be the same.

RMP:

How can they be different?

DG:

Please see your note 130. Doesn't it imply reality and the concept (idea) of reality are not the same?

RMP:

I don't see what you are referring to in Note 130. In the MOQ, laws are a species of intellectual patterns that are associated with a lot of social authority and are slow to change. I don't think they have any objective status at all. Ideas about laws are another set of intellectual patterns. Thus, they are both intellectual patterns, and as such, are the same.

DG:

I was referring to your statement: "The Buddhists would say it [the concept of "I"] is certainly central to a concept of reality but it is not central to or even a part of reality itself." It may be that I am interpreting your statement incorrectly, but it appears to me that the Buddhists are saying reality itself is not a concept or an intellectual pattern of value.

For instance, a materialist might dream that someday science will develop a theory of everything. On the other hand, an idealist might tend to side with the Buddhists in saying intellectual concepts of reality are not central to or even part of reality itself? That we will never develop a theory of everything? That there's no chance we can ever intellectually know reality?

RMP:

The confusion here seems to result from the two languages of Buddhism, the language of the Buddha's world and language of everyday life. In the language of everyday life, reality and intellect are different. From the language of the Buddha's world, they are the same, since there is no intellectual division that governs the Buddha's world.

RMP Annotation 99

Dynamic Quality and chaos are both patternless, and so it would seem they have a lot in common, particularly the fact that you can't say anything about them without getting into static patterns. But if you do, you can say that Dynamic Quality is good and precedes static improvement. It is the source of experience. Chaos, by contrast is the condition of total destruction. You can't call it either good or bad. It is not the source of anything.

DG:

This brings much clarity to a sentence on page 164 of Lila that had previously seemed a source of confusion for many contributors: "But Dynamic Quality is not structured yet it is not chaotic." After several days of pondering this however, I find I am still a bit confused. Pulling out the dictionary I found:

Chaos: n.

1. A condition or place of great disorder or confusion.

2. A disorderly mass; a jumble: the desk was a chaos of papers and unopened letters.

3. The disordered state of unformed matter and infinite space supposed in some cosmogonic views to have existed before the ordered universe.

4. Mathematics. A dynamical system that has a sensitive dependence on its initial conditions.

5. Obsolete. An abyss; a chasm.

Now it seems to me many times when contributors refer to chaos, they are referring to definition #4, which has nothing to do with definition #1, which I am assuming is the definition of the term as you are using it in your quote. Chaos in definition #1 has nothing to do with Dynamic Quality: "It is not the source of anything." On the other hand, chaos in definition #4 seems to hold some promise of representing some correlations of experience that at least point indirectly to Dynamic Quality?

RMP:

I think the mathematical definition of chaos deals exclusively with what the MOQ would call static objective patterns. The word "dynamical" is a term of physics that refers to changes in space and time. It is not the same as Dynamic Quality.

RMP Annotation 101

A materialist would say yes. An idealist would say no.

DG:

And the MOQ would say they are both right?

RMP:

Within their limitations. They seem to fit within the Hindu parable of the blind men and the elephant.

RMP Annotation 102

I see today more clearly than when I wrote the SODV paper that the key to integrating the MOQ with science is through philosophic idealism, which says that objects grow out of ideas, not the other way around. Since at the most primary level the observed and the observer are both intellectual assumptions, the paradoxes of quantum theory have to be conflicts of intellectual assumption, not just conflicts of what is observed. Except in the case of Dynamic Quality, what is observed always involves an interaction with ideas that have been previously assumed. So the problem is not, "How can observed nature be so screwy?" but can also be, "What is wrong with our most primitive assumptions that our set of ideas called 'nature' are turning out to be this screwy?" Getting back to physics, this question becomes, "Why should we assume that the slit experiment should perform differently than it does?"

I think that if researched it would be found that buried in the data of the slit experiment is an assumption that light exists and follows consistent laws independently of any human experience. If so, the MOQ would say that although in the past this seems to have been the highest quality assumption one can make about light, there may be a higher quality one that contradicts it. This is pretty much what the physicists are saying but the MOQ provides a sound metaphysical structure within which they can say it.

DG:

This seems to directly relate to my comments concerning your annotation on page 2 and your response to the mind-matter question in Lila: "So what the Metaphysics of Quality concludes is that all schools are right on the mind-matter question."

RMP:

As said in Note 101, "Within their limitations. They seem to fit within the Hindu parable of the blind men and the elephant."

DG:

Do you mean that you now believe philosophic idealism to be a higher quality intellectual pattern of value than materialism? If so, does the quote here still hold true but only in limited contexts? For it seems in rejecting materialism, "...the measuring instruments would just be measuring their own internal characteristics." (SODV paper)

RMP:

I think idealism is of higher quality for understanding the MOQ because most people understand materialism as "common sense" but few understand idealism as "common sense," and you need both. Although Dynamic Quality is neither an object nor an idea, I have always felt that someone who understands idealism will figure out the MOQ much faster than someone who only understands materialism will.

DG:

You mention philosophic idealism in Zen and the Art of Motorcycle Maintenance during your refutation of scientific materialism (Chapter 19) but you reject it as "too far fetched." Do you feel that's why so few people understand it?

RMP:

It seems outside "common sense," so most people don't believe it. But I believe it was the dominant school of philosophical thought in England during the Victorian period.

RMP Annotation 114

Eating cheeseburgers is biological quality.

DG:

And exercise?

RMP:

If your body seems to enjoy it. If your body, like mine, does not enjoy it, but you do it anyway because it's socially required, as in high school or the army, or because it's a fad, I would think that's social quality. If you do it anyway because it makes sense medically that's intellectual quality.

RMP Annotation 129

I've always thought this is incorrect because many forms of intellect do not have a subject-object construction. These include logic itself, mathematics, computer programming languages, and, I believe some primitive languages (although I can't remember what they are.)

DG:

I mentioned gorilla sign language in an earlier note. Watching a documentary on this, I noticed the gorilla was taught to refer to her "self" as an object.

RMP:

Not having seen the documentary, I can't analyze this. It sounds pretty advanced for a gorilla. I remember a story in which a "talking dog" was asked such questions as "What's sandpaper like?" and, "What's on top of a house?" The dog answered correctly each time (rough and roof).

DG:

It would seem the MOQ would regard the essence of any language as a biological sense and gorilla sign language as a Dynamic biological response to value?

RMP:

Those aspects of a language that a microphone or camera can pick up are objective and therefore biological. Those aspects of a language which a microphone or camera cannot pick up (i.e., meaning) are subjective and therefore social. If the gorilla understands what is meant in ways that are socially learned, then the gorilla is acting socially. If the gorilla can read and write and add and subtract then it is acting intellectually.

RMP Annotation 130

The word "I" like the word "self" is one of the trickiest words in any metaphysics. Sometimes it is an object, a human body; sometimes it is a subject, a human mind. I believe there are number of philosophic systems, notably Ayn Rand's "Objectivism," that call the "I" or "individual" the central reality. Buddhists say it is an illusion. So do scientists. The MOQ says it is a collection of static patterns capable of apprehending Dynamic Quality. I think that if you identify the "I" with the intellect and nothing else you are taking an unusual position that may need some defending.

DG:

It seems to me as value arises from experience that the "I" or "individual" must somehow be central to any concept of reality whether that is acknowledged or not.

RMP:

The Buddhists would say it is certainly central to a concept of reality but it is not central to or even a part of reality itself. Enlightenment involves getting rid of the concept of "I" (small self) and seeing the reality in which the small self is absent (big self).

DG:

Your space-theater analogy in Lila comes to mind here. We learn to play a game with reality and forget that we are just playing a game and that the game stops when the participant no longer participates.

RMP Annotation 132

It employs SOM reasoning the way SOM reasoning employs social structures such as courts and journals and learned societies to make itself known. SOM reasoning is not subordinate to these social structures, and the MOQ is not subordinate to the SOM structures it employs. Remember that the central reality of the MOQ is not an object or a subject or anything else. It is understood by direct experience only and not by reasoning of any kind. Therefore to say that the MOQ is based on SOM reasoning is as useful as saying that the Ten Commandments are based on SOM reasoning. It doesn't tell us anything about the essence of the Ten Commandments and it doesn't tell us anything about the essence of the MOQ.

DG:

I am beginning to see what you mean here. Direct experience does not mean direct experience per se but rather experience directly perceived. It may just be a matter of semantics but I have always argued there is no such thing as direct experience. Now I sense I have been looking at the question backwards, so to speak.

RMP:

Yes, see notes 25, 30, and 57.

RMP Annotation 137

Both "the genius" and the mentally retarded person are at the social level. At the intellectual level would be the law that requires them to be treated equally.

DG:

Could you elaborate on what you mean by being "at the social level"?

RMP:

My statement that "Both 'the genius' and the mentally retarded person are at the social level." is intended to refute the statement that "the genius appears to be on a higher evolutionary level." A person who holds an idea is a social entity, no matter what ideas he holds. The ideas he holds are an intellectual entity, no matter who holds them.

DG:

I must confess confusion at this point. At the intellectual level, doesn't prohibiting the marriage of mentally retarded people (see your note on eugenics) put them on a lower social standing than a "normal" person?

RMP:

Yes, it does, and it would have been better to have chosen a different example, but a difference in social standing is not a difference in evolutionary level in the MOQ, which was my point.

Conclusion

Rather than learning a thing or two in putting Lila's Child together, it seems as if I have had to unlearn a good deal. We all have preconceived notions of what reality is and what it should be. When we see or hear of something new we immediately set about categorizing and intellectualizing the newness until we know all about it or believe ourselves to. That's how I felt before beginning this project; sure of myself as I leafed through my worn copy of Lila filled with notes, highlights, and bracketing. I knew all about the MOQ. After all, had I not read Lila a dozen times or more until I could nearly recite it passage for passage? Hadn't I discussed the MOQ in depth with people from all over the world?

I was wrong. Maybe that's what real discovery is all about, being wrong, and I mean a deep down, "I'm feeling really dense," kind of wrong. After all, if a person is right about something new, then s/he already knows what that something new is. Perhaps it is that feeling of "Oh! I get it! But why didn't I see that before?" that indicates real discovery. In the end, I seem to have more questions than answers but I suspect it is my own inadequacy in letting go of what I know. The answers are here; I am simply not seeing them.

There isn't any professional proofreader or editor to blame for mistakes here, due to both the complexity of the work and (more chiefly) the lack of funds. Besides, I've seen mistakes in many professionally edited books and this work is too important to me to trust it to just anyone. Can you pay someone enough to care? The work here reminds me of a post I remember reading from the discussion group (I wish I could find it again now but Lord knows where it is) about watching a man raking out a gravel parking lot at a church early Sunday morning and wondering whether any of the parishioners would notice how smooth it was when they arrived hours later.

The reader may rest assured that I feel confident there is purpose behind any apparent "bumps" that remain and they are not mistakes at all. This is after all an international document. However, should anyone discover something amiss or perhaps just feel like commenting on anything, please feel free to holler at me (daneglover@hotmail.com) and perhaps it can be corrected in a future printing.

Over the last three years, I've spent countless hours scrutinizing every word, every line, and every nuance in the manuscript. ("If a book is going to be about Quality, it had damned well better be a Quality book.") There were times when I found it impossible to force myself to turn on the computer, much less to even look at Lila's Child; other times I found myself driven to put in up to eighteen hours a day for months at a time hammering the manuscript into shape. Yet I've played but a small part in the creation of Lila's Child, almost an invisible part. Actually, in a way Lila's Child created itself from the idea "seed" that Bodvar planted, blooming when the time was right to blossom and withering away when the time was right to rest, regenerating for the next big push.

A keen sense of loss accompanied the end of each flourish that would take several weeks or even months to run its course to where I could get back to feeling some semblance of normalcy. Now that the book is complete, the work finally done, I'll have to find something else to fill the suddenly too empty hours that always seem to grace the end of a great love affair, or perhaps it's better just to wait until something else finds me.

I have had a fantastic time putting this book together. There've been alternating feelings of heartache, exhilaration, despair, wonderment, embarrassment, and bewilderment, together with unrelenting misgivings that I should be the one doing this work in the first place or that Lila's Child would (or should) ever see print.

I doubt there will be any more books for me to put together. There's a Zen saying that work done then forgotten lasts forever. As time is apt to fold into itself, in several months I will barely remember working on Lila's Child. In a year, it will be as if someone else put the book together. I have no idea what I'll be doing then, but I am sure it will require all my attention.

Thank you for reading.

Dan Glover June 23, 2002

About the Author

Looking over the Lila's Child manuscript now, in 2012, ten years after I first compiled it, I can see many things that I would change... things I would do differently, questions I didn't think to ask... ways to perhaps make it better, but I think I might taking a risk as well of diminishing the work. So I haven't made any changes ... other than to add the hyperlinks to make for ease in navigating between the annotations.

Dan Glover lives in north-central Illinois with a tribe of mystic cats. He has free podcasts of his newest books available at his website and you may follow him on Twitter and connect with him on Facebook.

Thank you!

Dan Glover August 27, 2012

Books by Dan Glover

Philosophy

The Art of Caring: Zen Stories
The Mystery: Zen Stories
Apache Nation

Mermaid Series

Winter's Memaid
Mermaid Spring
Summer's Mermaid
Autumn Mermaid

Gathering of Lovers Series

Billy Austin
Lisa
Allison Johns
Tom Three Deer
Justine
Yelena

Short Stories

There Come a Bad Cloud: Tangled up Matter and Ghosts
Mi Vida Dinámica

Made in the USA
Las Vegas, NV
21 May 2021

23433636R00302